Chinese Cooking For Dummies®

Cheat Sheet

The Tools You Need for Chinese Cooking

Having the following items really makes your life easier when you're trying to prepare Chinese cuisine. They're all described in detail in Chapter 3.

- ✔ A wok that you've seasoned
- ✔ A sharp chef's knife
- ✔ A cutting board that you keep clean
- ✔ A small spice grinder
- ✔ A steamer
- ✔ A strainer
- ✔ Spatulas and ladles
- ✔ A claypot casserole
- ✔ An electric rice cooker
- ✔ Chopsticks

The Fundamental Ingredients for Chinese Cooking

Stocking your own Chinese pantry shouldn't require renting a U-Haul to carry your loot home from the store. By keeping only a few essential ingredients on hand, you can whip up an authentic Chinese meal on a moment's notice. Just add whatever fresh meat, fish, and produce catch your eye at the supermarket, and before you know it, you'll have a balanced, quick, and easy-to-make dish on your table. What can be more Chinese than that? Just stock up on the ingredients listed here:

Sauces and condiments:
- ✔ Soy sauce
- ✔ Rice vinegar
- ✔ Oyster-flavored sauce
- ✔ Hoisin sauce
- ✔ Chile paste or sauce
- ✔ Black bean sauce
- ✔ Plum sauce
- ✔ Vegetable oil
- ✔ Sesame oil
- ✔ Chile oil
- ✔ Rice wine (or dry sherry)

Spices and seasonings:
- ✔ Chinese five-spice powder
- ✔ Star anise
- ✔ Sichuan peppercorns
- ✔ Whole and crushed dried red chiles
- ✔ Chinese hot mustard
- ✔ White pepper

Canned and dried ingredients:
- ✔ Bamboo shoots
- ✔ Straw mushrooms
- ✔ Water chestnuts
- ✔ Broth (canned or home-made, see Chapter 9)

- ✔ Dried black mushrooms
- ✔ Long-grain rice (see Chapter 15)
- ✔ Cornstarch
- ✔ Sesame seeds

Noodles:
- ✔ Cellophane or bean thread noodles (see Chapter 15)
- ✔ Dried rice noodles (see Chapter 15)
- ✔ Dried egg noodles (stored in freezer if fresh, see Chapter 15)

IDG BOOKS WORLDWIDE

For Dummies™: *Bestselling Book Series for Beginners*

Chinese Cooking For Dummies®

Keeping Cooking Techniques Straight

Chinese cooking involves the use of all kinds of cooking techniques. Here are the basics:

Technique	The Results	What You Need	How Long?	Tips
Stir-frying	Crisp, brightly colored foods with lots of nutrition and flavor, but little fat	A wok or large frying pan	Lightning-quick — there's not time for waiting	Have all your ingredients and sauces prepared ahead of time; cook ingredients in stages.
Steaming	Healthful, almost fat-free foods whose fresh, natural flavors stand out	An electric steamer; a wok or pan with a steamer rack	Not too long — as long as it takes to fully cook the food	Be careful when removing the steamer lid so you don't get a painful steam burn.
Blanching	Softened — not fully cooked — foods that are now ready for complete cooking via another method	A wok or pot big enough to hold plenty of boiling water	Brief — only a few minutes or long enough to soften the food	Make sure to stop the cooking after removing the food by rinsing it with or plunging it into cold water.
Simmering	Gently cooked, tender, juicy, and flavorful food	A wok or pot that can hold enough water to cover the food	A while — from a few minutes to more than an hour	Gentle is the key word: After you bring the water to a boil, reduce the heat and gently cook the food until it's done.
Braising	Flavorful, tender, morsels from the toughest cuts of meats	Same equipment as simmering	A long time; normally a couple hours will do the trick	Browning the meat first adds flavor and color; just be patient and don't put too much meat in the pan at once.
Deep-frying	Food that's crisp and golden on the outside, tender and fully cooked on the inside	An electric fryer; a large pan or wok with a flat bottom or a ring stand	Not too long, because the quicker the food fries, the better the texture becomes	Don't let the oil temperature drop! Be careful working near the hot oil, too.
Roasting	Foods with a crisp, caramelized exterior and juicy, tender flesh (but they get that texture from dry, circulating heat rather than from hot oil, as in deep-frying).	An oven	Depends on the food's thickness, but generally a longer, less fuel-efficient method	Make sure that air circulates around the food, and baste it with the marinade or pan juices to add flavor and keep it moist.
Smoking	Foods with a distinctively smoky, aromatic flavor	A wok, which easily turns into a smoker	A longer, slower cooking method	Choose from many flavoring agents, such as tea and rice, to flavor your smoke.

For Dummies™: Bestselling Book Series for Beginners

Praise for Chinese Cooking For Dummies

There are two reasons that many of us in the West refrain from Chinese cooking: fear that the techniques are too hard to master and that the ingredients are too hard to find. Martin Yan blows away both of those fears. *Chinese Cooking For Dummies* is an excellent cooking school in a book. You learn techniques first, recipes second, with each lesson preparing you for the next. The solidity and universality of Chef Yan's approach is such that, by the end of his book, you will not only be able to cook Chinese cuisine with confidence and pleasure, you will be able to cook virtually anything.

> — Sara Moulton
> Host of *Cooking Live with Sara Moulton*, food editor of *Good Morning America* (ABC), and executive chef of *Gourmet* magazine

Martin Yan continues to be the most authentic and stimulating teacher of Chinese cooking today. His recipes are thoughtful, creative, and work blissfully. All of the energy and enthusiasm that excites me when watching him cook are transferred to Martin Yan's *Chinese Cooking For Dummies*. Martin makes it impossible not to be instantly successful when cooking from *Chinese Cooking For Dummies.*

> — Michael Lomonaco
> Executive Chef/Director, Window on the World

Forget Chinese takeout! Martin Yan's *Chinese Cooking For Dummies* is for everyone who craves good Chinese food any day of the week; the recipes are simple and authentic, and imbibed with just the right touch of Martin's humor. An added bonus is the wealth of technique, steps, and historical references that Martin shares from one of the world's most beloved cuisines.

> — Mary Ann Esposito
> PBS' *Ciao Italia!*

After a lifetime of cooking and teaching, Martin has boiled a complicated cuisine down to its essence. We can't think of a better, more entertaining way for Chinese food lovers to get out their woks and start cooking."

> — Mary Sue Milliken & Susan Feniger
> Chef-owners of Border Grills and Ciudad and authors of *Mexican Cooking For Dummies*

Are you, I wonder, one of those who count Martin Yan as a "trusted friend"? If so, welcome, because I am too! Over all the years I've known Martin, he has never, ever failed me. If he is new to you, then this book will rapidly help you to join our very satisfied gastronomic circle!

> — Graham Kerr
> International Culinary Consultant

Martin Yan is a master teacher as well as a master chef. His advice is lively, precise, and leads straight from page to kitchen to table. To follow him is a treat!

> — Anne Willan
> Founder and President of La Varenne Ecole de Cuisine
> and author of *From My Chateau Kitchen*

Martin Yan can get anyone to cook! He's witty, and he's smart about what people should know about cooking Chinese food. This book will have you on your wok-banging way into the kitchen! Chinese cuisine never translated so well!

> — Sam Choy
> Chef/Owner of Sam Choy's Restaurants and author of
> *Sam Choy's Island Flavors*

Chinese Cooking
FOR
DUMMIES®

by Martin Yan

IDG BOOKS WORLDWIDE

IDG Books Worldwide, Inc.
An International Data Group Company

Foster City, CA ◆ Chicago, IL ◆ Indianapolis, IN ◆ New York, NY

Chinese Cooking For Dummies®

Published by
IDG Books Worldwide, Inc.
An International Data Group Company
919 E. Hillsdale Blvd.
Suite 400
Foster City, CA 94404
www.idgbooks.com (IDG Books Worldwide Web Site)
www.dummies.com (Dummies Press Web Site)

Copyright © 2000 IDG Books Worldwide, Inc. All rights reserved. No part of this book, including interior design, cover design, and icons, may be reproduced or transmitted in any form, by any means (electronic, photocopying, recording, or otherwise) without the prior written permission of the publisher.

Library of Congress Catalog Card No.: 00-104231

ISBN: 0-7645-5247-3

Printed in the United States of America

10 9 8 7 6 5 4 3 2 1

1B/RS/QZ/QQ/IN

Distributed in the United States by IDG Books Worldwide, Inc.

Distributed by CDG Books Canada Inc. for Canada; by Transworld Publishers Limited in the United Kingdom; by IDG Norge Books for Norway; by IDG Sweden Books for Sweden; by IDG Books Australia Publishing Corporation Pty. Ltd. for Australia and New Zealand; by TransQuest Publishers Pte Ltd. for Singapore, Malaysia, Thailand, Indonesia, and Hong Kong; by Gotop Information Inc. for Taiwan; by ICG Muse, Inc. for Japan; by Intersoft for South Africa; by Eyrolles for France; by International Thomson Publishing for Germany, Austria and Switzerland; by Distribuidora Cuspide for Argentina; by LR International for Brazil; by Galileo Libros for Chile; by Ediciones ZETA S.C.R. Ltda. for Peru; by WS Computer Publishing Corporation, Inc., for the Philippines; by Contemporanea de Ediciones for Venezuela; by Express Computer Distributors for the Caribbean and West Indies; by Micronesia Media Distributor, Inc. for Micronesia; by Chips Computadoras S.A. de C.V. for Mexico; by Editorial Norma de Panama S.A. for Panama; by American Bookshops for Finland.

For general information on IDG Books Worldwide's books in the U.S., please call our Consumer Customer Service department at 800-762-2974. For reseller information, including discounts and premium sales, please call our Reseller Customer Service department at 800-434-3422.

For information on where to purchase IDG Books Worldwide's books outside the U.S., please contact our International Sales department at 317-596-5530 or fax 317-572-4002.

For consumer information on foreign language translations, please contact our Customer Service department at 1-800-434-3422, fax 317-572-4002, or e-mail rights@idgbooks.com.

For information on licensing foreign or domestic rights, please phone +1-650-653-7098.

For sales inquiries and special prices for bulk quantities, please contact our Order Services department at 800-434-4322 or write to the address above.

For information on using IDG Books Worldwide's books in the classroom or for ordering examination copies, please contact our Educational Sales department at 800-434-2086 or fax 317-572-4005.

For press review copies, author interviews, or other publicity information, please contact our Public Relations department at 650-653-7000 or fax 650-653-7500.

For authorization to photocopy items for corporate, personal, or educational use, please contact Copyright Clearance Center, 222 Rosewood Drive, Danvers, MA 01923, or fax 978-750-4470.

is a registered trademark under exclusive
license to IDG Books Worldwide, Inc.,
from International Data Group, Inc.

About the Author

Martin Yan, celebrated host of more than 1,500 cooking shows, highly respected food and restaurant consultant, and certified master chef, enjoys distinction as both teacher and author. His many talents are showcased in 24 best-selling cookbooks, including his two recent releases, *Martin Yan's Feast: The Best of Yan Can Cook* and *Martin Yan's Invitation to Chinese Cooking.*

As host of *Yan Can Cook,* Yan has captured the admiration and loyal following of millions of cooking and travel fans. He combines cooking artistry and teaching skill with humor and a unique personal style. Yan's programs are as entertaining as they are educational. He is dedicated to opening the mysterious world of Chinese and Asian cooking and furthering the understanding and enjoyment of these excellent cuisines and cultures.

Born in Guangzhou, China, Yan always possessed a passion for cooking. His formal introduction to the culinary world began at age 13 with an apprenticeship for a well-established Hong Kong restaurant. After earning a diploma from the Overseas Institute of Cookery in Hong Kong, he traveled to Canada and the United States. While earning an M.S. in Food Science from the University of California, Davis, Yan taught Chinese cooking for the University of California extension program.

Yan is the founder of the Yan Can International Cooking School in the San Francisco Bay Area. *Yan Can Cook* has received national and international recognition, including a 1998 Daytime Emmy Award, a 1996 James Beard Award for Best TV Food Journalism, and a 1994 James Beard Award for Best TV Cooking Show.

ABOUT IDG BOOKS WORLDWIDE

Welcome to the world of IDG Books Worldwide.

IDG Books Worldwide, Inc., is a subsidiary of International Data Group, the world's largest publisher of computer-related information and the leading global provider of information services on information technology. IDG was founded more than 30 years ago by Patrick J. McGovern and now employs more than 9,000 people worldwide. IDG publishes more than 290 computer publications in over 75 countries. More than 90 million people read one or more IDG publications each month.

Launched in 1990, IDG Books Worldwide is today the #1 publisher of best-selling computer books in the United States. We are proud to have received eight awards from the Computer Press Association in recognition of editorial excellence and three from Computer Currents' First Annual Readers' Choice Awards. Our best-selling *...For Dummies*® series has more than 50 million copies in print with translations in 31 languages. IDG Books Worldwide, through a joint venture with IDG's Hi-Tech Beijing, became the first U.S. publisher to publish a computer book in the People's Republic of China. In record time, IDG Books Worldwide has become the first choice for millions of readers around the world who want to learn how to better manage their businesses.

Our mission is simple: Every one of our books is designed to bring extra value and skill-building instructions to the reader. Our books are written by experts who understand and care about our readers. The knowledge base of our editorial staff comes from years of experience in publishing, education, and journalism — experience we use to produce books to carry us into the new millennium. In short, we care about books, so we attract the best people. We devote special attention to details such as audience, interior design, use of icons, and illustrations. And because we use an efficient process of authoring, editing, and desktop publishing our books electronically, we can spend more time ensuring superior content and less time on the technicalities of making books.

You can count on our commitment to deliver high-quality books at competitive prices on topics you want to read about. At IDG Books Worldwide, we continue in the IDG tradition of delivering quality for more than 30 years. You'll find no better book on a subject than one from IDG Books Worldwide.

John Kilcullen
Chairman and CEO
IDG Books Worldwide, Inc.

Eighth Annual
Computer Press
Awards ➤1992

Ninth Annual
Computer Press
Awards ➤1993

Tenth Annual
Computer Press
Awards ➤1994

Eleventh Annual
Computer Press
Awards ➤1995

IDG is the world's leading IT media, research and exposition company. Founded in 1964, IDG had 1997 revenues of $2.05 billion and has more than 9,000 employees worldwide. IDG offers the widest range of media options that reach IT buyers in 75 countries representing 95% of worldwide IT spending. IDG's diverse product and services portfolio spans six key areas including print publishing, online publishing, expositions and conferences, market research, education and training, and global marketing services. More than 90 million people read one or more of IDG's 290 magazines and newspapers, including IDG's leading global brands — Computerworld, PC World, Network World, Macworld and the Channel World family of publications. IDG Books Worldwide is one of the fastest-growing computer book publishers in the world, with more than 700 titles in 36 languages. The "...For Dummies®" series alone has more than 50 million copies in print. IDG offers online users the largest network of technology-specific Web sites around the world through IDG.net (http://www.idg.net), which comprises more than 225 targeted Web sites in 55 countries worldwide. International Data Corporation (IDC) is the world's largest provider of information technology data, analysis and consulting, with research centers in over 41 countries and more than 400 research analysts worldwide. IDG World Expo is a leading producer of more than 168 globally branded conferences and expositions in 35 countries including E3 (Electronic Entertainment Expo), Macworld Expo, ComNet, Windows World Expo, ICE (Internet Commerce Expo), Agenda, DEMO, and Spotlight. IDG's training subsidiary, ExecuTrain, is the world's largest computer training company, with more than 230 locations worldwide and 785 training courses. IDG Marketing Services helps industry-leading IT companies build international brand recognition by developing global integrated marketing programs via IDG's print, online and exposition products worldwide. Further information about the company can be found at www.idg.com.   1/26/00

Dedication

I dedicate this book to you, the reader. Whether it represents your first foray into Chinese cooking, or is yet another reference for your culinary library, your interest is ample compensation for my efforts.

Author's Acknowledgments

I've heard that too many cooks spoil the broth. But when putting this book together, the more spoons we had clanging around the pot, the better.

The project never would've come to fruition without our able and dedicated staff. Julie Tan-Salazar led the kitchen crew with professionalism, talent, and a whole lot of well-earned sweat. Without Kim Decker's tireless research and creative, stylish writing, I couldn't have brought the text portion of this book to life. And Jeannie Cuan, with her usual grace under pressure, made sure that everyone was on the ball.

Sandy Rust, Jan Nix, Winnie Lee, Eva Kwong, Susan Phan, Frankie Poon, Betty Poon, and William Chow all deserve plenty of thanks for logging so many hours in front of a hot stove.

Thanks so much to Ginny Bast for getting everything else — and I do mean *everything else* — done in the office when I was up to my ears in this and many other projects.

Tina Salter and, once again, Jan Nix contributed their familiarity with publishing, editing, and Chinese cuisine, along with plenty of honesty and encouragement; I'm so grateful for both of them. Eagle-eyed Susan Yoshimura saw that both text and recipes passed the first round of editorial muster. Ivan Lai's peerless sense of humor and ability to make a great book even better was also indispensable. Cheers to Roy Salazar whose expertise with wine and tea made the book's beverage chapter informative and fun to read. I sincerely thank Liz Kurtzman for her elegant and informative illustrations.

Let me also thank everyone else who contributed to the project. Without their work and enthusiasm, the book never would've developed the fabulous "flavor" it has now.

After working with Christy Beck, Tim Gallan, Linda Ingroia, Holly McGuire, and Tina Sims, I understand why IDG always turns out such top-notch publications. You're all pros!

Thanks to Colin and Devin for providing me with laughter. And of course, thanks to Sue, whose patience and support continue to amaze me.

Publisher's Acknowledgments

We're proud of this book; please register your comments through our IDG Books Worldwide Online Registration Form located at http://my2cents.dummies.com.

Some of the people who helped bring this book to market include the following:

Acquisitions, Editorial, and Media Development

Senior Project Editor: Tim Gallan

Senior Acquisitions Editor: Linda Ingroia

Copy Editor: Tina Sims

Technical Reviewer: Judith Sutton

Permissions Editor: Carmen Krikorian

Editorial Manager: Pam Mourouzis

Media Development Manager: Heather Heath Dismore

Editorial Assistant: Carol Strickland

Production

Project Coordinator: Maridee Ennis

Layout and Graphics: Amy Adrian, Angie Hunckler, Barry Offringa, Brent Savage, Kathie Schutte, Erin Zeltner

Proofreaders: Vickie Broyles, Susan Moritz, Marianne Santy, Jeannie Smith, Sossity R. Smith

Indexer: Sharon Hilgenberg

Illustrator: Liz Kurtzman

Special Help
Christine Meloy Beck, Ben Nussbaum

General and Administrative

IDG Books Worldwide, Inc.: John Kilcullen, CEO; Bill Barry, President and COO

IDG Books Consumer Reference Group

Business: Kathleen A. Welton, Vice President and Publisher; Kevin Thornton, Acquisitions Manager

Cooking/Gardening: Jennifer Feldman, Associate Vice President and Publisher

Education/Reference: Diane Graves Steele, Vice President and Publisher, Greg Tubach, Publishing Director

Lifestyles: Kathleen Nebenhaus, Vice President and Publisher; Tracy Boggier, Managing Editor

Pets: Dominique De Vito, Associate Vice President and Publisher; Tracy Boggier, Managing Editor

Travel: Michael Spring, Vice President and Publisher; Suzanne Jannetta, Editorial Director; Brice Gosnell, Managing Editor

IDG Books Consumer Editorial Services: Kathleen Nebenhaus, Vice President and Publisher; Kristin A. Cocks, Editorial Director; Cindy Kitchel, Editorial Director

IDG Books Consumer Production: Debbie Stailey, Production Director

IDG Books Packaging: Marc J. Mikulich, Vice President, Brand Strategy and Research

◆

The publisher would like to give special thanks to Patrick J. McGovern, without whom this book would not have been possible.

◆

Contents at a Glance

Introduction 1

Part I: What Is Chinese Cooking? 7
Chapter 1: How to Think Like a Chinese Chef 9
Chapter 2: A Wok Through China's Amazing Culinary Regions 13

Part II: Where to Begin? 21
Chapter 3: Tools of the Trade 23
Chapter 4: The Chinese Pantry and Refrigerator 35
Chapter 5: Common Chinese Cooking Techniques 55
Chapter 6: Edible Artistry: Garnishes to Prettify Your Plate 71

Part III: The Recipes 83
Chapter 7: Saucy Sauces and Dips 85
Chapter 8: Delectable Morsels: Appetizers, Snacks, and Salads 95
Chapter 9: Broth, Bones, and a Barrel of Soup 115
Chapter 10: Swimming with the Best of Them: Seafood 125
Chapter 11: Crying Fowl: Poultry Recipes 147
Chapter 12: Moo-ve In and Pig Out, My Little Lambs: Beef, Pork, and Lamb 173
Chapter 13: Healthy Tofu and Eggscellent Ideas 205
Chapter 14: The Green Revolution: Cooking Vegetables the Chinese Way 229
Chapter 15: Rice Bowls and Oodles of Noodles 251
Chapter 16: Sweet Sensations 273
Chapter 17: Bringing It All Together: Full-Fledged Chinese Meals 287

Part IV: The Part of Tens 297
Chapter 18: Almost Ten Tips for Enjoying the Chinese Restaurant Experience 299
Chapter 19: Ten Commandments: Secrets to Your Success 305
Chapter 20: Ten Martin-Tested Resources for Chinese Cuisine and Culture 311
Chapter 21: Drink Up: Ten Tips for Drinking Tea and Wine with Chinese Food 315

Index 319

Book Registration Information ....Back of Book

Recipes at a Glance

Chapter 6: Garnishes

Tomato Rose 76–77
Apple Wings 77–78
Cucumber Fan...79
Green Onion Brushes...80
Chili Pepper Flowers 81–82

Chapter 7: Sauces and Dips

All-Purpose Stir-Fry Sauce..86
Hot and Spicy Stir-Fry Sauce..87
Sweet and Sour Sauce..88
Master Sauce/Red-Cooking Sauce...89
All-Purpose Black Bean Sauce...90
All-Purpose Dipping Sauce..92
Chile Oil 92–93
Chinese Mustard Dip..93
Sichuan Spicy Salt 94

Chapter 8: Appetizers

Auntie Jessica's Party Chicken Wings 97
Cantonese Pickled Vegetables 98
Chinese Chicken Salad..99
Baked Pork Buns 100
Spring Rolls 104–105
Crispy Wontons 106–107
Potstickers...108–109
Steamed Shrimp and Chive Dumplings 110–111
Green Onion Pancakes...112
Shrimp Toast...113

Chapter 9: Soups and Broths

Chinese Chicken Broth 117
Egg Flower Soup 118
Fish Soup with Spinach and Tofu 119
Hot and Sour Soup 120

Sweet Corn and Crabmeat Soup..121
Winter Melon Soup..122
Wonton Soup..123

Chapter 10: Fish and Seafood

Braised Fish Hunan-Style..130
Fish Steaks in Fragrant Sauce..131
Smoke-Broiled Fish..132
Pan-Grilled Salmon Fillet with Black Bean Sauce..134
Steamed Whole Fish..135
Steamed Trout in Black Beans and Garlic..136
Sweet and Sour Shrimp..139
Spicy Salt Shrimp..142
Shrimp and Scallops with Snow Peas..143
Seafood Casserole..144
Oysters in Black Bean Sauce..145

Chapter 11: Chicken and Duck

Sichuan Bang Bang Chicken..156
Drunken Chicken..157
Kung Pao Chicken..158–159
Honey Garlic Chicken..159
Lemon Chicken..160
Moo Goo Gai Pan..161
Chicken Curry, Cantonese Style..162
Soy Sauce Chicken..166
Gingered Chicken..167
Chinese Roast Chicken..168
Pineapple Duck Stir-Fry..171–172

Chapter 12: Pork, Beef, and Lamb

Sweet and Sour Pork..179
Mu Shu Pork..180
Char Siu..181
Twice-Cooked Pork..182–183
Jing Tu Pork Chops..183
Sichuan Spareribs..184
Pork with Bean Threads..185
Steamed Cabbage Rolls..186–187
Shanghai Meatballs..188
Chinese Pork Chops..189

Tomato Beef 191

Tangerine Beef 192

Broccoli Beef 194

Beef Steak Over Glass Noodles 195

Spicy Beef with Leeks 196–197

Beef Stew 198–199

Uncle Phillips' Beef Tri-Tip 200

Mongolian Lamb in Hotpot 202–203

Lamb with Green Onions 204

Chapter 13: Tofu and Eggs

Tofu with Spicy Tomato Sauce 210–211

Tofu with Ham and Napa Cabbage 211

Tofu with Shrimp 212

Monk's Choice Tofu 214–215

Ma Po Tofu 216

Tofu and Spinach 217

Tofu Puffs with Three-Color Vegetables 218

Tofu with Mushrooms and Cashews 219

Scrambled Eggs with Crabmeat 223

Tomato Eggs 224

Steamed Eggs 225

Egg Fu Young 226–227

Tea-Flavored Eggs 228

Chapter 14: Vegetables

Braised Bamboo Shoots with Bok Choy 240

Stir-Fried Assorted Vegetables 241

Asparagus with Baby Corn and Oyster-Flavored Sauce 242

Ivory and Jade (Cauliflower and Broccoli with Creamy Egg White) 243

Sautéed Green Beans 244–245

Three Mushrooms 245

Eggplants with Spicy Sauce 246–247

Swiss Chard with Tender Pork Slices 248

Chinatown Chop Suey 249

Chapter 15: Rice and Noodles

Perfect Steamed Rice 254

Perfect Steamed Glutinous Rice 255

Fried Rice 257

Sweet Precious Glutinous Rice 258

Claypot Chicken and Mushroom Rice 259
Easy-to-Make Chow Mein..264–265
Hong Kong-Style Pan-Fried Noodles...266–267
Chinese Chicken Noodle Soup..267
Singapore Rice Noodles...268
Beef Chow Fun 269
Ja Jiang Mein 270
Eight Treasures Noodle Soup...271
Shanghai Fried Noodles 272

Chapter 16: Sweet Treats

Almond Jelly with Fruit Cocktail 276
Sweet Tapioca Pearls 277
Steamed Sponge Cake 278
Sweet Silken Tofu...279
Almond Cookies...280–281
Mango Pudding...281
Caramelized Bananas..282–283
Egg Custard Tarts 284–285
Lychee Ice Cream 286

Table of Contents

Introduction 1

A Guide to the Guidebook...1
What I Assume about You 2
Your Itinerary...3
    Part I: What Is Chinese Cooking?................................3
    Part II: Where to Begin?...3
    Part III: The Recipes 3
    Part IV: The Part of Tens.......................................4
Conventions Used in This Book 4
Icons Used in This Book...5
Where to Go from Here...6

Part I: What Is Chinese Cooking? 7

Chapter 1: How to Think Like a Chinese Chef 9

Chinese Cooking and I, We Go Way Back 10
The Three Tenets of Chinese Cooking................................10
    Keep it in balance 11
    Cook seasonally, buy locally 11
    If all else fails, improvise! 12

Chapter 2: A Wok Through China's Amazing Culinary Regions 13

    Beijing: A Land of Plenty in the Face of Hardship.............14
    Shanghai: China's Big Apple 16
    Guangzhou: South of Eden 17
    Sichuan: China's Wild, Wild West 18

Part II: Where to Begin? 21

Chapter 3: Tools of the Trade 23

The Wok...23
    Choosing the right wok for you 24
    Seasoning your new wok 25
    Caring for your wok 26
The Chinese Chef's Knife..26
    Keeping out of harm's way: How to use your knife safely.....27
    Staying on the cutting edge: How to sharpen your
    Chinese chef's knife...28

The Cutting Board 29
The Spatula and the Ladle 29
The Strainer or Skimmer 29
The Steamer 30
The Claypot Casserole...31
The Electric Rice Cooker 31
Spice Grinders 32
Chopsticks 32

Chapter 4: The Chinese Pantry and Refrigerator **35**
Market Forces: Where to Find Essential Chinese Ingredients 36
Getting Sauced: Classic Chinese Sauces and Condiments....................37
Black bean sauce (See tzup jeng; shi zhi jiang)....................38
Char siu sauce (Tza siu jeng; cha shao jiang)......................38
Chile pastes and sauces (Laut tziu jeng; la jiao jiang)....................38
Chile oil (Laut you; la you) 39
Hoisin sauce (Hoi seen jeng; hai xian jiang) 39
Oyster-flavored sauce (Hou yeo; hao you) 40
Plum sauce (Suin mui jeng; suan mei chiang) 40
Rice wine (Mike tziu; mi jiu)..40
Sesame oil (Ma you)...41
Sesame paste (Tzee ma jeng; zhi ma jiang).........................42
Soy sauce (Jeng yeo; jiang you)...42
Dark soy sauce (Lo ceo; lao chou) 43
Rice vinegar (Bok tzo; mi cu) 43
Black vinegar (Hok tzo; hei cu)...44
Spicing Up Your Life with Chinese Herbs and Spices 44
Chinese five-spice powder (Ng heung fun; wu xiang fen) 45
Chinese hot mustard (Gai mut; jie mo) 45
Ginger (Geung; jiang) 45
Sichuan peppercorns (Fa tziu; hua jiao)...............................46
Star anise (Bark gog; ba jiao) 46
Canned, Dried, and Otherwise Preserved: The Ultimate
in Long-Lasting Chinese Ingredients 47
Tofu (Dou fu; do fu) 47
Chinese sausage (Larp tzoen; la chang) 48
Baby corn (Siu gum soeun; xiao jin sun)...............................48
Bamboo shoots (Tzook soeun; zhu sun)................................49
Water chestnuts (Ma tike; ma ti) 49
Straw mushrooms (Tzo gu; cao gu) 50
Dried black mushrooms (Gon doan gu; gan dong gu) 51
Dried black fungus (Hok mook yee; gan mu er) 52

Chapter 5: Common Chinese Cooking Techniques **55**
Look Sharp: Getting Ready...55
Getting a grip on your knife 56
Slicing...57

Matchstick/julienne cutting 57
Cubing/dicing/mincing 59
Roll cutting 60
Parallel cutting 60
Crushing 61
Scoring 61
Tenderizing 62
Non-Knife Wielding Techniques 62
The Art of Cooking 63
Before you start cooking 63
Stepping up to the stove 64

Chapter 6: Edible Artistry: Garnishes to Prettify Your Plate **71**
From the Simple to the Sublime: Garnishes that Run the Gamut 72
The basics 72
The high end 72
Preparing to Pare: Principles for Successful Garnishing 74
Garnishing 1-2-3s 74
Preparation issues 75
Getting Down to Business: The Garnishes...............................76

Part III: The Recipes...**83**

Chapter 7: Saucy Sauces and Dips **85**
Sauce Smarts 86
Taking a Dip 91

Chapter 8: Delectable Morsels: Appetizers, Snacks, and Salads ...**95**
Scrumptious Starters...96
It's a Wrap!...101
Egg roll wrappers (Chun kuen pay; chun chuan pi) 102
Spring roll wrappers 102
Wonton and potsticker wrappers 103

Chapter 9: Broth, Bones, and a Barrel of Soup **115**
Chinese Soup for the Soul and Body 115
Broth-er, Can You Spare Some Time?....................................116

Chapter 10: Swimming with the Best of Them: Seafood **125**
A Shopping Spree by the Sea..126
Choosing a fish market: A lean, clean, fish-selling machine 127
Choosing a fish: Buy with your senses 127

What Do I Do with It Now? 128
Cooking Fish the Chinese Way...129
Don't Be Selfish with the Shellfish 137
    Shopping for shellfish 137
    Put it away right 138

Chapter 11: Crying Fowl: Poultry Recipes 147

Pickin' a Chicken (Or Any Other Bird, for That Matter) 148
Proper Poultry Practices: Handling and Storing It Safely 149
I Fall to Pieces: Deconstructing Your Chicken....................151
No Bones about It: Boning Chicken Legs 153
Little Drummer Bird: Making Chicken Drummettes 154
Great Chicken Recipes...155
Carving Out a Niche for Yourself: How to Carve a
    Bird Like the Chinese Do 163
Duck, Duck, Lucky Duck 169

Chapter 12: Moo-ve In and Pig Out, My Little Lambs: Beef, Pork, and Lamb 173

Buying Basics: How to Shop for Meat................................174
Safety First: Dealing with Meat at Home 175
In Praise of Pork 177
Purchasing the Perfect Pig Product: How to Buy Pork
    Like a Chinese Cook 178
What's Your Beef? 190
Better Beef for a Chinese Meal 190
On the Lamb 201

Chapter 13: Healthy Tofu and Eggscellent Ideas 205

Taking a Look at Tofu..206
    How tofu is made...206
    Tofu texture variations 207
    Frozen and fermented tofu? 209
    Tofu preparations 209
More Than It's Cracked Up to Be: The Egg in Chinese Cuisine 220
    Walking on eggshells: Safety tips for dealing with eggs 220
    Great egg preparations 223

Chapter 14: The Green Revolution: Cooking Vegetables the Chinese Way 229

Who's Who in the World of Chinese Vegetables 230
    Bean sprouts (Ah cai j dou ya) 231
    Bok choy (Bok choy; xiao bai cai)..............................232

Chinese broccoli (Gai lan; jie lan) 232
Chinese chives (Gou choy; jiu lai)............................232
Chinese eggplants (Aike gwa; qie zi) 233
Cilantro (Yim sike; yuan xi)......................................234
Daikon (Law bok; lou bu) 234
Napa cabbage (Siu choy; da bai cai)..........................234
Snow peas (Hor lan dou; xue dou) 235
Taro root (Woo tou; yu tou) 235
Winter melon (Doan gwa; dong gua) 236
Yard-long beans (Dou gog; dou jiao) 236
How to Get the Most Out of Your Vegetables
While Cooking Them the Least.....................................237

Chapter 15: Rice Bowls and Oodles of Noodles **251**
Rice to the Occasion..251
Which Rice Will Suffice? 252
Long-grain rice (Jim mike; chan mi)..........................253
Medium-grain rice (Fong loi mike; fung lai mi) 254
Glutinous rice (Nor mike; nuo mi) 255
What to Make with Your Perfectly Cooked Rice 256
Noodling Around 260
Choose a Noodle, Any Noodle 260
Fresh egg noodles (Darn min; ji dan mien) 261
Fresh rice noodles (Seen hor fun; xian he fen) 262
Dried rice noodles (Gon hor fun; gan he fen) 263
Cellophane or bean thread noodles (Fun xi; fen si)......263
Noodle Recipes..264

Chapter 16: Sweet Sensations **273**
Eastern Traditions 274
Western Influences..279

Chapter 17: Bringing It All Together:
Full-Fledged Chinese Meals **287**
The Chinese Family Meal 287
Eating a Chinese meal...288
Making a marvelous menu: Planning
a balanced Chinese meal 289
Sample Menus for Two, Four, and More...........................290
Two's company...291
A feast for four 293
A table for six..294

Part IV: The Part of Tens 297

Chapter 18: Almost Ten Tips for Enjoying the Chinese Restaurant Experience 299

Making Sense of Regional Chinese Restaurants.............................299
    Cantonese (Southern-style) 300
    Mandarin (Northern- or Beijing-style) 300
    Sichuan-Hunan 301
    Shanghai 301
Eating Your Heart Out: Dim Sum...302
A Not-So-Sticky Situation: Using Chopsticks 304

Chapter 19: Ten Commandments: Secrets to Your Success 305

Flexibility and Adaptation Are Key 305
Let Your Creative Instincts Loose 306
Cook with the Seasons 306
Let Your Senses Be Your Guide 307
Taste as You Cook 307
Portions Aren't Set in Stone..308
Respect the Leftover..309
Know Thy Stovetop..309
Mind the Details 310
Share the Food; Share the Fun!...310

Chapter 20: Ten Martin-Tested Resources for Chinese Cuisine and Culture 311

Chapter 21: Drink Up: Ten Tips for Drinking Tea and Wine with Chinese Food 315

Four Bits of Info for the Tea Drinker..315
Six Wine-Related Tips 316

Index 319

Book Registration Information ....Back of Book

Introduction

•••

Climb aboard for a tour of one of the most fascinating, tantalizing cuisines on Earth: Chinese cuisine. And don't worry if you don't have anything packed, because the only bags you'll need are the ones you find at the grocery store. Just rustle up a few down-to-earth ingredients, some basic pieces of equipment that you probably already have, and a curious, adventuresome spirit, and you're ready to go.

Before you head out the door, let me remind you of one more very important travel accessory you'll want to bring along. But since you're reading this right now, you probably already know what it is. Yes, this book is sort of a travel guide for your edible vacation, leading you to the wonders of China's regions, its history, its complex culture, and its unique sense of humor and beauty. Pretty impressive for a cookbook, isn't it? Well, because culture, history, and geography are as fundamental to Chinese cuisine as rice, tea, and togetherness are to the Chinese table, this cookbook necessarily introduces you to the Chinese way of life, as well as to the basics of its recipes and cooking techniques.

So prepare to learn, laugh, and lay into some delicious dishes that are classics both in North America and in China itself. If moving freely through China's culinary gold mines seems surprisingly easy to you, it'll surprise you more to learn that it gets easier with practice. After all, the way to a country's heart is through its kitchen!

A Guide to the Guidebook

Some travelers like to move methodically from one location to the next, planning ahead with reservations and schedules of which sites they're going to visit and when. Others travel with more of a "come-what-may" philosophy, following the maps of their hearts and whims, winding up wherever the train does, and wandering on again once their feet get itchy for greener pastures.

Culinary travelers are no different, falling into either of the two camps themselves, and this guidebook will satisfy both types. That's because it contains recipes, nuggets of wisdom, and stories that stand alone as keys to Chinese cooking – perfect for those who prefer roaming freely among their dinner table destinations. But reading this book from cover to cover before your culinary trip helps the more orderly among you establish a sturdy plan for understanding what it means to cook the Chinese way.

No matter which method you choose, consider this book your all-in-one resource for discovering the cuisine of China. Let it inspire you to travel further, too; pay repeat visits to the world of Chinese food, each time learning something new and delving even deeper into a cuisine that rewards exploration. You'll be glad you did.

What I Assume about You

This book is intended as an *introduction* to Chinese cooking, so I don't expect you to have a restaurant-quality supply of Chinese cooking equipment on hand. Luckily, you don't need one, although the recipes alert you when they require special items or gadgets. However, I do assume you have a kitchen, and that in your kitchen you have the following items:

- A chef's knife (the Chinese chef's knife I describe in Chapter 3 is ideal) and a paring knife for smaller, more intricate tasks.

- A 12- to 14-inch round-bottom wok and a lid with a ring stand, or a flat-bottom wok and lid, which works particularly well with electric burners (see Chapter 3). Whether or not you have a wok, you can prepare the stir-fries and a number of other dishes in this book in a similarly sized skillet, sauté pan, or frying pan with sides high enough to accommodate the ingredients.

- A large, covered pot or kettle for broths, soups, deep-frying, and steaming if you don't have a steamer (see Chapter 3 for instructions on steaming foods without a steamer).

- Saucepans and lids of various sizes for preparing some sauces and desserts. A double boiler is a plus for some recipes, but isn't necessary.

- A claypot and a lid (see Chapter 3), heavy Dutch oven and a lid, or a covered casserole for preparing claypot, stewed, or braised dishes.

- A large metal, ceramic, or glass roasting pan with a rack.

- Baking sheets and wire racks, glass or metal tart molds or a muffin tin, a glass or metal pie dish, and a 9-inch glass or metal cake pan.

- Liquid measuring cups (these are normally plastic or glass, with a spout and handle), dry measuring cups (usually metal or plastic and available in a different sizes that can be "nested" for storage), and measuring spoons.

- Wooden or metal mixing spoons, a wire whisk, and a spatula.

- Mixing bowls in various sizes.

- A large colander for draining noodles and vegetables.

Your Itinerary

You can tackle this book from many angles, but knowing how it's set up gets you where you want to go more efficiently. Once you pass the first few introductory chapters, its organization mirrors a Chinese restaurant menu, with chapters dedicated to appetizers, soups, seafood, poultry, meats, tofu and eggs, vegetables, rice and noodles, and desserts. I even toss in chapters on sauces and garnishes for good measure. Later chapters give you a chance to try your hand at entertaining and menu planning, Chinese-style.

Part I: What Is Chinese Cooking?

Do a little background reading about what really makes Chinese cooking distinctive – and it's not just ingredients, recipes, techniques, and equipment, either. Everything from the cuisine's history to basic Chinese cooking philosophies are in this section. It also officially sets us off on our edible tour of China. We visit the country's major regions and learn how the people, history, and location carved out the landscape of flavors in each region.

Part II: Where to Begin?

Find all the nitty-gritty basics here. This section contains clear, thorough descriptions of any equipment you may want to add to your kitchen as you work your way through the world of Chinese cooking. It also tells you how to stock your pantry and refrigerator with what's on my list of essential Chinese ingredients, and where to buy them. (In case you're shopping in Asian markets, I provide the Cantonese and Mandarin pronunciations for these ingredients.) I cover cooking techniques here, too — distinctly Chinese ones as well as some basic Western methods — with step-by-step instructions and illustrations. Before you move on, the chapter on garnishes gives easy instructions for making impressive plate decorations that help you dine with style.

Part III: The Recipes

Now you're ready to do some exploring on your own and in your own kitchen. Start with the basic sauces that pop up again and again in recipes throughout the book. Whet your appetite with classic Chinese appetizers and soups and then move on to the dishes that you know and love from menus at your favorite Chinese restaurants. In addition to those classics, this section includes plenty of dishes that may not be too familiar this side of the Pacific, as well as updates and twists on the tried-and-true, just to keep you on your toes.

Part IV: The Part of Tens

Every *For Dummies* book ends with top-ten lists. I offer you the commonsense scoop on successful Chinese cooking, some beverage tips for Chinese meals, and additional resources for more information.

Conventions Used in This Book

I wish I'd had this book when I was learning to cook. It makes things much more foolproof than the trial-and-error method that I practically perfected during my kitchen training. To take advantage of the tips, reminders, time estimations, illustrations, anecdotes, and experience-based advice — all of which make this book more than just a collection of recipes — read through the whole recipe before you start cooking.

Here are some other cooking conventions to keep in mind if you want to get the most out of this guide:

- All soy sauce is regular, naturally fermented soy sauce unless noted. (See Chapter 4 for more soy sauce tips.)

- Cut all meats, particularly beef, across the grain.

- Julienned or matchstick-cut ingredients should be cut to very thin dimensions — almost to the point of being shredded. (See Chapter 5 for explanations of julienne and matchstick-cutting; see Chapter 14 for a description of shredding.)

- Marinate foods in the refrigerator in sealed or covered containers before cooking.

- Sturdier proteins such as meats and poultry items can be marinated in the refrigerator in sealed or covered containers longer than specified in the recipes. Marinating fish and shellfish for long periods, however, may damage their texture and isn't recommended.

- When adding a cornstarch solution to a recipe, give it a thorough stir to blend the cornstarch and liquid before pouring the solution into the wok.

- Garlic burns easily in a hot wok, and when it does, it turns bitter and acrid. Ten seconds of stir-frying over medium heat, stirring frequently, is usually all that small amounts of garlic need to heat and release their fragrance without burning.

✔ Pay attention to whether recipe ingredient lists specify sauces or pastes. They're very different from one another, sauces being thinner than pastes, and aren't necessarily interchangeable. If you need a sauce but can only find a paste, you can always dilute the latter a little, or just use less of it. Going the other way around — from a sauce to a paste — is a little more challenging, and my only advice is to keep searching for the paste.

✔ Some of the Chinese rice wines used in certain recipes can be fairly high in alcohol content. If residual alcohol in a dish or sauce concerns you, make sure to bring the dish to a full boil to vaporize and drive off the alcohol.

Icons Used in This Book

A general good idea. A helpful hint.

Some advice that will keep you, or your food, from getting burned.

A food or cooking concept that you shouldn't forget.

When I talk about food from a particular region of China, I use this icon.

When I provide some interesting info on Chinese culture, I use this icon.

When I use this icon, you know I'm giving you advice that comes from my personal experience as a chef.

Where to Go from Here

China is a big country with an equally extensive culinary domain. Setting off to discover its cuisines can intimidate even seasoned cooks, let alone novices. But take it from this seasoned cook: The steps you've already taken put you on the fast track toward cooking Chinese food with the best. Stay the course as you make your way through this book, and you'll find that your journeys will give you a perspective on the cuisine that breaks right through intimidating boundaries. If more than a billion Chinese can cook it — and especially if I can cook it! — you can, too.

Part I
What Is Chinese Cooking?

The 5th Wave   By Rich Tennant

"It's General Gau's Stranger Flavored Chicken prepared by Mrs. Howel's odd looking husband."

In this part . . .

1 give you a little background on what really makes Chinese cooking distinctive — and it's not just ingredients, recipes, techniques, and equipment, either. Everything from the cuisine's history to basic Chinese cooking philosophies is in this part. It also officially sets us off on our edible tour of China. We visit the country's major regions and discover how the people, history, and location carved out the landscape of flavors in each.

Chapter 1

How to Think Like a Chinese Chef

In This Chapter

▶ Exploring the history of Chinese cuisine

▶ Three Chinese cooking guidelines

*1*f your idea of Chinese cooking is egg rolls, wonton soup, and fortune cookies, you're about to get quite a wake-up call. One of the most diverse and unique of the world's cuisines, Chinese cooking offers an endless variety of flavors, textures, shapes, and cooking techniques. But don't let that variety overwhelm you; at the heart of even the most elaborate imperial dish lies a no-nonsense simplicity and some common ingredients. Start thinking like a Chinese chef, and you'll soon become one.

So how do you think like a Chinese chef anyway? If you ask me, the best way to start is to remain flexible. Chinese cooking isn't fraught with strict rules or recipes that you have to follow to the fraction of a tablespoon. After all, you'll find China's best cooks not in the lavish hotel or restaurant kitchens, but rather in the home kitchens scattered throughout the country's towns and villages. These culinary magicians have learned to keep an open mind about how and what to cook, since access to ingredients and equipment is sometimes sketchy at best.

But, boy, have they turned scarcity into an art form. Chinese cuisine's flexible philosophy naturally breeds the creativity that makes Chinese foods so exciting to prepare and, of course, to eat. Just follow some basic guidelines — guidelines that will become second nature to you with the help of this book — and you can sharpen your Chinese culinary instinct and turn the contents of your pantry into authentic Chinese treats at the same time. It's this openness to invention that makes Chinese cuisine truly egalitarian. Power to the people!

Chinese Cooking and I, We Go Way Back

If you think that you spend a lot of time in the kitchen, consider this: Chinese people started cooking almost 500,000 years ago — and we're still at it! In northern China, Peking man used simple stone tools to hunt deer, tigers, water buffaloes, and other wild game. It's a pity that few of their cookbooks survived. I, for one, would be interested in finding out how to fillet a prehistoric wild boar.

Food, cooking, and agriculture have always played important roles in Chinese religion and society, too. For centuries, religious deities kept watch over all Chinese kitchens; poets and scholars sang praises of dining and drinking; and folk heroes were known for their appetites for good food and wine. Even today, faithful Chinese make offerings of fresh fruits, dumplings, barbecued meat, and whole chickens to the spirits of their departed love ones.

China has had its share of hard times and scarcity, however, and its people have learned to be resilient to keep food on the table in the face of floods, droughts, earthquakes, typhoons, and famines. Feeding one quarter of the world's population takes a lot of creativity and hard work, even under the best of circumstances.

That's why, over the centuries, Chinese cooking has adapted and changed while still paying homage to time-honored recipes handed down from generation to generation. Yet, it never shies from innovations — taking advantage of modern technology in food cultivation and preservation and incorporating new ingredients into the Chinese diet. Some recently "invented" Chinese dishes are actually modifications of older ones, with the addition of a few new ingredients and flavor twists. For example, common American-Chinese restaurant dishes such as chop suey and egg fu young were actually "invented" by Chinese immigrants to the United States; plenty of Chinese have never even heard of them. And what about those fiery, chile-packed Chinese recipes, or even tomato beef, a popular stateside menu choice? Well, neither chile peppers nor tomatoes entered Chinese kitchens until Western traders brought them there only a few hundred years ago.

The Three Tenets of Chinese Cooking

You don't have to be well versed in Confucianism or Taoist principles to think like a Chinese cook, and you don't have to master fancy cooking techniques or buy a ton of kitchen equipment either. You really need only a few simple tools (see Chapter 3) and the willingness to follow a few basic guidelines — not rules — that all Chinese cooks first followed as children in their own parents' kitchens. I talk about three of those guidelines in the following sections.

Keep it in balance

The Chinese pay a great deal of attention to contrast and harmony in their everyday existence. Balancing yin and yang is a way to achieve harmony in your life, as well as your culinary creations. These two elements complement and contrast each other, and a thorough understanding of them goes a long way toward understanding the Chinese philosophy in the kitchen. Here's what these two terms mean:

- ✔ Yin represents feminine, soft, cold, and wet forces.
- ✔ Yang is masculine, bright, hot, dry, and vigorous.

So how does this harmony translate to food? Chinese classify bland, low-calorie foods as yin, whereas richer and fattier items fall within the yang category. By harmonizing the yin and yang ingredients in a dish, the cook creates a good meal that maintains a healthy balance. If this concept sounds a bit too abstract, consider the popular dish sweet-and-sour pork — a clear example of the yin/yang balance of taste (sweet is yin, and sour is yang).

Balancing isn't restricted to taste alone. You can create texture contrast by combining soft, steamed items with crispy, fried ones. Or how about contrasting the color scheme with the spiciness in a single dish? Cooking techniques as opposite as deep-frying and steaming can join forces to create meals that are not only tasty but also philosophically stimulating.

Cook seasonally, buy locally

For much of China's history, its people have had to adapt their daily menus to those ingredients available in their own gardens and at local markets on that particular day. Chinese home cooks somehow managed to turn this liability into an asset, taking limited, simple ingredients and turning them into masterpieces. The popularity of wheat-flour dumplings and noodles and of root-based dishes in northern China; the deft preparation of fresh seafood in the regions running along the country's coast; and the prevalence of fresh produce and rice dishes in the semitropical south all attest to the use of local, seasonally accessible foods.

Perhaps the best place to start is at your local farmers market. Always ask what's in season. Fruits and vegetables that are in season are abundant and at their peak of flavor, color, and texture, while those out of season are few, and their quality can be questionable. Go with the numbers, and you have a better chance at getting high-quality ingredients.

Don't see what you want in your local market? Check out the seed store, and you may turn your backyard into a healthy Asian vegetable garden. You can rather effortlessly grow many vegetables that are common in Chinese dishes in small backyard plots or gardens. I know this because I consider myself a gentleman farmer on a small scale. Over the years, I've grown fresh chile peppers, Asian herbs and greens, and even a number of different cucumbers and squashes 15 feet from my bedroom window.

Granted, raising poultry and hogs in midtown Manhattan or catching live river shrimp in Nebraska may not be practical. Nevertheless, you should still think "fresh, fresh, fresh" when seeking these and other ingredients at your local market or your favorite butcher's counter.

Many substitutes are available for the traditional ingredients and cooking tools used in Chinese cuisine. But there is no substitute for freshness. None.

If all else fails, improvise!

Chinese chefs are experts in developing endless alternatives in ingredients and cooking methods in the face of scarcity and hardship. If you want to cook like the Chinese, you, too, should adopt a flexible approach when it comes to the availability of ingredients.

Many ingredients in traditional Chinese dishes sound foreign to novice cooks — and for good reason! Even with the ever-expanding stock of most supermarket chains, finding yard-long beans in suburban Detroit may still be a bit challenging. However, regular green beans can make a nice substitute. So be flexible: Buy fresh, crisp regular green beans and enjoy.

The next time you hit an ingredient-availability wall, don't give up on the whole recipe. Use your imagination to scope out attainable items that can take the place of ones not quite at peak freshness or still on the dock in Shanghai. No one but you will know the difference.

In all Chinese markets, you find an array of dried, pickled, salted, bottled, canned, or otherwise-preserved counterparts for seasonal or less-readily available ingredients. Take advantage of the assortment and stock up on dried noodles, grains, and dried black mushrooms, for starters.

If you don't have the time or inclination to make your own sweet-and-sour stir-fry sauce, the Asian foods section of your local store can pick up the slack with countless bottled versions. Remember that canned, sliced water chestnuts, bamboo shoots, and straw mushrooms — all easy to find — take the core out of your prep work. By throwing in a little patience and imagination, anyone can cook Chinese like the Chinese.

Chapter 2

A Wok Through China's Amazing Culinary Regions

In This Chapter

▶ Visiting Beijing

▶ Touring Shanghai

▶ Discovering Guangzhou

▶ Exploring Sichuan

China is a vast country. On a land mass of 3.8 million square miles, the "Middle Kingdom," as China is sometimes called, lays claim to almost every geographic and climatic region imaginable. Hot, arid deserts; lush, sub-tropical coastline; spectacular but flood-prone gorges; grassy plains that stretch as far as the eyes can see — you name it, and you'll find it in China. Over the millennia, these natural elements shaped the country's cuisines just as they shaped its culture. Chinese cooks must make do with what Mother Nature has given them, and in the process, they've proven themselves masters of frugality, resourcefulness, and, of course, good taste.

Environmental distinctions make it natural to classify Chinese cuisine by geographic regions: Beijing in the north, Shanghai on the eastern coast, Guangzhou in the south, and Sichuan at the western end of the river plains (see Figure 2-1). A good grasp of each region's history, geography, and culture is the first step to understanding China's rich and distinctive cuisines.

Figure 2-1:
A map of
China.

Beijing: A Land of Plenty in the Face of Hardship

Life isn't much of a picnic in northern China. Victim of Mother Nature's merciless whim, this region is cursed with bitterly cold winters. Bone-chilling winds from Manchuria and Siberia, Beijing's northerly neighbors, keep the ground frozen half the year. Once the earth thaws, the dry, sandy, infertile soil can't support a wide variety of crops even in the best weather. To make matters worse, year after year, the massive Yellow River (fittingly nicknamed "China's Sorrow") brings harvest-devastating and famine-spawning floods.

Harsh weather conditions make root vegetables and hearty cabbages the darlings of the northern palates. Rice dishes are rare because growing rice in the arid north is a losing proposition. Here, farmers plant grains that can thrive in the unforgiving soil, such as millet, barley, and primarily wheat, which they use to make noodles and a variety of dumplings. The Yellow River, magnificent as it may be, is no fertile ground for fish and edible shellfish, and northern Chinese cooks have to look elsewhere to fill their food baskets.

Out of these hardships a cooking style emerged that is as ingenious as it is hearty. Northern Chinese chefs seized upon what little nature has given them and turned it into the magnificent cuisine of China's Imperial Court. For more than eight centuries, Beijing served as the imperial capital of China, and it has retained all the historical and cultural splendors of an ancient civilization. The great Chinese culinary tradition is proudly passed on from one generation of imperial chefs to the next. The banquet halls in the Imperial Palace and today's Great Hall of the People have held the grandest and most elaborate feasts in history. In fact, historians say that the Forbidden City, as Beijing is often called, regularly had as many as 2,000 chefs in its kitchens. Obviously, the emperor didn't think that too many cooks would spoil his broth.

Today in Beijing, elegant restaurants such as Bianyifang Restaurant, the Tin Li Restaurant, and the Swan Palace have grabbed the baton from the ancient culinary masters. These restaurants create and serve food that is an amalgam of all China's cuisines, with a little worldly influence sprinkled in for good measure. A visit to these famous eateries is a journey through the Beijing culinary landscape: steamed buns, noodles, dumplings, and the world-famous Peking duck with crispy, honey-glazed skin and tender, succulent meat served in thin Mandarin pancakes doused with hoisin sauce and spring onions. Peking duck actually traces part of its origin back to Beijing's unbearably hot, dry summers. During that time, dressed and marinated ducks hung outside peasants' homes, where their skin quickly and naturally parched to the characteristic dry crispness that now takes chefs hours to achieve.

Today's Beijing cuisine also reflects the region's ties to its foreign neighbors. Throughout history, Beijing was invaded at different times by Mongols, Manchurians, and Muslims. Foreign invaders founded both the Yuan and Qing dynasties. In addition to palaces and historical monuments, these conquerors left behind many of their culinary habits and traditions. The lamb dishes in Beijing cuisine stem from Muslim influence. And the fonduelike hotpot (see Chapter 12) is a parting gift from the Mongols. To enjoy it, diners plunge thinly sliced sheets of meat — traditionally lamb, but now often pork and beef as well as seafood and vegetables — into pots of boiling broth. After the broth cooks the meat, diners dip it in a spicy sauce and chase it all down with pot-blanched cabbage and other vegetables. The grilled versions of the many dishes involve cooking the meat on a large, round, open griddle with vinegar and hot oil as seasoning. You'll find this type of Eastern grilling today in Mongolian barbecue restaurants.

With either choice, diners get a fair sample of the contrasts and melding of cultures and tastes inherent in Beijing's cuisine. Steeped in both elegance and modesty, at once worldly and nationalistic, the hotpot embodies many of the distinctive traits of this region's cooking.

Shanghai: China's Big Apple

Where Beijing is stark and dry, Shanghai, to Beijing's southeast, is colorful, rich, and blessed by the flowing, fish-filled waters of the Yangtze River. Water is life in these parts, and these waters — including many ponds, tributaries, and fish farms — have yielded enough bounty to sustain the population of Shanghai, one of the most populated cities on the planet.

The people of Shanghai and neighboring Yangzhou, Hangzhou, and Suzhou are among the wealthiest in China. They like to think of their fertile Yangtze River Valley as the "Land of Fish and Rice," and their daily diets celebrate this bounty. By Chinese standards, Shanghai is a relatively new city. It became incorporated only in the 1800s, so some may argue that there is no such thing as traditional Shanghai cuisine. In truth, this ever-growing metropolis, whose hustle and bustle rivals New York City's, has adopted the culinary styles of surrounding provinces such as Jiangsu and Zhejiang, and shaped them into a unique style of "Shanghai cuisine."

When you walk Shanghai's busy streets today — if you can squeeze through the crowds — and on every corner, you see provincial restaurants ready to feed the hungry masses rushing from one meeting or industrial complex to the next. A real hallmark of modern Shanghai's food style is street food — or should I call it fast food Shanghai style? Sidewalk stalls offer simple noodle and rice dishes and freshly steamed pork buns, which are breads stuffed with pork, cabbage, mushrooms, and onions. These foods provide today's always-on-the-go Shanghai diners a quick, tasty, and economical pick-me-up.

Although Shanghai proper has no deep-seated dining traditions of its own, the neighboring provinces that now lend the city irresistible flavors do possess more elaborate culinary resumes. Many of China's most recognized dishes come from nearby Yangtze Delta areas. Westlake fish, Lion's Head meatballs, Yangchow fried rice, salted fish, red-cooked pork, hundred-year-old eggs, sizzling spareribs, sweet vinegars, Dragon Well tea, and Shao Hsing rice wine all hail from this region of plenty.

Seafood lovers claim that the area's real culinary gold mine is the Shanghai hairy crab (actually caught in Yangcheng Lake a bit further up the Yangtze). True fans of these furry, black, autumn harvest treasures travel from all over the world and pay top dollar to enjoy the crustacean that they claim makes all other seafood dishes worthless by comparison. Look for them (the crabs that is, not the fans) during the autumn months, and you may just be the next convert.

Shanghai chefs generally prefer deep-frying, slow-braising, and red-cooking (a method of simmering meats in flavored and sweetened soy sauce) to the quicker stir-frying (see Chapter 5) method. Their dishes tend to be slightly oily and sweet, as they favor the combination of Shao Hsing rice wine with sugar, soy sauce, and vinegar. The region's ample bounty of vegetables, wild mushrooms, and fish balances these somewhat heavier dishes. The result is a cuisine that is rich in variety of ingredients, as well as more luscious and strongly flavored than any other Chinese regional offerings.

Guangzhou: South of Eden

Early Chinese immigrants to the West were primarily from the Guangzhou province (formerly Canton) in southern China. They brought with them the essence of Cantonese cooking: absolutely fresh ingredients; plenty of vegetables, fruits, and seafood; minimal seasoning other than salt, pepper, ginger, garlic, or spring onions; rice as a staple; and, above all, an overriding sense of simplicity. Over time, these ingredients have become the standard bearers for Chinese cuisine in the West because many of the first Chinese restaurants to open outside of China specialized in Cantonese fare. From moo goo gai pan (chicken with black mushrooms and snow peas) to egg flower soup and lemon chicken, most Westerners had their first taste of Chinese food in a Cantonese-style restaurant.

Cantonese enjoyment of food in all its forms is legendary. Although you won't find field mouse, anteater, or cobra on any Western menus, they're not entirely uncommon foods in Canton. The Chinese commonly say that the Cantonese eat anything with four legs except the dinner table or the chair. Or that they eat anything that flies but the kite and plane, or anything whose backbone points to heaven. In other words, the Cantonese eat anything that's edible. It's little wonder that Guangzhou is a truly unique, world-class dining capital.

An ancient Chinese saying sums up Guangzhou's lofty epicurean status nicely: Lucky people are born in Suzhou, home to the world's most beautiful women. Luck also visits those who dress in Hangzhou, where you find the world's finest silks. And if you are fortunate, you'll die in Guizhou, because the best wood for coffins grows there. But the truly luckiest of all are those who eat in Guangzhou, for nowhere else in the world do you find food as irresistible as what you find there.

Mother Nature smiles upon the Cantonese, giving them plenty of fresh seafood, three crops of rice per year, and six crops of exotic vegetables and fruits. Chiu Chow, Hakka, Hoklo, and Tanka fisherman — all "sea gypsies" who are ethnically related to the Cantonese — haul shrimp, lobster, eels, and other swimming delicacies, still thrashing in their nets, to market. There, lucky cooks snap them up for their family or restaurant kitchens. Lush, fertile farms and gardens reward the farmers who lovingly tend them with bounties of farm-fresh produce. The Cantonese home cooks who like to make multiple trips to the local market each day settle for nothing but the freshest that land and sea have to offer.

In Guangzhou, food is an all-day celebration. Pay an early-morning visit to any of Guangzhou's countless dim sum tea houses, where savvy diners choose from hundreds of delicately flavored and prepared finger foods and appetizer-sized delicacies. Chefs throughout China willingly acknowledge their Cantonese counterparts' leading roles in the kitchen. They admire the Cantonese preference of subtle seasoning, which brings out rather than covers a dish's natural flavors, and quick stir-frying and steaming, techniques that leave foods tasting light and natural.

With easy accessibility to nature's finest ingredients and the boundless imagination of the most inventive culinary minds, Guangzhou seems to be a culinary Paradise Found. If you want to discover these foods for yourself, travel there and experience some of the world's best food first-hand. Or find yourself an admirable Cantonese restaurant nearby and enjoy your own little slice of paradise.

Sichuan: China's Wild, Wild West

Deep in the heart of China, surrounded by mountains and closed off by the Yangtze River, lies hot and humid Sichuan (sometimes spelled "Szechuan"), China's spice — and rice — bowl. Along the bottom of this basin, millions of acres of thirsty fields drink from elaborate irrigation systems that have yoked water from the Yangtze and its four tributaries for more than a millennium. This is China's version of the Great Plains. To this day, it feeds more than a hundred million of the country's inhabitants.

The region's agricultural might, coupled with the influence of Western spices, created a culinary tradition appreciated the world over. Indian influence looms large in Sichuan life, from the Buddhist religion to the occasional curry dish and the spicy character of the food. It's only fitting that Sichuan cuisine, and the similar foods of nearby Hunan province, eventually got the chance to exert some culinary influence on neighboring cultures in Thailand, Burma, Laos, and Kampuchea. Sichuan cuisine's trademark is its heat, which coincidentally helps diners deal with that region's extreme climate: In the summer swelter, the sweating that a spicy dish induces cools the body, while in winter, a spicy meal readjusts diners' internal thermostats to "warm."

Categorizing Sichuan cuisine as simply hot-and-spicy doesn't give credit to the wealth of culinary delights that await the region's hungry explorers. Traders to India brought back foreign spices and cooking styles to Sichuan. They also introduced the Buddhist practice of vegetarianism that shows up today in many dishes using tofu and pungent Sichuan preserved vegetables — pickled or fresh kohlrabi, mustard greens, napa cabbage, and turnips spiced with chili powder and ground Sichuan peppercorn. You often find Sichuan peppercorn in stir-fried and red-cooked dishes, too, where along with spicier chili peppers, spring onions, garlic, sesame, and vinegar, it creates a piquant, flavorful profile that distinguishes Sichuan foods from those of China's other regions. In addition to stir-fries, slowly simmered dishes are popular with Sichuan diners, particularly the flavorful curries. In such a hot region know for fiery foods, it's appropriate that heat-heavy methods such as flash-frying and spit-roasting also figure prominently. And of course, Sichuan cooks have made a name for themselves as expert practitioners of the aromatic technique of smoking.

Sichuan chefs are also master blenders of flavors. By combining the sweetness of maltose or brown sugar, sourness from vinegar, saltiness from soy or salt, bitterness from spring onions, nuttiness from sesame flavors, and the essential heat from chiles, they create a flavorful painting that is wholly Sichuan.

Even though Sichuan is relatively landlocked, the Yangtze supplies the region's cooks and diners with freshwater crustaceans, eels, and fish that appear on local menus either fresh or salted and preserved. The Sichaunese love the taste and texture of poultry and pork combined with produce from the area's vast farmlands, as well as from the wilds of the mountains. Ask anyone familiar with Sichuan food, and he'll tell you unequivocally: Sichuan cooking is hot, in more ways than one!

Part II
Where to Begin?

In this part . . .

1 give you all the nitty-gritty basics here. I describe the
  equipment that you may want to add to your kitchen as
you work your way through the world of Chinese cooking.
I tell you how to stock your pantry and refrigerator with
essential Chinese ingredients. I also cover cooking techniques here, too — distinctly Chinese ones as well as
some basic Western methods — with step-by-step instructions and illustrations. At the end of this part, the chapter
on garnishes gives easy instructions for making impressive plate decorations that help you dine with style.

Chapter 3

Tools of the Trade

- -

In This Chapter

▶ Selecting everything from woks to chopsticks

▶ Caring for your kitchen tools

- -

Stepping into a typical kitchen in China may feel like a journey back in time. You probably won't find too many modern conveniences such as microwave ovens, food processors, or pots and pans in all different sizes to fit every dish. You may not even find an oven! The typical Chinese kitchen hasn't changed much over the centuries simply because it doesn't need to. Why change when the traditional method still works? Chinese cuisine is a simple cuisine, and so, naturally, are its essential kitchen accoutrements.

Many skilled Chinese cooks get by with nothing more than a wok, a matching lid, a spatula, a chef's knife, and a heavy-duty cutting board. A *really* well-stocked Chinese kitchen may even come with a ladle, a bamboo steamer, a claypot, a few pots, and, of course, lots and lots of chopsticks.

Before you run to your housewares store and snap up every gadget necessary to create a top-notch Chinese kitchen, consider that you may already have sevcral of these functional items. Furthermore, you may be surprised at how easily you can adapt everyday Western cooking tools to make authentic-tasting Chinese dishes. If you decide to purchase a few items, choose high-quality pieces that will last as long as Chinese cooking has. Here's what you may want to buy new and what you can improvise from your current kitchen stock.

The Wok

The wok is the single most essential and functional piece of equipment in the Chinese kitchen, shown in Figure 3-1. The traditional concave, bowl-shaped pan can do the job of a number of pots and pans. It stir-fries, steams, deep-fries, boils, simmers, braises, smokes, and can also pop your corn. In a pinch, it can even be a portable kitchen sink! A wok's depth makes it spillproof when you toss foods quickly, its concave shape spreads heat efficiently over its surface, and its round bottom allows cooks to use less oil in their stir-fries and deep-fried dishes. What an invention!

Figure 3-1:
The kind of
traditional
well-
stocked
kitchen that
you can find
all over
China.

Spatula Strainer

Ladle

Steamers

Chopsticks

Chef's
knife

Cutting Board

Wok Claypot

TRADITIONAL CHINESE KITCHEN SCENE

Choosing the right wok for you

Even this ancient, deceptively simple tool has a few bells and whistles. Woks come in all sizes, ranging in diameter from 9 inches for small home woks, to 24 inches for restaurant woks, to massive 4-foot woks that you can find in Buddhist temples. For family use, I suggest a deep 12- or 14-inch wok, which should give you enough room to prepare a hearty stir-fry for four to six people.

In addition to picking the right size, you have to choose among woks made from spun carbon steel, stainless steel, an aluminum/stainless steel amalgam, or the latest offering — anodized aluminum with or without a nonstick surface. You also have the option of a round or flat bottom. The latter works well with most electric cooktops because the increased surface contact between its flat base and the burner heats the wok more efficiently.

If you go for a round wok (shown in Figure 3-1), you may need a wok stand — a metal ring placed on top of the cooktop that stabilizes your wok. Round-bottomed woks work better on gas ranges. And no matter which wok you choose, a high, domed lid turns it into an excellent roaster and steamer. (If the wok you buy doesn't come with a lid, you can purchase one separately. Look for a lid that's slightly smaller in diameter than the wok so that it sits solidly just below the wok's rim.)

When some people travel, they take everything but the kitchen sink. Personally, I like to stick with my electric wok, another one of the woks available today. Because it has its own built-in heating element and temperature control, it works independently from the stove, making it a real boon to those who just can't spare an extra burner. That built-in thermostat also gives you plenty of control over the temperature, making electric woks great for deep-frying. And thanks to their mobility, you can use them as "chafing woks" for buffet dishes. The one drawback of the average electric wok: It just doesn't heat to high enough temperatures to produce really vibrant, authentic stir-fries, so if you do have room on the stove for a traditional wok, I'd recommend using it.

Seasoning your new wok

Patience is the key to good wokking. Instead of firing up your brand-new wok immediately, season it first. New woks (except for the nonstick variety) need some initial pampering, or "seasoning," to give them an oil coating that creates a resistant cooking surface.

To season your wok, follow these steps:

1. **Scrub it thoroughly with hot, soapy water and a scouring pad.**

   This is one of the few times that you need to use heavy soap on the wok's surface.

2. **Place it over low to medium heat to dry it thoroughly.**

3. **Using an old towel, rub a small amount (maybe a teaspoon) of vegetable oil evenly over its surface, gently heating the wok while rubbing with the oiled towel. Add a bit more oil if the wok's surface starts looking dry. Use a little elbow grease while you're at it, making sure that the oil really gets into the wok's "pores."**

4. **Continue this rubbing process for about 15 to 20 minutes, depending on the wok and how vigorously you rub, until the wok's surface gets a darkened look.**

   Your goal is to develop the "homemade" nonstick surface that's the telltale sign of a seasoned wok. If the center of the wok has a dark-brown, "stained" appearance, you've reached that goal.

5. **Let the wok cool, wash it in warm water with a soft, nylon pad or brush, and briefly dry it on the stove over high heat.**

From here on, it only gets better with each use.

Caring for your wok

Rinse your wok after each use with water only; use none or, at the very most, a little soapy water. You don't have to scrub it very vigorously after each use. If the wok rusts, scour it with an abrasive cream or fine salt to remove the surface rust. Before storing your wok, make sure to thoroughly dry it by setting it over low heat on the cooktop for a couple minutes. Then rub a little oil into the surface if you don't plan to use it for a few weeks. Over time, you and your wok will become the best of buddies in the kitchen.

The Chinese Chef's Knife

The Chinese have used a type of single-blade food processor in the kitchen since centuries before the invention of electricity. What's more, this age-old food processor is a lot easier to clean and store than an electric model. It is the Chinese chef's knife (refer to Figure 3-1).

The modest chef's knife, with its large, wide blade and slightly curved edge, is the ideal slicer, dicer, shredder, and mincer. Aside from cutting and dicing, you can tenderize meats by pounding them with the dull side of its blade. You can use the flat of the blade as a scooper and smasher for herbs and spices such as garlic and ginger. Even the handle comes in handy: Use it to crush black peppercorns, Sichuan peppercorns, and other dried spices.

But before you rush out to buy your first Chinese chef's knife, take into account these purchasing and usage guidelines that will keep you chopping effectively for years to come:

- Select a Chinese chef's knife that's made from quality, high-carbon stainless steel, one that feels comfortable and well balanced in your hand. Don't pick a knife that feels awkward or heavier on one end than the other.

- Its center of gravity should be right where the wooden part of the handle meets the metal part of the blade.

- And once you find the knife of your dreams, what's the secret to the lightning-fast chopping skill and accuracy of an accomplished Chinese master chef? Three words — practice, practice, practice.

Keeping out of harm's way: How to use your knife safely

Any professional chef will tell you that "a sharp knife is a safe knife." Always make sure that your knife holds its sharp edge and that it sharpens easily when needed. Your chef's knife is not a heavy cleaver for hacking through dense bones, because that will ruin its edge. You can use your knife for cutting poultry carcasses, but not bones and joints of beef, lamb, and pork. Protect your knife's blade during storage; knocking it against other knives and tools can dull it quickly. After using it, clean your knife with hot, soapy water, rinse it, and wipe it dry. To preserve its wooden handle, never soak your chef's knife in water and never put it in the dishwasher.

No matter how you look at it, a Chinese chef's knife is a big, sharp tool that, if used improperly, can cause serious injury. And although fast and furious chopping is an important skill in my bag of tricks and I've spent my whole career honing it, I never for a minute let theatrics take precedence over safety when working with knives. I just can't afford to lose these nimble fingers.

You probably want to keep all your fingers, too, and there's no reason why you can't, even when wielding a big, intimidating-looking Chinese chef's knife. When getting ready to chop, slice, or dice, just calm down, focus on the task at hand — namely, safely preparing ingredients for a recipe — and follow the same tips that have kept me injury-free all these years:

- **A sharp knife is a safe knife.** Sharp knives slice effortlessly through even tough foods, whereas dull blades force you to push against the food — just think of sawing through a tomato with a dull knife. The extra force that you apply makes you more likely to slip and cut yourself. Besides, using a dull knife results in messy-looking food and longer prep times.

- **Cutting boards save not only your countertop — but also your hands.** These boards are built to be sturdy and are much safer cutting surfaces than bare glass, metal, or marble. The commonly used plastic or wood provides a stable surface for your knife to grip and keeps it from slipping.

- **Match form with function by using a knife appropriate to the chopping technique.** Although your Chinese chef's knife is an all-purpose tool, you don't want to peel grapes with it. For those delicate tasks, stick with smaller paring knives. By the same token, don't chop through chicken bones with a bread knife.

- **Carry a knife as you would have carried scissors in front of your first grade teacher: point-down and perpendicular to the floor.** Keep it close to your body, with its edge facing away from you. And never run with a knife. What would your teacher think?

✔ **If you drop your knife, don't try to catch it.** Chances are, you'll miss the handle and end up with a handful of sharp blade. Just step back out of the line of fire and let it fall.

Staying on the cutting edge: How to sharpen your Chinese chef's knife

Although my mom's chosen sharpening method is scraping the knife blade against the rough underside of an unglazed earthenware bowl, I recommend using a sharpening steel. True, honing your knife's edge to a razor sharpness takes some practice, but having this skill will keep you slicing, dicing, and mincing with the same trusty knife for years. Just follow these steps (see Figure 3-2) to get — and keep — your knife blade as sharp as the ones the pros use.

USING A STEEL TO SHARPEN A KNIFE

1. GET A GOOD GRIP ON THE STEEL'S HANDLE AND REST ITS TIP ON THE CUTTING BOARD.

2. HOLD KNIFE AT A 20 DEGREE ANGLE AGAINST THE STEEL, BLADE DIRECTED DOWN, HANDLE JUST BELOW STEEL'S HANDLE.

3. PUSH BLADE DOWN ALONG STEEL WHILE YOU PULL STEEL UP TOWARD YOU. STOP! WHEN BLADE REACHES STEEL'S TIP.

4. BRING THE BLADE BACK TO THE POSITION IN STEP 2, PLACING THE OTHER SIDE OF THE BLADE AGAINST THE STEEL.

☆ REPEAT 6 to 8 TIMES ON EACH SIDE OF THE BLADE.

Figure 3-2: The basic steps for keeping your knife blade razor-sharp.

1. **Get a good grip on the sharpening steel's handle and rest its tip on your cutting board.**

2. **Hold the knife at a 20-degree angle against the steel, with the blade directed down and the handle just below the steel's handle.**

3. **Push the blade down along the steel while you pull the steel up toward you.**

   Stop when the blade reaches the steel's tip.

4. **Bring the blade back to the position shown in Step 2, placing the other side of the blade against the steel.**

   Repeat the sharpening motion shown in Figure 3-2.

5. **Repeat Steps 3 and 4 six to eight more times on each side of the blade.**

The Cutting Board

A good, solid hardwood cutting board preserves not only your knife's edge but also your countertops. My mom's cutting board was actually the cross section of a pine tree (refer to Figure 3-1) — how's that for cooking with nature? But you don't have to fell a tree for a cutting board. You can simply visit your favorite department, discount, or grocery store. There, you will find a wide assortment of cutting boards in all sizes, materials, and weights to suit your kitchen. And if you make a trip to a well-appointed Chinese market, you can actually find one of those tree-trunk cutting boards, perfect for that rustic, country kitchen look.

No matter which type of board you select — hardwood or plastic — work with it only on a steady, level surface that doesn't tip or slip. Placing a damp cloth on the work surface underneath the board gives it traction. Be sure to follow my first rule on chopping board usage: "Those who won't lift a finger to assure stability of their board now won't have too many fingers to lift later."

Always clean your cutting board thoroughly with hot, soapy water between uses. This advice is especially important when you're switching from raw meat and poultry preparation to vegetable preparation. A thorough cleaning is the most effective way to prevent cross-contamination. Investing in two different boards is another possibility. To remove the odors of strong foods, thoroughly wash your cutting board and then rub the cutting surface with a freshly cut lemon half.

The Spatula and the Ladle

The wok's unique shape led to the Chinese development of the long-handled, shovel-shaped metal spatula (refer to Figure 3-1), whose perfectly curved scoop fits the wok's sloping sides. The spatula makes quick stirring and tossing of foods a snap, preventing burning. With its shovel-type base, it also doubles as a serving utensil. The ladle (shown in Figure 3-1) often works with the spatula to help toss and scoop meats and vegetables quickly while they're cooking.

The Strainer or Skimmer

When deep-frying or scooping out the food in your wok, use a wire strainer or skimmer. The Chinese like to call them "spiders." Take a look at the skimmer in Figure 3-1, and you'll understand how it got that name. A typical Chinese skimmer is a shallow, copper-wire mesh bowl attached to a long, flat bamboo handle. But if you can't find this traditional variety of skimmer, any strainer or basket with a handle long enough to keep you a safe distance from the hot oil will do. A 6- or 8-inch skimmer is most functional. To clean the bamboo-handled variety, just rinse it in hot, soapy water and dry.

The Steamer

Steaming is a popular way to cook many healthy and tasty Chinese dishes. Traditional basket steamers, for use in a wok, are made of bamboo (refer to Figure 3-1) and come in different sizes perfect for using in different sizes of woks. Nowadays, you can also find aluminum or stainless steel steamer sets that resemble double boilers, but with perforations in the top tier's base. Chinese chefs generally prefer the age-old bamboo variety, which have woven lids that allow excess steam to escape without condensing and dripping back onto the food. You can buy a few of these steamers and only one lid and then stack the baskets one atop the other to steam or to reheat several dishes at one time.

When shopping for a steamer basket, choose one slightly smaller than your wok's diameter; a 12-inch steamer works well in a 14-inch wok, for example. After each use, simply wash, rinse, and thoroughly dry it before storing in an open shelf or cupboard for maximum air circulation. (Keep it cooped up and it may mildew.)

If you don't have a steamer, you can still steam the really old-fashioned way: Fill a wok about one fourth to one third the way up with water. Arrange four chopsticks tic-tac-toe style slightly above the water level (see Figure 3-3). Bring the water to a boil, place the food you want to steam on a heatproof dish or glass pie plate, and set the dish on the "chopstick steamer" rack. As an alternative, use one to three empty cans, such as tuna or water chestnut cans, with both ends removed, as supports to hold the plate of food above the water. (You can do this easily in a large kettle or soup pot if you don't have a wok.) Either way, cover the wok with its lid and let the steam power go to work for you.

Figure 3-3:
Four chopsticks arranged in a tic-tac-toe pattern or empty tin cans provide support for a steaming dish of food.

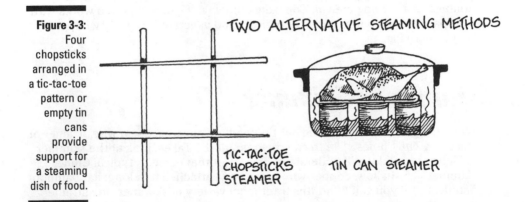

TWO ALTERNATIVE STEAMING METHODS

TIC-TAC-TOE CHOPSTICKS STEAMER

TIN CAN STEAMER

The Claypot Casserole

The best way to serve a slowly cooked, stewed, or braised Chinese dish is in a rustic-looking earthenware pot commonly called a Chinese claypot (refer to Figure 3-1). These covered casseroles usually have a dark brown, lead-free glaze on the inside, and an unglazed exterior that is sometimes encased in wire mesh for protection and strength. They come in all sizes, from small ones that are perfect for dinner for two (or one very hungry person!) to larger ones that can feed a big party of diners. If you don't have a claypot, use any heatproof, covered casserole as a substitute.

When purchasing a claypot, ask the salesperson to let you dip it in water to check for any cracks or leaks, indicated by small bubbles floating to the water's surface. Before using a claypot, soak it (and its lid, if it has one) in water for several hours, drain, and then let it dry overnight. You don't have to soak it any further after this. Never set an empty pot over direct heat and never place a hot claypot on a damp, cool surface or in cold water; the sudden change of temperature may cause it to crack. You can use claypots in the oven, but make sure to warm them up beforehand so the oven's heat won't be too much of a shock to the clay.

The Electric Rice Cooker

The Chinese have been cooking rice long before the invention of the electric rice cooker. These days, however, this handy and inexpensive modern convenience is a common sight in practically every Chinese household. If nothing else, it frees your stove from one more pot and lets you tend to other dishes while the rice cooks to perfection by itself.

Sold at all gourmet stores and housewares sections of department stores, rice cookers come in many sizes and often boast several different bells and whistles — quite literally. For example, some models chime when the rice is done, and others switch to a "warm" setting that keeps fully cooked rice at a comfortable serving temperature for several hours. More expensive models are equipped with timers that allow you to set the cooking time in advance. Set it right, and you will come home to a perfectly cooked pot of rice. Choose a rice cooker with a nonstick cooking pot inside for easy cleaning. I also recommend cookers with a 3- to 5-cup capacity, as these can easily handle enough rice to feed up to four to six people.

All in good measure

Most electric rice cookers come with small, clear or colored plastic cups for measuring rice. They usually have gradations (¼ cup, ½ cup, ¾ cup) and accompanying fill lines etched onto the outside of the cup so you'll really be able to nail the perfect amount of rice. But a quick test shows that ½ cup of rice measured in one of the small plastic cups doesn't necessarily correspond exactly to ½ cup as measured with a standard dry measuring cup. Turns out that the rice steamer cup actually gives you a little bit less as compared to the standard measure. So what does the conscientious cook do? Don't lose that little measuring cup, that's what. And use it, if you happen to still have one, following the manufacturer's instructions. And although it won't ruin your steamed rice to have the measurement of rice a little bit "off," proportions *are* important in rice cooking, and the steamer manufacturer calibrated its cups the way it did for a reason. So if precision and accuracy are your goal, keep a close eye on that plastic cup, or at least figure out its equivalent capacity as measured in a standard cup.

Spice Grinders

I learned about grinding spices and herbs the old-fashioned way — with a heavy mortar and pestle. It worked, and it was quaint, but boy was it hard on the elbows! For my money, I'd invest in an electric spice grinder or a mini food processor. They save both time and aching joints!

Coffee grinders make excellent spice grinders, but unless you like the taste of coffee in your Sichuan peppercorn, or vice versa, I recommend purchasing a small grinder — which isn't that expensive — to use solely for herbs and spices. The coffee drinkers in your house will thank you.

In a pinch, when none of these are available, put the spices in a bowl and use the end of the handle on your trusty Chinese chef's knife to pound the spices.

Chopsticks

No Chinese kitchen is complete without plenty of chopsticks. Long or short, wooden, bamboo, lacquer, plastic, bone, or ivory, these deceptively simple devices make excellent cooking and eating tools. Master their use, and you will never miss having knives or forks at your dining table again. In most Chinese families, kids learn how to use chopsticks as soon as they are ready for solid food.

CULTURAL TIDBIT

Although the Chinese don't object to modern cutlery, they do prefer to cut up meat in the kitchen and not at the dining room table. Confucius forbade enlightened people from bringing their knives and other weapons to the table. Hence, Chinese chefs cut their food into bite-sized pieces behind the scenes so that refined diners need only lightly and effortlessly grasp the little morsels with their slender, elegant chopsticks.

Chopsticks aren't used just for eating. I use them to beat eggs for omelets, mix sauces, and give a good swirl to soups and broths. I even use them to stir-fry food in a wok. Chinese markets and cookware shops sometimes carry long cooking chopsticks that range anywhere from 1 to 1½ feet. These long sticks are great for cooks who "can't take the heat"; their added length keeps flames and the hot oil literally at arm's length. And because they're wooden or bamboo, they don't conduct heat like a metal spoon.

Clean your chopsticks by rinsing them with warm, soapy water and dry them soon thereafter. Long soaking and frequent dishwashing can result in water-logged, warped chopsticks. Although ivory or plastic chopsticks can go in the dishwasher, it's still much easier to clean them separately and set them in the dish drainer to dry. If you are the proud owner of a pair of silver chopsticks like I am, take care of them as you would all fine silverware — with plenty of silver polish.

Chapter 4

The Chinese Pantry and Refrigerator

• •

In This Chapter

▶ Shopping for basic Chinese ingredients

▶ Stocking up on sauces and condiments

▶ Adding flavor with herbs and spices

▶ Picking out preserved products

• •

A trip to Chinatown always leaves me breathless. I'm totally amazed by the breadth of products I can find in the markets: farm-fresh produce, live fish and shellfish, and barbecued pork and Cantonese roast duck at crowded deli counters, among other treats. And the shelves at the packed-to-the-gills Chinese grocery stores contain every dry Asian ingredient imaginable. Even a culinary glutton such as myself can get a case of sensory overload.

And if the experience overwhelms me — albeit pleasantly so — I can imagine how intimidating it can be to any novice of Chinese cooking. But don't worry. Just focus on the basics of Chinese ingredients, and in no time, you'll be shopping Chinatown like the pros. Doing so is a lot easier than you may think.

First of all, you don't really need an entire Chinatown to stock your pantry. The single most positive retail food trend of the past decade (in my opinion, at least) has been the expansion of the average supermarket's Chinese ingredients section from just one shelf to, in many cases, a whole aisle. Granted, some rare ingredients are bound to call for a trip into Chinatown, but always check your local supermarket first, just in case. You can put the time you save to better use in your kitchen.

This chapter is your tip sheet to the basic necessities for a good Chinese pantry. I compiled it by taking an inventory of my own pantry and picking out all those items that I really couldn't live — or at least eat — without.

Market Forces: Where to Find Essential Chinese Ingredients

The Chinese are pros at shopping. My mom used to visit the local market twice a day. Back in those days, shopping twice daily was customary. How else could she get the freshest fruits, roots, gourds, and greens, often with clumps of earth still attached?

If I could, I'd still do the same, but busy schedules and the lure of the modern supermarket sometimes get the best of me. Well, I make sure to get the best ingredients by making the most of my shopping trips, wherever they lead me. And usually, they lead me to the following types of stores. You'd do well to head to similar locations; I'm sure that you can find each ingredient in this chapter in at least one of the suggested outlets.

- **Supermarkets:** Both the variety and quality of Chinese ingredients available in supermarkets nationwide keep growing. Nowadays, most stores have a specific aisle or aisles dedicated to Chinese sauces, pastes, vinegars, oils, and seasonings, as well as to rice, noodles, and preserved foods. In addition to Chinese ingredients, these sections often carry other Asian specialties such as Thai curry pastes, Japanese bread crumbs, and Korean barbecue sauces. For time saving and convenience, look for packaged mixes for soups and rice or noodle dishes.

- **Natural food stores and co-ops:** Chinese cuisine advocates lots of fresh, locally grown produce, plenty of grains, and a wide acceptance of soybeans and sprouts in all their forms. For that reason, Chinese food is a logical match for the current natural foods eating trend in North America. It is, therefore, not surprising that many natural food stores carry a wide array of Chinese ingredients, especially items that are harder to find at conventional stores — certain soy and tofu products, wheat gluten, exotic mushrooms and fungi, and bulk spices, for example. Look for fresh produce at natural food markets; they often carry greens, sprouts, and leafy items that may not be so popular at major chain markets.

- **Chinatown markets:** I can't emphasize enough the wealth of Chinese cuisine and culture that you'll experience at these shopping heavens. Produce stalls and butcher and seafood shops carry the freshest ingredients. For prepared foods such as Chinese roast pork, crispy-skinned duck, or Chinese sausages, visit your friendly Chinese deli. You can't miss them, because they usually hang their deli meats right behind glass windows.

Crossing the shopping language gap

The language gap in Chinatowns is really less of a gap than a crack in the sidewalk. As foreign and exotic as Chinatowns may seem, they *are* still part of North America. And to function profitably in North America, the employees in Chinatown shops, delis, and restaurants need to develop at least some proficiency in English. Be patient, explain slowly, and chances are, they may know what you need even better than you know it yourself.

Your biggest problem is most likely your own unfamiliarity with Chinese names, pronunciations, and Chinese language characters for foods. But even if the deli counter or fish tank doesn't have English translations for its contents — most of them do, by the way — if you can manage a well-aimed point of the finger, the crack employees at your local Chinese market are glad to assist with an explanation.

Make good use of their expertise when searching the aisles of jars, bottles, and canned goods, especially if the labels are almost entirely in Chinese. Again, giving employees just a brief description of the ingredient should lead you right to it.

Tell the server at the counter what and how much of an item you want. And don't be shy — if you see a piece of meat that is leaner and juicier, point to it. The server is there to take care of your needs and cater to your preferences. If only all shopping were so satisfying!

Chinese supermarkets stock every dried and preserved ingredient imaginable. Many are also excellent places to shop for Chinese cooking utensils and equipment such as woks and steamers of all sizes and makes. If you can't find it here, you may not even find it back in China.

Getting Sauced: Classic Chinese Sauces and Condiments

If you were to create a library of Chinese ingredients, you'd have to build an entire wing for the sauces and condiments alone. Chinese cooks have thousands of pastes, potions, sauces, and seasonings at their ready, and thanks to your supermarket's Asian food aisle, you can get in on some of that action yourself. These condiments are already prepared and conveniently packaged for you, too, so they let you inject real Chinese flavor into a dish without any fuss. Start your browsing of the Sauce and Condiment Wing with some of the following suggestions. (By the way, in the following headings, the first Chinese pronunciation is Cantonese; the second is Mandarin.)

Black bean sauce (See tzup jeng; shi zhi jiang)

This ready-to-use sauce made of salted black beans and rice wine is a popular addition to dishes all over China, where its savory, slightly salty flavor sometimes gets a little kick from garlic and hot chiles. It's a great way for introducing people to the wonderful flavor of salted black beans — not exactly the most common of Western ingredients.

Add it to stir-fries and sauces near the end of their cooking times because the prepared sauce only needs to be heated through. This feature makes it a super time saver for appetizers and quick meals. Refrigerate the jar upon opening, and the sauce should last for about a year.

Char siu sauce (Tza siu jeng; cha shao jiang)

Because I'm such a fan of char siu, Chinese roast pork, I just love this thick, sweet and savory, ready-made sauce. A combination of fermented soy beans, vinegar, tomato paste, chile, garlic, sugar, and Chinese spices, it has a vibrant reddish brown color and unmistakable flavor that are synonymous with Chinese barbecued spareribs and roast pork. If you've ever seen the glistening, caramelized red strips of pork and ribs hanging in Chinese deli windows, you know what I mean. That shiny color comes from the caramelization of the sauce during barbecuing and roasting, and if you think it *looks* good, just wait until you taste it.

Use char siu sauce as you would Western barbecue sauce — in marinades, basting sauces, and dips for meats and poultry. And of course, use it in barbecue cooking, where its sweet and spicy flavor livens up anything from grilled meats to vegetables.

Char siu sauce comes in a range of sizes. Refrigerate it after opening, and it will keep for about a year.

Chile pastes and sauces (Laut tziu jeng; la jiao jiang)

These fiery pastes and sauces come in a range of flavors, degrees of heat, and consistencies, but most are made from a blend of fresh and dried chiles and vinegar. Different regions in China make different chile sauces, but generally they all contain seasonings such as garlic, ginger, soybeans, or sesame oil.

Chile sauces and pastes run from mild to wild, so start slowly when adding them to stir-fries or noodle soups. Keep in mind that your spice tolerance may increase with time. The sweeter versions of chile pastes and sauces make nice accompaniments to roast chicken, by the way.

Most Asian markets sell an assortment of popular brands of chile pastes and sauces, some even coming from different countries. You may want to initiate yourself and your palate with a small bottle or jar because a little goes a long way. Refrigerate it after you've opened it, and it should keep for about a year.

Chile oil (Laut you; la you)

Another spicy addition to your Chinese pantry, this reddish orange oil comes from infusing whole, dried red chiles or crushed red pepper flakes in oil. Used primarily as a flavoring agent during cooking or as a condiment at the table, it has surprised many unexpected diners who didn't realize how much punch a few drops can pack. Be careful! Start with adding just a drop or two and then add more if you have an asbestos tongue.

Chile oil is a perfect flavoring agent for stir-fries and, when combined with soy sauce, vinegar, and a little sugar or garlic, makes an eye-opening dipping sauce for dim sum (see Chapter 8) and Chinese appetizers.

Chile oil comes in small bottles, often with convenient, no-drip spouts. Store the bottles in a cool, dry place for up to several months.

Hoisin sauce (Hoi seen jeng; hai xian jiang)

This dark, rich, pastelike sauce is one of the most popular Chinese condiments in the West. Its spicy-sweet flavor and reddish brown color are great matches for Western roasts as well as for Asian stir-fries and barbecues. It's normally made from fermented soybeans, vinegar, garlic, sugar, and Chinese spices, all of which add to its complex flavor.

If you've ever had Peking duck or mu shu dishes, you've probably spread a thin coating of hoisin on the accompanying Mandarin pancakes or steamed buns. Hoisin also makes a great dipping sauce or barbecue sauce base. Try adding a little hoisin to your own sauce recipes to give them an intriguing Asian sweetness and smokiness.

Jars and bottles of hoisin come in lots of sizes. I prefer the big ones because I can never have enough of this stuff. In addition, the larger jars' wide mouths make serving the thick sauce easier. Refrigerate opened bottles or jars for up to a year.

Oyster-flavored sauce (Hou yeo; hao you)

The name of this sauce is a little deceptive: It really doesn't have a flavor much like oysters. Instead, the thick, brown, all-purpose sauce made from oyster extracts, sugar, seasonings, and cornstarch has sweet and smoky notes that make it indispensable in a wide variety of Chinese meat and vegetable dishes.

I practically grew up on oyster-flavored sauce because it's one of the most common ingredients in Cantonese cuisine. Whether drizzled over simple steamed Chinese broccoli and savory egg custards, mixed into a sizzling stir-fry or a wok of fried rice, or simply used as a dip for roast pork or chicken, oyster-flavored sauce enhances the natural flavors of any dish.

You'll find plenty of brands, sizes, and types of oyster-flavored sauce. You can even choose mushroom-based "oyster-flavored" sauces with the same smoky character as the original that should please vegetarians. Whichever kind you buy, refrigerate it after opening, and it will keep for a year.

Plum sauce (Suin mui jeng; suan mei chiang)

Although this sauce may look like something you'd want to spread on a piece of toast, it's made from a combination of salted plums, apricots, yams, rice vinegar, chiles, sugar, and other spices. These flavors make the sauce better suited as a dipping sauce for roast duck, deep-fried appetizers, and barbecued meats.

Depending on the brand, plum sauce (also known as "duck sauce" thanks to its popularity as a condiment for Cantonese roast ducks) can run the gamut from sweet-tart to salty, and from smooth to chunky and jamlike. Try all the varieties to discover the flavor, composition, and consistency that you like best. I've found that certain styles go better with some dishes than others. It's really a mix-and-match ingredient.

You can buy plum sauce in jars, bottles, and cans. Refrigerate jars and bottles after opening. Transfer the contents of an opened can to a storage container with a tightly fitting lid and refrigerate. All should keep for a year.

Rice wine (Mike tziu; mi jiu)

Chinese cookbooks regularly call for this amber-colored liquid from the fermentation of glutinous rice and millet. As with Western grape-based wines,

Chinese rice wines come in a wide range of qualities, with some of the finest made in the city of Shao Hsing in eastern China, the Napa Valley of the East.

After 10 to even 100 years of aging, these wines have developed a delightful aroma that stir-frying helps release. Just remember to add the wine toward the end of cooking, or the high heat will flash off those pungent volatile notes. In braised "drunken" dishes, those that are marinted in plenty of wine, the mildly acidic rice wine adds flavor while helping tenderize tough meats.

You can find rice wines from many locales and at just as many different quality levels. And as with everything else in life, you get what you pay for when it comes to rice wines. Generally speaking, the more expensive the wine, the better the quality. If you have a hard time finding Chinese rice wine, you can substitute dry sherry or Japanese sake. All will keep, once opened, for several months in a cool, dry place.

Sesame oil (Ma you)

You don't use this dark amber, aromatic oil pressed from toasted sesame seeds for cooking, but rather for the subtle and unmistakably Chinese flavor it gives to a finished dish. As with rice wine, its flavor and aroma can vaporize if exposed to high heat for a long time, so be patient and add it at the end of cooking.

Use sesame oil anywhere you'd like to add a nutty aroma and richness — marinades, salad dressings, and soups come to mind. I love tossing it with a bowl of cooked noodles, slivered carrots, and green onions. That's a nutritious yet elegant lunch, and it's so quick and easy to make.

The best-quality oils are 100 percent pure, as opposed to blends of sesame oil with a greater proportion of soybean oil. The latter oils just don't have the same nutty, toasted flavor as the all-sesame oils. Whichever kind you choose, you can refrigerate it for up to several months after opening.

It may seem strange to refrigerate oil, as I suggest you do with sesame oil. But, even though they're shelf stable, oils can experience some pretty significant flavor changes from exposure to sunlight, and they definitely deteriorate over time, even at mildly warm temperatures. A cool refrigerator — and a tightly closing lid to keep out the oxygen that turns oils rancid — ensures that your sesame oil tastes fresh and flavorful well into its shelf life.

Sesame paste (Tzee ma jeng; zhi ma jiang)

This thick, peanut buttery, golden brown to light gray-brown paste made from toasted white sesame seeds plays an important role in Sichuanese dishes. Try it in your Sichuanese creations and in any other dish that could use a nutty flavor and aroma. It's also perfect for salad dressings and marinades. If the paste is too thick to add to dressings, sauces, or marinades, just soften it with a little fresh oil or water.

If you can't find Chinese sesame paste, go ahead and substitute Middle Eastern tahini, made from *un*toasted white sesame seeds, or even peanut butter mixed with some sesame oil. But if you do land some of this rich, flavorful paste, stir the layer of oil at the top of the jar back into the paste itself. Or, if you prefer it in a thicker style, pour off the oil before each use and then top off the jar with a fresh layer of sesame oil or lightly flavored vegetable oil before storing the paste in the refrigerator. It should keep there for several months.

Soy sauce (Jeng yeo; jiang you)

Anyone who has ever eaten in a Chinese restaurant, opened a Chinese cookbook, or paid Chinese cooking any attention at all must be well acquainted with soy sauce. Perhaps the single most important ingredient in Chinese kitchens, soy sauce plays a role in virtually every Chinese dish I've ever made or eaten. The best-quality soy sauces, made from traditionally fermented soybeans and wheat, have a dark color emblematic of Chinese foods and a slightly sweet, mildly salty flavor that isn't overpowering or parchingly salty.

Soy sauce gives an unequivocally Chinese note to marinades, stir-fry sauces, braising liquids, roasting glazes, soups, and salad dressings. Chinese restaurants often serve a mixture of soy sauce and vinegar as a table condiment for roast meats and Chinese appetizers.

Always choose a "naturally brewed" or fermented soy sauce rather than the artificially colored and chemically processed soy sauces that you can find on the market. Read the labels! The naturally brewed varieties proudly state that distinction on their labels. Store soy sauce in a cool, dry place, or in the refrigerator if you're a slow user. Because they're fermented and contain plenty of salt, soy sauces are naturally preserved and will keep for several months. However, be mindful that they will darken and become more concentrated over time.

Reduced-sodium soy sauce

With today's interest in health and a greater awareness of special dietary needs, some cooks prefer to use reduced-sodium or "lite" soy sauce. Most lite soy sauces have about 40 percent less sodium than regular, which makes them welcome alternatives for those who need or wish to reduce their total sodium intake.

Though they taste less salty, reduced-sodium soy sauces still have a rich flavor. Use them just as you would regular soy sauces, but keep this caveat in mind when storing them: Salt is a natural preservative. Because reduced sodium soy sauce contains less salt, it's more susceptible to spoilage and thus should go in your refrigerator, where it will keep for several months.

Dark soy sauce (Lo ceo; lao chou)

The addition of molasses and a bit of cornstarch gives a sweeter, more full-bodied flavor and a syrupy consistency to dark soy sauce, setting it apart from the regular variety. This is the soy sauce of choice for Shanghai-style red-cooked meats and stewed dishes, as well as for any application that requires a richer, slightly sweet flavor and deeper mahogany color.

Many dark soy sauce bottles have labels that are solely in Chinese, but don't let that discourage you from trying to find them. Ask and the clerk at the Chinese market can locate a bottle for you. In a pinch, you can tell whether that mysterious bottle contains dark soy sauce by tilting both it and a bottle of regular soy sauce upside down and then right side up again. Watch as the sauces run down the necks of their respective bottles. While regular soy sauce drains quickly with little residue, dark soy sauce coats the bottle neck and runs down the sides more slowly.

Dark soy sauce is not interchangeable with regular, although the two often appear together in recipes. If you've given up on finding a bottle of dark soy sauce, use a mildly sweet regular soy sauce, such as Kikkoman brand, as a substitute. As with regular soy sauce, store dark soy sauce in a cool, dark place, or in the refrigerator if you're a slow user, for up to a year.

Rice vinegar (Bok tzo; mi cu)

Compared to distilled white vinegar, rice vinegar is milder, less pungent, and sweeter. Popular Chinese rice vinegars range in color from clear or slightly golden to rich amber brown. "Seasoned" rice vinegars are spiked with sugar, which adds an even stronger sweetness.

Rice vinegar contributes the sweetness and sourness essential to sweet and sour sauces and also helps season cooked and raw vegetable dishes, salad dressings, and marinades. In addition to its specifically Chinese applications, rice vinegar gives vibrancy to foods from other cuisines as well, Japanese cuisine in particular.

Store bottles of rice vinegar in a cool, dry place. They'll keep for several months, albeit with some loss in intensity and flavor. (If your rice vinegar smells slightly sour, good. It's supposed to!)

Black vinegar (Hok tzo; hei cu)

As a direct contrast to rice vinegar's mild flavor and color, black vinegar has a bold, sweet-tart, and smoky flavor and a deep, dark color. The fermentation of a mixture of rice, wheat, and millet or sorghum gives black vinegar its unique characteristics.

Chinkiang vinegar, a specific variety of black vinegar produced in eastern China, has an esteemed reputation with Chinese cooks, who swear by it for braised dishes or as a table condiment for dumplings and hot and sour soups. As an alternative to black vinegar's robustness, you can also turn to Chinese red vinegar for a mild, light, and smooth flavor. The latter works just as well in just as many applications.

Both black and red vinegar come in variously sized bottles. If you can't find either, substitute balsamic vinegar, but decrease the amount of sugar listed in the recipe. Store Chinese black and red vinegars in a cool, dry place for several months, although, as with rice vinegar, they will lose some flavor and intensity.

Spicing Up Your Life with Chinese Herbs and Spices

The Chinese have a long tradition of using herbs and spices to boost not only a dish's flavor but also its nutritional benefits. Walk into any Chinese herb shop or pharmacy, and you'll quickly discover that the line between food and medicine in China is a pretty blurry one. So considering that the meal is often the medicine itself, you won't need that spoonful of sugar to help it go down. Just try adding some of the flavorful ingredients listed in this section. (For more on China's medicinal foods, see Chapter 14.)

Chinese five-spice powder (Ng heung fun; wu xiang fen)

The Chinese have long believed that the number five has special curative and healing powers, which is why this light cocoa-colored powder originally contained five specific spices. But nowadays, it contains quite a few more, including cinnamon, star anise, fennel, clove, ginger, licorice, Sichuan peppercorn, and dried tangerine peel.

I love the unmistakable cinnamon and anise flavor that Chinese five-spice powder gives braised meats, roasts, and barbecues — it's an essential ingredient in hoisin sauce and in red-cooked dishes.

Most grocery stores carry Chinese five-spice powder, either in jars or small plastic packages. If you can't find it in the spice section, give the trusty Chinese food section a try, and I bet you'll locate some there. Store loose powder in a jar with a tight-fitting lid in a cool, dry place, and it will keep for a year.

Chinese hot mustard (Gai mut; jie mo)

Most people who have had egg rolls in American-Chinese restaurants have given Chinese hot mustard a try. It's the condiment with the pungent, horseradish-like fieriness that goes so well with Chinese appetizers and cold meat platters. Try adding Chinese hot mustard to chicken salad dressings and dipping sauces for fresh vegetables. It's so piquant and distinctive that it makes a perfect crossover flavoring agent and condiment for many Western recipes. Go ahead and spread it on a burger or stir it into a macaroni salad. You may surprise yourself and delight your guests.

Chinese hot mustards are available already prepared or in powdered form. Store the loose powder in a jar with a tightly fitting lid in a cool, dry place. Store opened containers of prepared mustard in the refrigerator. Both will keep for several months.

Ginger (Geung; jiang)

No matter where or when I smell it, fresh ginger signals the prelude of Chinese cooking to me. This pale golden, knobby, hand-shaped rhizome (it's not actually a root, but rather a special type of underground-growing stem) has the perfect combination of enchanting aroma, spicy bite, and natural sweetness. Figure 4-1 provides a nice illustration of a "hand" of ginger, as it's called.

Slice, julienne, mince, or grate fresh ginger for use in dressings, sauces, and marinades. And remember to include it in poultry, meat, seafood, and vegetable dishes. Come to think of it, I don't know of a single dish that a little fresh ginger can't improve. I bet that it will say "Chinese food" to you when you smell it, too.

Choose ginger that is hard, heavy, and free of wrinkles and mold. It's available year-round. You can also find young ginger, which is more delicate in flavor and texture, during summer and fall. Store mature ginger in a cool, dry place for up to a couple weeks. Alternatively, peel and place it in a jar with rice wine sherry and refrigerate for up to several months. (For tips on peeling ginger, see Chapter 5.)

Sichuan peppercorns (Fa tziu; hua jiao)

Black peppercorns are no substitute for these dried, reddish brown berries with a unique woodsy fragrance and pleasantly numbing tang (see Figure 4-1). In fact, the two aren't even related. To give red-cooked dishes and stir-fries a distinctive Chinese flavor, stick with Sichuan when it comes to peppercorns.

The cuisine of western China relies a great deal on Sichuan peppercorn as well as Chinese five-spice powder. Get the most out of your Sichuan peppercorns by toasting a handful of them in a dry frying pan over low heat until they become fragrant and then add them to your recipe. You can work with either whole peppercorns or ones that are crushed to a fine or coarse powder in a mortar and pestle or spice grinder.

Sichuan peppercorns are available in plastic bags. Some packages label them "wild" or "red" pepper. But don't let the latter name confuse you — these are *not* the same things as red chile peppers. Store the peppercorns in a jar with a tightly fitting lid in a cool, dry place. They'll keep for several months.

Star anise (Bark gog; ba jiao)

Another essential in Chinese five-spice powder, star anise is hard to miss. Shown in Figure 4-1, these approximately 1-inch, star-shaped pods have points, each containing a shiny, mahogany-colored seed. And like the anise seed of the West, star anise has a licorice flavor that complements meats and poultry in red-cooked and barbecued dishes.

Most cooks use star anise to make rich braising sauces and stews. You don't want to eat the whole spice; just let it infuse the sauce or braising liquid with its warm, mild spiciness. Ground star anise goes into flavoring powders, Chinese five-spice powder being a fine example, and in dipping sauces.

You can find whole and ground star anise in plastic packages and small jars. And I challenge you to find a bag with no broken stars — it's impossible, given their delicate points. Nevertheless, eight broken points still equal one whole pod. Store whole and powdered star anise in separate jars with tightly fitting lids in a cool, dry place. They'll keep there for several months.

Figure 4-1:
Various seasonings spice up Chinese culinary life, including ginger, Sichuan pepper-corns, and star anise.

SICHUAN PEPPERCORNS

GINGER

STAR ANISE

Canned, Dried, and Otherwise Preserved: The Ultimate in Long-Lasting Chinese Ingredients

The Chinese are masters at making foods last for the long haul. When you've had as much experience battling Mother Nature, the seasons, and pesky foreign invaders as China's cooks have, you're bound to learn some preservation tricks. And even though the Western world's food supply is predictable and stable enough to make stockpiling long-lasting ingredients unnecessary, these preserved ingredients have become such important players in Chinese cuisine that omitting them will leave you with a less-than-authentic dish.

Tofu (Dou fu; do fu)

This is the chameleon of Chinese ingredients. Tofu (also known as bean curd) comes in a variety of textures, from silky-soft, which is best for soups and puddinglike dishes, to a dense yet slightly spongy firmness that stands up to hearty stir-fries and also works well cold and crumbled into salads. Its neutral taste lets it absorb the flavors of other foods and sauces like a sponge. No wonder it's such a popular meat substitute.

You can find soft, regular, or firm tofu in plastic containers and cartons in the refrigerated sections and produce departments of most supermarkets these days. Check the package for its best storage method and its expiration date. If you frequent Asian markets or health food stores, you may find tubs of water holding cubes of loose tofu. Store these cubes in a container with a tightly fitting lid, fill it with water, and refrigerate. It will keep for several days if you change the water daily. If your tofu develops a strong odor, discard it.

By the way, this is only part of the book's treatment of tofu. Do check Chapter 13 for a more complete discussion — and celebration — of this versatile ingredient.

Chinese sausage (Larp tzoen; la chang)

Whenever I need to add a savory, flavorful, specifically Chinese note to a rice dish or stir-fry, I reach for Chinese sausages. You may have seen these slender, deep brownish red, wrinkled links hanging from racks in Chinese deli windows. I see them even more often in my refrigerator because I make a point of always having some of these secret ingredients on hand.

Most Chinese sausages are made from pork, pork fat, duck, or beef. They get a simple seasoning treatment from salt, sugar, and rice wine, giving all varieties a delicious savory sweetness. But no matter which kind you buy, cook them before serving to bring the pork to a safe temperature and to remove excess fat. A quick turn in a steamer, in a pot of boiling water, or in the wok with the rest of the stir-fry should do the trick.

Chinese delis sell these sausages in pairs held together with colored string, the color representing each different type of sausage. (Approximately four pairs give you a pound of sausage.) You can also find them in vacuum-sealed packages. Store them in your refrigerator in their original packaging or in a zippered plastic bag for up to a month or freeze them for up to several months.

Baby corn (Siu gum soeun; xiao jin sun)

These little mellow-yellow gems never fail to impress diners in Chinese restaurants or dinner guests at home — my sons can appreciate eating a vegetable that's just the right size for them. Normally 2 to 3 inches long and found in cans, baby corn, or young corn, as it's sometimes called, is completely edible, cob and all. Chalk up another point for convenience!

Enjoy the sweet taste and crunchy texture of baby corn in stir-fries, soups, and salads. I sometimes serve it on its own as a snack or part of a vegetable platter. When using canned baby corn, drain and rinse it under water to remove any trace of the salty canning brine. And if the corn has a metallic taste, blanch the ears in boiling water, as described in Chapter 5.

After you open a can, transfer the ears to a container with a tightly fitting lid, fill it with water, and refrigerate. The baby corn will keep for a week if you change the water daily.

Bamboo shoots (Tzook soeun; zhu sun)

Another classic Chinese food ingredient, bamboo shoots come in so many forms — whole tips, young tips, sliced shoots, and diced shoots (see Figure 4-2) — that you should have no problem finding the variety that suits your tastes and your recipe. All of them have a mildly sweet flavor, but their individual textures vary with how much fiber the shoots contain. Young winter shoots are most tender, while older, sliced shoots are more fibrous.

For a quick and easy vegetarian treat, combine bamboo shoots with Chinese mushrooms and vegetables to make a stir-fry, or just add the crunchy shoots to salads, light soups, and savory dumpling fillings.

Most bamboo shoots in Western markets come in cans, and as with other canned ingredients, you'll want to rinse them under water to remove excessive saltiness, or blanch them to rid them of tinny flavors. Transfer the contents of an opened can to a container with a tightly fitting lid, fill it with water, and refrigerate for up to a week, changing the water daily. If you can find fresh shoots in bins of water in your market's produce section, go ahead and try them. Store fresh shoots in your refrigerator the same way you would canned shoots.

Water chestnuts (Ma tike; ma ti)

Fresh water chestnuts, shown in Figure 4-2, are proof that you can't judge a book by its cover. These squat, dingy brown, pointy-topped tubers that are rarely bigger than golf balls have a sweet, slightly starchy taste and pale beige flesh that belies their homely exteriors. I wish I had a year-round supply of them, and I also wish that they were easier to peel.

Luckily for me (and water chestnut lovers all over), many grocery stores carry cans of whole and sliced water chestnuts. They may not be as sweet as the fresh kind, but they keep their crunchy texture long after cooking, just like the fresh ones, making them perfect for stews as well as stir-fries and salads. (Use them in salads as you would jícama, a slightly sweet and crunchy, white-fleshed root vegetable available in most grocery stores' produce sections. In fact, if you can't find water chestnuts at all, jícama makes an excellent substitute.)

If you can find fresh water chestnuts, choose ones with no wrinkles or mold and store them in a breathable paper bag in the refrigerator for up to a week. (Fresh water chestnuts, by the way, are not at all related to the chestnuts that you roast over an open fire as Jack Frost nips at your nose.) You can also peel fresh ones and freeze them for up to a month. Treat the canned ones as you would any other canned ingredient: Drain and rinse them with cold water, blanch them if necessary, and store them for a week in the refrigerator in a container with a tightly fitting lid and enough water to cover them, changing the water daily.

Straw mushrooms (Tzo gu; cao gu)

These cute little mushrooms may look like props from the set of *Alice in Wonderland*, but I promise that they're quite edible (and deliciously so). You're probably most familiar with the peeled variety — the kind that look like little toadstools with their brown, dome-shaped caps and thick, straw-colored stems. But Chinese cooks actually prefer the unpeeled variety, which resembles little brown eggs with a slightly flat bottom. Both kinds are shown in Figure 4-2. The delicate sweetness and firm, meaty texture of the peeled and unpeeled mushrooms make either perfect for stir-fries of the meat or vegetarian variety.

For canned straw mushrooms, drain and rinse before using and blanch them in boiling water if they still have that tinny flavor. Although most supermarkets carry only peeled straw mushrooms, do keep your eyes "peeled" for the unpeeled variety that comes in cans and jars as well. To store the unused portion of a can, transfer the contents to a container with a tightly fitting lid, fill it with water, and refrigerate. If you change the water daily, the mushrooms should keep for a week.

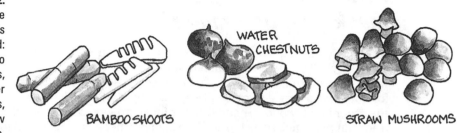

Dried black mushrooms (Gon doan gu; gan dong gu)

You can find just as many types of dried mushrooms in Chinese markets as you can find dishes in which to use them. The favorite of most Chinese cooks by far is the dried black mushroom, the same one that the Japanese refer to as the *shiitake*. I just can't resist the rich, meaty texture and wild-mushroom flavor of these preserved treats, and judging by their popularity, I'm not alone!

You can spot them by their tan undersides and their brownish black caps, which are sometimes cracked in a chrysanthemum-shaped pattern and are sometimes smooth, as shown in Figure 4-3. Before cooking, soak them in warm water until they're soft (usually a half hour to an hour will do) and then cut off the hard, knobby stem. And remember to strain and save that soaking liquid — it adds so much flavor to sauces and soups. After your dried mushrooms are rehydrated, chop them and add them to stuffings for poultry or dumplings. Larger slices work best in stir-fries, where their substantial texture can stand up to and complement the textures of other ingredients.

Dried black mushrooms are available in plastic packages in Asian markets. Increasingly, small specialty companies and organic farms are marketing them to large Western supermarkets and health food stores, so look for them in those outlets if you don't have an Asian market nearby. Store mushrooms in a tightly sealed container in a cool, dry place. They will keep for several months.

Dried black fungus (Hok mook yee; gan mu er)

Not to be confused with dried black *mushrooms*, dried black fungus is actually a catchall term for some different fungus varieties, including cloud ear, wood ear, and tree ear. As you can imagine, cloud ear fungus gets its name from its resemblance to clouds — apparently, dark, black storm clouds. On the other hand, wood ear and tree ear fungi grow on old pieces of wood and tree stumps, hence their imaginative names. Check out Figure 4-3 for a good visual representation of these creatively named items. But no matter which type of dried, leathery-looking chips you choose, the slightly crispy/slightly gummy bite and smooth surface of black fungus add a whole new textural dimension to your dishes. And to boot, their bland flavor goes with just about any dish, from mu shu to wonton soup.

Soak dried black fungus in warm water until soft before using, and remove the knobby stem end. Because these thirsty characters really expand — up to three times their dried size — prepare only a few pieces for use in a recipe. Slice them into strips or bite-sized chunks depending on the texture and appearance you want. You can find whole or shredded dried black fungus in plastic packages. Look for the bags with small, thin ears, which are better quality than the thick, large ones. Store them in a tightly sealed container in a cool, dry place for several months.

Figure 4-3:
Black mushrooms and their cousins, black fungus, make great additions to Chinese dishes.

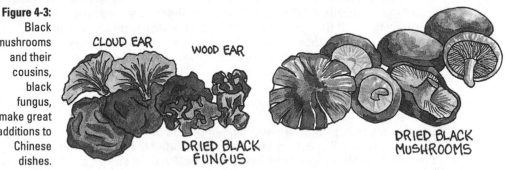

CLOUD EAR

WOOD EAR

DRIED BLACK FUNGUS

DRIED BLACK MUSHROOMS

Pantry primer: The fundamental ingredients

I know from experience how easily you can go overboard when shopping for Chinese ingredients. Combine an empty stomach, this handy chapter, and a well-stocked Chinese market, and you've got a surefire recipe for a hefty grocery bill. And who could blame you for giving into the temptation to go hog-wild? All those brightly colored vegetables and jars and the heady aromas practically beg you to "Try me! Try me!" It's hard not to want to give them all a home.

But stocking your own Chinese pantry shouldn't require renting a U-Haul to carry your loot home from the store. Actually, by keeping only a few essential ingredients on hand, you can whip up an authentic Chinese meal on a moment's notice. Just add whatever fresh meat, fish, and produce catch your eye at the supermarket, and before you know it, you'll have a balanced, quick, and easy-to-make dish on your table. What can be more Chinese than that? Just stock up on the ingredients listed here — some of which you probably already have and most of which are described in this chapter — and enjoy having a Chinese mini-market in your own home.

Sauces and condiments:

- Soy sauce
- Rice vinegar
- Oyster-flavored sauce
- Hoisin sauce
- Chile paste or sauce
- Black bean sauce
- Plum sauce

- Vegetable oil
- Sesame oil
- Chile oil
- Rice wine (or dry sherry)

Spices and seasonings:

- Chinese five-spice powder
- Star anise
- Sichuan peppercorns
- Whole and crushed dried red chiles
- Chinese hot mustard
- White pepper

Canned and dried ingredients:

- Bamboo shoots
- Straw mushrooms
- Water chestnuts
- Broth (canned or homemade, see Chapter 9)
- Dried black mushrooms
- Long-grain rice (see Chapter 15)
- Cornstarch
- Sesame seeds

Noodles:

- Cellophane or bean thread noodles (see Chapter 15)
- Dried rice noodles (see Chapter 15)
- Dried egg noodles (stored in freezer if fresh, see Chapter 15)

Chapter 5

Common Chinese Cooking Techniques

In This Chapter

▶ Cutting stuff

▶ Doing prep work

▶ Frying, steaming, roasting, and more

*I*f the word *technique* sounds too technical, relax. You don't need to struggle with complicated techniques to cook like a true Chinese chef. Basic Chinese cooking techniques are never more complicated than the ones that you already know and practice daily in your own kitchen. With a little planning and some practice (and practice is the fun part!), anyone can master Chinese cooking.

SAFETY TIP

Always work with clean equipment. That includes countertops, cutting tools, and especially your hands. You can keep the risk of cross-contamination at bay if you wash cutting boards, knives, bowls, and other equipment in warm, soapy water before allowing them to come in contact with the next raw ingredient.

Look Sharp: Getting Ready

Good Chinese cooking starts with good ingredient preparation. The key to effective stir-frying — the most popular Chinese cooking technique — is cooking all the ingredients in the pan (or wok) quickly over high heat. For this reason, it's a good idea to first cut all the meat and vegetables into bite-size dimensions so that they will cook quickly and evenly.

Those who are familiar with my cooking show know that I am quite fond of my Chinese chef's knife (see Chapter 3). I use it to slice, dice, and chop, and I can work up quite an appetite with all that exercise. But speed isn't everything. In fact, when it comes to knife skills, I recommend starting slowly and carefully. Here are some cutting basics to give you the edge.

Getting a grip on your knife

Although holding your knife properly may seem *really* basic, you'd be surprised to find how many people don't understand the importance of this simple technique. But you won't get too far in Chinese cooking without having a firm handle on holding your knife, so to speak.

As I mention in Chapter 3, the first step to razor-sharp knife skills is finding a knife that fits your hand — as well as one that fits the task at hand. After you've met those two requirements, familiarize yourself with your knife and with the different ways that you can grip it. After all, although there are some generally accepted "correct" ways to hold a knife, the ultimate grip decision is up to you, based on what makes you most comfortable in different chopping situations.

I offer some general descriptions of the most basic grip styles. Take a look at them, try them out with your own knife, and modify them according to your own ergonomic needs (see Figure 5-1).

Grip Number 1

Grip Number 1, the most basic grip, is a particularly comfortable and effective way to hold your Chinese chef's knife. Grasp the handle with three fingers while placing your index finger on one side of the blade and your thumb on the opposite side. By holding the knife near its center of gravity this way (for more on a knive's center of gravity, see the section on the Chinese chef's knife in Chapter 3), you gain additional control and stability.

Grip Number 2

A slight variation on Grip Number 1, Grip Number 2 has you holding the handle with all four fingers and firmly placing your thumb against the side of the blade near the front edge of the handle.

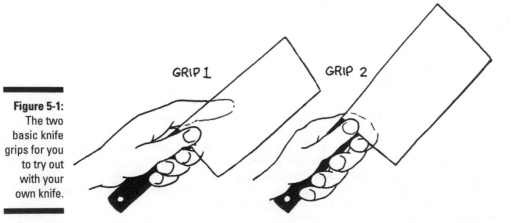

Figure 5-1:
The two basic knife grips for you to try out with your own knife.

GRIP 1   GRIP 2

Your guide hand

After you choose the appropriate way to hold your knife, you're going to find yourself with a free hand. Well, don't just let it lie idle! That free hand, called the guiding hand, performs some pretty important functions, from guiding the food you're cutting, to keeping the knife from slipping, to controlling the size of the cuts you make.

No matter what you do with your free hand, make sure to keep it out of the knife's way. When holding food, use your guiding hand's fingertips to steady the item while you keep your thumb back away from the blade. Tuck your fingertips under a bit so that your knuckles abut the blade's flat side, as shown in Figure 5-2. This hand position lets you slice, chop, and otherwise move the knife freely without putting those fingertips in danger. "Fingers" may be a nice nickname for a piano player, but not a chef.

Slicing

Hold the food securely on the cutting board, making sure that the fingers on your guiding hand are curled under and are out of the way of the knife's edge (see Figure 5-3). Press straight down with the knife, slicing into the food to get pieces of the desired thickness.

Matchstick/julienne cutting

The words matchstick and julienne mean essentially the same thing: thin strips of food that are cut to the size of matchsticks. To julienne or matchstick-cut an ingredient, cut it into thin, evenly sized slices, stack them, and slice vertically through the stack to create a bundle of thin strips resembling matchsticks, as shown in Figure 5-4. If you want to julienne or matchstick-cut meat or chicken, I suggest chilling it in the freezer for about 15 to 20 minutes. Doing so firms the flesh and makes slicing more manageable.

Technically, julienned foods are cut to dimensions of ⅛ inch x ⅛ inch x 1 to 2 inches. But in Chinese cooking, we generally julienne or matchstick-cut items thinner – almost to shreds, in fact. The thinner the vegetables or meats, the quicker they cook, and that's an important quality when using a quick-cooking method such as stir-frying (described in detail later in the chapter). In addition to julienne-cutting or matchstick-cutting ingredients very thinly, make sure that all ingredients in a recipe are cut to similar dimensions. Having the foods roughly the same size ensures that they'll cook at the same pace.

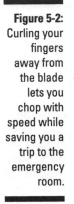

Figure 5-2:
Curling your fingers away from the blade lets you chop with speed while saving you a trip to the emergency room.

SAFE FINGER PLACEMENT WHEN SLICING

Figure 5-3:
The basic technique for slicing . . . anything! Remember to curl the fingers of your guiding hand away from the blade.

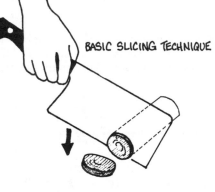

BASIC SLICING TECHNIQUE

Figure 5-4:
The basic technique for julienne cutting, as performed on a bell pepper.

MATCHSTICK/JULIENNE CUTTING

Cubing/dicing/mincing

The main difference between cubes, dices, and minces is the size. Other than that, they're all basically cube-shaped pieces of food. Cubes are the largest of the three, while a dice can measure ¾ inch cubed down to ¼ inch cubed. Mincing produces the smallest pieces, usually ⅟₁₆ inch cubed. To cube, dice, or mince a food, first cut it into long sticks by using the julienne/matchstick technique, Vary the sticks' cross-sectional dimensions depending on whether you want to cube, dice, or mince. Then cut across the sticks to create whatever size cubes you want. Figure 5-5 illustrates the dicing technique.

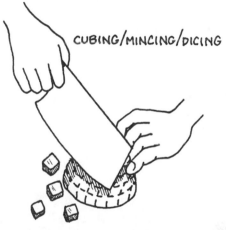

Figure 5-5: The basic cubing, mincing, and dicing technique; to vary among the three, just make the cuts larger or smaller.

CUBING/MINCING/DICING

Not your basic minced meat

Many Chinese recipes call for minced chicken, pork, beef, or shrimp. Over the years, Chinese chefs have developed a quick and exciting way to mince their meats. Hold a cleaver in each hand (double the cleaver, double the fun) and rapidly alternate chopping the meat with each cleaver as if you were playing a drum-roll. Periodically scoop the meat off the board by using the flat of the knife's blade as a scooper, flip the meat over, and start chopping again along a different direction. After a couple more flips and turns, you'll have the ingredient down to a finely minced texture.

Some chefs can mince with one knife, but you'd best leave that fancy blade work to the pros. One blade or two, this technique takes a little practice. If you're in a bit of a rush, you may want to buy store-ground meats or run slightly frozen meat through a food processor to achieve the same effect.

Roll cutting

Roll cutting is a great technique for cutting long, cylindrical vegetables such as carrots, zucchini, and eggplants. To begin, cut a diagonal slice off the tip of the vegetable, as shown in Figure 5-6. Then roll it a quarter turn, make another diagonal cut along the same angle as the first, roll a quarter turn again, and make another cut. Continue rolling and cutting until you come to the end of the vegetable. This convenient technique creates attractively shaped ingredients and exposes more of the food's surface to heat to speed cooking.

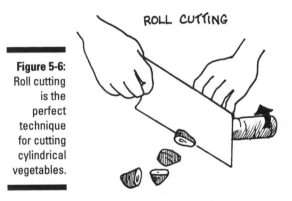

Figure 5-6: Roll cutting is the perfect technique for cutting cylindrical vegetables.

Parallel cutting

When you need to cut wide, thin slices from meats or want to slice a block of tofu into two layers, parallel cutting is your technique of choice (illustrated in Figure 5-7). Just place the piece of food near the edge of your cutting board and lay your guiding hand flat on top of it. With your other hand, hold your Chinese chef's knife at a slight angle downward so that it's not quite parallel to the board. Use a slow and careful back-and-forth motion to slice the food.

PARALLEL CUTTING
A CHICKEN FILLET
HOLD THE KNIFE AT A
SLIGHT ANGLE DOWNWARD

Figure 5-7: Parallel cutting into very thin slices.

☆ BE SURE TO KEEP FINGERS
OUT OF THE WAY!

When parallel cutting food into very thin slices, your fingers come awfully close to the knife's blade. So, as always, be very careful to keep that knife angled slightly downward and away from your hand.

Crushing

To release the essential oils in pungent ingredients such as garlic, ginger, or salted black beans, crush them. Doing so bursts the cellular "sacks" containing those oils. Place the ingredient on a cutting board and hold a knife over it horizontally with the blade's edge facing away from you. Then slap the flat of the blade onto the board with your free hand, crushing the food underneath it. Use the flat of the knife's blade as a scoop to pick up the newly crushed ingredient (see Figure 5-8).

Figure 5-8:
Turning your
Chinese
chef's knife
into a handy
crusher/
scooper.

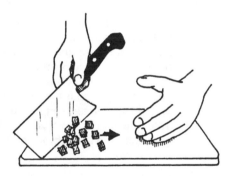

CRUSHING FOOD WITH A KNIFE...   ... AND USING THE KNIFE AS A SCOOP

How's this for easy garlic and ginger peeling? For garlic, just crush an unpeeled clove by using the technique described in this section, and the peel will slide right off. Peeling ginger calls for a different skill. Although the skin of young ginger is so thin that you don't really need to peel it, older hand-shaped chunks of ginger — actually called hands of ginger — have thick, rough skin that you'll probably want to remove. Beware, however, that most of ginger's flavor is concentrated right below its skin, so peeling too deeply may remove the flavor along with the skin. The solution? Use a teaspoon to scrape off the skin (gingerly, of course).

Scoring

Ever ordered a fish fillet and noticed the diamond pattern sliced into its surface? If so, you already know what happens when you score food. Simply make a few slightly angled cuts, about ⅛ inch deep, at the food's surface, being careful not to cut all the way through. These marks help the food cook faster and more evenly. You can also slip slices of garlic, herbs, and other aromatic flavorings into the score marks to enhance the flavor. Remember, you'll always be a winner in the kitchen if you know how to keep . . . scores.

Tenderizing

Save your money on a tenderizer hammer. Put your handy Chinese chef's knife to work instead. Use the blunt edge to pound tough cuts of meat in a crisscross pattern. This action helps break down some of the stronger fibers that give meat a tough texture.

Non-Knife Wielding Techniques

Chinese cooking gives you plenty of opportunities to put your knife skills to work. But several prep steps don't require that you pick up a blade at all. For example, a recipe may ask that you *marinate* meat, poultry, or seafood before cooking. This process not only adds flavor but also helps tenderize tougher cuts of meat. About a half hour is all a typical Chinese marinade needs to work its magic. Just place the marinade and meat in a nonreactive plastic or glass bowl or sealable plastic bag and keep the bowl or bag in the refrigerator while marinating. If you leave the food at room temperature, you could encourage the growth of potentially dangerous bacteria such as *E. coli* or *Salmonella*.

Similar to marinating, *velveting* involves coating food with a mixture of unbeaten egg white, cornstarch, and salt and then deep-frying it quickly before stir-frying it later. Chinese restaurant cooks take this extra step to prevent overcooking and seal in the food's flavor and texture. And as the name suggests, it gives foods a temptingly glossy appearance and smooth velvety texture. To make sure that the coating sticks to the food, professional cooks refrigerate it for 20 to 30 minutes before starting the dish. Velveting is not a necessary step for home cooking, and most home cooks (myself included) skip right over it with no notable consequences.

For dried ingredients such as mushrooms and dried shrimp, you need to *soak* them before preparing the meal. As a general rule, soak dried ingredients for about a half hour in lukewarm water to make sure that they rehydrate sufficiently. If you want to get a jump on preparing your ingredients, soak the dried ones the night before and store them in the refrigerator until cooking time. Also, because the soaking liquid takes on some of the flavor of dried ingredients, it makes a great addition to sauces and stir-fries. So don't dump it out!

Toasting whole spices and seeds such as Sichuan peppercorns and sesame seeds really enhances their aroma and flavor, and it's such an easy thing to do. Just place the ingredients in a small, dry pan and cook over low heat, swirling the pan to expose all surfaces of the ingredients to the heat. When the items look slightly darkened and release their fragrance — after 3 to 4 minutes — remove them from the heat. If you need to toast larger quantities of larger ingredients, such as walnuts or peanuts, place them in a single layer on a tray and roast them in a 350° oven for 8 to 10 minutes or until golden brown. You may want to plan ahead by toasting more than you need for the specific recipe and storing the rest in plastic bags or jars in your pantry. They keep for months.

Toasting is *not* burning. Burnt seeds, nuts, and spices have an acrid, burnt flavor that will spill over to your food. Remove the spices from heat when you notice their change of color, and always err on the undertoasted side.

The Art of Cooking

Chinese cooking really is an art form, with the ingredients serving as canvases that spices, sauces, herbs, and other "paints" help decorate. And what does the skillful Chinese culinary artist use as a brush? The cooking techniques themselves, of course. Study up on this section, and with a little practice, you'll be wielding those "brushes" with plenty of skill and confidence, too, creating masterpieces in your very own kitchen.

Before you start cooking

You've equipped your kitchen and stocked your shelves with the essentials of Chinese cooking. But as any worthy Chinese cook does, you should keep this old motto in mind: Be prepared. (And you thought the Boy Scouts came up with that one.) It's true: the first step in any Chinese cooking technique is preparation. It's the key to success in every kitchen from Grand Rapids to Guangzhou. So follow this step-by-step approach, and you'll be ready to sidle up to the stove in no time.

1. **Wash your hands in warm, soapy water.**

2. **Wash all ingredients, cut ingredients to the recommended dimension (don't worry if the pieces don't look perfect — you'll get better with practice), and measure quantities.**

3. **If the recipe requires that you soak ingredients or marinate meats, and if you haven't already begun to do so the night before, get it started now.**

4. **If you're making your own sauce, combine the sauce ingredients in a bowl or prepare it according to the recipe's instructions.**

   Set it within easy reach.

5. **Line up all the recipe's components or arrange them in groups on the kitchen counter according to their order in the recipe.**

   This way, you'll know what to grab, when to grab, and where to grab it.

6. **Preheat your wok or frying pan.**

   A hot wok makes foods less likely to stick. To tell whether it's hot enough, splash a few droplets of water into it. If the water evaporates immediately, the wok is ready.

7. **Check the recipe one more time to finalize your plan of attack.**

8. **Now relax and have some fun. The hardest part of cooking is already behind you!**

Stepping up to the stove

Here's a quick explanation of the different types of techniques that are common in Chinese cooking.

Stir-frying

This is the most common Chinese cooking technique. Its simplicity makes it the perfect starting point for novice cooks, too. In no time, you'll be hooked by the crispy textures, bright colors, and delicious flavors of stir-fried dishes. To keep up with the fast pace of this cooking method and to get the best results, pay attention to the three cardinal rules of stir-frying:

- **Organize, organize, organize.** Stir-frying is a quick cooking method, leaving little time to reach into cabinets or chop ingredients after you start cooking. Have everything chopped, measured, and within easy reach and have the sauce mixed and ready to pour.

- **Hot, hot, hot.** High heat gets the best stir-fry results. Intense cooking temperatures and the small size of stir-fry ingredients help your stir-fry go from stove to serving dish in no time. Keeping things hot also seals flavor, juices, and nutrients into the ingredients while leaving them crisp.

- **Stir, stir, stir.** That's how the technique got its name. Rapidly toss and stir the ingredients to expose all their surfaces to the heat. Don't load the wok with vegetables and meat and just stand there and stare at it. Good stir-fry dishes require plenty of elbow grease. Remember that it's *stir*-fry, not *stare*-fry!

Now that you've got everything chopped and on the counter and your wok is sizzling hot, it's time to wok and roll. And although each stir-fry recipe is slightly different, they all tend to follow the same basic pattern of steps:

1. **Preheat the wok (remember the second cardinal rule of stir-frying, "hot, hot, hot"), add the oil, and let it heat up.**

2. **Add the aromatic flavoring ingredients such as garlic, ginger, chiles, and green onions.**

   Cook these ingredients for a few seconds until they become aromatic and release their flavors into the oil.

3. **Add the meat or seafood.**

   If your home stove doesn't reach very high temperatures (which is likely if you have an electric range), you may want to let the meat rest in the hot wok for up to a minute to begin cooking its surface before you start stir-frying in earnest. After you do, remember to toss, stir, and toss some more. You're sealing in the juices and keeping the food from sticking at this point.

   When the meat or seafood is done, you may want to remove it from the wok to a platter, or it will overcook and toughen. Cooking the meat or seafood first flavors the oil and releases juices into the wok, adding flavors to the vegetables that come next.

4. **Add the vegetables.**

   Add the dense, tough ones first, followed by the smaller, more tender ones. Continue tossing and stirring now that you are a stir-frying expert.

5. **When the vegetables are done, return the meat and any accumulated juices to the wok, along with the sauce called for in the recipe.**

   Stir this well and allow everything to heat through.

   Chinese stir-fry sauces often call for the addition of a solution of cornstarch and water near the end of cooking. The solution helps thicken the sauce and gives it a smooth, glossy appearance. (For more on sauce-making basics, refer to Chapter 7.)

6. **Taste the dish to decide whether the seasonings are balanced.**

   Don't be shy about taste-testing — this is one perk of doing the cooking.

7. **Don't forget to add a garnish that echoes one of the other ingredients in the dish: a green onion blossom for lamb with green onions, or some toasted, sliced almonds to decorate a dish of almond chicken.**

   Garnishes don't make the dish, but they are small details that can turn an ordinary stir-fry into something that impresses our eyes as well as our palates.

8. **Remove the wok from the heat, place the stir-fry on a serving platter, and get ready to take your bow!**

Steaming

Steaming is another popular cooking technique in China. Steam power cooks foods quickly and lets their natural flavors come through. Nutritionists and weight watchers love it, too, because it introduces little or no fat and leaves the ingredients' nutrients intact. And as if these advantages weren't enough, it's also easy to do.

Many steamers are readily available at your culinary store (see Chapter 3); however, you can make do, as I prefer to, with a wok or a large pan. Bring water to a boil in a large wok or large pan with a rack in it. (Refer to Chapter 3 for some ideas for making your own steaming rack.) Place your food in a heatproof dish or glass pie plate and put that on the rack over the boiling water. Cover with a tightly fitting lid and let the moist heat circulate around the food, cooking it to a tender finish. Add water to the wok or pan if the level gets too low.

To tell whether my steamer is out of steam, I like to place a marble at the bottom before I start cooking. It quietly rolls around in the water while the level is high, but once that level reaches zero, it clangs against the bottom of the steamer to tell me that I need to add more water. The hotter the water, the better — and boiling is best — but just be careful to gently pour the water around the food or underneath the steamer basket into the bottom of the steamer.

Be especially careful when removing the lid from your steamer. Always open it away from you, letting the steam — which is hotter than boiling water — escape out of your way before you remove your food.

Blanching

Chinese cooks use blanching to precook many of their ingredients before the final cooking process. It softens tough, hardy vegetables, such as broccoli, carrots, and potatoes, and makes peeling vegetables and fruits such as tomatoes and peaches easier. Blanching is also a quick and easy way to get rid of the tinny, metallic taste of some canned vegetables such as bamboo shoots, straw mushrooms, and water chestnuts.

Bring a wok of water to a boil and plunge the vegetables into the water for a few minutes until they're crisp-tender and their color has brightened. Remember, blanching is not cooking, so remove your ingredients quickly from the wok and rinse them under cold water. Or better yet, plunge them into a cold water bath to stop the cooking and set the color.

Do you ever wonder how your favorite stir-fried dishes from Chinese restaurants get their rich, flavorful character? Is it the oil? The chef's expert technique? A well-guarded secret passed from generation to generation of Chinese restaurant owners? Well, all of those factors help. But between you and me, the real secret is oil blanching. By quickly submerging bite-sized pieces of meat or seafood in moderately hot oil (300° to 325°) rather than in boiling water, Chinese chefs seal in juices and give foods a tantalizing richness and shiny finish that Chinese restaurant diners crave. Although I usually follow this practice when I cook in a restaurant, I leave it out in my home kitchen. The stir-frying recipes in this book are for home cooking, and they taste wonderful without oil blanching.

Simmering

In cooking as in life, faster isn't always better. Simmering, a slow cooking method that leaves foods tender and juicy, is a perfect example. It's the technique of choice to make broths, soups, and some sauces.

To simmer, fill a wok or pot with just enough water or liquid to cover the food you want to simmer, bring the solution to a boil, and add the food. Reduce the temperature to just below the boiling point and let the food cook gently until it's done.

Braising

When you combine simmering with stir-frying, you get *braising,* a cooking method that's especially effective with larger, tougher cuts of meat.

Braising is a two-step process. Stir-frying comes first: Lightly brown chunks of meat in a wok or pot to caramelize them. Do not overcrowd the pot with too much meat, or you'll lower the temperature and prevent all the pieces from contacting the cooking surface evenly.

After you've browned the meat, add the seasonings and braising liquid — stock, water, soy sauce, or rice wine. Bring this to a boil, lower the heat to a simmer, cover, and cook gently for a couple hours (or whatever the recipe requires) so that the braising liquid's flavors permeate and tenderize the meat.

Deep-frying

Deep-fried Chinese foods, including wontons, egg rolls, and sweet and sour dishes, are crowd pleasers inside China as well as outside. Who can refuse rich flavors and a crispy exterior contrasted with a moist, delicate inside? I certainly can't! For easy deep-frying at home, follow these simple guidelines:

1. **Pour oil into a wok or deep frying pan to a depth of about 2 inches and turn on the heat.**

2. **Regulate the oil temperature according to the recipe.**

   If the temperature is too hot, you'll burn the food or cook the outside too quickly before the inside has a chance to cook. If the temperature is too low, your foods will take a long time to cook, absorbing so much oil in the process that they end up soggy and greasy. Properly heated oil seals the food's surface, creating a crispy outer layer while fully cooking what's inside.

Red-cooked and ready to eat

Red-cooking refers to the slow cooking process that is popular in Shanghai and its neighbors — Jiangxi, Fujian, and Zhejiang provinces. In red-cooking, food is simmered in a fragrant mixture of soy sauce, sugar, and other flavorings. After cooking slowly and gently, meats develop a mahogany glaze and take on the rich flavor of the red-cooking sauce.

How can you tell whether your oil has reached the correct temperature? Most electric frying pans come with a temperature control, thereby eliminating guesswork. You can also use a deep-frying thermometer to get an even more accurate measure. But if you don't have either of these tools, I have an age-old trick that Chinese chefs have used for centuries: Dip the tip of a dry, wooden chopstick into the hot oil. If the oil bubbles around the chopstick, it's hot enough for the food.

3. **After the oil is hot enough, add the food. But don't add too much at once or you'll lower the oil temperature and end up with greasy food.**

4. **Very carefully slide the food into the oil a few pieces at a time, pointing them away from your body.**

You don't want oil that's been heated to 300° or hotter splashing on you. If you deep-fry in a wok, use a flat-bottom one or stabilize a round-bottom one by setting it in a ring stand (see Chapter 3 for more on woks).

5. **Turn the food frequently as it cooks to ensure even browning.**

6. **After the food floats to the top of the wok and stays there (some foods float initially but then sink), it's ready.**

Remove it with a wire strainer or slotted spoon and drain on paper towels.

Roasting

Oven-baked dishes are not very common in traditional Chinese kitchens, with fuel scarcity in China being a major reason for their rarity. In the old days, most ovens were found in restaurants and community bakeries rather than in homes. But even though Chinese home cooks don't roast foods every day, you can still find plenty of roasted Chinese delicacies, such as Peking roast duck or barbecued Cantonese spareribs (despite the name, the ribs are really roasted or baked).

Traditional Chinese cooks hung marinated meat or poultry on a hook and cooked it over a wood-burning fire. You can simulate this process by roasting marinated meat or poultry on a rack in a foil-lined baking pan. Turn the meat occasionally to ensure even cooking. To keep the meat moist and tasty, baste it with the marinade and juices that collect in the pan.

Smoking

Like barbecuing and roasting, variations on smoking are at home both in Western and Chinese kitchens. Smoking is a flavoring technique that involves slowly cooking meats in an enclosed container with a smoky fire. The Chinese often smoke in a wok, using black tea leaves, citrus peel, raw rice, brown sugar, and whole spices to add flavor.

For easy smoking in your own home, line a large wok with foil and sprinkle in smoking seasonings listed in this section or in the recipe. Place the meat on a rack inside the wok. Tightly cover the wok, turning the excess foil up to cover the wok's lid and sealing in the heat and flavor. Increase the heat and let the scented smoke permeate the meat, giving it a very distinctive smoky flavor. Follow the smoking time recommended in your recipe.

An old-fashioned Eastern barbecue?

Barbecuing involves cooking marinated meats or poultry over a dry heat — normally a charcoal fire or heated grill surface. Although grilling may not be the most popular cooking method in China, the famous Mongolian barbecue provides a good example of a Chinese use of this technique: Chefs sizzle slices of marinated meats and poultry — lamb being among the chief favorites — on a huge, table-sized griddle, and serve the pleasingly charred and smoky treats to hungry diners. Mongolian barbecue restaurants have sprung up in various parts of North America, but the tradition originated with the Mongolian nomads who wandered northern China, leaving valuable souvenirs of their culture in their wake. Take advantage of your own griddle or barbecue grill and give an Asian-style barbecue a try.

Chapter 6

Edible Artistry: Garnishes to Prettify Your Plate

In This Chapter

▶ Understanding the basics of garnishing

▶ Discovering garnishing's rules and tools

▶ Making your own garnishes

Recipes in This Chapter

▶ Tomato Rose
▶ Apple Wings
▶ Cucumber Fan
▶ Green Onion Brushes
▶ Chili Pepper Flowers

*N*o matter how much my wife fusses over choosing my shirt, my jacket, and the right pair of pants, I'd always feel underdressed if I left home without a watch. And I think the same applies to my dinner. Now I'm not suggesting that you buy your roast chicken a Rolex (although a timer for your egg isn't a bad idea). But just as the right accessory completes an ensemble, the right garnish goes a long way in transforming a simple dish into a memorable culinary masterpiece.

Chinese cooking is judged by four elements: color, smell, texture, and taste. Long before your guests take their first bite, they dine with their eyes and their noses, and few things get mouths watering faster than a dish that's a feast for those senses. Enter the garnish. Like a snazzy silver belt buckle, the proper garnish — and "proper" can mean anything from a smattering of sesame seeds to a pineapple carved to resemble a fishing boat — gives a dish that "special something." And although carving elaborate pagodas from carrots may be a task for the truly gifted, the everyday home cook can master plenty of simple yet elegant garnishes with a little practice.

Remember, a naked chef may be entertaining, but never a naked dish. Garnish it!

From the Simple to the Sublime: Garnishes that Run the Gamut

Among other things, Chinese imperial cuisine is famous for its beautiful and elaborate garnishes — each a miniature food sculpture in its own right. But not all garnishes have to take on such a grand scale. If you're interested in injecting some garnishing flair into your next dinner party, you'd do well to adopt a start-small philosophy. Take heart in knowing that many of the most attractive ways to adorn your plate don't require years of apprenticeship in a sculptor's studio.

The basics

At the most basic level, a garnish can be as simple as one of the dish's component ingredients scattered strategically atop the plate. Here are just a few examples of quick and easy eye-pleasers:

- A sprinkling of toasted sesame seeds
- Rings of sliced green onion
- Sprigs of fresh cilantro
- Thin, half-moon slices of citrus fruit, tomato, or cucumber
- Nests or puffs of fried bean thread noodles
- A bed of shredded lettuce or fresh iceberg lettuce-leaf "cups"
- Deep-fried strips of wonton skins
- Mint and basil leaves
- A tomato cut into six or eight wedges

Let this short list get your mental garnishing-gears turning. Just take a look around your stash of ingredients the next time you're in the kitchen. I'd bet that you can find the perfect edible accessory, ready for service, right in front of you. It's really that simple.

The high end

But as much as I enjoy the simplicity — and appreciate the ease — of these subtle plate decorations, I must pay homage to the high end of the spectrum by telling you about the handiwork of the imperial artists/chefs. To call these sculptors merely gifted is to call the Great Wall just a stack of old bricks.

Garnishing was a specialty in the imperial kitchen. Chefs who are trained in this time-honored craft still often decorate hollow winter melons with bas-relief designs, creating bowls and soup tureens whose iridescent, closely shaved rinds make them look like pearly, glowing lanterns. And a gifted food sculptor can do truly amazing things with a carrot! I've seen carrot horses, fish, eagles, and dragons, each carved to the last anatomically precise detail.

Needless to say, these are handiworks of culinary professionals. So please, don't try them at home — unless, of course, you crave the frustration of attempting to turn a clove of garlic into a blossoming magnolia. But you may want to test your mettle with some garnishes that go beyond simply scattered sesame seeds or an artfully placed orange wedge. If so, just head to the next section for tips and how-to's to make completely doable garnishes that turn eating into an aesthetic journey.

Imperial garnishes aren't all pomp and stuffiness; they can be whimsical and playful, too. Imagine transforming a common carrot or winter melon into a pagoda, a flower pot, or a soup bowl decorated with creatures from ancient Chinese myths (see Figure 6-1). I must tip my chef's hat to these witty artists, who certainly bring a sense of history and culture to the dining table.

Figure 6-1: Some examples of the edible art of the Chinese garnish.

CARVED VEGETABLE GARNISHES

Preparing to Pare: Principles for Successful Garnishing

Before packing your bags for seven years of garnishing school, take a good look through this chapter. The garnishes here are easy enough for the all-thumbs crowd to tackle, yet deceptively impressive enough for the most discerning and sophisticated audience. I like to think of them as the garnishing equivalents of designer accessory knockoffs!

Garnishing 1-2-3s

It's tempting for your imagination to write checks that your garnishing know-how can't cash. Therefore, start slowly, familiarizing yourself with the basic garnishing principles before venturing out into more complicated terrain. Here are a few simple rules that will let you pull off a garnishing feat without going overboard:

- **A garnish should complement the dish it decorates.** This is why a simple ingredient from the recipe often provides the best enhancement. Chinese cuisine prides itself in balancing appearance with aroma and flavor; hence, the most attractive garnish may still be unsuitable if it clashes with the dish's other sensory attributes.

- **A garnish works its magic by way of contrast.** What's the use of having a garnish if it blends right into the main dish? A camouflaged garnish doesn't do much for the balanced yin-yang aspect of the presentation. By contrasting textures and colors, you'll not only bring the dish's elements into sharper focus but also make it a more satisfying sensory experience at the same time.

- **The home cook's most foolproof garnishing choices are the simplest.** Don't get carried away. It's "garnish," not "garish." Overindulging in complicated garnishes or using too much of the same garnish will only detract from, not enhance, the dish. You don't want your guests to wonder what, exactly, they're supposed to eat. So don't get carried away.

- **Don't use the same garnish over and over in the same meal.** For one thing, a single garnish probably won't "match" every single dish; for another, it won't make an impact if you overuse it. Remember that you don't *have* to garnish every plate.

- **All garnishes have to be edible.** Here's where I put my foot down. No aluminum foil, no twigs, no matchsticks, and no Barbie dolls — unless they're made of sugar. (Flowers? Fine, but only so long as they're edible. Ask your florist which ones haven't been sprayed and are safe to eat.)

> ✔ **After you've taken all the previous suggestions to heart, the most important guideline is to be creative and have fun.** You're going to need patience and practice, but after a while, you'll develop the necessary carving proficiency and stealthy garnish-seeking sense. Before you know it, you'll be spotting potential pagodas where, before, you only saw potatoes.

Preparation issues

Every trade has its tools, and garnishing is no exception. A custom-made, professional garnishing kit in China is a real bag of tricks. It includes cleavers, scoops, chisels, scalpels, scrapers, and plenty of other pieces of equipment that seem more suitable for a surgical bag than a kitchen cupboard. But as good news to all you amateur garnishers, you have it much easier than the pros in China. To create the garnishes in this book, you need only a few common utensils that you probably have in your kitchen already. Check out this list to find out.

- ✔ A Chinese chef's knife works well for some of the less delicate garnishes.

- ✔ Paring knives or kitchen scissors make quick and safe work of the precise cuts that smaller garnishes require.

- ✔ Small metal cookie cutters in any shape you like easily cut figures out of sturdy vegetables; choose cutters about 1 to 2 inches in diameter, or no bigger than the diameter of a wide carrot or cucumber.

- ✔ Bamboo skewers or toothpicks poke eyeholes into animal-shaped garnishes. (The tip of your paring knife works well in a pinch.)

- ✔ For garnishes that need soaking, have a medium bowl of ice water at the ready.

If there's ever a time when you want your knives to be sharp, it's when you're preparing garnishes. In fact, all garnishing tools should be razor sharp to get the cleanest, most precise carvings. A dull knife is imprecise and dangerous.

Bear in mind that while having a sharp knife can steer you clear of injury — sharp knives are safe knives — the close, precision carving that some of these items call for could have you turning your precious digits into part of the garnish *if you're not careful.* Pay close attention to where you maneuver the knife, always direct it away from your body when you cut, and always work with a stable, well-secured, bump-free cutting board. You may want to consult Chapter 5 for a refresher of proper cutting techniques.

Your sharp knives deserve only the firmest, freshest, most colorful foods on which to work their garnishing magic. Rotten tomatoes don't make very perky tomato roses. Be picky when selecting produce for garnishes. Also, to keep items such as apples, potatoes, and pears from browning after you carve them, soak them in a bowl of ice water with a squirt of lemon juice before you start carving them.

And if you've reached the end of the meal and no one has dared eat your stunningly lifelike garnishes, save them, sealed safely in a zippered plastic bag, for the next dinner party. Just refresh them in a bowl of ice water for about 10 minutes if they look a little tired.

Getting Down to Business: The Garnishes

In this section, you find the instructions for making a few of my favorite simple yet elegant garnishes. All of them are easy enough for anyone with even rudimentary knife skills, and the necessary equipment is probably already in your kitchen drawers. Go ahead and impress your guests with your creations.

Tomato Rose

This one's a real classic. Practically everyone has at some point had one dish or another decorated with a delicate tomato rose. Now you can make as many as you'd like, yourself.

What you'll need: *Sharp paring knife; firm, ripe tomato of your choice*

1 With a paring knife, begin slicing a paper-thin piece of the tomato's skin, ¾ inches wide, at the nonstem end of the tomato, as shown in Figure 6-2. Continue to slice in a circle around the tomato until you have one long strip.

2 Holding the nonstem end of the strip, curl it up to form a small pistil. Continue to curl the rest of the strip into a circle to form the shape of a rose (see Figure 6-2).

Remember: Use a ripe yet firm tomato to get a rose with the ideal form and shape. Roma tomatoes make attractive smaller rosebuds, while large or beefsteak tomatoes make the best fully bloomed roses.

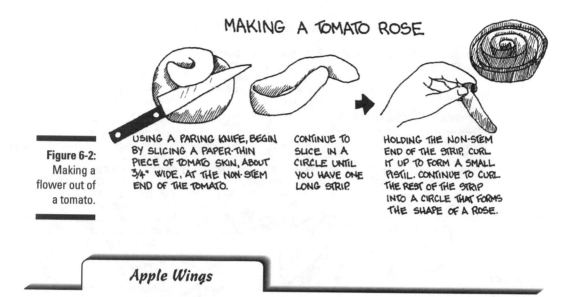

MAKING A TOMATO ROSE

Figure 6-2:
Making a
flower out of
a tomato.

USING A PARING KNIFE, BEGIN BY SLICING A PAPER-THIN PIECE OF TOMATO SKIN, ABOUT 3/4" WIDE, AT THE NON-STEM END OF THE TOMATO.

CONTINUE TO SLICE IN A CIRCLE UNTIL YOU HAVE ONE LONG STRIP.

HOLDING THE NON-STEM END OF THE STRIP, CURL IT UP TO FORM A SMALL PISTIL. CONTINUE TO CURL THE REST OF THE STRIP INTO A CIRCLE THAT FORMS THE SHAPE OF A ROSE.

Apple Wings

This is a simple way to turn an apple — a firm, unblemished, red one is best, such as a Macintosh, Red Delicious, or Rome apple — into a spectacular three-dimensional plate decoration.

What you'll need: *Sharp paring knife; firm, clean, red apple; 2 cups water mixed with juice of half a lemon*

1 Cut an apple in half and place the two halves on a cutting board.

2 On each half, make two diagonal cuts, angling the knife inward to cut out a small wedge (see Figure 6-3). Carefully place the wedge in a bowl of 2 cups water mixed with the juice of half a lemon to prevent discoloration.

3 Cut out four more wedges, each ¼ inch wider than the previous one, using the same technique as noted in Step 3. Place each in the water-juice mixture.

4 Remove the wedges from the water-juice mixture and reassemble them in their original order, stacking the smaller wedges atop the larger ones, as shown in Figure 6-3.

5 With your thumb, gently press the edges of the stacked wedges to spread them out and form the layers of "feathers" in the wing, as shown in Figure 6-3.

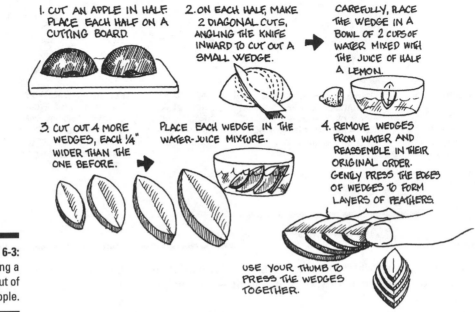

MAKING APPLE 'WINGS'

1. CUT AN APPLE IN HALF. PLACE EACH HALF ON A CUTTING BOARD.

2. ON EACH HALF, MAKE 2 DIAGONAL CUTS, ANGLING THE KNIFE INWARD TO CUT OUT A SMALL WEDGE.

CAREFULLY, PLACE THE WEDGE IN A BOWL OF 2 CUPS OF WATER MIXED WITH THE JUICE OF HALF A LEMON.

3. CUT OUT 4 MORE WEDGES, EACH ¼" WIDER THAN THE ONE BEFORE.

PLACE EACH WEDGE IN THE WATER-JUICE MIXTURE.

4. REMOVE WEDGES FROM WATER AND REASSEMBLE IN THEIR ORIGINAL ORDER. GENTLY PRESS THE EDGES OF WEDGES TO FORM LAYERS OF FEATHERS.

USE YOUR THUMB TO PRESS THE WEDGES TOGETHER.

Figure 6-3: Making a wing out of an apple.

My cooking philosophy draws much from Chinese imperial cuisine, and using garnishes to make food a multisensory treat is a big part of that philosophy. Garnishing dates all the way back to the Tang dynasty (618-907 A.D.). Since then, garnishes have continued integrating food's beauty with its symbolism in China. I can't imagine a better example of yin-yang balance, a topic I discuss in Chapter 1, than combining simple food (the basic substance that sustains life) with the grandeur of intricately designed, meticulously prepared garnishes.

Carving out a niche: Garnishes in Chinese cuisine

To appreciate fully the importance of garnishes in Chinese cuisine, we need to understand the dichotomy that is ever-present in Chinese culture. China is full of contrasts — between the ancient and the modern, Confucianism and Communism, and, of course, between yin and yang. But instead of conflicts, these contrasts actually create balance, and this intricate balance has kept Chinese life and cuisine interesting for thousands of years.

The Chinese attitude toward visual presentation of food reflects that contrast. From modest homecooked meals to elaborately garnished banquet dishes, the basic philosophy of garnishing remains the same: Contrasts create balance, and balance brings beauty.

Cucumber Fan

This elegant garnish echoes graceful folding fans — classic artistic elements in Chinese culture. Make sure to use English or pickling cucumbers for these garnishes because they're firmer and have smaller seeds.

What you'll need: *Sharp paring knife (or Chinese chef's knife if you have sharp knife skills); firm cucumber with few, small seeds, or seedless cucumber*

1 Cut a cucumber in half lengthwise. Cut off the ends.

2 Trim off the sides of the cucumber halves to give each one a rectangular shape, as shown in Figure 6-4.

3 Make thin slices, about ⅛ inch wide, from the top of the cucumber to the bottom. Do *not* cut all the way through both ends of the cucumber, but rather leave one end intact so it forms a "hinge" that holds the cucumber fan together (see Figure 6-4).

4 Push down on the hinge end with your fingers to fan out the slices. Or, alternatively, fold every other slice inward to form a fan pattern. Both options are shown in Figure 6-4.

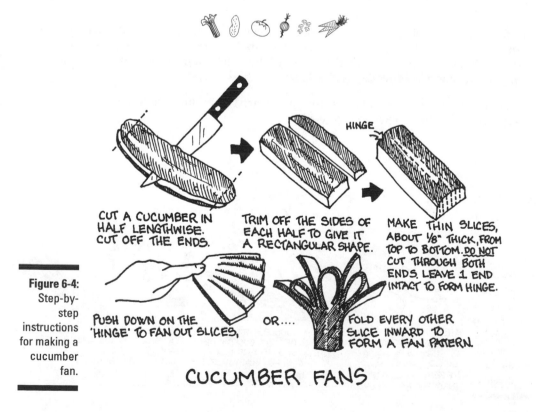

Figure 6-4: Step-by-step instructions for making a cucumber fan.

CUT A CUCUMBER IN HALF LENGTHWISE. CUT OFF THE ENDS.

TRIM OFF THE SIDES OF EACH HALF TO GIVE IT A RECTANGULAR SHAPE.

MAKE THIN SLICES, ABOUT ⅛" THICK, FROM TOP TO BOTTOM. DO NOT CUT THROUGH BOTH ENDS. LEAVE 1 END INTACT TO FORM HINGE.

PUSH DOWN ON THE 'HINGE' TO FAN OUT SLICES,

OR....

FOLD EVERY OTHER SLICE INWARD TO FORM A FAN PATTERN.

HINGE

CUCUMBER FANS

At a formal Chinese banquet, you'll find all sorts of intricately designed dragon and phoenix garnishes. Dragons and phoenixes are creatures that play important roles in Chinese myths and legends, and their presence on the dining table is highly symbolic. Take time to examine the jaw-dropping delicacy of these creations; the experience will no doubt give new depth to the term "food art." Of course, every one of these wonders is edible, but I dare anyone to take a bite out of these pint-size masterpieces.

Green Onion Brushes

I love the sense of whimsy that these little brushes add to a dish. Make single or double brushes as directed and mix them up among the dishes in a meal.

What you'll need: *Sharp paring knife; green onion; strip of green part of green onion, blanched to soften slightly and tied into a ring (optional); bowl of ice water*

1 Trim the root end and green tops on the green onion, as shown in Figure 6-5.

2 To make a single-sided brush, make repeated slashes into the green onion, starting at the top and extending about a third of the way down the length of the onion (see Figure 6-5).

3 To make a double-sided brush, fully slice off the bottom of the root end, making it the same diameter as the top of the onion (see Figure 6-5). If you wish, slide the ring of green onion or red pepper onto the center of the onion. Make repeated slashes on both ends of the onion, as directed in Step 2.

4 Place the onions in a bowl of ice water for at least 1 hour, until the slashed ends curl up to form the brushes shown in Figure 6-5.

GREEN ONION BRUSHES

Figure 6-5: The steps for making single or double green onion brushes.

TRIM THE ROOT END AND GREEN TOPS. TO MAKE A SINGLE-SIDED BRUSH, MAKE REPEATED SLASHES INTO THE GREEN ONION.

FOR A DOUBLE-SIDED BRUSH, SLICE OFF THE BOTTOM OF THE ROOT END AND MAKE IT THE SAME DIAMETER AS THE TOP

YOU CAN SLIDE A RING OF RED CHILI PEPPER ONTO THE CENTER.

PLACE THE ONIONS IN A BOWL OF ICE WATER FOR AT LEAST 1 HOUR, UNTIL THE SLASHED ENDS CURL UP.

Chili Pepper Flowers

Jalapeño and Fresno chiles are ideal for this garnish because of their size and firmness. Use any color you wish, but just make sure to buy what's fresh and available in the market.

Chiles have oils that irritate the skin and mucous membranes in the eyes and mouth, so wear gloves when working with chiles unless you want your fingers and everything they touch to burn. And don't touch your eyes and mouth with the gloves either.

What you'll need: *Kitchen scissors or a sharp paring knife; small, firm peppers such as jalapeños or Fresnos with stem end intact; bowl of ice water*

1 Using kitchen scissors or a paring knife, cut off the tip of the pepper to the desired length. Keep the stem end intact.

2 Make 4 or 5 lengthwise slits around the pepper to form 4 or 5 petals (see Figure 6-6), being careful *not* to cut all the way through to the stem end. Trim the tip of each petal to a point.

3 Remove the membrane and seeds of the chile. (These parts can really make you "feel the burn," so be careful here.)

4 Place the pepper in a bowl of ice water for at least 1 hour, until the "petals" start to curl up a bit (see Figure 6-6).

Figure 6-6:
Turning a
chili pepper
into a
flower.

Part III
The Recipes

The 5th Wave   By Rich Tennant

©RICHTENNANT

"Here's a recipe for Chinese Thousand Year Old Eggs. Thank goodness for microwave ovens."

In this part . . .

Here's the heart and soul of the book. I start by presenting the basic sauces that pop up again and again in recipes throughout the book. Then it's on to classic Chinese appetizers and soups. Then I move on to the dishes that you know and love from menus at your favorite Chinese restaurants. In addition to those classics, this part includes plenty of dishes that may not be too familiar this side of the Pacific, as well as updates and twists on the tried-and-true, just to keep you on your toes.

Chapter 7

Saucy Sauces and Dips

· ·

In This Chapter

▶ Sauces for cooking

▶ Dips for dipping

· ·

Recipes in This Chapter

▶ All-Purpose Stir-Fry Sauce

▶ Hot and Spicy Stir-Fry Sauce

▶ Sweet and Sour Sauce

▶ Master Sauce/Red-Cooking Sauce

▶ All-Purpose Black Bean Sauce

▶ All-Purpose Dipping Sauce

▶ Chile Oil

▶ Chinese Mustard Dip

▶ Sichuan Spicy Salt

*Y*ou know the old saying, "the suit makes the man"? I think the better analogy is "the sauce makes the meal," and it's as true in Chinese cuisine as in French. But traditional Chinese sauces aren't the complicated reductions or egg- and cream-thickened concoctions of classic French cooking, nor are they the hearty tomato-based ragus characteristic of Italian cuisine. Instead, the inventory of Chinese sauces and dips is based upon simple, yet flavorfully potent, combinations of basic seasonings and widely available bottled sauces.

In Chapter 4, I introduce you to many of those prepared sauces available in supermarkets and Chinese groceries. Most of these work wonders on their own — it doesn't take much more than a spoonful of hoisin to bring Peking duck and Mandarin pancakes together in culinary harmony. Yet, by mixing that hoisin with fresh garlic, ginger, dried chili peppers, and any of a number of other flavorings, Chinese cooks build an elegant sauce with complex character. Now it's your turn to do the same and experiment a little. You'll be amazed at all the creative sauces and dips you can make with just a few basic building blocks.

And the beauty of most Chinese sauces and dips is that you can make them in quantity ahead of time and store them in tightly sealed containers in the refrigerator, where they'll keep for weeks at a time. Whenever you want to add a little sweet-and-sour to your pork with peppers, you can have that sauce prepared and ready to go without a lot of last-minute kitchen confusion. The recipes and sidebars in this chapter give you plenty of ideas how.

Sauce Smarts

The entire strategy behind Chinese sauce making involves building a more complex sauce out of simpler elements. But achieving complexity of flavor while keeping the overall sauce balanced is key here. Just as in any other aspect of Chinese cuisine, when one flavor dominates all others — even if you really like that one flavor — you've missed the mark.

The following recipes guarantee that your Chinese sauces will hit the mark every time.

All-Purpose Stir-Fry Sauce

The culinary equivalent of a simple white shirt, this sauce goes with just about anything. Start with the basics — soy sauce, rice wine, and an honest broth — and add a little garlic, ginger, and sesame oil, and you have yourself a sauce that truly deserves the name "all-purpose."

Preparation time: *15 minutes*

Cooking time: *5 minutes*

Yield: *About 1¾ cups*

⅔ cup soy sauce	¼ teaspoon white pepper
½ cup chicken broth	2 tablespoons cooking oil
⅓ cup Chinese rice wine	1 tablespoon minced garlic
3½ tablespoons sugar	1 tablespoon minced ginger
1 tablespoon sesame oil	2 tablespoons cornstarch dissolved in ¼ cup water

1 In a bowl, combine the soy sauce, chicken broth, rice wine, sugar, sesame oil and white pepper.

2 Place a pan over high heat until hot. Add the cooking oil, swirling to coat the sides. Add the garlic and the ginger; cook, stirring, until fragrant, about 15 seconds.

3 Add the mixture from Step 1; bring to a boil. Reduce the heat to medium and cook for 1 minute. Add the cornstarch solution and cook, stirring, until the sauce boils and thickens.

Hot and Spicy Stir-Fry Sauce

Sometimes an all-purpose sauce needs a little bit of kick, and this variation of the standard all-purpose stir-fry sauce packs just such a wallop by way of two different types of pepper and a liberal dose of chile garlic sauce.

Be sure to taste your sauce as you make it. That way, you can put the brakes on the hot chile if it gets a little too racy for you.

Preparation time: *15 minutes*

Cooking time: *7 minutes*

Yield: *1½ cups*

⅔ cup Chinese rice wine

⅓ cup soy sauce

⅓ cup chicken broth

3 tablespoons sugar

½ teaspoon white pepper

2 tablespoons thinly sliced green onions

1½ tablespoons chile garlic sauce

2 tablespoons cooking oil

1½ tablespoons minced garlic

1½ tablespoons minced ginger

2 tablespoons cornstarch dissolved in ¼ cup water

1 In a bowl, combine the rice wine, soy sauce, chicken broth, sugar, white pepper, green onions, and chile garlic sauce.

2 Place a wok or medium pan over high heat until hot. Add the cooking oil, swirling to coat the sides. Add the garlic and ginger; cook, stirring, until fragrant, about 30 seconds. Add the wine mixture, bring to a boil, reduce the heat to medium, and cook for 2 minutes. Add the cornstarch solution and cook, stirring, until the sauce boils and thickens. Let cool.

Sweet and Sour Sauce

North America's favorite Chinese restaurant sauce has finally come to your own kitchen. And when you make it yourself, you can control the sweet and sour flavors to the proportion that's just right for your palate.

The sauce balances the flavors of any stir-fry, but it's especially good at cutting the richness of batter-dipped meats and fish, as well as deep-fried appetizers such as egg rolls.

Preparation time: *15 minutes*

Cooking time: *15 minutes*

Yield: *2 cups*

½ cup water	1½ tablespoons soy sauce
½ cup ketchup	1½ teaspoons crushed dried red chiles
⅓ cup packed brown sugar	2 tablespoons cooking oil
⅓ cup orange juice	2 tablespoons minced ginger
⅓ cup rice vinegar	1½ tablespoons cornstarch mixed with ¼ cup water

1 In a bowl, combine the water, ketchup, brown sugar, orange juice, rice vinegar, soy sauce, and dried chiles.

2 Place a medium pan over high heat until hot. Add the cooking oil, swirling to coat the sides. Add the minced ginger and cook, stirring, until fragrant, about 20 seconds. Add the mixture from Step 1; bring to a boil and cook until the sugar dissolves. Add the cornstarch solution and cook, stirring, until the sauce boils and thickens.

Remember: Sweet and sour sauce wouldn't be sweet and sour without an ample helping of acidic ingredients such as rice vinegar and orange juice. But any starch-thickened sauce becomes thin and watery if you add too much acid. So if you're playing with proportions, don't get out of hand when upping the sour. (For more tips on working with starch solutions in sauces, see the sidebar "Through thick and thin" in this chapter.)

Master Sauce/Red-Cooking Sauce

Like a well-seasoned wok, this richly flavored sauce that hails from eastern China gets better with each use, so don't pour it down the drain after using it in a stew or a claypot casserole. Rather, strain it and store it in a tightly sealed container in the refrigerator or freezer (the latter if you'd like to keep it longer) until you're ready to red-cook again — and again, and again. Every item that you cook in it deepens and enriches the sauce with its own flavors. That's my idea of sauce recycling!

Preparation time: *15 minutes*

Cooking time: *23 minutes*

Yield: *About 3½ cups*

3 cups chicken broth

½ cup soy sauce

⅛ cup dark soy sauce

⅛ cup Chinese rice wine

¼ cup packed brown sugar

2 whole star anise

2 pieces dried tangerine peel or 4 pieces fresh orange peel

2 tablespoons cooking oil

8 slices ginger

6 cloves garlic, crushed

1 tablespoon sesame oil

1 In a bowl, combine the chicken broth, soy sauce, dark soy sauce, rice wine, brown sugar, anise, and tangerine peel.

2 Place a medium pan over high heat until hot. Add the cooking oil, swirling to coat the sides. Add the ginger and garlic; cook, stirring, until fragrant, about 20 seconds. Add the broth mixture; bring to a boil, reduce the heat, cover and simmer for 20 minutes, stirring occasionally.

3 Stir in the sesame oil.

Remember: Some of the aromatics and fresh ingredients in a red-cooking sauce need replenishing now and again. The volatile flavors of dried tangerine peel, ginger, and garlic can "flash off," or vaporize, during cooking. Taste your sauce each time; if it seems a bit weak, by all means add fresh ginger, onions, soy, or any other flavoring ingredient that could use some refreshing.

All-Purpose Black Bean Sauce

This is truly a sauce for all seasons — and a seasoning for just about every situation. Try it with pork ribs, meat dishes, vegetable stir-fries, and especially with seafood. When it comes to pairing black beans with the flavors of the sea, anyone who's done any eating in Guangzhou can vouch that no match is more well seasoned.

Preparation time: *9 minutes*

Yield: *About ¾ cup*

2 tablespoons black bean garlic sauce

1 tablespoon chicken broth

1 tablespoon sesame oil

1 tablespoon sugar

2 tablespoons sliced green onion

1 tablespoon minced ginger

1 teaspoon minced garlic

In a bowl, combine all the ingredients; stir to mix well.

The power of pepper: White pepper in Chinese cuisine

A rose by any other name may smell as sweet, but substituting black pepper for white in a Chinese dish yields very different results. White pepper is actually more common than black in Chinese dishes, and without it, the cuisine loses some of its distinct character. Although using black pepper in lieu of white won't ruin a recipe, it may rob it of that pungency-transcending, subtle warmth that only white pepper gives.

What makes white pepper so different from black? Both do come from the same tropical plant. But instead of being picked green and then sun-dried, as are the berries destined for black peppercorns, those destined for white pepper ripen on the tree until they turn red. Processors then ferment them and wash off their outer layer of skin.

Beware: Some processors make "white pepper" by mechanically removing the dark skins of black peppercorns. Don't get fooled! This isn't the real McCoy, and doesn't have the same delicate fragrance and flavor as genuine white pepper. To tell the difference, look for the term "decorticated" on the label. If you find it, you've found the fake.

Through thick and thin

Getting a smooth, thick consistency out of a Chinese sauce depends on stove-top magicians called slurries. *Slurries* are bland solutions of starch — normally cornstarch, tapioca, arrow-root, or rice flour — mixed with about twice as much water, broth, or other liquid. Thoroughly stir one into a heating sauce, and in minutes, the mixture develops a rich, velvety texture. So how do slurries work their magic in the first place?

When you add a starch-and-water mixture to a sauce on the stove, the heat helps the starch granules absorb liquid. The more they heat, the more they absorb. The more they absorb, the more they swell. Eventually, the swollen gran-ules burst, releasing the starch into the sauce where it does its thickening duty. Granules of different starches burst at specific tempera-tures, known as the *gelation temperature*. But you should start paying extra attention to a sim-mering sauce when it hovers near the boiling point — the ballpark temperature at which most starches hit their gelation temperatures.

As you approach the gelation temperature, the sauce may seem discouragingly thin. But resist the temptation to heat it violently or stir in more slurry because right when those granules burst, the sauce *will* thicken — I promise. And once it does, too much heat or starch solution will turn your silky sauce into glue. Just bring the sauce to a gentle boil and exercise patience, or you'll end up with a gloppy mess that's better suited to hanging wallpaper.

If you're making a sauce ahead of time to store in the refrigerator, leave out the slurry until you begin the actual cooking process. Starch-thick-ened sauces turn into solid, even sliceable, gels as they cool, because the freed starch mole-cules that give the sauce body when warm collapse back in upon themselves — a process called *retrogradation* — when their motion slows at low temperatures. (Incidentally, the same process causes bread to stale.) Try reheating that jellied sauce on the stove, and it'll "break" into a thin, separated, watery mess. The moral of the story: Don't hurry the slurry.

Taking a Dip

The distinction between sauces, dips, oils, and dressings isn't always very clear in Chinese cuisine — or in any cuisine, for that matter. But the recipes that follow all provide you with plenty of pleasing condiments that are great for appetizer-dunking or splashing onto stir-fries and salads. Give them a try, and you won't let your food go naked again.

All-Purpose Dipping Sauce

Is it a sauce, or is it a dip? Who cares? When you have hoisin and Worcestershire sauces, ketchup, and two flavored oils contributing to this complex mixture, what you call it really doesn't matter. Its thick consistency makes it heavenly for fried finger foods, giving it a number-one rank in my list of favorite dips.

To make chile oil for all-purpose dipping sauce, see the recipe later in the chapter.

Preparation time: *3 minutes*

Yield: *About 2 cups*

1 cup ketchup

⅓ cup soy sauce

¼ cup hoisin sauce

¼ cup chicken broth

2½ tablespoons sugar or honey

2 tablespoons Worcestershire sauce

2 tablespoons sesame oil

1 teaspoon chile oil

⅛ teaspoon white pepper

Combine all the ingredients in a medium bowl and mix well.

Chile Oil

Sure, you can buy chile oil at the grocery store or Asian market. But when you make it yourself, you control its heat and its freshness — a real plus, because chile sauces lose some of their flavor over time.

Keeping a bottle of this homemade chile sauce on hand for stir-fries, sauces, salad dressings, and dips saves you plenty of time. It even makes a mouth-watering dip on its own.

Preparation time: *5 minutes*

Cooking time: *1 minute*

Yield: *About 1¼ cups*

1 cup cooking oil

2 tablespoons sesame oil

2 tablespoons crushed dried red chiles

2 teaspoons crushed garlic

Place a small pan over high heat until hot. Add the cooking oil for about 1 minute. Remove from the heat and add the sesame oil, dried chiles, and garlic. Let stand overnight, strain out the seasonings, and then transfer to an airtight jar.

Chinese Mustard Dip

As sure as the Yangtze River flows to the East China Sea, an order of egg rolls will come with a little bowl of pungent Chinese mustard. Like sweet and sour sauce — another common egg roll accompaniment — Chinese mustard dip has a mild tartness that, along with the bite of the mustard itself, provides the perfect foil for deep-fried appetizers.

Preparation time: *7 minutes*

Yield: *About ¾ cup*

⅓ cup rice vinegar

¼ cup water

1 tablespoon sugar

¾ cup dry mustard powder

2 tablespoons sesame oil

¾ teaspoon cooking oil

In a small bowl, whisk all the ingredients to a smooth paste. Set aside for at least 1 hour before serving.

Martin Says: Like a fine wine, Chinese mustard improves with age. When you first mix up a batch, it may seem particularly sharp, a little bitter, and even powdery. But let it spend the night in a covered container in the fridge, and it will wake up mellowed, smooth, and ready to enhance the flavor of your egg rolls or fried wontons.

Sichuan Spicy Salt

Table salt will never seem the same after you taste some of this warm and spicy seasoned salt. Serve it in a bowl as a "dry dip" for chunks of roast chicken or the popular restaurant dish, salt and pepper prawns. The Chinese five-spice powder, Sichuan peppercorns, chiles, and white pepper that it contains lend just a subtle flavor and aroma, so it's an excellent substitute for ordinary salt in recipes as well. Turn to Chapter 5 to find out how to toast the peppercorns.

Preparation time: *5 minutes*

Cooking time: *5 minutes*

Yield: *About ⅓ cup*

⅓ cup salt

½ teaspoon white pepper

¾ teaspoon ground red chiles

1½ teaspoons Chinese five-spice powder

1½ teaspoons ground toasted Sichuan peppercorns

Place a wok over medium heat until hot. Add all the ingredients. Cook, stirring, until fragrant, about 3 minutes. Let cool.

Chapter 8

Delectable Morsels: Appetizers, Snacks, and Salads

- -

In This Chapter

▶ Preparing appetizers

▶ Working with wrappers

- -

Recipes in This Chapter

▶ Auntie Jessica's Party Chicken Wings

▶ Cantonese Pickled Vegetables

▶ Chinese Chicken Salad

▶ Baked Pork Buns

▶ Spring Rolls

▶ Crispy Wontons

▶ Potstickers

▶ Steamed Shrimp and Chive Dumplings

▶ Green Onion Pancakes

▶ Shrimp Toast

Many people had their first "fling" with Chinese food in the privacy of their supermarket's frozen food aisle. There, they encountered their first glimpse of frozen egg rolls, spring rolls, maybe even a pack of wontons or two. Now, if your Chinese appetizer repertoire is still limited to these few items, you're missing out on some of the most flavorful and fanciful foods in all of Chinese cuisine. From steaming, slightly sweet little pork buns to spicy chicken wings, from savory shrimp and vegetable dumplings to fluffy rice flour crepes filled with savory fillings, Chinese appetizers are much more than a fling. These pleasures call for a lifelong commitment.

The Chinese may be the world champions of finger foods, and the proof is *not* in the pudding, but rather in the *dim sum*. Dim sums — the words literally mean "touches the heart" — are small, sweet or savory morsels that traditionally accompany morning tea in China. Chinese dim sum chefs have developed approximately 2,000 distinctive dim sum items over the centuries, so the definition of dim sum seems rather bland and inadequate. Some of these creations are so imaginative and intricate that you'll wonder whether they're fine food or fine art. My opinion is "both!" Regardless of the answer, they certainly take the saying "Great things come in small packages" to a whole new level.

The only way to experience dim sum is to do so at a leisurely pace. Enjoy each morsel slowly; appreciate the complex form, taste, aroma, and texture; sip a little tea; and then move on to the next item. Variety is the key here, so don't "touch your heart" with just one dish.

But wait — I have more good news about dim sum: You no longer have to board the next plane for Hong Kong (the undisputed dim sum capital) to have a great dim sum experience. Just visit a local Chinatown dim sum restaurant. Or better yet, turn your own house into a teahouse and prepare dim sum (and then some) all on your own. Trying your hand at a few appetizer items can give you an overview of the wonderful world of Chinese snacks, and you'll find recipes to do just that in this chapter. So, no more sneaking around the freezer aisle. Head for the Chinatown teahouses and your own dim sum kitchen because it's time to start a long and beautiful friendship. (For more on dim sum, see Chapter 18.)

If you're unaware of any dim sum restaurants in your area but would really like to give these specialties a try before making them yourself, study the appetizer portion of the menu at your favorite local Chinese restaurant. You'll probably find some of the real classics right there, such as egg rolls, wontons, barbecued spareribs, and foil-wrapped chicken. Or, you can always call the Chinese restaurants in your area and ask them whether they have special dim sum menus or perhaps serve dim sum at midday on weekends — always a popular dim sum time.

Scrumptious Starters

What better way to start a meal, and this chapter, than with a few recipes for Chinese appetizer classics, as well as some updates on those traditional starter themes? I even include some Asian takes on Western favorites, too. So let's get the party rolling!

Auntie Jessica's Party Chicken Wings

Western palates favor chicken breast or thigh meat, but the Chinese hold the wings, with their gelatinous juiciness, in highest esteem. But whether East, West, North, or South, no one on earth can resist the temptation of this spicy Chinese version of fried chicken wings — courtesy of my family's good friend, "Auntie" Jessica Ozorio.

Preparation time: *10 minutes*

Cooking time: *30 minutes*

Yield: *4 to 6 servings*

2 pounds chicken wings, rinsed and patted dry

⅓ cup cornstarch

2 tablespoons powdered chicken broth mix

1 teaspoon Chinese five-spice powder

1 teaspoon salt

Cooking oil for deep-frying

1 Separate the chicken wings into sections. Combine the cornstarch, chicken broth mix, five-spice powder, and salt in a large bowl. Add the chicken; mix well. Let stand for 10 minutes.

2 In a wok, heat the cooking oil to 375°. Deep-fry the chicken wings, a few at a time, turning occasionally, until golden brown, 7 to 8 minutes per batch.

Tip: The convenient size and simple preparation of these wings make them perfect finger foods for a party. Just place them on a serving platter and keep them warm, and they'll still taste great at the end of the festivities, if there are any left.

Cantonese Pickled Vegetables

This common Chinese side dish is normally served as a pre-meal appetizer but often isn't actually listed on restaurant menus. It highlights the Chinese knack for preserving perishable foods by pickling and brining.

Preparation time: 25 minutes (and 3 hours standing time)

Cooking time: None

Yield: 4 to 6 servings

1 cup julienned daikon (white radish)	1½ teaspoons salt
1 cup julienned carrots	¼ cup rice vinegar or distilled white vinegar
1 cup julienned cucumber	2½ tablespoons sugar

1 In a bowl, combine the daikon, carrots, cucumber, and salt; mix well. Let stand for 3 to 4 hours.

2 To make the pickling dressing, bring the vinegar and sugar to a boil in a small saucepan. Let cool.

3 Rinse the vegetables; drain well and return to the bowl. Add the vinegar mixture. Let it stand for another 3 hours at room temperature, or overnight in the refrigerator.

Tip: Save the pickling dressing in a tightly covered container in the refrigerator for the next time you make pickled vegetables. You can even save the pickled vegetables in the fridge, too, because they taste better after a day of two of chilling. Like a fine wine — and like a certain fine Chinese chef I know every time I look into the mirror — the more they age, the better they get!

Regional Note: The clean, fresh taste of this pickle dressing is quintessentially Cantonese. But for extra zing and to shunt the dish more toward Sichuan, add some slices of ginger and fresh red chiles to the pickle mix.

Chinese Chicken Salad

Guess what: Chinese chicken salad, like a number of dishes common in American-Chinese restaurants, is actually a Western invention. Even so, it's a simple, classic, and refreshing dish that successfully combines Asian flavors such as rice vinegar and sesame oil with the Western penchant for salads. Now, that's my idea of fusion cuisine. To keep the salad crisp and crunchy, be sure to dress it right before serving.

Preparation time: 30 minutes

Cooking time: 7 to 8 minutes

Yield: 4 to 6 servings

⅓ *cup rice vinegar*

2 tablespoons honey

2 teaspoons hot pepper sauce or chile garlic sauce

2 teaspoons sesame oil

1 teaspoon dry mustard

1½ cups shredded iceberg lettuce

1 cup julienned carrots

½ *red onion, julienned*

1½ cups shredded cooked chicken

1 tablespoon toasted sesame seeds

1 To make the dressing: Mix the rice vinegar, honey, hot pepper sauce, sesame oil, and dry mustard in a bowl and set aside.

2 Arrange the lettuce on a serving plate. In a small bowl, toss the carrots, onion, and chicken with the dressing. Place on top of the lettuce. Sprinkle with the toasted sesame seeds.

Variation: Three cheers for flexible recipes — this one included! If you like your dressing richer and creamier, add 2 teaspoons chunky peanut butter and 1 tablespoon cooking oil to the other dressing ingredients and mix thoroughly.

Variation: To add some extra crunch to the salad, deep-fry ¼-inch strips of wonton skins in 350° oil for a couple minutes until crisp and golden brown, and sprinkle them liberally over the top of the salad. If you don't feel like firing up the wok for deep-frying, just buy some already prepared crispy Chinese noodles — available in the Chinese food sections of most grocery stores — and sprinkle those on instead. And of course, a sprightly garnish of cilantro leaves can only improve the overall picture.

Baked Pork Buns

These are some of the more popular dim sum items with American diners, perhaps owing to the filling's mild sweetness. They're almost like little self-contained barbecued pork sandwiches with a little Chinese accent.

Preparation time: *2½ hours*

Cooking time: *25 minutes*

Yield: *12 servings*

Dough

4 tablespoons sugar

½ cup milk

⅓ cup warm water

2 teaspoons active dry yeast

1 tablespoon shortening

2 teaspoons baking powder

3 cups all-purpose flour

½ teaspoon salt

Filling

2 tablespoons cooking oil

½ cup chopped onions

½ cup water

2 tablespoons hoisin sauce

1 tablespoon sugar

2 teaspoons cornstarch dissolved in 2 tablespoons water

1 cup chopped char siu (deli-bought or see Chapter 12)

1 egg yolk, lightly beaten

1 To make the dough: Dissolve 2 tablespoons of the sugar in the milk and water. Sprinkle in the yeast; let stand in a warm place until bubbly, about 15 minutes. Gradually mix in the remaining 2 tablespoons of sugar, shortening, baking powder, 2½ cups of the flour, and the salt. Add more flour as needed until the dough is no longer sticky.

2 Place the dough on a lightly floured board and knead until smooth and elastic, 6 to 8 minutes. Place in an oiled bowl, cover, and let rise in a warm place until doubled in bulk, about 2 hours.

3 Heat a wok over high heat. Add the oil, swirling to coat the sides. Add the onions; stir-fry until slightly softened, about 2 minutes. Stir in the water, hoisin sauce, and sugar. Add the cornstarch solution and stir until the sauce boils and thickens. Stir in the char siu. Set it aside to cool.

4 Punch down the dough and then roll it into a cylinder. Cut the cylinder into 8 equal pieces, as shown in Figure 8-1. Roll each into a ball and cover. Flatten each ball and roll into a circle, 4 to 6 inches in diameter. Place 1 heaping tablespoon of the filling in the center. Gather the edges of the circle over the filling; twist and pinch the edges together to seal. Place the buns, seam side down, 2 inches apart on an oiled baking sheet. Cover and let rise in a warm place until puffy and light. Brush the tops with the egg yolk.

5 Preheat oven to 350°. Bake the buns until golden brown, 18 to 20 minutes.

Tip: A light brush of egg yolk before popping these buns into the oven gives them that glossy golden sheen you see on the baked pork buns at dim sum restaurants. If you want more of a caramelized effect, brush the tops with a simple syrup of two parts water to one part sugar brought to a simmer (a microwave works well for this) and cooled.

MAKING DOUGH FOR BAKED PORK BUNS

1. AFTER PUNCHING DOWN THE DOUGH THAT YOU'VE LET RISE UNTIL DOUBLED IN SIZE, ROLL INTO A CYLINDER. CUT INTO 8 EQUAL-SIZE PIECES.

2. ROLL EACH PIECE INTO A BALL AND COVER

3. FLATTEN EACH BALL. ROLL INTO A CIRCLE 4 TO 6 INCHES IN DIAMETER.

4. PLACE 1 HEAPING TABLESPOON OF FILLING IN THE CENTER.

5. GATHER THE EDGES OF THE CIRCLE OVER FILLING; TWIST AND PINCH THE EDGES TOGETHER TO SEAL.

6. PLACE THEM SEAM SIDE DOWN, 2 INCHES APART ON AN OILED BAKING SHEET. COVER, LET RISE IN A WARM PLACE TILL PUFFY AND LIGHT. BRUSH TOPS WITH EGG YOLK.

Figure 8-1: Step-by-step instructions for making bun dough.

It's a Wrap!

Much of dim sum making is all about wrapping. And as future dim sum chefs, all of you owe a great debt to the companies that produce and conveniently package fresh wrappers — they've done the work of rolling and cutting the dough for you. You can now find a wrapper with the right size, thickness, and shape to accommodate any appetizer you want to make. To avoid confusion and make sure that you have the right wrap for the right reason, familiarize yourself with the basics listed in this section. It'll make your next dim sum wrapping experience sheer "wrapture."

Egg roll wrappers (Chun kuen pay; chun chuan pi)

These classic wrappers are made from wheat flour, eggs, and water. The dough gets rolled into thin, large, pliable squares with a golden yellow, wheaty color. As the name implies, they are designed to wrap the crunchy American-Chinese (Cantonese-Chinese, in particular) restaurant favorite called the egg roll. But you can also wrap egg roll wrappers around other fillings: savory leftover vegetables and even dried fruit and crunchy nuts. Deep-fry these packages until they're golden brown, crispy-crunchy, and bubbly on the outside, and you have a tasty treat that dares you to stop at one. Dip the savory rolls in sweet-and-sour sauce or soy sauce for a complete treat.

Don't try to make egg rolls with spring roll wrappers. Although the two are used in similar ways — and although many restaurants mistakenly call egg rolls spring rolls and vice versa — the finished items are not the same, nor are their respective wrappers.

Store the wrappers in a zippered plastic bag in the refrigerator for up to a week or freeze them for up to several months. Defrost frozen wrappers in the bag so that they retain their moisture. When working with the wrappers, remove only a few from the bag at a time and cover the rest with a damp cloth to prevent drying.

Spring roll wrappers

Unlike egg roll wrappers, spring roll wrappers contain no eggs — just wheat flour and water. Cooks pour the thin batter onto the wok surface and steam it to form a paper-thin pancake that is thinner than egg roll wrappers and a lighter, grayer color (due to the lack of eggs in the batter). Spring rolls also fry up crispier and have a smoother, lighter-textured surface.

Egg rolls trace their roots to southern China and Guangzhou, the reason they're so popular in American-Cantonese restaurants. The thinner, more delicate spring rolls have a larger following in central and northern China.

You can fill spring roll wrappers the same way you would egg roll wrappers — with precooked meats and vegetables — and then deep-fry them to make all kinds of delicious hot snacks. Dip them in a variety of different sauces such as soy sauce and Chinese hot mustard, or even Western Worcestershire sauce. Let your imagination guide you when enjoying these delicate delights.

Fresh square and round spring roll wrappers are sold in plastic packages similar to those for egg roll wrappers. Store them in a tightly sealed, zippered plastic bag in the refrigerator for up to a week or freeze them for up to several months. Defrost the frozen wrappers in the bag to retain their moisture. When working with them, take out only a few at a time and cover the rest with a damp cloth to prevent drying.

Wonton and potsticker wrappers

Like egg roll wrappers, wonton and potsticker wrappers contain eggs as well as wheat flour and water. Thus, they have the same texture and tawny color as their egg roll cousins. However, these wrappers are much smaller in size — usually around 3½ inches in diameter. They also come in a greater variety of thicknesses and shapes, from round, thin wrappers used to make *siu mai*, to the thicker wrappers for potstickers, and even to the traditional square shape used for wontons. In fact, Chinese cooks have found so many applications for these little sheets of pasta that calling them just "wonton" or "potsticker" wrappers doesn't give them enough credit.

The thickness and type of wrapper you choose depend ultimately on what you want to do with them. Thicker wrappers stand up better to deep-frying and pan-frying (they won't break when flipped inside the wok). Thinner wrappers work best in steamed dishes or as wrappers for soup dumplings.

You find all sorts of fresh wrappers in plastic packages at most Chinese or Asian markets. If you can't find the round wrappers in some locations, just use a round cookie cutter or pair of scissors to cut a circle from a square wrapper. Store wrappers in the refrigerator in a zippered plastic bag for up to a week or freeze them for up to several months. Defrost frozen wrappers in the bag to hold moisture, and remove only a few wrappers from the package at a time when working with them. Cover the rest with a damp cloth in the meantime to prevent them from drying.

Now that you know your dim sum wrappers backward and forward, how about putting that knowledge to use in the following wrapped-up recipes?

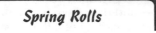

Spring Rolls

The secret to making the perfect spring roll is having the oil hot enough, but not too hot. Make sure you heat it to 360° rapidly. Then comes the most important step: adding the spring rolls. Without them, all you have to show is a pot of hot oil!

Serve the spring rolls hot with a dipping sauce. I recommend the All-Purpose Stir-Fry Sauce, the Chinese Mustard Dip, or the Sweet-and-Sour Sauce from Chapter 7, but any bottled dipping sauce works, too.

Preparation time: *1 hour*

Cooking time: *18 minutes*

Yield: *12 spring rolls*

6 dried black mushrooms

2 tablespoons cooking oil

½ pound boneless pork, finely julienned

1 cup shredded cabbage

2 green onions, coarsely chopped

2 tablespoons oyster-flavored sauce

⅛ teaspoon white pepper

¼ cup chicken broth

1 cup bean sprouts

1½ teaspoons cornstarch dissolved in 1 tablespoon water

12 spring roll wrappers

Cooking oil for deep-frying

1 Soak the mushrooms in warm water to cover until softened, about 20 minutes; drain. Discard the stems and thinly slice the caps.

2 To make the filling: Place a wok over high heat until hot. Add the cooking oil, swirling to coat the sides. Add the pork; stir-fry for 2 minutes. Add the mushrooms and cabbage; stir-fry for 2 minutes. Add the green onions, oyster-flavored sauce, and white pepper; cook for 1 minute. Add the chicken broth and the bean sprouts; stir to coat. Add the cornstarch solution and cook, stirring, until the sauce boils and thickens. Remove from the heat and cool.

3 To make each spring roll: Mound 2 heaping tablespoons filling across a wrapper (see Figure 8-2). Fold the bottom corner over the filling to cover and then fold over the right and left corners. Roll over once to enclose the filling. Brush the sides and top of the triangle with water. Fold over to seal. While filling the remaining spring rolls, cover the filled spring rolls with a dry towel to prevent drying.

4 In a wok, heat the cooking oil for deep-frying to 360°. Carefully lower the spring rolls, several at a time, into the hot oil with a slotted spoon. Deep-fry, turning occasionally, until golden brown, 2 to 3 minutes. Remove with a slotted spoon; drain on paper towels.

Cultural Tidbit: Although any time is a good time for these light and crispy treats, the Chinese often serve spring rolls during the Chinese New Year (which normally falls in February of our calendar year) as a prelude to the coming spring season. Golden brown and looking like gold bars, spring rolls symbolize wealth and future prosperity.

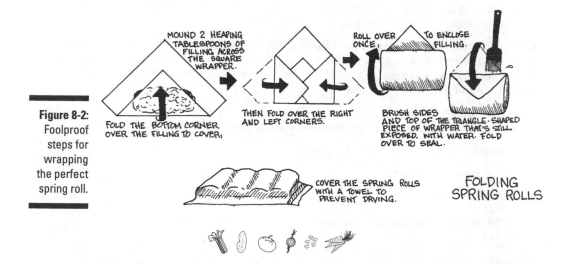

Figure 8-2: Foolproof steps for wrapping the perfect spring roll.

MOUND 2 HEAPING TABLESPOONS OF FILLING ACROSS THE SQUARE WRAPPER.

FOLD THE BOTTOM CORNER OVER THE FILLING TO COVER,

THEN FOLD OVER THE RIGHT AND LEFT CORNERS.

ROLL OVER ONCE, TO ENCLOSE FILLING.

BRUSH SIDES AND TOP OF THE TRIANGLE-SHAPED PIECE OF WRAPPER THAT'S STILL EXPOSED, WITH WATER. FOLD OVER TO SEAL.

COVER THE SPRING ROLLS WITH A TOWEL TO PREVENT DRYING.

FOLDING SPRING ROLLS

A sticky situation

According to the legend of potstickers (we have a legend about practically every food in China), the origin of this delectable treat was actually the result of an imperial chef's carelessness. While teaching his apprentice son to make dumplings, instead of minding them as they cooked, he forgot about them until he heard sizzling coming from the wok. Sure enough, it was the potstickers, which were far more browned and crispy on the bottom than usual. Fearing reprisals from the emperor, the chef panicked. But his son — in a show of filial piety that would've done Confucius proud — offered to serve the dumplings to their boss and take the blame himself, rationalizing that since he was only a chef's apprentice, the emperor would cut him some slack rather than cut off his head. So the young chef purposely served the "dumplings" burnt side up, taking the fall for his dad's inattention. But much to both of their surprise — and relief — the apprentice received praise instead of a death sentence! The emperor inquired as to the dish's name, and quick as a flash, the son labeled them "potstickers," for obvious reasons. And the tag has "stuck" ever since.

Crispy Wontons

One is never enough with these snacks. To save time, fold your crispy wontons in advance and then freeze them in a single layer on a baking sheet. If they touch while freezing, they tend to stick together, and when you try to separate them, they'll crumble. Either that, or you'll have one very big wonton.

Once the wontons have been individually frozen, you can store them in freezer bags. When you're ready, you can fry them straight from the freezer by using the instructions in this recipe, but just remember to let them fry a little longer because they'll need the extra time to fully cook and brown.

In fact, all these "wrappetizers" work well when made ahead, frozen individually, and fried at a later time. Just goes to show how convenient Chinese cooking really is.

Preparation time: 1 hour and 45 minutes

Cooking time: 50 minutes

Yield: 48 wontons

¼ pound medium raw shrimp, shelled and deveined

¼ pound ground pork

6 whole water chestnuts, finely chopped

3 tablespoons minced green onions

2 tablespoons oyster-flavored sauce

2 teaspoons wine

1 teaspoon sesame oil

2 teaspoons cornstarch

48 wonton wrappers

1 egg, lightly beaten

Cooking oil for deep-frying

1 To make the wonton filling: With a cleaver, chop the shrimp into a fine paste (or use a food processor). Place the chopped shrimp in a bowl with the pork, water chestnuts, green onions, oyster-flavored sauce, wine, sesame oil, and cornstarch; mix well.

2 To make each wonton: Place 1 heaping teaspoon filling in the center of a wonton wrapper, as shown in Figure 8-3; keep the remaining wrappers covered to prevent drying.

3 Brush the edges of the wrapper with the beaten egg; fold the wrapper in half to form a triangle and pinch the edges to seal.

4 Pull the two opposite corners together, moisten one corner with the egg, and overlap with another corner; press to seal. Cover the filled wontons with a dry towel to prevent drying.

5 In a wok, heat the cooking oil to 350°. Deep-fry the wontons, a few at a time, turning occasionally, until golden brown, 3 to 3½ minutes. Remove with a slotted spoon and drain on paper towels. Keep them warm in a 200° oven while cooking the remaining wontons.

Variation: Making the filling for these wontons gives you a great opportunity to try dried black mushrooms. (See Chapter 4 for an introduction to dried black mushrooms.) Most traditional wonton fillings include them, soaked and finely chopped to the same size as the rest of the filling's ingredients. If you're in a mushroom mood, go ahead and add some — use as much or as little as suits your tastes.

Figure 8-3:
Step-by-step instructions for wrapping crispy wontons.

PLACE 1 HEAPING TEASPOON OF FILLING IN THE CENTER OF THE WRAPPER.

BRUSH THE EDGES OF THE WRAPPER WITH THE BEATEN EGG.

FOLD THE WRAPPER IN HALF TO FORM A TRIANGLE. PINCH EDGES TO SEAL.

PULL 2 OPPOSITE CORNERS TOGETHER. MOISTEN ONE CORNER WITH EGG. OVERLAP WITH OTHER CORNER. PRESS TO SEAL.

FOLDING WONTONS

Potstickers

Not too long ago, potstickers, called "Beijing dumplings" in some places, were practically unheard-of in the West. Not anymore, thankfully. These little dumplings have become almost as popular in American-Chinese restaurants as the tried-and-true egg rolls and wontons. The combination of steaming and pan-frying gives their wrapper's texture an irresistible balance between smooth and noodlelike on top, and crispy and caramelized on the bottom.

By the way, despite the name, I recommend that you brown the bottom of the dumplings without letting them stick to the wok or pan. Nonstick pans can help you prepare this recipe correctly. A pot*sticker* is what you want, not a pot*stucker*.

Preparation time: *1 hour*

Cooking time: *About 30 minutes*

Yield: *30 potstickers*

8 dried black mushrooms	*2 teaspoons Chinese rice wine*
4 cups shredded napa cabbage	*1 teaspoon sesame oil*
1 teaspoon salt	*1½ tablespoons cornstarch*
¾ pound ground pork, chicken, or beef	*¼ teaspoon white pepper*
4 green onions, chopped	*30 potsticker wrappers*
1½ tablespoons minced ginger	*3 tablespoons cooking oil*
2 tablespoons oyster-flavored sauce	*1 cup chicken broth*

1 Soak the mushrooms in warm water to cover until softened, about 20 minutes; drain. Discard the stems and mince the caps.

2 In a large bowl, toss the napa cabbage with the salt; squeeze to remove the excess liquid.

3 To make the filling: Combine the mushrooms, napa cabbage, ground pork, green onions, ginger, oyster-flavored sauce, rice wine, sesame oil, cornstarch, and white pepper in a bowl; mix well.

4 To make each potsticker (see Figure 8-4): Place a heaping teaspoon of the filling in the center of a potsticker wrapper; keep the remaining wrappers covered to prevent drying. Brush the edges of the wrapper with water; fold the wrapper in half, crimping one side, to form a semicircle. Pinch the edges together to seal. Set the potsticker, seam side up, in a baking pan. Cover the potstickers with a wet towel to prevent drying.

5 Place a wide frying pan over medium heat until hot. Add 1 tablespoon of the cooking oil. Add 10 potstickers, seam side up; cook until the bottoms are golden brown, about 3 minutes. Add ⅓ cup chicken broth; reduce the heat to low, cover, and cook until the liquid is absorbed, 4 to 5 minutes. Remove from the heat. Repeat with the remaining potstickers, cooking oil, and chicken broth.

Tip: Most potsticker wrappers come in 1-pound packages. The number of actual wrappers in a 1-pound package varies depending on the wrapper thickness. But because potsticker wrappers should be a little bit on the thick side to survive pan-frying without tearing, scope out those packages that appear to have fewer, thicker wrappers.

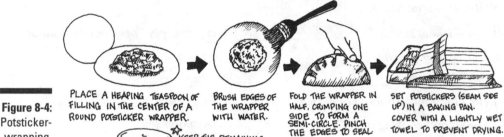

Figure 8-4: Potsticker-wrapping, made easy.

PLACE A HEAPING TEASPOON OF FILLING IN THE CENTER OF A ROUND POTSTICKER WRAPPER.

BRUSH EDGES OF THE WRAPPER WITH WATER.

FOLD THE WRAPPER IN HALF, CRIMPING ONE SIDE TO FORM A SEMI-CIRCLE. PINCH THE EDGES TO SEAL.

SET POTSTICKERS (SEAM SIDE UP) IN A BAKING PAN. COVER WITH A LIGHTLY WET TOWEL TO PREVENT DRYING.

KEEP THE REMAINING WRAPPERS COVERED TO PREVENT DRYING.

FOLDING POTSTICKERS

Steamed Shrimp and Chive Dumplings

Here's your chance to make your own dumpling dough — the tender "hot-water dough" at the heart of many of the typical dim sum wrappers. It's not hard to make, although you'll want to use caution when stirring the boiling water into the dry ingredients. The elastic texture that results is the perfect complement for these dumplings. In a pinch though, prepared potsticker wrappers do the trick.

Preparation time: *2 hours (including ½ hour for rolling and folding)*

Cooking time: *35 minutes*

Yield: *40 dumplings*

1⅓ cups wheat starch	*¾ cup finely chopped bamboo shoots*
⅓ cup tapioca starch	*1 egg white*
½ tablespoon salt	*2 teaspoons wine*
1 cup plus 2 tablespoons boiling water	*1 teaspoon sesame oil*
1 tablespoon cooking oil	*¼ teaspoon salt*
¾ pound medium raw shrimp, shelled and deveined	*⅛ teaspoon white pepper*
1 cup chopped Chinese chives	*Cabbage leaves as a lining for the dumplings*

1 To make the wrappers: Combine the wheat starch, tapioca starch, and salt in a bowl. Add the boiling water, stirring with a wooden spoon or chopsticks, until the side of the bowl is clean. Cover and let cool for 5 minutes. When the dough is cool enough to handle, knead until smooth and no lumps exist. The dough should not stick to your hands. Cover until ready to use.

2 Prepare the filling: Coarsely chop the shrimp and place in a bowl with the chives, bamboo shoots, egg white, wine, sesame oil, salt, and white pepper; mix well.

3 Divide the dough into 4 equal parts. Work with 1 part and cover the other parts to prevent drying. Roll each part into a half-inch cylinder and cut into 1-inch pieces. Roll the pieces into round balls. With a rolling pin, roll out the balls into 3- to 3½-inch circles.

4 To wrap: Place a rounded teaspoon of filling in the center of the dough. Fold the dough over the filling to form a semicircle. Pinch the edges together to seal. Cover with a damp cloth while shaping the remaining dumplings.

5 Prepare a wok for steaming (see Chapter 3). Line the bottom of a steamer with the cabbage leaves. Arrange the dumplings on the leaves without crowding. Cover and steam until the dumplings are translucent, about 8 minutes.

6 Serve the dumplings hot with a dipping sauce of your choice (see Chapter 7).

Tip: To make truly authentic steamed shrimp and chive dumplings, use green Chinese chives — either the flat or flowering variety. (See Chapter 14 for a description of these and other Chinese vegetables.) Considering that a full cup of them goes into the filling, they obviously contribute a hefty amount to the dumplings' character. In fact, maybe I should call the dish "Steamed Chive and Shrimp Dumplings" instead.

Green Onion Pancakes

You can find green onion breads and pancakes throughout northern China and in North America, too. Green onion *breads* are thick, doughy items that are often rolled into a snail shape. This recipe is for the thinner, batter-based pancake version. Because the batter doesn't require the extensive rolling that the bread dough does, it's a quicker and more convenient, but just as appetizing, option. Savor it with a soup or the meal's main course.

Preparation time: *15 minutes*

Cooking time: *50 minutes*

Yield: *About 8 pancakes*

1 egg

1½ cups water

¼ cup plus 2 tablespoons cooking oil

1 teaspoon sesame oil

¾ teaspoon salt

¼ teaspoon Chinese five-spice powder

2 cups all-purpose flour

½ cup thinly sliced green onions

1 In a bowl, combine the egg, water, the 2 tablespoons cooking oil, sesame oil, salt, and five-spice powder. Gradually add the flour and mix into a smooth batter. Add the green onions, blending well. Let stand for 30 minutes to 1 hour.

2 Place a nonstick frying pan over high heat until hot. Add 1½ teaspoons of the remaining ¼ cup cooking oil, swirling to coat the sides. Reduce the heat to medium; remove the frying pan from the heat, and pour ¼ cup of the batter into the hot pan. Spread to make a 6-inch circle.

3 Return the pan to the heat and cook until the pancake is golden brown and crispy, 2½ to 3 minutes. Flip the pancake over and lightly brown the other side for another 2½ to 3 minutes, pressing the pancake down with a wide spatula or pancake turner to flatten.

4 Repeat with the remaining oil and batter. Cut into wedges and serve with soup or other dishes.

Cultural Note: These savory, pan-fried street foods of northern China are perfect examples of Chinese foods with a Mongolian accent. Vendors sell both the thin ones in the recipe as well as their puffy, yeast-raised cousins from carts and stalls all over northern China.

Martin Says: Here in North America, I've heard people compare Green Onion Pancakes to Mexican tortillas. Come to think of it, the richness and succulence they get from quick pan-frying remind me of quesadillas without the cheese. And I don't miss the cheese one bit — I'm not a cheesy kinda guy, especially not with my jokes.

Shrimp Toast

This example of a blending of Eastern and Western ingredients and cuisines — Western-style sandwich bread is *not* a traditional staple in Chinese kitchens — makes great use of day-old bread. If you don't have leftover sandwich slices on hand, you can always let fresh bread dry for a few hours on a rack or baking sheet. The problem with using bread that's too fresh and soft: It absorbs too much oil when deep-fried.

Preparation time: *25 minutes*

Cooking time: *10 minutes*

Yield: *12 toasts*

6 slices day-old sandwich bread

½ pound medium raw shrimp, shelled and deveined

1 large egg white

1 teaspoon cornstarch

1 teaspoon wine

⅛ teaspoon salt

⅛ teaspoon white pepper

1 green onion, minced

Cooking oil for deep-frying

1 Trim the bread crust and cut each slice diagonally in half to make 12 triangles.

2 Set aside 6 shrimp for the topping. Make the shrimp paste by placing the remaining shrimp, egg white, cornstarch, wine, salt, and white pepper in a food processor. Process until the mixture forms an almost smooth paste. Transfer to a bowl and stir in the green onion.

3 Spread the shrimp paste, about ¼ inch thick, on one side of each bread triangle. Cut the reserved shrimp in half lengthwise. Curl one shrimp half on top of each bread triangle, pressing it firmly into the shrimp paste.

4 In a wok, heat the cooking oil for deep-frying to 350°. Deep-fry the triangles, shrimp side down, a few at a time, for about 45 seconds. Turn over and cook until golden brown, about 30 seconds longer. Remove with a slotted spoon; drain on paper towels. Serve warm.

Variation: If you don't have a food processor, preparing the shrimp with your good old Chinese chef's knife does the trick just as easily. (See the sidebar on mincing meats in Chapter 5.) After you mince it to a paste, use some elbow grease to combine it with the egg white, cornstarch, wine, salt, and pepper. And if you want to make these Shrimp Toasts ahead of time, deep-fry them until they're only light beige, let them cool, and store them in a zippered plastic bag in the freezer for later. To reheat, just arrange them in a single layer on a baking sheet and heat them in a 350° oven for 10 minutes.

Chapter 9

Broth, Bones, and a Barrel of Soup

- -

In This Chapter

▶ Understanding the role of soup in the Chinese diet

▶ Making soups, Chinese style

- -

Recipes in This Chapter

▶ Chinese Chicken Broth
▶ Egg Flower Soup
▶ Fish Soup with Spinach and Tofu
▶ Hot and Sour Soup
▶ Sweet Corn and Crabmeat Soup
▶ Winter Melon Soup
▶ Wonton Soup

The Chinese put a lot of stock in their soups. In Guangzhou, meals begin with a savory soup and often end with a sweet soup as dessert. And although soup is associated with home-cooked meals in every culture, the Chinese regard it as the premier comfort food.

Chinese soups are usually clear broths with some greens, a handful of dumplings, or a few strips of barbecued pork or chicken added for flavoring. Instead of a formal first course, they can be served together with other dishes at meals or as palate cleansers between courses. Diners sip them as a hot beverage, picking up the chopsticks only when they need to grab that hunk of shredded duck or beancurd from the bottom of the bowl. In comparison to heartier Italian minestrones or thick American split-pea porridges, Chinese soups are light and simple fares. That doesn't mean that Chinese cooks don't make hearty soups that could be meals in their own right. But even so, the typical Chinese soup is still a far cry from a thick chowder or a cream bisque.

Chinese Soup for the Soul and Body

The Chinese find something restorative and curative in a warm bowl of soup. And with a few carefully chosen herbs, they can turn an everyday soup into a tonic. I guess that chicken soup really is good for your soul (and your body, too), whether you're in Hoboken or Hong Kong. The Chinese have a tradition of adding a wide repertoire of dry medicinal herbs and exotic ingredients to their soups. From sharks' fins (reputedly a cure for bad skin), green turtle, and birds' nests to ginseng and good old ginger, Chinese cooks have an endless list of adjuncts that get the yin in balance with the yang. Dare I say that the Chinese are up to their yin yangs with herbs?

Chinese soups, like any other type of Chinese food, display regional variations. In Guangzhou, you find the world-famous wonton soup, with its meat- and vegetable-filled dumplings, while the Mongolian hotpot of the north consists of a hot broth that diners use to cook strips of vegetables and meat. And who among you hasn't ordered the famous Sichuan hot and sour soup at your favorite Chinese restaurant? There's a good reason why these soups are crowd pleasers: They're all delicious! They're also popular because they're relatively easy to prepare. Try the following recipe for a simple Chinese chicken broth, and you'll find out what I mean.

Broth-er, Can You Spare Some Time?

The recipe road to any good chicken stock has its secret twists and turns, and there are just as many paths as there are travelers. But a few key elements distinguish Chinese chicken broth from its Western counterpart.

Waste not, want not

To call Chinese cooks frugal is like calling Siberia just a little chilly in January. They've perfected the art of the leftover in China, making delicious meals out of days-old rice and animal bones. But nowhere do they make better use of seemingly useless scraps than in their soups. Here are some ways to adopt the Chinese-leftover ethic to your cooking style and make some unbeatable soups at the same time:

✔ **Use the whole bird, fish, or pig.** If you don't know what to do with the neck, giblets, feet, or backbone, save them for the stockpot. Chicken feet, "oxtails" (they're actually cowtails), and pig snouts (nothing to thumb your nose at) also add flavor and succulence to a stock that no other animal parts can imitate.

✔ **Nothing's off limits when using vegetable scraps.** When cleaning and trimming greens, store the ribs and stems in a zippered plastic bag. You can also save mushroom stems, carrot tops, cabbage cores, onion stems, potato and ginger peels, and anything else that might otherwise go into the compost pile.

✔ **Don't pour cooking liquids down the drain.** If you boiled a chicken just for its meat or steamed some vegetables as a side dish, the leftover cooking water is already halfway to becoming a stock, so save it. Even liquid used to soak dried mushrooms has a flavor that makes it a perfect addition to a broth or sauce.

✔ **If you're not in a big hurry, buy whole chickens and quarter and debone them yourself, saving the parts you weren't planning to eat for stock or soup.** You'll save money and have a tastier soup as a result. (On the other hand, if you crave convenience, buy the precut chickens and ask your friendly butcher for the giblets, neck bones, and the other stock fixings that he might otherwise throw out.)

For example, the key difference that sets the classic Chinese chicken broth apart from Western stocks is the lack of a *mire poix* — that classic French combination of onions, carrots, celery, and bay leaf that flavor Western broths. Instead, Chinese stocks get their flavors from ginger and green onion — maybe even a little rice wine if the cook's feeling frisky.

Chinese Chicken Broth

Don't even think of throwing away that chicken after you use it to make your broth! Although most of its flavor gets distilled into the stock, its shredded meat still makes a delicious treat when dipped in a little oyster-flavored sauce.

Should you choose to make the stock with just the chicken, duck, or turkey bones, remember to use three to four carcasses — you need the extra bones to boost the stock's flavor.

Preparation time: *10 minutes*

Cooking time: *2 hours*

Yield: *About 9 cups*

1 whole chicken (about 3 pounds)

8 slices ginger, lightly crushed

6 green onions, halved

⅛ teaspoon salt

⅛ teaspoon white pepper

1 Clean the chicken by removing the giblets and extra fat.

2 Place the chicken in a large pot and add enough cold water to cover. Add the ginger, green onions, salt, and white pepper; bring to a boil. Skim off any foam that forms. Reduce the heat and simmer, covered, for 2 hours. Strain.

Variation: Pork, fish, and ham bones, vegetable scraps, and any other flavorful ingredients lying around the kitchen are all fair game for making a rich, succulent Chinese soup stock, too. Everything and anything goes — every Chinese chef should have a diversified "stock" portfolio.

Tip: Skimming the fat from the top of a warm or hot broth can be particularly tricky because, at high temperatures, the fat liquefies and blends right in with the broth. Refrigerating the pot of broth or placing it in an ice bath reduces the temperature to the point where the fat solidifies, allowing you to easily scoop it off the broth's surface.

Egg Flower Soup

Sometimes called egg drop soup, this version of egg flower soup is surprisingly quick and easy to make. It's a great dish when your cupboards are almost bare and you just can't summon the energy to fix anything more complicated.

Preparation time: *12 minutes*

Cooking time: *About 15 minutes*

Yield: *4 to 6 servings*

6 cups chicken broth

1 tablespoon wine

¼ cup julienned carrots

1 cup snow peas, stem ends snapped off and fibrous strings removed

1 teaspoon cornstarch dissolved in 2 teaspoons of water

1 sheet of 8-x-7-inch nori, cut into ⅛-inch strips (see the sidebar "A note about nori")

1 egg, lightly beaten

1 teaspoon sesame oil

⅛ teaspoon salt

⅛ teaspoon white pepper

1 In a medium soup pot, bring the chicken broth and wine to a boil. Reduce the heat and simmer for 5 minutes. Add the carrots and snow peas; cook for 30 to 40 seconds.

2 Add the cornstarch solution and cook, stirring, until the soup comes to a boil. Stir in the nori. Turn off the heat.

3 Slowly pour in the egg, stirring with a chopstick in a circular motion until long threads form. Stir in the sesame oil, salt, and white pepper.

Variation: To give this recipe a little bit more green, add baby bok choy, spinach, or any other leafy green that you like. And to create a more substantial soup for those meat lovers, a half cup of leftover barbecued pork, cooked shrimp, or ham lunch meat also makes a nice addition.

Regional Note: Cantonese chefs "invented" egg flower soup when some onions and a few eggs were all they had on hand in the kitchen. Imagine what they could have made if they had some stones as well!

Cultural Tidbit: The name "egg flower soup" often confounds Western diners: For one thing, the soup contains no flowers, and flowers don't grow on eggs anyway. The name actually came from the beaten egg white's apparent "blossoming" as it's slowly drizzled into the hot broth. And even though many American-Chinese restaurants call it "egg drop soup," cooks don't "drop" the egg into the soup either.

A note about nori

I "borrowed" the *nori,* Japanese-style dried seaweed, for the Egg Flower Soup recipe in this chapter from China's neighbors in Japan. There, chefs lightly toast the deep green sheets before using them to wrap *sushi,* the hand-held delicacies of raw fish and rice. In China, on the other hand, cooks turn to strips of nori and purple Chinese-style dried seaweed (which is a bit more roughly textured than nori) primarily for use in soups and seafood dishes.

You can find nori and Chinese-style dried seaweed in plastic packages or bundles at Asian markets. If your grocery store is particularly well stocked, you may even be able to find some in the Asian food aisle there. If not, ask a local Japanese restaurant to sell you some — I'm sure that it has plenty on hand. Store either type of dried seaweed in a zippered plastic bag in a cool, dry place for up to several months.

Fish Soup with Spinach and Tofu

Soft tofu works best in this and most other soup recipes. It has a smooth, tender texture that is the perfect complement to clear, mildly flavored broths such as this one. For more of the lowdown on tofu — and for more tofu recipes — head to Chapter 13.

Preparation time: 15 minutes

Cooking time: 12 minutes

Yield: 8 servings

10 ounces white fish fillet, thinly sliced	*3 slices ginger, julienned*
2 teaspoons cornstarch	*¼ cup thinly sliced carrots*
¾ teaspoon salt	*4 cups spinach leaves*
¼ teaspoon white pepper	*½ package (8 ounces) soft tofu, cut into ¼-inch strips*
5 cups chicken broth	*8 to 10 sprigs cilantro*

1 Pat the fish pieces dry with paper towels. Make a marinade by combining the fish with the cornstarch, salt, and white pepper in a large bowl.

2 In a medium soup pot, bring the chicken broth to a boil. Add the fish and ginger; reduce the heat and simmer for 1 minute. Add the carrots, spinach, tofu, and cilantro; simmer for 2 minutes.

Tip: If you use store-bought chicken broth in this or any other recipe, be sure to taste it first before adding salt. Canned broths often contain considerable salt already, and a quick taste may convince you that you don't need to add any more.

Hot and Sour Soup

You can adjust the heat and bite of this Chinese restaurant classic by experimenting with the amounts of white pepper and vinegar you add. Keep in mind, however, that the Sichuan cooks who concocted it didn't name it hot and sour soup for nothing — like most of the foods from that region, it's supposed to be fiery. But finding the right balance between the hot and the sour tastes is still the secret to this creation.

Preparation time: *35 minutes*

Cooking time: *20 minutes*

Yield: *4 to 6 servings*

4 dried black mushrooms	*⅔ cup white vinegar*
2 cloud ears	*1 tablespoon dark soy sauce*
6 cups chicken broth	*½ teaspoon salt*
4 ounces pork, shredded	*1 teaspoon white pepper*
½ cup julienned bamboo shoots	*4 tablespoons cornstarch dissolved in 5 tablespoons water*
1 cup julienned firm tofu	

1 In separate bowls, soak the mushrooms and cloud ears in warm water to cover until softened, about 20 minutes; drain. Discard the stems of the mushrooms; cut the cloud ears and the mushroom caps into thin strips.

2 In a medium soup pot, bring the chicken broth to a boil. Add the pork, mushrooms, cloud ears, and bamboo shoots; cook for 3 to 4 minutes. Add the tofu, vinegar, soy sauce, salt, and white pepper; cook for 1 to 2 minutes. Add the cornstarch solution and cook, stirring, until the soup boils and thickens.

Tip: To guarantee uniform cooking in this soup, and in most other quickly cooked dishes, cut all the ingredients into the same dimensions. In the case of the Hot and Sour Soup recipe, that means cutting or shredding them into thin strips.

Tip: Although the quantity of cornstarch in the recipe may seem like too much, this sour soup actually needs a little more than usual to reach the right consistency. All the acid from the vinegar would prevent a smaller amount of cornstarch from thickening the soup effectively.

Sweet Corn and Crabmeat Soup

What could be simpler and tastier than this comforting Sweet Corn and Crabmeat Soup? The sweetness of the corn marries well with the subtle crabmeat in this tasty soup.

Preparation time: 10 minutes

Cooking time: 8 minutes

Yield: 4 to 6 servings

6 cups chicken broth

1 can (15 ounces) cream-style corn

1 cup cooked crabmeat

⅛ teaspoon salt

⅛ teaspoon white pepper

3 tablespoons cornstarch dissolved in ¼ cup water

2 egg whites, lightly beaten

½ teaspoon sesame oil

1 In a medium soup pot, bring the chicken broth and corn to a boil. Reduce the heat and simmer for 3 minutes. Add the crabmeat, salt, and white pepper and heat through.

2 Add the cornstarch solution and cook, stirring, until the soup boils and thickens. Slowly pour in the egg whites, stirring with a chopstick in a circular motion until long threads form. Stir in the sesame oil.

Regional Note: This soup is another genius Cantonese creation, and a relatively recent one at that. Corn — a New World food — was adopted by the Chinese with relish. Of all the popular Chinese soups, this chowderlike concoction probably resembles Western soups the most.

Variation: Fresh, cooked crabmeat isn't always easy to find, but surimi is. Surimi is the red-tinted, artificial "krab" that you can find in almost any grocery store's refrigerated section. It's made from a processed fish paste that's flavored, colored, and molded to resemble actual crabmeat. Surimi is usually based on Alaskan halibut, but it may also contain real crab or shrimp, depending on the brand. No, it doesn't have the fresh, sweet flavor of "crab-with-a-*c*," but it also doesn't have its shards of crab shell or steep price tag either. So if it's not crab season when you get a craving for this soup, go ahead and use surimi.

Winter Melon Soup

This is a simplified version of a winter melon soup often served in Chinese restaurants. Winter melon itself is actually a relatively bland ingredient on its own; it functions as more of a yin-yang "tonic" in this recipe than as a flavoring agent (see the sidebar "The winds of winter in a melon" in this chapter and the description of winter melon in Chapter 14). The other ingredients really help pick up the slack by adding their own flavor.

Ideally, you'd make this recipe with the cured and smoked hams from Yunnan, a province near Sichuan in southwestern China that's famous for having some of the best hams in the country — and I'm not talking about its stand-up comics either. But because China doesn't export Yunnan ham to the West, you'll have to make do with a substitute. Most Chinese cooks outside China use Smithfield ham, a flavorful, salty product from Virginia with a firm, dry texture that can pass for Yunnan ham. But if Smithfield ham is as rare in your area as the Yunnan variety, just use some Italian prosciutto, a salted and air-cured ham that's a convincing substitute as well.

Preparation time: 30 minutes

Cooking time: About 25 minutes

Yield: 4 to 6 servings

6 dried black mushrooms	*½ cup shredded carrots*
1 pound winter melon	*⅛ teaspoon white pepper*
6 cups chicken broth	*¼ teaspoon sesame oil*
½ cup shredded smoked Virginia ham	

1 Soak the mushrooms in warm water until softened, about 20 minutes; drain. Discard the stems and slice the caps into ¼-inch pieces.

2 Cut off the melon rind and discard; remove the seeds and stringy fibers. Cut the winter melon into ½-inch cubes.

3 In a medium soup pot, bring the chicken broth to a boil. Add the mushrooms, winter melon, ham, carrots, and white pepper; cook, covered, until the vegetables are tender, about 10 minutes. Reduce the heat and simmer for 5 minutes. Stir in the sesame oil just before serving.

Variation: Considering that this is a winter melon soup, winter melon is obviously an important ingredient. But if your local market doesn't carry it, the cooling flavor of a peeled cucumber can serve as a stand-in in a pinch.

The winds of winter in a melon

If my mom didn't make winter melon soup as often as she did when I was young, I don't think that my internal balance would be nearly so . . . well, so *balanced* as it is today.

Winter melons keep our insides cool — sipping winter melon soup in midsummer is like taking in a cool refreshing breeze. The Chinese believe that winter melons calm the overbearing yang in our food. The melon's rind (not used in the soup itself) is particularly cooling, and artistic chefs often use the hollowed gourd as a soup tureen, carving its skin with beautiful and elaborate designs (see Chapter 6). But don't worry, because the soup tastes just as yummy in a conventional tureen.

Wonton Soup

Who doesn't crave a bowl of savory wonton soup? Maybe I should ask who *does* crave one right this moment. Lucky for you, you can make it yourself in a jiff with this simple recipe. Just use the wonton recipe in Chapter 8 to prepare the wontons themselves — but don't fry them, of course — and you're well on your way to enjoying this ever-present Chinese restaurant favorite.

Preparation time: 10 minutes

Cooking time: 12 minutes

Yield: 4 servings

20 pre-made wontons

6 cups chicken broth

½ cup julienned carrots

4 to 6 whole baby bok choy, quartered lengthwise

½ teaspoon sesame oil

1 teaspoon salt

⅛ teaspoon white pepper

1 Bring a pot of water to a boil. Add the wontons and cook for about 4 minutes; drain.

2 In a medium soup pot, bring the chicken broth to a boil. Add the carrots and baby bok choy; cook until the vegetables are tender-crisp, 2 to 3 minutes. Add the sesame oil, salt, white pepper, and cooked wontons. Cook until they are heated through.

Tip: Cook the wontons right before you add them to the soup — if you let them sit around too long, they'll stick together. If you wish, you can even cook them in the soup stock itself, but you may end up with a starchier, cloudier soup.

Chapter 10

Swimming with the Best of Them: Seafood

In This Chapter

▶ Finding the best fish on the market

▶ Storing your catch safely

▶ Cooking fish to perfection

▶ Shopping for and storing shellfish

Recipes in This Chapter

▶ Braised Fish Hunan Style

▶ Fish Steaks in Fragrant Sauce

▶ Smoke-Broiled Fish

▶ Pan-Grilled Salmon Fillet with Black Bean Sauce

▶ Steamed Whole Fish

▶ Steamed Trout in Black Beans and Garlic

▶ Sweet and Sour Shrimp

▶ Spicy Salt Shrimp

▶ Shrimp and Scallops with Snow Peas

▶ Seafood Casserole

▶ Oysters in Black Bean Sauce

Ah, fresh seafood! It's a topic near and dear to my heart, and even nearer to my stomach! It's the birthright of everyone from the region of Guangzhou (formerly called Canton), for it's well known all over China that when it comes to preparing seafood, Cantonese cooks lead the pack. The easy access to every type of fresh seafood imaginable has spoiled the Cantonese palate over the centuries. From humble country farmers to savvy business tycoons, Cantonese have the highest seafood expectations, so only the freshest and the best can satisfy them. And after centuries of taming the wild of the deep in their kitchens, cooks throughout China must have recipes for every seafood item imaginable.

Even in this era of industrial fishing fleets, Chinese by the tens of thousands still make their living by fishing the South China Seas. For some, fishing is more than a 9-to-5 job; many of them live on board their vessels with their entire families, just as their forefathers before them. Statistics show that the coastal region of China has the highest consumption of protein in the world, and most of it comes from fish. Maybe that's why we Cantonese are so healthy and smart. You know what they say when it comes to fish and smarts: It's a no-brainer.

An ocean full of luck

Fish has long held an auspicious position not only in the Chinese kitchen but also in Chinese culture. The Chinese word for fish, *yu*, is a homonym for another *yu*, meaning abundance or prosperity. Always in tune with symbolism, the Chinese have thus associated fish with the same luck and success as its homonym.

That symbolism shows up in all sorts of places: Fish are popular wedding motifs because it's believed (although not necessarily proven) that they always swim in pairs. Because of their lucky associations, fish are popular decorations for everything from building entrances to robes and gowns. It's no wonder that a big fried or steamed whole fish appears on virtually every dinner table at Chinese New Year. What better way to ring in a lucky and prosperous new year!

As the Chinese population surges, so does its demand for fish and seafood. This gave rise to the fish-farming industry, or *mariculture*. In truth, fish farming has been around for hundreds of years. Chinese fish farmers rustled up herds of carp, grouper, sole, and mullet in the fish ponds that dotted the countryside. Nowadays, fish farming is more high-tech, and it involves herding young marine fish and shellfish into large, floating "corrals" where they remain until sufficiently plump, mature, and tasty for the market. Whether nature or nurture, China's fish and seafood supply keeps the nation's appetite for the freshness of the sea satisfied.

A Shopping Spree by the Sea

The most widely stocked fish market in the West still pales in comparison to the average Chinese fish bazaar by the docks. Fishermen and fish farmers bring their catch straight off the boat or out of the pond — without a moment's delay — to the eager eyes of hungry customers. As an ultimate guarantee of freshness, much of what they sell is still alive and swimming. No wonder Chinese cooks wouldn't think of eating fish that had already sat around a fish market for a couple of days.

And the saying "beauty is only skin deep" couldn't be more appropriate than in the Chinese seafood market. Even the ugliest, scaliest, gnarliest-looking fish in the South China Seas may turn out to be one of the tastiest. In addition to bass, cod, grouper, halibut, crab, and other standards, the average Chinese seafood lover also enjoys more obscure varieties such as bream, mullet, sturgeon, eel, jellyfish, carp, and mackerel — even the prized abalone, sea cucumber, and shark's fin.

Regardless of which fish you choose, follow some of the same guidelines that Chinese shoppers use when they hunt for fresh fish. I am always saddened when I hear people say that they don't care for fish because it smells fishy. Good-quality, fresh fish doesn't smell fishy at all. Instead, its odor reminds me of the seashore and my childhood home. (And no, we didn't live behind a fish market.)

Choosing a fish market: A lean, clean, fish-selling machine

When you can't get your fish straight off the boat, follow these rules for choosing the best of what your local fishmonger has to offer:

✔ Buy fish — or any perishable products, for that matter — only from a clean, well-run market. This tip is almost so obvious that it's easy to forget. If the fish counter has lots of dirty, melted ice and castaway fish trimmings, or if it doesn't have some sort of sneezeguard separating you from the fish, these signs mean that it's time to find a new fish market.

✔ If there's low turnover — the fillets that you saw on Monday are still lounging around on Thursday — you're better off saving your money and buying frozen.

✔ Frequent a fish market where the staff is friendly, knowledgeable, and helpful. Say that you need a salmon fillet, but all that's available is the whole, big fish. If you know a fishmonger who'll slice you up a fillet or two to order, you've found yourself a gem of customer service — a rare find these days.

Choosing a fish: Buy with your senses

The best fish-selecting tools are right under your nose, in front of your eyes, and at your fingertips, so to speak. So use those innate senses to get the real clues as to which fish to choose:

✔ *Feel* how cold it is in your local fish market. Is the fish in a refrigerated case? Has the fishmonger displayed it on plenty of clean, fresh ice? Fish and visitors may smell after three days, but fish that isn't kept at a chilly 30 to 40 degrees will start to smell fishy even sooner.

✔ Ask your fishmonger whether he will let you *touch* the fish. Why? For one thing, the flesh should be firm and springy — if you poke your finger in the side of a fish, the indentation should spring right back up. And the fish should not feel slimy. If it does, that's a bad sign. Put it back.

✔ While you have up-close access to the fish, *smell* it. You shouldn't be able to smell much more than a pleasant, salty-marine aroma. If you do detect a "fishy" smell reminiscent of ammonia, choose another fish. And if that unpleasant odor pervades the entire fish market, definitely find somewhere else to buy your fish.

✔ Beauty is only skin deep, and it's true that some of the ugliest fish taste delicious. But if the fish at your market *look* obviously out-of-date, it definitely indicates that they have passed their prime. Don't buy fish with any of the following signs: cloudy eyes, gills that have turned from deep red to a dull pink or brown, flesh that's dark and bruised, ragged fins, or scales with a distinctive slimy sheen. As for fillets, if they've begun to curl or appear dried out along the edges, don't waste your money on them either.

Now for a few words about frozen seafood: As much as my mom would turn her nose up at it, I know that fish frozen via high-tech flash-freezing methods often retain as high a quality as fresh fish. And if I have to pick between iffy "fresh" or quality frozen, I'd pick the latter any day. You can keep a stash of frozen fish on hand (it'll keep for a few months in a subzero-degree freezer) for whenever a fish fancy strikes you. Just remember to keep it fully frozen until ready to use, at which point you'll want to defrost it in the refrigerator.

What Do I Do with It Now?

Now that you've found the perfect fresh fish — whether whole, fillet, or steak — it's time to turn it into a delicacy that would do a Cantonese cook proud. Ideally, you'd prepare your fish the same day that you caught — or, more likely, *bought* — it. But if you just can't fit a fish meal into your schedule that day, your fish will keep its freshness a couple days longer if you store it properly by using these guidelines:

✔ Before you stow it, rinse the fish with cold water, pat it dry with a lint-free towel, and place it in a zippered plastic bag.

✔ Keep fish in the coldest part of the refrigerator — usually the back corner of the top shelf. The few degrees of difference among shelves may not appear to make much of a difference, but with a commodity as perishable as fish, trust me, they do.

✔ Better yet, set the wrapped fish on an ice pack or in a bowl of shaved ice. (Shaved is actually better than cubed because the cubes can bruise the fish's delicate flesh.)

Proper refrigeration methods help extend your fish's shelf life by a few days. But when estimating how long your fish will stay fresh, always factor in the time the fish takes to reach the market, especially if you live fairly far inland. I always go by the simple rule that if I don't plan to cook the fish that day, I freeze it below 0 degrees (the colder the freezer, the longer the fish will last) in a zippered plastic bag.

Cooking Fish the Chinese Way

How do you cook your fish with a Chinese accent? (No, the answer is not Berlitz.) Doing so is actually a lot easier than you may think. The Chinese love to steam fish because this simple cooking method accentuates the clean, natural flavor of the fish. Just add a little simple seasoning from a marinade of green onions, soy sauce, sugar, and pepper, and the result is pure magic.

Deep-frying is also a popular way to prepare fish in China. A particularly festive New Year's dish is a deep-fried whole fish garnished with green onions and topped with a sweet and sour sauce whose red color symbolizes life, energy, wealth, and prosperity. It makes me feel successful — and hungry — just thinking about it!

But fish's real beauty is in its variety and versatility. There are literally thousands of edible fish in the sea, and each can make a delicious meal all by itself. Chinese cooks often make an entire dinner out of one fish: soup, appetizer, and entree. It's a pity that so many Western home cooks shy away from fish, fearing it difficult to prepare and easy to ruin. The truth is, you can do just about anything to fish that you can to chicken, beef, and pork. The key is matching the method and flavorings to the fish. Read on for more tips:

✔ More delicate varieties — sole, orange roughy, and red snapper — merit similarly subtle cooking methods to showcase, but not cover, their clean flavors. They could come apart in red-cooking or braising. Stir-frying and steaming these delicate textured fish bring the best results.

✔ Varieties such as tuna, sea bass, halibut, salmon, and other fish that have a more pronounced flavor and sturdier consistency complement stronger spice treatments and less-forgiving cooking methods, including stewing and grilling.

If a recipe calls for a thick cod steak but the market has only halibut, don't give up and order take-out. Just substitute halibut, and your guests will be none the wiser.

The following recipes give you an idea of how you can combine simple ingredients and techniques to create truly inventive seafood dishes. After preparing a few of them, you'll probably find yourself familiar enough with the methods and flavorings to invent a few Chinese seafood creations of your own.

Braised Fish Hunan Style

Hunan province in central China is known for having spicy cuisine similar to that in neighboring Sichuan, and this recipe proves it. And even though both regions are miles from the nearest coast, their rivers and lakes provide plenty of freshwater fish perfect for pairing with the zesty sauce in this recipe.

Preparation time: *15 minutes*

Cooking time: *10 minutes*

Yield: *4 servings*

1 pound fish steaks or fillets, about 1 inch thick

¼ teaspoon salt

¼ cup chicken broth

2 tablespoons Chinese rice wine

2 teaspoons black bean garlic sauce

1½ teaspoons sugar

1 teaspoon chile garlic sauce

1 teaspoon sesame oil

½ teaspoon soy sauce

2 tablespoons cooking oil

1 green onion, thinly sliced

1 teaspoon cornstarch dissolved in 2 teaspoons water

1 Cut the fish into 4 pieces. Pat the fish dry with a paper towel. Rub the salt all over; let stand for 10 minutes.

2 Make the sauce: Combine the chicken broth, rice wine, black bean garlic sauce, sugar, chile garlic sauce, sesame oil, and soy sauce in a bowl.

3 Place a wok over high heat until hot. Add the cooking oil, swirling to coat the sides. Reduce the heat to medium and add the fish; pan-fry until golden brown, about 2 minutes on each side.

4 Add the sauce and bring to a boil. Add the green onion, cover, and braise over low heat for 3 to 5 minutes. Add the cornstarch solution and cook, stirring, until the sauce boils and thickens.

Variation: Any type of firm, moist white fish works in this dish. Choose one with a slightly fatty texture to provide a counterpoint to the sauce's piquancy. My personal favorites are sea bass, cod, and halibut.

Fish Steaks in Fragrant Sauce

This recipe asks you to take the extra step of dredging the fish in cornstarch before pan-frying it. Doing so gives the surface a crispy texture that contrasts nicely with the smooth, moist flesh inside. A firm, fatty whitefish such as cod, halibut, or even monkfish will keep its shape without flaking or falling apart even after pan-frying and simmering in its aromatic sauce.

Preparation time: *12 minutes*

Cooking time: *25 minutes*

Yield: *4 servings*

¾ cup chicken broth

2 tablespoons oyster-flavored sauce

1 tablespoon dark soy sauce

1 tablespoon soy sauce

1 green onion, thinly sliced

1 teaspoon sugar

½ teaspoon chile flakes

4 fish steaks (4 ounces each), about 1 inch thick

½ teaspoon salt

¼ teaspoon white pepper

2 tablespoons cornstarch

¼ cup cooking oil

2 tablespoons chopped shallots

1 teaspoon minced fresh ginger

1 teaspoon minced garlic

¾ teaspoon cornstarch dissolved in 2 teaspoons water

1 Make the sauce: Combine the chicken broth, oyster-flavored sauce, soy sauces, green onion, sugar, and chile flakes in a bowl.

2 Just before pan-frying, season the fish steaks with the salt and white pepper. Dust the fish steaks with the cornstarch.

3 In a wide frying pan, heat the oil over medium heat until hot. Pan-fry the fish until golden, about 5 minutes on each side. Remove with a slotted spoon and drain on paper towels.

4 In the same pan, add the shallots, ginger, and garlic; stir-fry until fragrant, about 1 minute.

5 Add the sauce and bring it to a boil. Add the cornstarch solution and cook, stirring, until the sauce boils and thickens.

6 To serve, place the fish on a platter and pour the sauce on top.

Smoke-Broiled Fish

Spiciness isn't the only classic sign of a Sichuan-inspired dish. Cooks in this region have perfected the art of smoking foods, and this recipe pays homage to their talent. You don't even have to build your own smokehouse to make it, either, because a regular broiler oven and a few easy-to-find smoking ingredients will do the trick just as well. Serve this fish smoking-hot, at room temperature, or even chilled as a light lunch on a hot day.

Preparation time: *18 minutes*

Cooking time: *About 30 minutes*

Yield: *4 servings*

Marinade

3 tablespoons hoisin sauce

3 tablespoons Chinese rice wine

2 tablespoons dark soy sauce

2 tablespoons brown sugar

2 teaspoons minced ginger

½ teaspoon toasted ground Sichuan peppercorns or black pepper

1½ pounds firm white fish fillets (sea bass or rock cod), cut into 4 pieces, ¾ inch thick

Smoking mixture

¾ cup packed brown sugar

½ cup black or oolong tea leaves

½ cup uncooked rice

1 teaspoon Sichuan peppercorns (optional)

1 Combine the marinade ingredients in a bowl. Add the fish and turn to coat. Let stand for 10 minutes.

2 Preheat broiler. Remove the fish from the marinade, reserving the marinade. Place the fish on a rack about 2 inches from the heat. Broil for about 5 minutes on each side, basting the fish with the marinade once during broiling.

3 Line a wok with foil. Combine the ingredients for the smoking mixture and spread it evenly in the wok. Place the wok over high heat and cover until the mixture starts to smoke, about 3 to 4 minutes.

4 Set a rack over the smoking mixture and place the fish on the rack. Cover the wok with a tight-fitting lid. Smoke for 15 minutes.

5 Turn off the heat; let the fish stand for 3 to 4 minutes, covered, before serving.

Tip: If the idea of smoking foods conjures up images of blaring smoke alarms and a fume-filled kitchen, this is the perfect smoked fish recipe for you. Because hardly any smoke actually results from the smoke-broiling method, the only precaution you may want to take is turning on your oven fan or cracking open a window.

Variation: You can even skip the smoking step if you want. The marinade is so flavorful that it gives the fish a marvelous, slightly smoky character all by itself.

Steak your claim to a tasty fillet

Some fish recipes call for steaks, while others ask for fillets. And unless the sign in the fish case specifies one or the other, you may not know what you're bringing home. But don't worry, because differentiating between a fish fillet and a fish steak is actually very easy.

First, imagine a whole fish. Now, cut it in cross sections, each section containing a portion of the backbone and a strip of skin around the edge. Bingo, you've got fish steaks. So when you see pieces of fish that are shaped like an upside-down U with a thickened base where the backbone is located, as shown in the accompanying figure, you'll know that these are the steaks. Salmon and cod are good examples of large fish that often get cut into steaks. Sometimes, in the case of very large fish, fishmongers cut the U-shaped steak into smaller portions, partitioning it along the line that runs from the top of the steak down to the bottom of the backbone (see the accompanying figure again). You often find tuna, swordfish, and halibut steaks in this form. These sectioned steaks have an advantage over the U-shaped steaks: They're boneless.

Fillets, also boneless cuts of fish, are slices of flesh that run horizontally along either side of the backbone. So imagine the whole fish again, and make a top-to-bottom cut parallel to the backbone from the fin on the fish's back down to the belly and from the head back to the tail. This technique gives you fillets that you can further slice into smaller individual portions if the original fillet is large enough. Depending on the fish and the diners' tastes, the skin may or may not be removed. Although the idea of eating the skin may take some getting used to, the skin actually gives the fish a moist and luscious flavor.

U-STEAK

Pan-Grilled Salmon Fillet with Black Bean Sauce

A grilled salmon fillet, even if it's grilled indoors on a grill pan, may not seem like the most authentically Chinese dish. But the flavors in this recipe's marinade — ginger, green onions, and a pungent black bean sauce — give this fish an undeniably Chinese character. The slight crispness and caramelization of pan grilling accentuate those lingering marinade flavors, too.

Preparation time: *8 minutes*

Cooking time: *15 minutes*

Yield: *4 servings*

3 tablespoons chicken broth

2 tablespoons black bean garlic sauce

1 tablespoon minced ginger

1 tablespoon Chinese rice wine

1 tablespoon sugar

2 teaspoons sesame oil

4 green onions, sliced

4 pieces (about 4 ounces each) salmon fillets, ¾ inch thick

2 tablespoons cooking oil

1 Make the marinade: Combine the chicken broth, black bean garlic sauce, ginger, rice wine, sugar, sesame oil, and green onions in a bowl. Add the salmon fillets; turn to coat. Let stand for 10 minutes.

2 Lift the salmon fillets from the marinade and drain, reserving the marinade in a small pan. Place a nonstick grill pan over high heat until hot. Add the oil, swirling to coat the pan. Add the salmon fillets to the pan and cook to sear, about 4 minutes on each side.

3 While the salmon is cooking, simmer the reserved marinade until slightly reduced, about 3 minutes.

4 To serve, place the salmon fillets on a platter and pour the sauce over.

Variation: Placing the fillets under the broiler and cooking them for 4 minutes per side also brings out that crispy charred texture that's so hard to resist.

Steamed Whole Fish

Chinese restaurant aficionados often judge the quality of a restaurant by its steamed whole fish. Such a simple cooking method makes it practically impossible to hide a second-rate fish (and chef!) underneath heavy seasonings or the masking flavor of a thick sauce. Test your own steaming prowess with this simply sublime Cantonese classic.

To make it really Cantonese, use carp instead of sea bass. Although carp isn't a very popular fish in the West, it's a Chinese favorite, and if you live near a Chinese market, you can probably find it still alive and swimming in the store's fish tanks.

Preparation time: *15 minutes*

Cooking time: *12 to 14 minutes*

Yield: *4 servings*

1 sea bass, cleaned with head left on	*2 green onions, cut into 1½-inch pieces and thinly julienned*
¼ teaspoon salt	*¼ cup cooking oil*
¼ cup finely shredded ginger	*¼ cup soy sauce*

1 Pat the fish dry and score it on both sides. Lay it on a heatproof serving dish with slightly raised sides. (If your wok or steamer is rather small, the fish can be halved). Sprinkle with the salt; spread the ginger on the fish and some in the cavities.

2 Prepare a wok for steaming (see Chapter 5). Cover and steam the fish over high heat, until the fish is cooked and the flesh flakes off, about 13 minutes. Remove from the heat and sprinkle with the green onions.

3 Heat the cooking oil in a small saucepan over high heat until it begins to smoke. Pour the hot oil over the fish and the green onions. Pour the soy sauce over the fish.

Martin Says: Although a freshly steamed fish, lightly flavored with ginger and green onion, is reward enough on its own, what really gets me anxious to steam a whole fish is actually the prospect of eating the fish cheeks. That's right, the flesh in a fish's cheeks is among the most tender, flavorful flesh in its entire body, and the Chinese often politely "battle it out" at the table for this coveted culinary prize.

Variation: Setting the fish on two whole green onion stalks as it steams not only adds to the meal's flavor but also gives the steaming process a helpful nudge by letting the steam circulate more fully around the fish. Try it yourself. (You and I both can thank my mom for that hint.) Also, those score marks you've made are the perfect "pockets" for holding any additional seasonings — slices of ginger, green onion, or even slices of black mushrooms — that you may want to use to give an extra jolt of flavor.

Steamed Trout in Black Beans and Garlic

As with the steamed whole fish, this recipe asks you to score the fish. Refer to Chapter 5 and to Figure 10-1 for a refresher course on scoring food. This little step helps the fish steam more evenly and lets the flavor of the black bean sauce permeate the moist flesh.

Preparation time: *8 minutes*

Cooking time: *10 minutes*

Yield: *4 servings*

2 tablespoons black bean garlic sauce	*2 green onions, thinly sliced*
1 tablespoon Chinese rice wine	*1 teaspoon sesame oil*
2 tablespoons sugar	*1 trout (about 1 pound), with head left on*
1 teaspoon cornstarch	*5 sprigs mint, chopped*
1½ tablespoons julienned ginger	

1 Make the black bean sauce: Combine the black bean garlic sauce, rice wine, sugar, cornstarch, ginger, green onions, and sesame oil in a bowl.

2 Score the fish with 4 diagonal cuts almost touching the bone on both sides and lay it on a heatproof pie dish (up to ¾ inch deep). Spread the black bean mixture evenly on the fish and some in the cavity.

3 Prepare a wok for steaming (see Chapter 5). Cover and steam the fish over high heat, until cooked and the flesh flakes off, about 10 to 12 minutes. Garnish with mint sprigs.

Figure 10-1:
Make score marks about ⅛ inch deep and 2 inches long on the fish in the Steamed Trout in Black Beans and Garlic recipe.

SCORING FISH FILLETS

Don't Be Selfish with the Shellfish

Most of the seafood dishes on any Chinese restaurant menu feature some sort of shellfish: kung pao shrimp, wok seared scallops, crab with ginger and green onion, just to name a few. Chinese chefs crave shellfish of all sizes and shapes. Shrimp, scallops, crab, lobster, clams, oysters, and mussels all rank highly in their books. Whether steamed, fried, stir-fried, served with a savory sauce, or accompanied by a simple salt-and-pepper dip, shellfish sure get the royal treatment in China.

To get the same delicious results, give your shellfish the same royal treatment, starting with the purchase and storage of high-quality, extremely fresh products.

Shopping for shellfish

Most of the shellfish that you purchase are still alive (surprise!), but how do you know whether you're picking out the best that your market has to offer? Follow these guidelines, and you'll pick winners every time:

- The shells of clams, mussels, and oysters should be tightly closed. Tap any that are open; if they don't go shut in response, toss them out because they're probably dead already (or in a deep coma). Never waste hard-earned clams on dead ones.

- Don't purchase a lazy lobster. Make sure that it's moving about its tank as you're window-shopping on the other side of the glass. This activity is a sign that the lobster is indeed alive — and healthy.

  Buy lobsters that are live because bacteria quickly decompose the dead flesh and make it unsafe to eat. If that prospect sounds unappetizing, that's because it is.

- Although live crab does taste better, precooked varieties make for an easier purchasing option. Just be sure to clean all the way through the meat to make sure that no shards of shell remain. Search with your fingers as much as with your eyes because distinguishing the shell from the meat is sometimes hard.

- Buying shrimp is a bit easier than buying other types of shellfish because shrimp are generally dead by the time they reach market. (Purchasing dead shrimp is perfectly safe.) But you still get to choose among different species and sizes, as well as between peeled or unpeeled, vein-in or deveined, and head-on or head-off varieties. Choose based upon what the recipe calls for and on how much effort you want to spend. If peeling and deveining 2 pounds of shrimp sound like more work than you're willing to do, the higher price of peeled and deveined is worth it.

SAFETY TIP

- Although it's nice to cook shrimp with the heads on — they add a delicious, unmistakable flavor — doing so isn't always convenient (and may not appeal to some of your guests).

- Smaller shrimp may be less expensive but are very easy to overcook.

- Because most shrimp in U.S. markets have been previously frozen, freshness isn't as much of an issue. Nevertheless, make sure that the shrimp has a clean aroma, that the shells are firm, and that the flesh isn't mushy.

- You can find large sea scallops (up to 3 inches) and smaller bay and calico scallops (the latter are bay scallops' warm-water cousins) at most markets. The large sea scallops are expensive and harder to find, whereas bay and calico are more readily available. Of these two, bay scallops are generally higher in quality. If you aren't sure which one your seafood market has in the cases, don't be shy — ask!

Put it away right

Shellfish are delicate creatures — especially when it comes to storage issues. If you've paid attention to selecting the freshest shrimp, clams, or scallops at the market, you'll want to prolong that freshness by following these storage rules:

- Mollusks need to breathe, so don't store them in sealed, zippered plastic bags or under ice. Simply keep them refrigerated in a mesh or opened bag with a light weight on top to hold the shells closed.

- Store shrimp and scallops as you would fish: wrapped or in a closed container, and on ice.

- When you purchase live shellfish such as crab or lobster, it will probably come wrapped in damp paper. Keep it that way because this is the best material in which to store it. Just keep the live shellfish away from fresh water because fresh water will kill it.

- Cook live critters as soon after purchase as possible. But for shrimp and scallops, follow the same storage timing guidelines as you would for finfish.

Now you're ready to take a crack at the following recipes. As diverse as they are, they only skim the surface of Chinese shellfish cookery. I have yet to see a definitive book on Chinese seafood, a subject that's as deep as the deep blue sea itself. Discover whether the harmony of ingredients, flavors, and textures inspires you to dive a little deeper and discover your own shellfish cooking secrets.

Sweet and Sour Shrimp

Every American-Chinese restaurant has its own version of this North American favorite. We've come to associate this dish with Cantonese cuisine — it's a fixture on Cantonese restaurant menus. But we actually owe northern Chinese cooks for coming up with its characteristically bright flavor and texture combinations that create a perfect yin-yang balance. Now you can make it at home by using the Sweet and Sour Sauce from Chapter 7. If you can't resist giving it a little more restaurant flair, add some colorful contrast with red and green bell peppers and juicy cubes of pineapple.

Preparation time: *12 minutes*

Cooking time: *10 minutes*

Yield: *4 servings*

1 pound medium raw shrimp, shelled and deveined

1 teaspoon minced garlic

1 teaspoon minced ginger

¼ teaspoon white pepper

1½ tablespoons cooking oil

2 stalks celery, cut at an angle, ¼-inch thick

⅔ cup Sweet and Sour Sauce (see Chapter 7)

¼ cup chicken broth

½ cup canned pineapple chunks

¼ cup crystallized ginger chips (optional)

1 Combine the shrimp, garlic, ginger, and white pepper in a bowl. Let stand for 10 minutes.

2 Place a wok over high heat until hot. Add the oil, swirling to coat the sides. Add the shrimp and cook until they turn pink, about 2 minutes. Remove and set aside.

3 Add the celery; stir-fry for 1 to 2 minutes. Add the Sweet and Sour Sauce and the chicken broth; cook until the sauce boils and reduces slightly. Add the pineapple and return the shrimp to the wok; stir to coat well.

4 To serve, place the shrimp on a serving plate and garnish with the ginger chips, if desired.

In vein or not in vein

Although the little black veins that run along the backs of shrimp aren't dangerous, poisonous, or otherwise hazardous to eat, they're definitely unappetizing. Most cooks remove these gritty, slightly muddy-tasting, and just plain ugly tubes before cooking the shrimp. If you're in a big pinch for time, you can safely leave them in the shrimp, but the resulting dish will suffer for it. And although most markets sell deveined shrimp — at a higher price, of course — extracting these mini-intestinal tracts yourself actually doesn't take much work.

You can buy little gadgets such as plastic deveiners at your local kitchen supply shop, but they're not much more helpful than a simple paring knife. Hold the shrimp under cold, running water and make a shallow slit with a knife down the shrimp's back along the line of the vein. Then wash the vein and grit away with the water, as depicted in the accompanying figure.

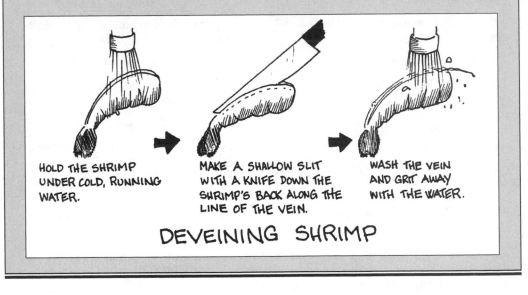

HOLD THE SHRIMP UNDER COLD, RUNNING WATER.

MAKE A SHALLOW SLIT WITH A KNIFE DOWN THE SHRIMP'S BACK ALONG THE LINE OF THE VEIN.

WASH THE VEIN AND GRIT AWAY WITH THE WATER.

DEVEINING SHRIMP

Coming out of their shells: Easy instructions for shelling shrimp

I grew up eating shrimp cooked with the shell, tail, and even the head left on. Chinese cooks still normally prepare shrimp this way, for a number of reasons. For one, shrimp with the shells and head intact retain a more intense, fresh-shrimp flavor that you just can't get from shelled shrimp. Also, these little shields of armor protect the shrimp from being overcooked and help keep its shape.

But what if you find staring your shrimp in the face a little disarming and you would rather remove the shells in the kitchen than at the table? If so, you can easily take them off before cooking by following these steps and the instructions in the accompanying figure. By the way, the shells are excellent candidates for making a shrimp broth, so be sure to save them. (These instructions work equally well for raw and cooked shrimp.)

1. Holding the shrimp by the tail with one hand, use the thumb and forefinger of the free hand to grasp the shrimp's legs and edge of the shell.

2. Simply pull the legs and shell off the shrimp. They should easily slip off in one piece.

3. Leave the shrimp's tail intact for a slightly fancier presentation or pull it off to save you work at the dinner table.

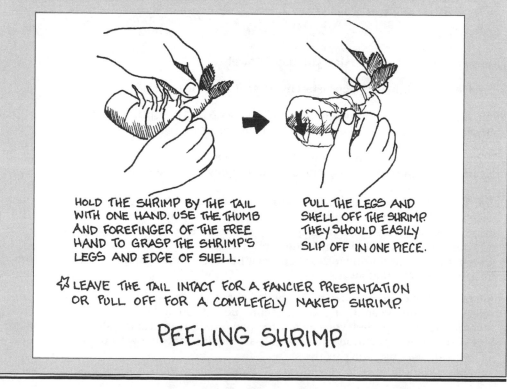

HOLD THE SHRIMP BY THE TAIL WITH ONE HAND. USE THE THUMB AND FOREFINGER OF THE FREE HAND TO GRASP THE SHRIMP'S LEGS AND EDGE OF SHELL.

PULL THE LEGS AND SHELL OFF THE SHRIMP. THEY SHOULD EASILY SLIP OFF IN ONE PIECE.

☆ LEAVE THE TAIL INTACT FOR A FANCIER PRESENTATION OR PULL OFF FOR A COMPLETELY NAKED SHRIMP.

PEELING SHRIMP

Spicy Salt Shrimp

There's just something mouth-watering about fried shrimp; no wonder they're so popular from China to Charleston. Frying them as in this recipe — in their shells with a light dusting of cornstarch and the heads and tails intact — is classically Chinese. The addition of a quickly toasted, aromatic spicy salt complements the shrimp's naturally sweet flavor without concealing it.

During certain parts of the year and in certain parts of the country — parts that are far from significant bodies of water, for example — good-quality fresh shrimp are as easy to find as an unexploded firecracker after the Chinese New Year. In those cases, take advantage of the plentiful supply of excellent frozen shrimp available. Just be sure to defrost the shrimp thoroughly in the refrigerator and in the packaging in which you stored them. Give them a quick rinse in cold water before adding them to the recipe as well.

Preparation time: *15 minutes*

Cooking time: *30 minutes*

Yield: *4 servings*

1 pound medium raw shrimp in the shell, parts of heads and tails trimmed

¼ cup cornstarch

Cooking oil for deep-frying

2 teaspoons Sichuan Spicy Salt (see Chapter 7)

1 Rinse and pat the shrimp dry with paper towels.

2 Dredge the shrimp in the cornstarch and shake off the excess.

3 In a wok, heat the oil for deep-frying to 350°. Deep-fry the shrimp, a few at a time, 30 to 40 seconds. Remove with a slotted spoon and drain on paper towels.

4 Wash, dry, and reheat the wok until hot. Over medium heat, add the Sichuan Spicy Salt, return the shrimp to the wok, and toss thoroughly, 20 to 30 seconds.

Tip: You don't have to use shrimp with heads. You don't have to leave the tails intact either. But I highly recommend that you keep the shells on because they protect the meat from the intense heat of deep-frying and leave it succulent and tender even after cooking. And the audible crunch the shells make when you first bite into them announces the tantalizing textural contrast between their crispness and the shrimp meat's moistness that awaits you.

Remember: Of course, you can use shelled shrimp if you wish. And you can also prepare the shrimp via another cooking technique. Although the classic dish as served in restaurants is deep-fried, you can stir-fry, pan-fry, or even grill the shrimp. But regardless of the cooking method you choose, pair the final product with the aromatic spicy salt, or the dish just won't be the same.

Shrimp and Scallops with Snow Peas

What a combination! The tender, luscious textures of the seafood combine with the crunchy snow peas to make your mouth cry out for more. Go ahead and satisfy your mouth. This recipe — like so many others in this book — is light and healthful, too.

Preparation time: *30 minutes*

Cooking time: *10 minutes*

Yield: *4 servings*

½ pound medium raw shrimp, shelled and deveined (remove tails, if desired)

½ pound sea scallops, halved horizontally

2 teaspoons minced ginger

1 teaspoon minced garlic

2 tablespoons chicken broth

2 tablespoons oyster-flavored sauce

1½ tablespoons cooking oil

¼ cup sliced water chestnuts

¾ cup (about 3 ounces) snow peas, stem ends snapped off and fibrous strings removed

1 Pat the shrimp and scallops dry with paper towels and place in a bowl. Add the ginger and garlic; stir to coat. Let stand for 10 minutes.

2 Make a sauce by combining the chicken broth and oyster-flavored sauce in a small bowl.

3 Place a wok over high heat until hot. Add the oil, swirling to coat the sides. Add the shrimp and scallops; stir-fry until the shrimp are slightly pink and the scallops are slightly firm, about 2 minutes.

4 Add the water chestnuts and snow peas; stir-fry for about 30 seconds. Return the seafood to the wok. Add the sauce; bring to a boil and cook until the sauce reduces slightly.

Tip: Once your shrimp begin to turn pink and curl up or your scallops become firm and opaque, they're done. So take them off the heat ASAP, or you'll wind up with tough, dry, and overcooked shellfish that won't make your mouth cry out for more, but rather will make it cry, period.

Seafood Casserole

This casserole is another nutritional winner. Even if it didn't taste so tempting, the combination of seafood and vegetables would make me feel just as invigorated inside and out. To give it even more nautical appeal, add 6 ounces of a firm-fleshed white fish such as cod or sea bass to the pot with the other seafood.

Preparation time: 25 minutes

Cooking time: 10 minutes

Yield: 4 servings

6 dried black mushrooms	½ teaspoon white pepper
½ cup chicken broth	1 tablespoon cooking oil
3 tablespoons Chinese rice wine	1½ cups cauliflower florets
2 tablespoons soy sauce	1 cup small button mushrooms
12 medium raw shrimp, shelled and deveined, tails intact	1 zucchini, halved lengthwise, then roll cut into ¾-inch pieces
6 sea scallops, halved horizontally	½ cup diced onion (½-inch)
1 teaspoon minced ginger	2 teaspoons cornstarch dissolved in 1 tablespoon water
1 teaspoon salt	

1 Soak the mushrooms in warm water to cover until softened, about 20 minutes; drain and discard the stems.

2 Make a sauce by combining the chicken broth, rice wine, and soy sauce in a bowl; set aside.

3 Combine the shrimp, scallops, ginger, salt, and white pepper in a bowl.

4 Place a claypot over low heat; gradually increase the heat to medium-high. Add the oil, swirling to coat the sides. Add the shrimp and scallops and stir-fry for about 1 minute.

5 Add the cauliflower, mushrooms, zucchini, and onion and the sauce from Step 2; cover and simmer over low heat for about 10 minutes. Add the cornstarch solution and cook, stirring, until the sauce boils and thickens. Serve immediately.

Variation: Don't worry if you don't have a traditional Chinese claypot for preparing this recipe. (See Chapter 3 for a description and illustration of one.) A Dutch oven or a burner-safe casserole dish with a cover works just as well.

Oysters in Black Bean Sauce

Tomatoes and basil, corned beef and cabbage, peanut butter and jelly: They're all entic-ing edible engagements. But none of them quite have the chemistry of one of my favorite culinary couples: seafood and black bean sauce. You can taste the essence of Cantonese flavors within this simple combination: fresh, clean treasures from the deep, kissed with the smokiness of black beans, and bitten by garlic's vibrancy.

If you're lucky enough to find some fresh, *in-season* oysters — and if you don't mind shucking them yourself — by all means, enjoy them in this dish. If not, the jars of shucked oysters that you can find year-round at grocery stores come in very handy.

Preparation time: *5 minutes*

Cooking time: *5 minutes*

Yield: *4 servings*

2 jars oysters (or 16 fresh oysters)	*1 teaspoon chile garlic sauce*
½ cup chicken broth	*1 tablespoon cooking oil*
2 tablespoons Chinese rice wine	*2 to 3 whole dried chiles*
2 teaspoons black bean garlic sauce	*8 slices ginger, julienned*
1 teaspoon oyster-flavored sauce	*4 green onions, thinly sliced*

1 Blanch the oysters in boiling water for 30 seconds. Drain and pat dry; set aside.

2 Make the black bean sauce by combining the chicken broth, rice wine, black bean garlic sauce, oyster-flavored sauce, and chile garlic sauce in a bowl.

3 Place a wok over high heat until hot. Add the oil, swirling to coat the sides. Add the chiles, ginger, and green onions; cook, stirring, for about 2 minutes.

4 Add the oysters and sauce. Reduce the heat to low and simmer for 3 minutes.

 I crave the combination of seafood and black bean sauce so much that I wish I could've included more than three black bean sauce dishes in this seafood chapter. (In addition to this recipe, try Pan-Grilled Salmon Fillet with Black Bean Sauce and Steamed Trout in Black Beans and Garlic). If you're as smit-ten with these pairings as I am, rest assured: The treasure trove of Cantonese cuisine has plenty more sand-and-sea combinations where these came from.

Chapter 11

Crying Fowl: Poultry Recipes

· ·

In This Chapter

▶ Selecting and handling your bird

▶ Cutting up a chicken

▶ Removing the bone from chicken legs

▶ Fixing chicken drummettes

▶ Carving a cooked chicken

▶ Dining on duck

· ·

Recipes in This Chapter

▶ Sichuan Bang Bang Chicken

▶ Drunken Chicken

▶ Kung Pao Chicken

▶ Honey Garlic Chicken

▶ Lemon Chicken

▶ Moo Goo Gai Pan

▶ Chicken Curry, Cantonese Style

▶ Soy Sauce Chicken

▶ Gingered Chicken

▶ Chinese Roast Chicken

▶ Pineapple Duck Stir-Fry

*I*n recent years, chicken has become the darling in Western kitchens. Consumers appreciate it as a healthy, versatile source of protein, inexpensive as well as nutritious, and low in fat when prepared the right way. Its mild character makes it the perfect partner to a variety of flavorings and cooking methods. Chinese cooks have recognized this versatility for ages. They fry, roast, steam, and boil the whole bird; stir-fry dices, shreds, or slices of it; mince it for dumpling stuffings; and turn its carcasses into luscious soups. It's the meat with a million uses!

Even in this industrial age, some Chinese families still raise their own chickens. The birds need very little space, live off last night's dinner scraps, and reward their owners with eggs and meat, so it's no wonder that they're among the most popular domesticated animals in China. Size-wise, these homegrown chickens may not measure up to the plump, industrially raised ones sold in U.S. supermarkets, but they do have a sweet, beguiling flavor that has generations of Chinese diners hooked.

In fact, Chinese cooks customarily turn their noses up at frozen or frozen-and-defrosted birds that are common in the West; if it wasn't running around the henhouse just a few hours ago, they probably wouldn't want it. I take a more practical approach. Today's modern freezing technology means that you should have no qualms about purchasing chickens at your local supermarket. Use the following buying guidelines and keep your eyes on the birdie.

Pickin' a Chicken (Or Any Other Bird, for That Matter)

The variety of poultry products at supermarkets these days is truly amazing. For whole birds, I get my picks from free-range, organic, or kosher birds, as well as the choice between standard store brands and national brands. Any of these options work well in Chinese poultry dishes. Of course, the freshness of a recently butchered bird would be ideal — and would make my choosy mother very happy — but unless you live near Chinatown or a poultry farm, such an option may be hard to come by. However, if you do happen to live near a source of freshly butchered chickens, by all means, take advantage of it. I'm sure that you'll find the clean, fresh flavor quite a treat.

Regardless of the type of chicken you choose, keep these caveats in mind when browsing the poultry case:

✔ **Always check the "sell-by" dates stamped on fresh poultry.** These dates generally indicate when two weeks have passed since the processor butchered and packaged the bird. Be warned: The closer you are to that date, the closer you are to eating a two-week-old chicken. That's *not* what I call fresh. So don't be afraid to dig through the poultry case to find a package with a sell-by date as far in the future as is available. Doing so gets you a fresher bird.

✔ **A frozen bird lasts longer, whether it was frozen at the processing plant or in your own freezer after you put it there.** But it won't last indefinitely, because the high proportion of unsaturated fat in chicken and poultry skin goes rancid even under freezer conditions. When that happens, expect off-flavors and off-aromas. Thus, as a general rule, you won't want to eat a bird that's been frozen for more than six months. And never buy a frozen bird that appears soft or slightly defrosted — a sure sign that its flavor, freshness, and safety have been compromised.

✔ **Is the whole really the sum of its parts? When it comes to chicken, it is.** Whole birds are great for roasting and for soups. You can skin, bone, and cut them into pieces. But if time is of the essence, go ahead and buy the precut chicken parts or the boneless, skinless strips, often marked "for stir-fry." Just make sure that what you buy looks moist and fresh, and always check that sell-by date.

✔ **The color of a chicken's skin tells more about its diet and where it was raised than its freshness and quality.** However, dry, bruised skin or depressions and dimpling in the meat are signs that the bird isn't fresh and probably hasn't been treated too carefully. Pass it up.

A poultry report card: What those USDA stamps mean

If you've ever taken a good look at a poultry package, a pair of official-looking government stamps should appear familiar to you. The United States Department of Agriculture (USDA) gives these stamps to birds as proof that USDA agents have inspected and graded the birds, respectively.

All poultry destined for public sale and consumption must undergo USDA *inspection,* which guarantees that the birds are fit to eat and have been processed according to strict guidelines. And although inspection doesn't tell you anything about quality, grading does. This voluntary procedure, which has actually become pretty standard in the industry, assigns grades of A, B, or C to poultry. To get a USDA grade of A, a bird must have thick flesh and a well-developed layer of fat but cannot have any deformities, pinfeathers, lacerations, broken bones, discoloration, or, in the case of frozen birds, handling or storage defects. Birds graded B and C, on the other hand, usually just go into processed poultry products.

Neither grading nor inspection tells us anything about a poultry product's tenderness — a very important characteristic for cooks and diners. Poultry *classification,* based partly on the bird's age, is the key to that characteristic. For example, if a chicken is classified as a "roaster," it is more tender than an older "hen/stewing" chicken.

Proper Poultry Practices: Handling and Storing It Safely

After you bring home your prime piece of poultry, follow a few basic safe handling and storage procedures. These guidelines will maintain the flavor and quality of your bird and prevent you and your dinner guests from coming down with food poisoning.

These highly perishable birds are extremely susceptible to salmonella contamination. Some statistics estimate the number of contaminated birds in markets can be as high as 50 percent. That means that you should never gamble with your health when handling and cooking chickens. Keep the following precautions in mind when you bring fowl into the kitchen:

- **Once again, mind the sell-by date.** It not only indicates freshness for aesthetics' sake but also gives you an idea of how safe your bird is to eat. The older it is, the greater the likelihood that bacteria in it have multiplied to unsafe levels.

- **Don't dawdle on your way home from the store.** The sooner you get poultry home and into the refrigerator — the safest range is between 32 and 34 degrees — the better off you are. And never let raw poultry get above 40 degrees, the doorway to the danger zone for raw foods. Poultry stored under proper conditions keeps for two to three days. If you don't plan to cook it during that time, move on to the next point.

✔ **Freeze a bird that you don't plan on cooking within a couple days of its purchase.** You're best off storing it in its original package in a freezer set at 0 degrees or below as soon as you get home. However, don't freeze poultry at home that has been commercially frozen and thawed. Double freezing with a thaw cycle in between results in inferior meat — and it may make you sick.

✔ **Defrost your chicken gradually in the refrigerator and keep it on a plate or tray that can catch any juices as they drip.** Expect the chicken to take a couple days to defrost this way. Don't defrost your chicken on the countertop, because that spot has prime conditions for bacterial growth. If you absolutely need to defrost your chicken quickly, place it in a plastic bag and then submerge it in a large bowl of cold water on the counter. Change the water periodically as the chicken defrosts.

✔ **Never cook a partially frozen bird, no matter how rushed you are.** The inside will never reach temperatures that are high enough to kill dangerous bacteria unless you completely char the outside to a crisp. And don't cook the bird halfway one day and finish cooking it the next. Bacteria that didn't get wiped out the first time around will definitely multiply to dangerous levels before you give it its second cooking.

✔ **Always wash any equipment — cutting boards, knives, towels, countertops, and hands — that come into contact with raw meat or its juices in hot, soapy water.** *I can't stress this step enough.* When you're done with all the preparation, it's also a good idea to clean cutting boards, bowls, and any other exposed equipment in a dishwasher (and towels in a washing machine) to achieve full sterilization.

✔ **Keep raw poultry and its juices away from cooked foods and raw foods that you plan to eat raw.** Be careful when opening packages of raw poultry — those juices can splash out onto other raw or cooked ingredients. Refrigerate poultry on a low shelf so juices won't drip onto any cooked foods below it, and remember to keep it on a plate. And never place cooked foods in a raw poultry marinade or use a marinade as a sauce unless you cook it to 160°.

✔ **That 160° temperature is a very important benchmark.** Always cook poultry to this temperature. Insert an instant-read thermometer into the thickest part of the flesh or the thigh joint to make sure that you do. If you don't have a thermometer, you can tell that the bird is fully cooked when its juices run clear and the flesh is no longer pink at the bone.

I Fall to Pieces: Deconstructing Your Chicken

When I was young, choosing a chicken was a catch-as-catch-can experience, literally: The slowest bird running around the backyard was the one we'd catch! Today, chicken lovers have it much easier. You don't have to train for the hundred-meter dash to get a bird for dinner. Instead, you can buy conveniently packaged and prebutchered chicken parts — legs, thighs, wings, breasts, halves, and quarters — with or without skin or bones, at your grocery store or butcher shop.

I guess that parts of me still long for those good old days when I was swift, quick, and in my chicken-catching shape. Today, I'd probably starve if I had to get chickens that way. But if I feel nostalgic, I can always jog up to the checkout counter with my supermarket chicken. I like buying whole chickens because cutting up poultry yourself can really save money. I also think that the whole birds just taste fresher and more flavorful.

Cutting your own poultry at home takes only a little extra effort. I've whittled the whole process down to eight seconds, flat. And although speed is not a requirement, safety is. Make sure that you end up with as many digits when you finish as you had when you started. All you need is a sharp Chinese chef's knife and a sturdy cutting board. Here's how I do it (shown in Figure 11-1):

1. **Set your bird on the cutting board, breast up, and slice through the skin and meat on either side of the breastbone.**

2. **Flip the chicken over so that it's now breast down and make another cut along one side of the backbone from neck to tail.**

   You may feel tempted to saw back and forth as you work the knife down the backbone, but it's actually easiest to do this in one quick motion.

3. **Turn the chicken on its side and cut through the shoulder joint to sever it, leaving the wing attached to the breast.**

4. **Use the heel of your cleaver to secure the chicken to the cutting board and tug the wing to pull the breast away from the body.**

   Cut through the skin to fully separate the breast from the body, leaving the breast "fillet" still attached.

5. **To remove the fillet, cut along the rib cage with the tip of your cleaver. Grab the tough, white ligament nestled in the fillet and use it as a handle with which to pull away the fillet.**

6. **To remove the ligament, set the fillet on the cutting board with the ligament facing down, anchor the ligament to the board with your fingertip, and just push the meat off the ligament.**

7. **Move to the leg and bend it back to break the thigh joint.**

   Cut the whole leg from the body, being sure to include the small muscle called the "oyster" that's between the thigh and the backbone.

8. **Repeat Steps 3 through 6 on the other side of the chicken, and you're done.**

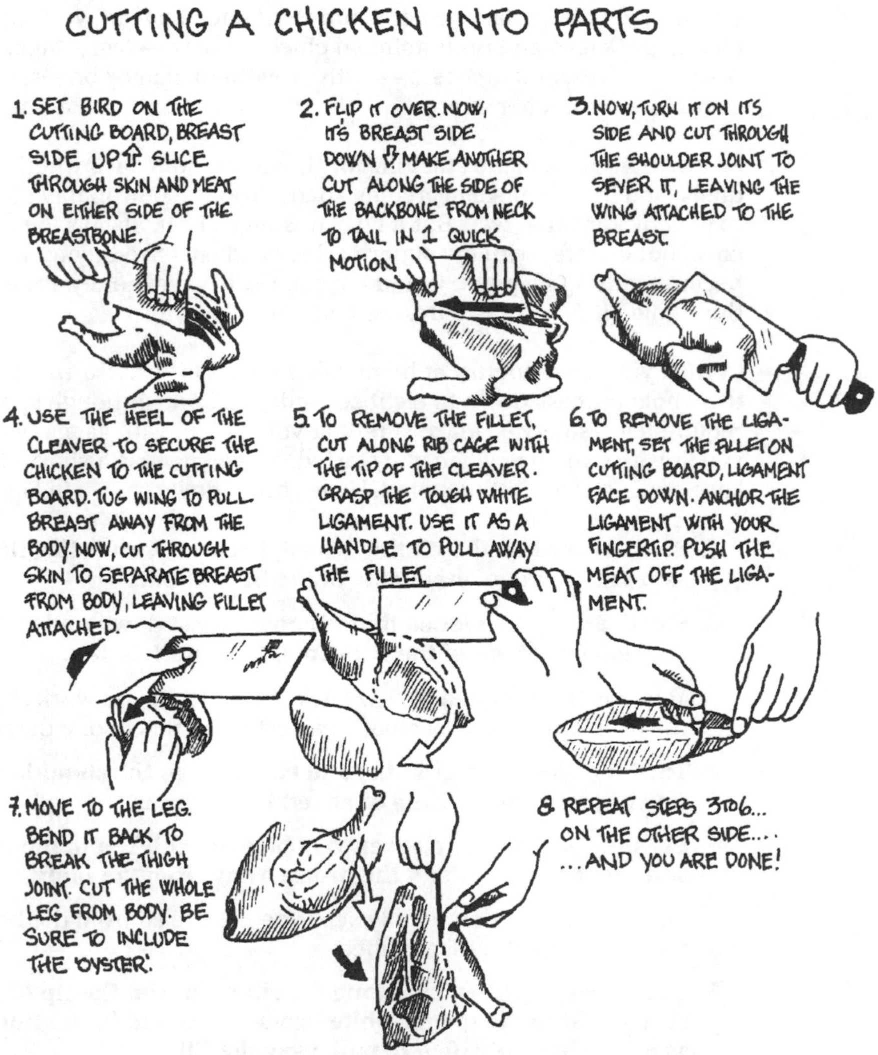

CUTTING A CHICKEN INTO PARTS

1. SET BIRD ON THE CUTTING BOARD, BREAST SIDE UP ⇧. SLICE THROUGH SKIN AND MEAT ON EITHER SIDE OF THE BREASTBONE.

2. FLIP IT OVER. NOW, IT'S BREAST SIDE DOWN & MAKE ANOTHER CUT ALONG THE SIDE OF THE BACKBONE FROM NECK TO TAIL IN 1 QUICK MOTION.

3. NOW, TURN IT ON ITS SIDE AND CUT THROUGH THE SHOULDER JOINT TO SEVER IT, LEAVING THE WING ATTACHED TO THE BREAST

4. USE THE HEEL OF THE CLEAVER TO SECURE THE CHICKEN TO THE CUTTING BOARD. TUG WING TO PULL BREAST AWAY FROM THE BODY. NOW, CUT THROUGH SKIN TO SEPARATE BREAST FROM BODY, LEAVING FILLET ATTACHED.

5. TO REMOVE THE FILLET, CUT ALONG RIB CAGE WITH THE TIP OF THE CLEAVER. GRASP THE TOUGH WHITE LIGAMENT. USE IT AS A HANDLE TO PULL AWAY THE FILLET.

6. TO REMOVE THE LIGAMENT, SET THE FILLET ON CUTTING BOARD, LIGAMENT FACE DOWN. ANCHOR THE LIGAMENT WITH YOUR FINGERTIP. PUSH THE MEAT OFF THE LIGAMENT.

7. MOVE TO THE LEG. BEND IT BACK TO BREAK THE THIGH JOINT. CUT THE WHOLE LEG FROM BODY. BE SURE TO INCLUDE THE 'OYSTER'.

8. REPEAT STEPS 3 TO 6... ON THE OTHER SIDE... ...AND YOU ARE DONE!

Figure 11-1: Cutting a whole chicken in eight easy steps.

No Bones about It: Boning Chicken Legs

Don't stir-fry a whole chicken leg. It wouldn't fly. (Nor, for that matter, would chicken wings, which explains why you don't see airborne chickens more often). Stir-frying calls for rapid stirring and high temperatures, and chicken — or any other ingredient — has to be in cut into relatively small bits, chunks, or strips.

So if stir-frying is your goal, after you've deconstructed your bird, you have to get rid of those bones. Of course, you can always buy the boneless, skinless chicken thighs that are already sliced into strips and labeled "for stir-fry." However, being able to bone a chicken leg is a nice skill to have. Follow these steps and look at Figure 11-2 to get that skill yourself:

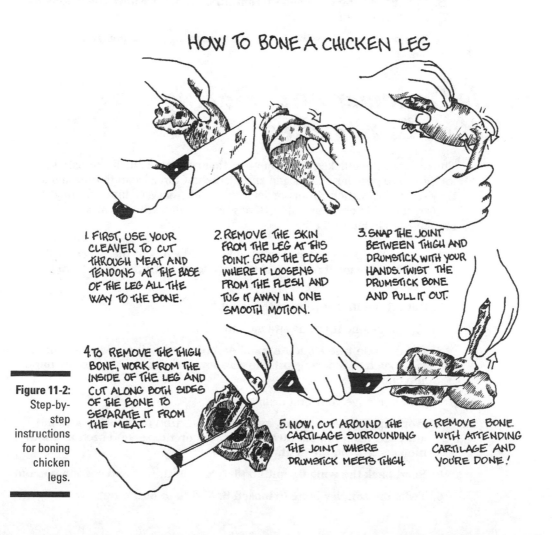

HOW TO BONE A CHICKEN LEG

1. FIRST, USE YOUR CLEAVER TO CUT THROUGH MEAT AND TENDONS AT THE BASE OF THE LEG ALL THE WAY TO THE BONE.

2. REMOVE THE SKIN FROM THE LEG AT THIS POINT. GRAB THE EDGE WHERE IT LOOSENS FROM THE FLESH AND TUG IT AWAY IN ONE SMOOTH MOTION.

3. SNAP THE JOINT BETWEEN THIGH AND DRUMSTICK WITH YOUR HANDS. TWIST THE DRUMSTICK BONE AND PULL IT OUT.

4. TO REMOVE THE THIGH BONE, WORK FROM THE INSIDE OF THE LEG AND CUT ALONG BOTH SIDES OF THE BONE TO SEPARATE IT FROM THE MEAT.

5. NOW, CUT AROUND THE CARTILAGE SURROUNDING THE JOINT WHERE DRUMSTICK MEETS THIGH.

6. REMOVE BONE WITH ATTENDING CARTILAGE AND YOU'RE DONE!

Figure 11-2: Step-by-step instructions for boning chicken legs.

1. Working with the whole leg and a sturdy cutting board, first use your Chinese cleaver to cut through the meat and tendons at the base of the leg all the way to the bone.

2. Remove the skin from the leg.

   Just grab the edge of the skin where it loosens from the flesh and tug it away in one smooth motion. If any bits of skin or fat remain, just pick them off the meat.

3. Snap the joint between the thigh and drumstick with your hands.

   Twist the drumstick bone and pull it out.

4. To remove the thigh bone, work from the inside of the leg and cut along both sides of the bone to separate it from the meat.

5. Cut around the cartilage surrounding the joint where the drumstick and thigh meet.

6. Remove the bone with its attending cartilage, and you're done.

Little Drummer Bird: Making Chicken Drummettes

Those cute little chicken "drummettes" that resemble small drumsticks or lollipops are popular snacks and appetizers in China. Despite their name, they're not drumsticks from particularly small chickens. Instead, they're slightly modified chicken wings. Here's how to make them yourself, shown step-by-step in Figure 11-3:

1. Locate the point where the wing bone attaches to the breast and cut through the meat and any skin there to remove the wing from the breast.

2. Cut off the first section of the wing.

   That's the one that was attached to the breast.

3. Cut the skin free from the small end of this section and use a small knife such as a paring knife to scrape the meat and skin to the opposite end.

   Now you have your first drummette.

4. Working with the second, and largest, section of the wing and the attached wing tip, cut through the skin on the second section about ½ inch away from the joint.

5. Bend back the wing tip until both bones in the second section pop out.

6. Twist the smaller bone to loosen it, and then pull it out.

MAKING CHICKEN DRUMMETTES

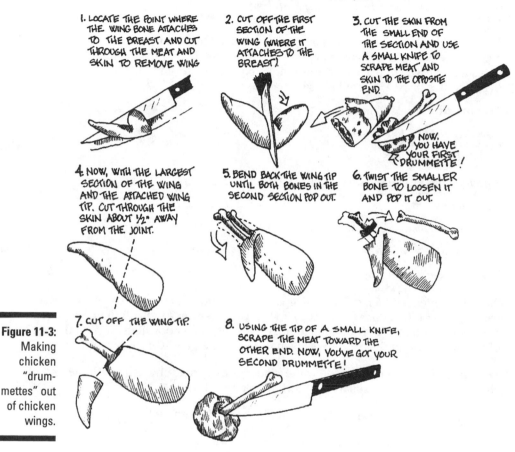

Figure 11-3:
Making chicken "drum-mettes" out of chicken wings.

7. **Cut off the wing tip.**

8. **Using the tip of a small knife such as a paring knife, scrape the meat toward the other end of the bone as you did with the first section.**

   Now you have your second drummette.

Great Chicken Recipes

Now that you know exactly how to prepare poultry for cooking, head into the following recipes to start enjoying the wide world of Chinese chicken — and duck and turkey — cuisine.

Sichuan Bang Bang Chicken

This dish goes by a number of names. Some call it "bon bon," "pon pon," or "pang pang" chicken as well as the "bang bang" name I've chosen here. But no matter what you call it, it's a great way to use leftover shredded chicken or turkey. Serve it as an appetizer, over noodles or rice, or chilled as a salad.

Preparation time: 15 minutes

Cooking time: 7 to 8 minutes

Yield: 4 to 6 servings

¾ pound boneless, skinless chicken	3 tablespoons chunky peanut butter
2 teaspoons salt	1 tablespoon chile garlic sauce
3 tablespoons white vinegar	2 teaspoons sugar
2 tablespoons soy sauce	¼ small head of iceberg lettuce, julienned
2 tablespoons chicken broth	1 teaspoon toasted sesame seeds

1 Place the chicken in a medium saucepan; add enough water to cover. Add the salt and bring it to a boil. Reduce the heat to low and simmer for 7 to 8 minutes. Remove the chicken and discard the cooking liquid. Let the chicken cool slightly. With the flat blade of a cleaver, pound the cooked chicken until softened and shred by hand.

2 Make a sauce by combining the white vinegar, soy sauce, chicken broth, peanut butter, chile garlic sauce, and sugar in a bowl; whisk it well with a fork.

3 Place the lettuce on a serving dish and place the chicken on top of the lettuce.

4 Pour the sauce over the chicken and sprinkle with the toasted sesame seeds.

Variation: Traditionally, Sichuanese cooks made the sauce for this dish with sesame paste, but because you may find chunky peanut butter an easier catch, go ahead and use that ingredient instead. You may want to mix that peanut butter with a little water or chicken broth first to thin it out a little. It's really up to you and your personal tastes. Any leftover sauce can go into a tightly sealed container in the fridge for a salad the next day.

Cultural Tidbit: This spicy Sichuanese dish gets its name — or names — from the many pronunciations of the Chinese word for the "stick" or "rod" that cooks traditionally used to pound and tenderize the chicken in the dish. But you needn't resort to blunt instruments to tenderize your chicken; American birds are already tender enough to require only a little thumping with a Chinese chef's knife.

Drunken Chicken

This recipe doesn't call for chickens who've had one too many martinis. It actually gets its name from the step of marinating moist, cooked chicken pieces overnight in Chinese rice wine mixed with sugar, ginger, and other flavorings.

Because this dish is served cold and improves with longer marination, you can prepare it well in advance. Served as an appetizer or a cold main dish, it's a foolproof (80 proof even) recipe.

Preparation time: *25 minutes*

Cooking time: *50 minutes*

Yield: *4 servings*

6 boneless, skinless chicken thighs (about 2¼ pounds)

¾ cup chicken broth

1 cup Chinese rice wine

3 tablespoons brandy

3 tablespoons soy sauce

6 pieces thinly sliced ginger, lightly crushed

2½ teaspoons sugar

⅛ teaspoon white pepper

1 Discard lumps of fat from the chicken. Place the chicken in a 1½-quart heatproof bowl. Add the chicken broth, rice wine, brandy, soy sauce, ginger, sugar, and white pepper; evenly coat the chicken with the mixture.

2 Prepare a wok for steaming. Steam the chicken over high heat until the chicken is no longer pink when cut, 45 to 50 minutes.

3 Remove the chicken from the steaming juices; let cool slightly. Cut the chicken into ½-inch-thick slices. Strain the juices and skim the fat. Place the sliced chicken in a serving bowl. Pour enough juices into the bowl to cover the chicken; cover and refrigerate for 24 hours.

4 Serve the chicken chilled with the gelatinized juices.

Martin Says: The steaming liquid in which you marinate the cooked chicken overnight contains a heady mix of the bird's own juices and fats, so don't be surprised if that potion has gelatinized by the time you remove it from the fridge. In fact, this palate-pleasing gel is really one of the best parts of the dish. Serve it with the chilled chicken and enjoy its rich, sumptuous texture and flavor.

Kung Pao Chicken

In recent years, kung pao chicken has gotten a bad rap in the Western press as a "typical fattening Chinese meal." The truth is, like any other dish, Chinese or otherwise, it's only as fattening as its ingredients and the techniques used to prepare them. Although some American-Chinese restaurants deep-fry the chicken pieces and add a generous portion of oil to the sauce, this is *not* how cooks normally prepare kung pao chicken in China. By stir-frying skinless lean chicken in minimal oil, you can create a lean, delicious dish that beats the stereotypes.

Preparation time: *10 minutes*

Cooking time: *10 minutes*

Yield: *4 servings*

1 tablespoon oyster-flavored sauce

1 tablespoon Chinese rice wine

½ teaspoon cornstarch

¾ pound boneless, skinless chicken, cut into ½-inch cubes

3 tablespoons chicken broth

2 tablespoons white vinegar

2 tablespoons dark soy sauce

2 teaspoons sugar

1½ tablespoons cooking oil

1 teaspoon minced garlic

6 whole dried red chiles, halved

1 red bell pepper, cut into ½-inch dice

1 green bell pepper, cut into ½-inch dice

1 cup sliced bamboo shoots

½ teaspoon cornstarch dissolved in 1 teaspoon water

⅓ cup unsalted roasted peanuts, walnuts, or cashew nuts

1 Combine the oyster-flavored sauce, rice wine, and cornstarch in a bowl to make a marinade. Add the chicken and stir to coat. Let stand for 10 minutes.

2 Make a sauce by combining the chicken broth, vinegar, dark soy sauce, and sugar in a bowl.

3 Place a wok over high heat until hot. Add the oil, swirling to coat the sides. Add the garlic and chiles; cook, stirring until fragrant, about 10 seconds. Add the chicken and stir-fry for 3 minutes.

4 Add the red and green peppers and bamboo shoots; stir-fry for 1 minute. Add the sauce; bring it to a boil. Add the cornstarch solution and cook, stirring until the sauce boils and thickens. Add the peanuts and stir to coat.

Remember: Make sure to use skinned peanuts for this recipe. The ones that you find in jars or cans at the store will do just fine.

Cultural Tidbit: There's an interesting story behind this famous Sichuan/Hunan dish. A big, gluttonous general named Kung Pao, known for eating around the clock, drowsily knocked a jar of chiles right into the stir-fried chicken he was making as a midnight snack. Instead of being overwhelmed by the dish's spiciness, he loved it and decided to name it after himself. You can increase the heat in your own version by breaking open the chile pods to expose the heat-containing seeds and ribs.

Honey Garlic Chicken

Honey's smoothness mellows the intense flavor of 12 cloves of garlic in this simple stir-fry. Pairing the two may not seem like an obvious combination at first, but after trying this honey of a sauce, I bet you'll be sweet on it yourself.

Preparation time: *15 minutes*

Cooking time: *8 minutes*

Yield: *4 servings*

2 tablespoons oyster-flavored sauce

1 tablespoon Chinese rice wine

1 teaspoon cornstarch

⅛ teaspoon Chinese five-spice powder

1 pound boneless, skinless chicken, cut into 1-inch cubes

⅓ cup chicken broth

1 tablespoon dark soy sauce

2 tablespoons honey

1½ tablespoons cooking oil

12 cloves garlic, crushed

3 whole dried red chiles

1 cup cubed water chestnuts or jícama (½-inch pieces)

1 To make the marinade, combine the oyster-flavored sauce, rice wine, cornstarch, and five-spice powder in a bowl. Add the chicken and stir to coat. Let stand for 10 minutes.

2 To make the sauce, combine the chicken broth, soy sauce, and honey in a bowl.

3 Place a wok over high heat until hot. Add the oil, swirling to coat the sides. Add the garlic; cook, stirring, until golden brown, about 2 minutes. Add the chiles and cook until fragrant, about 10 seconds. Add the chicken and stir-fry until done, 4 to 5 minutes. Add the water chestnuts and the sauce; bring to a boil until the sauce reduces slightly and the chicken is fully glazed, about 2 minutes.

Remember: If the thought of peeling 12 cloves of garlic drives you out of your own skin, just remember that a good smash with the flat of your knife's blade makes quick work of slipping off those papery peels.

Lemon Chicken

Another Cantonese classic, this citrusy treatment of chicken combines sweet and sour flavors with savory meats. No wonder you find versions of it on almost every Chinese restaurant menu in the West.

Preparation time: *15 minutes*

Cooking time: *15 minutes*

Yield: *4 servings*

⅓ cup chicken broth

⅓ cup fresh lemon juice

½ teaspoon dark soy sauce

¼ cup packed brown sugar

2 teaspoons lemon zest

1 egg

½ teaspoon salt

¼ teaspoon white pepper

¾ pound boneless, skinless chicken breasts, butterflied

¼ cup cornstarch

⅓ cup cooking oil

1½ teaspoons cornstarch dissolved in 1 tablespoon water

1 teaspoon toasted sesame seeds

1 Make a sauce by combining the chicken broth, lemon juice, soy sauce, brown sugar, and lemon zest in a small saucepan; set aside.

2 In a bowl, beat the egg lightly with the salt and white pepper. Dredge the chicken with the cornstarch; dip into the egg batter and dredge in the cornstarch again. Let it stand for 5 minutes. Just before cooking, shake off the excess cornstarch.

3 In a wok, heat the oil until hot. Pan-fry the chicken, a couple pieces at a time, turning occasionally, until golden brown, about 3 minutes on each side. Remove with a slotted spoon and drain on paper towels.

4 Bring the sauce to a boil over medium heat; add the cornstarch solution and cook, stirring, until the sauce boils and thickens.

5 Cut the chicken across the grain into ½-inch slices. Place the chicken on a serving plate. Pour the sauce on top and sprinkle with the sesame seeds.

Tip: The breast, with its tenderness and mild flavor, works best for lemon chicken, as does a simple garnish of lemon slices and cilantro. The lemon echoes the citrusy sauce, while the cilantro brings its own bright colors and flavor notes to the dish.

Tip: Toast the sesame seeds before adding them to this recipe — refer to Chapter 5 for the instructions. Toasting rids the seeds of any raw flavor and enhances their warm nuttiness. It gives them a prettier color, too.

Moo Goo Gai Pan

Westerners get a kick out of this dish's name. It sounds kind of funny even to me! But in Cantonese, it actually makes perfect sense: "Moo goo" refers to Chinese mushrooms, "gai" is Cantonese for "chicken," and "pan" means "slices." Put them together, and you have sliced chicken with mushrooms.

Preparation time: *30 minutes*

Cooking time: *8 minutes*

Yield: *4 servings*

¾ pound boneless, skinless chicken breast

½ cup chicken broth

2½ tablespoons oyster-flavored sauce

1 tablespoon Chinese rice wine

1½ tablespoons cooking oil

1 teaspoon minced garlic

4 ounces asparagus spears, cut into 1-inch pieces

1 cup thinly sliced carrots

4 ounces fresh small white mushrooms, sliced

4 ounces fresh shiitake or crimini mushrooms, sliced

½ teaspoon cornstarch dissolved in 1 teaspoon water

1 Slice the chicken breast thinly (about ⅛ inch thick) across the grain.

2 Make a sauce by combining the chicken broth, oyster-flavored sauce, and wine in a bowl.

3 Place a wok over high heat until hot. Add the oil, swirling to coat the sides. Add the garlic and cook, stirring until fragrant, about 10 seconds. Add the chicken; stir-fry until the chicken turns white, 2 to 3 minutes. Add the asparagus, carrots, and white and shiitake mushrooms; stir-fry for 2 to 3 minutes.

4 Add the sauce and bring it to a boil. Add the cornstarch solution and cook, stirring, until the sauce boils and thickens.

Remember: The savory oyster-flavored sauce in this recipe enhances the dish's overall flavor. Don't leave it out!

Chicken Curry, Cantonese Style

Is chicken curry a Chinese dish? In the same way that pizza has become an American meal, it is. Chinese food has assimilated the influence of all sorts of neighboring cuisines, and in this chicken curry, a vibrant — but pleasantly mild — curry paste marries the taste of India with the smoothness of coconut milk that's straight out of Southeast Asia.

This combination may seem like a match made in heaven, but it's actually more commonly put together in Guangzhou (close enough, if you ask me), where mild curries blending Indian and Southeast Asian ingredients are very popular. But to reassure the tender-tongued out there: Cantonese curries are traditionally more mild than wild. So enjoy as much as you like.

Preparation time: *10 minutes*

Cooking time: *40 minutes*

Yield: *4 servings*

1 large russet potato, about 8 ounces, peeled and roll cut (Chapter 5 explains roll cutting)	*6 pieces chicken wings or drumsticks, about 1¼ pounds*
1 tablespoon cooking oil	*¾ cup thick coconut milk*
3 tablespoons curry sauce (purchased)	*1 teaspoon sugar*
1 teaspoon turmeric	*2 tablespoons salt*
½ cup diced onion (½-inch pieces)	*1 large or 2 small tomatoes, cut into wedges, then halved*

1 Place the potato slices in a medium saucepan and barely cover with water. Bring to a boil. Reduce the heat, cover, and simmer until the potatoes are slightly soft when pierced, about 8 minutes. Drain and set aside.

2 Place a deep pan over high heat until hot. Add the oil, swirling to coat the sides. Add the curry sauce and turmeric; cook, stirring, until fragrant, about 30 seconds. Add the onion and cook, stirring, until soft, about 1 minute.

3 Add the chicken, stirring for 4 minutes. Add the coconut milk, sugar, and salt; reduce the heat to medium. Cover and cook for 12 to 15 minutes. Add the potatoes and tomatoes and continue to cook for an additional 10 minutes.

CULTURAL TIDBIT

Unfamiliar parts: What to do with the chicken parts you don't normally use

What more can you do with chicken wings? Ask some Chinese chefs, and they'll give you quite a few ideas. Although the chicken wing may be something of a castaway part to some Western diners, its crispy skin and little nuggets of flavorful meat make it a favorite in China. So aside from turning it into a tasty little drummette as described in the section "Little Drummer Bird: Making Chicken Drummettes," how about marinating it in a pungent mixture of Chinese five-spice powder and soy sauce and then frying it to a crispy finish — another classic Chinese preparation? Either way gives you the opportunity to truly appreciate chicken wings for the delicacy that they are.

Chinese love chicken wings for the same reason that they love another chicken part unfamiliar to many American palates: the feet. Both the feet and the wings have that perfect combination of moist and flavorful skin, gelatinous tendon,

crunchy bone, and hints of silky, dark meat to make them truly prized items at any Chinese table.

Don't forget the *oyster* either. It's the extremely tender little pearl of meat that's attached to the thigh and nestled right next to the backbone. When you're cutting up a chicken at home, be sure to include it with the thigh as you cut the leg off. You wouldn't want to miss out on it.

And what to do with that backbone, as well as the neck, gizzards, liver, and other organ meats that come with the bird? Do as all wise Chinese cooks do: Keep them, store them in a zippered plastic bag in the freezer, and when you've gathered a big-enough collection (I'd say, about two to three chickens' worth of parts and bones), use them to make a chicken broth that will do your mom proud.

Carving Out a Niche for Yourself: How to Carve a Bird Like the Chinese Do

It's a classic Western scene: the head of the household carving the holiday bird and dispensing servings to those seated around the table. Turns out that it's a classic Chinese scene as well, with a few important twists.

Westerners usually prefer to feast on thin slices of boneless meat while Chinese would rather cut up the bird, *bones included*, into rectangular chunks small enough to pick up with chopsticks, and then reassemble those pieces (yes, the head, too) back into a shape of the chicken. Here are the steps for a carving method that blends East and West techniques harmoniously. See Figure 11-4 for visual help.

CARVING POULTRY CHINESE STYLE

1. FIRST, LET THE BIRD _COOL_ SLIGHTLY! IT'S EASIER AND CLEANER TO SLICE.

2. PLACE ON A CUTTING BOARD, BREAST SIDE UP. SLICE THROUGH SKIN AND FLESH ALL AROUND THE LEG JOINT BETWEEN LEG AND BODY. AFTER CIRCLING THE JOINT, BEND THE LEG BACK SO THE JOINT IS EXPOSED. SLICE THROUGH THE JOINT TO FREE THE LEG.

3. FLIP BIRD SO IT'S BREAST DOWN. CARVE THE WINGS AS DESCRIBED FOR THE LEGS.

4. FLIP AGAIN AND MAKE A CLEAN CUT THROUGH THE BREASTBONE FROM NECK TO TAIL TO SEPARATE THE BREAST IN HALF.

5. OPEN THE BIRD AT THE _CUT_ BETWEEN THE BREAST HALVES. USE THE SAME PROCEDURE TO CUT THE BIRD IN HALF AT THE BACKBONE. REMOVE BACKBONE.

6. PLACE EACH HALF ON THE CUTTING BOARD, CUT SIDE DOWN. LOCATE THE END OF THE RIB CAGE. CUT IN HALF IN 2 PIECES ALONG THAT LINE.

7. RETURN TO THE LEGS. CHOP THROUGH BONES TO MAKE 4 OR 5 CHOPSTICK-SIZED PIECES.

8. CHOP THE WINGS AT THE ELBOW JOINTS AND RE-ASSEMBLE AT THE TOP OF THE PLATTER.

9. WITH THE 4 BODY PIECES, CHOP EACH CROSSWISE INTO RECTANGLES 1" WIDE. ARRANGE ON THE PLATTER, GENERALLY IN THEIR ORIGINAL SHAPE.

10. PUSH THE PIECES TOGETHER ON THE PLATTER TO GIVE THE BIRD A COHESIVE, MOUNDED APPEARANCE. FILL IN GAPS WITH APPROPRIATE GARNISH.

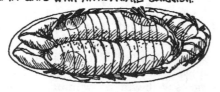

Figure 11-4: Carving a roast bird the Chinese way.

1. **Let the bird cool slightly to firm its flesh and make it easier and cleaner to slice.**

   If you have to slice it while it's hot, use a very sharp knife and have a bowl handy to catch any escaped juices.

2. **Place the slightly cooled bird, breast up, on the cutting board and use your chef's knife to slice through the skin and flesh all around the leg joint between the leg and the rest of the bird's body.**

   After you've circled the joint, bend the leg back so the joint is exposed and slice through the joint to free the leg. Repeat with the other leg.

3. **Flip the bird over so it's facing breast down and use the carving technique described in Step 2 for the wings.**

   You should find it easier to hack through the smaller, more delicate wing joints.

4. **Turn the bird breast up again and make a clean cut through the breast bone from neck to tail to separate the breast in half.**

   If the bird is still too hot, slice along, but not through, the length of bone and finish the job by cutting through with a sturdy pair of scissors.

5. **"Open" the bird at the cut between the breast halves and use the same cutting or scissoring procedure to fully cut the bird in half at the backbone.**

   Cut or scissor along the other side of the backbone to remove it.

6. **Place each half of the bird on the cutting board with the cut side facing down, locate the end of the rib cage, and cut each half into two pieces by cutting along that line.**

7. **Return to the legs and chop through the bones to make three or four chopstick-sized pieces.**

   Reassemble them into a leglike shape at the bottom of a serving platter.

8. **Chop the wings into two at the "elbow" joint and reassemble them at the top of the platter.**

9. **Working with each of the four body pieces, chop them crosswise into rectangles about 1 inch wide and arrange them on the platter between the legs and wings, generally in their original shape.**

10. **After laying all the pieces on the platter, push them together gently to give the bird a cohesive, mounded appearance, filling in any gaps or unattractive spots with appropriate garnishes such as slices of ham, mushroom, or green onion.**

    Feast your eyes, and your stomach, on that lovely sight!

Better yet, try out your new Chinese carving skill in the following chicken recipes.

Soy Sauce Chicken

This chicken — sold halved, whole, or even over rice in Chinese delis — is a great example of a dish cooked with the red-cooking method introduced in Chapter 5. The rich braising liquid of dark soy sauce, rice wine, and sesame oil flavored with brown sugar, star anise, dried tangerine peel, and ginger gives meats and poultry a slightly sweet flavor and red glaze.

Preparation time: 8 minutes

Cooking time: 1 hour, plus 20 minutes for the chicken to rest

Yield: 4 to 6 servings

4 cups chicken broth

¾ cup soy sauce

½ cup dark soy sauce

½ cup rice wine

½ cup packed brown sugar

1½ tablespoons sesame oil

10 slices ginger, crushed

8 cloves garlic, slightly crushed

3 whole star anise

2 pieces dried tangerine peel (about 1 inch)

1 whole chicken (3 to 3½ pounds)

1 Make the master sauce by combining all ingredients except the chicken in a large pot.

2 Place the chicken, breast side down, in the pot over high heat; cover and bring the sauce to a boil. Reduce the heat to low, cover, and simmer for 20 minutes. Turn the chicken over in the sauce and continue to simmer, covered, for another 20 minutes. Turn off the heat and let it stand, covered, for 15 minutes. Remove the chicken and cool on a platter for 20 minutes before cutting.

3 Cut and arrange the chicken on a platter back to the shape of a chicken. Drizzle a bit of the cooked sauce over the chicken before serving.

Tip: After you finish cooking the dish, don't pour the red-cooking sauce down the drain. Instead, use it as a starter or master sauce for other dishes, even hard-boiled eggs. Simply cool it, strain it, and store it in a closed container in your freezer. The next time you red-cook, pull it out of storage to defrost in the refrigerator, refresh some of the original ingredients (add new soy sauce, garlic, ginger, and tangerine peel, for example), and red-cook with it again. Over time, juices from the different meats add to the master sauce's richness and complexity, giving it a well-aged, sumptuous character.

Gingered Chicken

Another common deli food, gingered chicken uses the "white-cut" or "crystal boiling" cooking technique of gently simmering a chicken in broth or water until it's barely cooked. Food cooked this way stays tender and clean-tasting — characteristically Cantonese. A couple spoonfuls of the ginger-laced dipping sauce, as well as the slices of ginger tucked into the chicken's cavity, earn this dish its name.

Preparation time: *40 minutes*

Cooking time: *1 hour and 30 minutes*

Yield: *4 servings*

1 whole chicken (about 3 to 3½ pounds), cleaned and patted dry

1½ teaspoons salt

1 teaspoon white pepper

3 pieces thinly sliced ginger, crushed

4 green onions, minced

2 tablespoons minced ginger

1 teaspoon sesame oil

¾ teaspoon salt

Enough chicken broth or water to cover the chicken, about 5 cups

½ cup cooking oil

1 Rub the chicken, inside and out, with the salt and white pepper. Place the ginger slices in the cavity. Let stand in the refrigerator for 30 minutes.

2 Make the dipping sauce by combining the green onions, ginger, sesame oil, and salt in a small bowl.

3 Place the chicken in a large saucepan, breast side up; add the chicken broth or water. Cover and bring to a boil over high heat. Reduce the heat to low and simmer until the chicken is cooked, about 30 minutes. Let stand, uncovered, in the cooking liquid for an additional 30 minutes.

4 Remove the chicken from the liquid; set aside for 30 minutes. Cut into serving-size pieces.

5 In a small saucepan, heat the cooking oil until smoking. Add the dipping sauce and stir. To eat, spoon the mixture over the chicken pieces. Serve with steamed rice (see Chapter 15).

Safety Tip: To ensure that your white-cut gingered chicken is served juicy yet fully cooked, follow this recipe carefully. Although eating undercooked poultry is clearly unsafe, overcooked chicken is hard on the teeth and harder on the cook's ego.

Chinese Roast Chicken

How do you roast a chicken? Ask three Chinese chefs, and you'll get four different recipes. Fortunately all of them are delicious. Here's one of my favorite examples.

Preparation time: *10 minutes, plus 2 hours to marinate*

Cooking time: *1 hour and 30 minutes*

Yield: *4 to 6 servings*

3 tablespoons Chinese rice wine

3 tablespoons honey

2 tablespoons soy sauce

1 teaspoon sesame oil

½ teaspoon white pepper

1 roasting chicken (3 to 3½ pounds), cleaned

1 To make the marinade, combine all ingredients except the chicken in a bowl.

2 Place the chicken in a resealable plastic bag. Pour the marinade into the bag and seal the bag. Place in the refrigerator for up to 2 hours, turning the bag occasionally.

3 Preheat the oven to 350°. Remove the chicken from the bag, reserving the marinade. Place the chicken on a rack in a roasting pan, breast side up. Roast for 35 minutes, basting occasionally. When the chicken starts to brown, cover it loosely with foil. Turn the chicken and roast for a further 35 minutes, basting it with the reserved marinade. Turn the chicken again and roast until the meat near the bone is no longer pink when cut, about 20 minutes.

4 Cut the chicken into 2-inch pieces with a Chinese cleaver or a kitchen shear or carve it Western style.

Tip: Letting the chicken rest on the rack for 20 minutes after it cooks not only brings it down to a temperature that makes carving easier but also allows its juices to "resorb" back into the meat itself. If you carve it too soon, all those juices will come running out, and you end up with a much drier chicken.

Black, blue, and eaten all over China: Chinese blue-black chickens

White-meat chicken only? Not here. If you've ever been in a Chinese market and seen Cornish hen-sized birds that are black and blue in color, you know what I'm talking about. No, those aren't bruises on those birds. Their flesh just happens to be as blue-black as the feathers that used to cover it.

And yes, these birds are perfectly safe to eat. In fact, their flavor is a special treat for their die-hard fans. And as if flavor alone weren't enough, the darkly colored birds are believed to have medicinal, elixir, and aphrodisiac qualities that make them very expensive both in China and in the United States — if you're lucky enough to find them in the West. Not surprisingly, Chinese chefs pick blue-black chickens over anything else when making a curative chicken soup to restore health.

You can't always find these exotic delicacies in the West, and when you do, they're normally frozen and pricey. But for a special occasion, splurge on a blue-black chicken if you should stumble upon one. It gives a soup or stew healing and aesthetic qualities that will soothe and surprise family and guests.

Duck, Duck, Lucky Duck

Though not as much of a staple as chicken because they're not as easy to raise, duck still gets plenty of respect in the Chinese kitchen. The first dish that comes to mind is the world-famous Peking roast duck — the epitome of Chinese dining elegance. And there's a lot more where that came from: From Nanking duck to Cantonese *pei pa* duck, it's safe to say that when it comes to fowl plays, Chinese chefs never "duck."

Ducks have a distinct flavor, fattiness, and meaty texture that don't blend well with as many ingredients, seasonings, or cooking techniques as do a chicken's. But when you roast a duck, those rich distinctions become an asset rather than a liability. While the skin crisps to a sticky, succulent golden-brown, the melting layer of fat underneath bastes the bird's flesh in its own juices. What a mouth-watering thought, indeed!

Season duck with bean pastes, mushrooms, and smoky tea notes, all of which go well with duck's gamey flavors. Slow braising in a claypot, roasting, and steaming with warm spices such as ginger, Sichuan peppercorn, and star anise also tame the wild flavor of this domestic bird.

Peeking in on Peking duck

No discussion of Chinese poultry is complete without a few comments on Peking roast duck, an ancient dish dating back to Mongolian invaders. Although those raiders may have invented the dish while they roamed across China, the imperial kitchens of the Ming dynasty refined it during the 1600s into the type of dish served in restaurants today.

But today's Peking duck is a very different affair from the original. Instead of roaming around ponds and streams, today's plump birds live short but decadent lives in special duck farms where farmers specially feed them to produce the subcutaneous layer of fat and hearty breast meat that Chinese diners crave.

When preparing the ducks, chefs first blanch them to melt some of their fat away. They then pump air under the skin to separate it from the layer of fat below. Doing so ensures that the skin cooks up to the characteristic crispy texture. Next, they lacquer the ducks by plunging them into a maltose solution prior to roasting. The high heat in the roaster caramelizes this glaze and produces the salty-sweet taste and copper color that make Peking ducks such a delicious treat. Actually, in imperial times, the nobles ate only the succulent skin, wrapping it in papery Mandarin pancakes with spring onions and a salty-sweet sauce. They gave the peasants the meat and the bones for soups and stocks. Nowadays, wise diners enjoy the whole bird — the meat as well as the glistening cracklings. It doesn't hurt to save the bones for broth, and the juices for sauce, either!

If making Peking duck the old-fashioned way sounds like more of an ordeal than you or your kitchen equipment can handle, don't frown. Many Chinese restaurants in North America have Peking duck on their menus, so enjoy it in the restaurant and take home the leftovers. Or just place a take-out Peking duck order and have a duck fete at home. Beware that a real Peking duck takes time to prepare; most restaurants requires that Peking duck orders be placed one day in advance, so plan accordingly.

Pineapple Duck Stir-Fry

Cooks in so many cultures pair duck with fruit for a good reason: The sweetness of the fruit is just the thing for tempering the duck's slightly gamey flavor. Fruit enhances the mild flavor of chicken breast just as well, in case your store's supply of duck has "flown south" for the winter when you prepare this dish.

Preparation time: *30 minutes*

Cooking time: *8 minutes*

Yield: *4 servings*

2 tablespoons oyster-flavored sauce

2 tablespoons Chinese rice wine

1 tablespoon dark soy sauce

¾ pound boneless duck breast, thinly sliced

¼ cup chicken broth

3 tablespoons orange juice

2 tablespoons plum sauce

1 tablespoon cooking oil

4 pieces thinly sliced ginger

½ cup diamond-cut red bell pepper, ¾-inch (see the sidebar "A real gem of a cutting technique" in this chapter)

1 cup pineapple chunks

2 teaspoons orange zest

¾ teaspoon cornstarch dissolved in 2 teaspoons water

2 tablespoons julienned pickled ginger

1 To make the marinade, combine the oyster-flavored sauce, rice wine, and soy sauce in a bowl; add the duck breast and stir to coat. Let stand for 10 minutes.

2 To make the sauce, combine the chicken broth, orange juice, and plum sauce in a bowl.

3 Place a wok over high heat until hot. Add the oil, swirling to coat the sides. Add the ginger and cook, stirring until fragrant, about 10 seconds. Add the red pepper and stir-fry for 1 minute. Add the duck and stir-fry until almost cooked through, about 3 minutes. Remove the excess duck fat from the wok.

4 Stir in the pineapple chunks and orange zest. Add the sauce and bring it to a boil. Add the cornstarch solution and cook, stirring until the sauce boils and thickens. Return the duck to the wok; add the pickled ginger, and heat through.

Variation: Canned pineapple works well in the dish, although the increased availability of fresh, precut pineapple in grocery produce departments means that you can easily opt for fresh without the extra work. Using leftover duck or duck from a deli counter — Asian or otherwise — also saves you some time: no marinating beforehand, and less time in the wok.

Remember: A citrus fruit's *zest* is simply the thin, colored layer on the outside of its peel. But as thin as it may be, the zest still stores most of the aromatic essential oils that make it a powerful "secret" ingredient in this and many other citrus-flavored dishes. But getting at that zest can sometimes be a bit tricky. The key is to remove only the thin top portion of the peel; the white pith underneath is notoriously bitter and will make your dish taste the same. Gently run a vegetable peeler along the surface of a clean, unpeeled citrus fruit to harvest some of its zest. If it comes off in wide strips but the recipe calls for thin ones, simply matchstick-cut or julienne them as described in Chapter 5. Alternatively, many kitchen supply shops sell zesters — tools that, with a quick swipe, shave off conveniently thin curls of zest that are ready for action.

Safety Tip: Slice or cut bell peppers with their skin sides facing the work surface. Bell pepper skin is so tough and resilient that it takes some pushing on the knife blade to break through it. Because it's also slippery, if you push too hard, your knife may end up slipping off the pepper's skin and onto your fingers. Better to handily slice through the more tender flesh underneath than slice off your precious digits.

A real gem of a cutting technique

You may not think of the kitchen as the best place to cut diamonds. But when those diamonds are cut from jewel-toned bell peppers, I can't think of a better place to set up your culinary jeweler's shop. So how do you turn peppers — or zucchini, carrots, pineapple, and any other ingredient — into a precious gem? Just follow these steps:

1. Slice the ingredient into relatively flat pieces that are several times larger than the dimensions of the diamond cuts called for in the recipe.

2. Make several cuts along the length of the ingredient, holding those slices together or stacking them — whichever feels more comfortable to you.

3. Turn those slices about 45 degrees from their original position and slice through them once again — cutting on the diagonal — to create individual diamond-shaped chunks.

It's that simple, and the eye-catching diamonds are an attractive break from squares, rectangles, and other standard shapes. I guess that diamonds can actually be a cook's best friend!

Chapter 12

Moo-ve In and Pig Out, My Little Lambs: Beef, Pork, and Lamb

. . . .

In This Chapter

▶ Shopping for meat

▶ Handling meat properly at home

▶ Picking out pork products

▶ Beefing up your menu

▶ Pairing lamb with aromatic flavors

. . . .

Recipes in This Chapter

▶ Sweet and Sour Pork

▶ Mu Shu Pork

▶ Char Siu

▶ Twice-Cooked Pork

▶ Jing Tu Pork Chops

▶ Sichuan Spareribs

▶ Pork with Bean Threads

▶ Steamed Cabbage Rolls

▶ Shanghai Meatballs

▶ Chinese Pork Chops

▶ Tomato Beef

▶ Tangerine Beef

▶ Broccoli Beef

▶ Beef Steak Over Glass Noodles

▶ Spicy Beef with Leeks

▶ Beef Stew

▶ Uncle Philip's Beef Tri-Tip

▶ Mongolian Lamb in Hotpot

▶ Lamb with Green Onions

🍴 🍵 🥢 ⚄ 🌿

Throughout China's history, eating high on the hoof has been a real luxury. Meat is traditionally expensive and scarce; hence, the Chinese don't consume as much of it as do Westerners. But then, absence can make the meat grow fonder. Chinese cooks employ meats to *complement* and *enhance*, rather than overpower, the vegetables, starches, and other ingredients in dishes.

You'd be hard-pressed to find a big, thick cut of prime rib or a grilled two-fisted pork chop on too many tables in China. Rather than slabs of flesh, you're more likely to find bite-size chunks of roasted and glazed spareribs, strips of flank steak in stir-fries, and thin slices of lamb loin dipped into a Mongolian hotpot. These chopstick-friendly meat treats really take the cake in Chinese cooking.

Even loyal porterhouse aficionados will be impressed by the Chinese style of meat eating. You'll be surprised by just how easy it is to stretch out a relatively small cut of meat when it's part of a meal's ensemble cast rather than its starring lead. So don't limit yourself to the same old T-bone, lamb chops, and pork tenderloin. Give the Chinese way a try and see how quickly you trade in your carving knife for a pair of chopsticks.

Most Chinese would rather feast on a plateful of freshly cooked vegetables lightly accented with meat than on a big hunk of red muscle. But life in ancient China was more than a veggie stir-fry. Menus from ancient banquets and the inventory records from medieval Chinese markets indicate that the Chinese have consumed — among other exotic treats — dog, horse, donkey, bear, panther, camel, fox, and even rodent in addition to the more mundane pork, beef, and lamb over the years. And I thought venison sounded exotic. (They ate that, too, by the way.)

When preparing meat for any of these recipes, remember to cut it across the grain. That means identifying the direction in which the meat's fibers run and making your slices perpendicular to that direction. Doing so makes for a more tender cut of meat and a much more forgiving chewing experience. The bundled fibers of a crosscut piece of meat essentially "unbundle" easily with chewing, whereas the long, stringy meat fibers of a chunk cut along the grain just never seem to break down no matter how long you gnaw on them. In fact, even the most tender meat cut along the grain is a challenge to chew compared to a tougher cut of crosscut meat.

Buying Basics: How to Shop for Meat

Meat may be something of a pricey commodity in parts of China, but Western markets have plenty of it to go around. Nose up to the meat case in any supermarket, and you'll find yourself up against a whirlwind of cuts, qualities, and kinds of meat. Your options become even greater at an actual butcher's shop.

Of course, an overwhelming variety can never make up for meat that isn't fresh. The number one rule in meat shopping should be as follows: Choose your meat purveyor wisely. If the local market doesn't have a very high turnover in its meat cases, find one that does. And don't be too shy to ask the meat department manager directly for specifically fresh cuts. I also recommend patronizing smaller butcher shops where the focus is squarely on meats. Not only is the product fresher, but you're more likely to get a wider selection and more personalized service.

This doesn't mean that you have to give up supermarket meat-shopping entirely. By following a few rules, you'll know how to spot the freshest cuts on every trip:

 ✔ **Check out the meat's color and general appearance.** Pork should be pink and have a moist, but not slimy, appearance. Anything that's brown, gray, or dry-looking doesn't warrant your attention. As for beef and lamb, the freshest cuts have a reddish pink bloom and look moist but not slimy. Dry, dark, and gray beef or lamb is past its prime.

Never buy beef that has an iridescent green sheen either; that's an indication of bacterial growth. On the other hand, beef that's not bright red may not look too attractive, but is safe to eat. Turns out that the meat has this duller color simply because the muscle pigments haven't had exposure to enough oxygen to turn them a brighter, more appetizing shade of red.

✔ **If you notice a pool of blood or meat juices in the meat's Styrofoam tray, put it back.** Those signs usually indicate that the meat has sat out for a while or has already gone through at least one freeze-and-defrost cycle. This process damages the meat's texture and flavor. Put it back. The abundance of fresh meat on the market makes buying frozen meat an avoidable compromise in quality anyway. If you need to have a supply of meat on hand for the long haul, you're probably better off buying it fresh and freezing it yourself.

✔ **Pay attention to the meat's texture.** Even if the meat is shrink-wrapped on a Styrofoam tray, you can still give meat a gentle poking to determine whether it has the firm, springy texture that tells you it's still fresh.

✔ **Remember the all-important sell-by or packed-on date.** The former should be at least three days away (unless you plan to freeze the meat), and the latter should be fairly recent, if not that very day.

✔ **Check for marbling.** Most people know that leaner is better when it comes to meat. But a little bit of fat — seen as white streaks, or marbling, in a steak or chop — gives meat a sumptuous flavor and texture that you just don't get with extremely lean cuts. Consult the following sections on pork, beef, and lamb for more specifics on how to find a juicy, tasty cut.

✔ **If you make the effort to buy the freshest meat, make the effort to keep it that way.** That means putting it at the end of your shopping list so it's one of the last items you grab on your way out of the store. Head right home and get the meat into the refrigerator as soon as you arrive. Unless you plan to freeze it, try to use the meat the day you buy it or perhaps the day after. Preparing meat with this farm-to-fork-in-a-flash philosophy ensures the freshest, best-tasting product.

Safety First: Dealing with Meat at Home

Pork, beef, and lamb require careful treatment after you get the product home — all are perishable and can harbor pathogenic organisms. With ground beef, there's the concern about *E. coli* infection, which can result from eating meat, especially ground beef, that hasn't been cooked thoroughly. And even though modern breeding practices have made trichinosis in domestic pork extremely rare, you should always adhere to safe handling and preparation practices, which help eliminate the risk entirely. Here are some basic precautions to keep in mind:

✔ **Refrigerate meat early.** Don't dilly-dally on the way home from the store. Stow the meat in the coldest part of the refrigerator — somewhere with a temperature between 30° and 35°, which is usually the back corner of the top shelf — on a plate that can catch any leaking juices. If you don't plan on using the meat within a few days, freeze it. Defrost it on a plate in the refrigerator once you decide to prepare it.

✔ **Store meat in airtight packaging.** If you bought your meat from a butcher shop and it comes wrapped in butcher paper, rewrap it in plastic and transfer it to a zippered plastic bag or container with a tightly fitting lid. As for meat from the grocer's case, you're fine leaving it in its original Styrofoam tray wrapped with plastic. This goes for meat you intend to freeze as well as for that which you'll refrigerate.

✔ **Don't let raw or cooked meat sit out.** Raw cuts contain live bacteria that can thrive in comfy kitchen temperatures, as well as anywhere between 40° and 140°. And even though cooked meats have already been exposed to temperatures high enough to kill some of these bugs, the heartier pathogens and bacterial spores that survived cooking may find the warm conditions a green light to start reproducing. So get meats into cold storage immediately after returning from the store, always marinate meats in the refrigerator, don't let dinner sit out any longer than it takes to eat it, and then store the leftovers soon after eating.

✔ **Keep meat and meat juices away from foods that you've already cooked or plan on eating raw.** Always open packages of raw meat a safe distance away from fruits and raw vegetables, salads, or other dishes that are ready for service. Those juices have a tendency to splash about when you tear off the plastic wrapping.

✔ **Anything that touches raw meat or its juices deserves a good scrub in hot, soapy water.** Clean your hands, knives, cutting boards, bowls, and the counter before using them to prepare the next ingredient. This prevents cross-contamination. Consider your dishwasher a sterilization device and use it to disinfect dishwasher-safe items.

✔ **Boil raw meat marinades before using them as sauces.** If the meat that a marinade contained was contaminated, you can bet that the marinade is now contaminated as well, and only high heat can eradicate that problem.

After you have these fundamentals down, you're ready to hit the meat trail. By the way, it's only taken me 500 years (and a few trips to my doctor) to learn the tips and advice that I'm imparting to you. Trust me, you wouldn't want to learn about food safety the hard way.

In Praise of Pork

Neutral in flavor, nonfibrous in texture, and easy to raise on small plots with last night's leftovers as feed, pork is China's undisputed king of meats. Except for those pockets with sizable Muslim populations, people everywhere in China relish pork. Estimates hold that 70 percent of the meat dishes that Chinese chefs make include some part of the pig. Nothing is off limits: Tails, snouts, ears, feet, internal organs, and even the pig skin become a delicacy when placed in a Chinese chef's deft hands (this may explain why no Chinese teams have been in the Super Bowl).

Chinese diners eat "everything but the squeal," according to an old saying. They also prepare it in just about every way imaginable. Strips of pork butt go into stir-fries, while chunks of pork belly soften slowly when simmered in a slow-cooking claypot casserole. Chinese chefs mince pork and mix it with vegetables and seasonings for potstickers and dumplings. Plenty of Western diners are familiar with glistening-red barbecued spareribs as restaurant appetizers. And, after a meal of Cantonese roast suckling pig, who could forget that juicy, rich-flavored meat with the crispy layer of fat and skin? It's a truly auspicious dish for special occasions.

Roasting an entire pig on your own can be a bit of a chore, but you can buy as much or as little as you want from most Chinese delis.

Check out all the delicious preserved pork products that the Chinese have "invented" to make their king of meats last through leaner times and beyond. Sweet-savory pork sausages, shredded dried pork (a Chinese version of pork jerky), and Yunnan ham, which makes a good soup stock even better, all kept the Chinese well fed during times of scarcity — so well fed, in fact, that they kept eating these "peasant foods" even after prosperity returned. But don't wait until the next stock market crash to untie a string of Chinese pork sausages, which I discuss in Chapter 4. Toss a few chunks of ham or slices of sausage into a stir-fry or atop steaming rice tonight and discover how a little bit really does go a long way toward great flavor and texture.

Purchasing the Perfect Pig Product: How to Buy Pork Like a Chinese Cook

In addition to following the general guidelines for buying fresh meat in the section "Buying Basics: How to Shop for Meat," pay attention to a few hints for choosing the cuts of fresh pork that make a meal truly Chinese. Because the cooking methods and seasonings typical to Chinese cuisine can be a far cry from what you may be used to, qualities such as the fat-to-lean ratio and texture requirements may differ as well. Here's what to look for:

✔ Leaner cuts such as the loin and chops may be too lean for stir-frying. Because stir-frying uses relatively little oil in the first place, you'll want pork with enough marbling to give the dish moisture and flavor of its own. If you choose meat that's too lean, you'll probably end up adding more oil to the wok, but that extra oil won't be nearly as flavorful as that coming from a richer cut of meat.

✔ You can definitely use the leaner pork loin or chops in recipes that have rich sauces or that call for only small amounts of pork. In these cases, the leanness of the meat isn't that much of a flavor and texture liability. And if you find yourself with no other alternative than pork chops or loin, opt for those with a hearty band of fat around the edges. You can dice it up and toss it in if the dish cooks up too dry.

What kind of cut would I recommend for most Chinese recipes? I prefer pork butt with a fat-to-lean ratio right around 15 percent fat to 85 percent lean. This cut gives just enough juiciness and flavor for quick, light stir-fries, but it can also stand up to long, slow red-cooking and braising without becoming tough. True, most pork butts at the grocery store are pretty large, but you can get so many uses out of just one: chunks of pork for stews, strips for stir-fries, and ground pork butt for dumplings and potstickers.

You can always ask your butcher or the supermarket meat department manager to grind part of the butt for you on the spot. Because some of the ground pork sold at supermarkets may contain more than just pork — spices, inferior cuts, and even meats other than pork find a way of sneaking in — having the butt ground specially gives you a better idea of what you're getting.

So once you choose your perfect piece of pork, discover why it's such a star in Chinese cuisine by trying the following recipes. And what a better way to start than with a classic stir-fry.

Sweet and Sour Pork

This recipe pays its respects to one of the most popular dishes in American-Chinese restaurants, and it does a pretty good job of it to boot. Everything from the lightly crispy pork to the mildly tangy sauce with bell pepper, onion, and pineapple chunks will take you back to your favorite neighborhood spot for Chinese food.

I take the liberty of making one change, however: Many restaurant versions dip the pork in a heavy batter before deep-frying. I've lightened the dish by coating the pork in a light dusting of cornstarch instead. This method is simpler and less greasy, but it still achieves that delightful crispiness that makes sweet and sour pork such a winner.

Preparation time: *12 minutes*

Cooking time: *15 minutes*

Yield: *4 servings*

1 cup Sweet and Sour Sauce (see Chapter 7)

¼ cup chicken broth

¾ pound boneless pork, cut into ¾-inch cubes

½ cup cornstarch

2 tablespoons cooking oil

½ cup diced onion (½-inch)

½ cup diced green bell pepper (½-inch)

¾ cup pineapple chunks

1 Combine the Sweet and Sour Sauce and the chicken broth in a bowl.

2 Dust the pork with the cornstarch.

3 Place a wok over high heat until hot. Add 1 tablespoon of the oil, swirling to coat the sides. Add the pork and stir-fry until golden brown, about 3 minutes. Remove and drain on paper towels. Keep warm.

4 Return the wok to high heat; add the remaining oil, swirling to coat the sides. Add the onion; stir-fry for 2 minutes. Add the bell pepper; stir-fry for 1 minute.

5 Reduce the heat to medium-high. Add the sauce, stirring until the sauce boils and thickens. Return the pork to the wok and add the pineapple chunks; turn to heat through, about 1 minute.

Variation: Whether store-bought or homemade from the recipe in Chapter 7, any sweet and sour sauce that gets your mouth watering is good enough for this recipe.

Mu Shu Pork

To make this simple pork, vegetable, and mushroom stir-fry officially *mu shu*, you should eat it the way people do in China and in Chinese restaurants. That means wrapping a few tablespoons of the meat and vegetable mixture in thin, crepelike Mandarin pancakes that you've spread with some hoisin sauce.

Chinese groceries carry the pancakes, and if you're lucky, your supermarket may have a selection as well. But if you can't find Mandarin pancakes, flour tortillas make a convenient substitute.

Preparation time: *25 minutes*

Cooking time: *15 minutes*

Yield: *4 servings*

6 dried black mushrooms

4 cloud ears or wood ears (see Chapter 4)

¼ cup chicken broth

2 tablespoons soy sauce

1 tablespoon cooking oil

2 teaspoons minced garlic

½ pound boneless pork, julienned

3 cups julienned cabbage

1 cup julienned carrots

2 green onions, julienned

1½ teaspoons cornstarch dissolved in 1 tablespoon water

3 tablespoons hoisin sauce

10 to 12 tortilla wraps

1 In separate bowls, soak the mushrooms and the cloud ears in warm water to cover until softened, about 20 minutes; drain. Discard the mushroom stems and thinly slice the mushroom caps and the cloud ears.

2 Make the sauce by combining the chicken broth and soy sauce in a bowl.

3 Place a wok over high heat until hot. Add the oil, swirling to coat the sides. Add the garlic and cook, stirring, until fragrant, about 10 seconds. Add the pork and stir-fry until lightly browned, about 2 minutes. Add the mushrooms, cloud ears, cabbage, and carrots; stir-fry for 1 to 2 minutes. Add the green onions and sauce; bring it to a boil. Add the cornstarch solution and cook, stirring, until the sauce boils and thickens.

4 To eat: Spread ½ teaspoon hoisin sauce on a tortilla wrap and place about 1½ tablespoons mu shu mixture over the sauce and serve.

Variation: A quick glance at a Chinese restaurant menu shows that mu shu dishes are the picture of versatility: mu shu pork, mu shu chicken, mu shu vegetables, combination mu shu . . . you get the picture. So, mu shu any way you want to, adding new ingredients and taking others out. Mu shu is up to you!

Char Siu

A little bit of char siu goes a long way — except, of course, when it's in my refrigerator. That's why I'm glad that I have this recipe, which makes char siu easy to prepare in your own kitchen.

It takes advantage of some of the same techniques that make deli-made char siu so good — take roasting the pork over a pan of water, for example. When the water heats up, it creates steam that circulates around the pork and moderates the oven temperature as well, both of which prevent the pork from drying out.

Preparation time: *20 minutes, plus 1 hour marinating time*

Cooking time: *45 minutes*

Yield: *4 to 6 servings*

1½ pounds boneless pork butt (with a bit of fat and marbling)

¼ cup hoisin sauce

¼ cup soy sauce

2 tablespoons sugar

1 tablespoon Chinese rice wine

1 tablespoon cooking oil

1½ teaspoons salt

¼ cup honey

1 Cut the pork into long strips, 2 inches wide. Score each strip of meat with 3 or 4 shallow diagonal cuts for better absorption of the marinade.

2 Make the marinade: Combine the hoisin sauce, soy sauce, sugar, rice wine, oil, and salt in a large bowl. Add the pork and turn to coat. Cover and refrigerate for 1 hour.

3 Preheat the oven to 375°. Remove the pork from the marinade; reserve the marinade and add to the honey. Place the strips on a wire rack in a baking pan. Pour water into the pan just below the level of the rack. Roast for 20 minutes. Turn the strips over, brush with the honey marinade, and continue to roast until the meat is no longer pink when cut in the thickest part, about 20 minutes. Cut into slices. Serve hot or cold.

Martin Says: When you feast on Chinese roast pork, that little health-conscious voice in you — with a little coaxing from your arteries — may be whispering, "Remove that crackling skin and fat!" But just this once, don't listen! Do your taste buds a favor and give it a try. After all, the Chinese have savored this rich treat in measured mouthfuls for ages, and they're doing just fine. Even if the thought of eating pork skin really leaves you cold, don't throw it out (the economically minded side of me is speaking now), but rather save it to make an unbeatable gravy.

Twice-Cooked Pork

Chinese cooks learned early on that applying multiple cooking methods to meats not only ensures that they pass the yin-yang test but also layers the meat with complex flavors and textures that are actually simple to achieve.

This recipe is a great example. Simmering the pork in a fragrant mixture of rice wine, ginger, and green onions tenderizes it and keeps it moist, while finishing the dish by stir-frying the sliced, simmered pork with garlic and a chile-laced sauce gives it a final flavorful punch.

Preparation time: *12 minutes*

Cooking time: *About 40 minutes*

Yield: *4 servings*

1 pound boneless pork butt	*1 teaspoon chile garlic sauce*
3 cups water	*3 tablespoons cooking oil*
2 tablespoons Chinese rice wine	*6 dried or fresh red chiles*
3 to 4 pieces thinly sliced ginger	*1 tablespoon minced garlic*
2 green onions, cut into 2-inch lengths	*½ small head of napa cabbage, cut into 1-inch lengths*
⅓ cup chicken broth	
3 tablespoons oyster-flavored sauce	*1 teaspoon cornstarch dissolved in 1 tablespoon water*
1 teaspoon sugar	

1 Place the whole pork butt in a pot with the water, rice wine, ginger, and green onions and bring to a boil. Reduce the heat to low, cover, and simmer for 30 minutes. Remove from the heat and set aside to cool. When cool, drain and cut the meat into large slices, about ⅛ inch thick.

2 Make the sauce by combining the chicken broth, oyster-flavored sauce, sugar, and garlic sauce in a small bowl.

3 Place a wok or frying pan over high heat until hot. Add 2 tablespoons of the oil, swirling to coat the sides. Add the chiles and garlic; cook, stirring until fragrant, 10 seconds. Add the pork slices and the napa cabbage; stir for about 1 minute.

4 Add the sauce; cover and cook until the cabbage begins to soften, about 4 minutes. Remove the cover; add the cornstarch solution and cook, stirring, until the sauce boils and thickens.

Variation: To lend the dish a more traditional taste, toast ¼ to ½ teaspoon ground Sichuan peppercorn with the chiles and garlic for about 25 to 30 seconds. When the peppercorn releases its unmistakable aroma, you'll know that you've "awakened" its flavor. Toss in some shredded bamboo shoots, too, if you're looking for a little extra crunch.

Tip: Keeping some of the sauces from Chapter 7 stored in the refrigerator can give you a helping hand if you're pressed for time. Just ½ cup of the Hot and Spicy Stir-Fry Sauce rather than the sauce in the recipe, and you'll still get a delicious dish but with one fewer step.

Jing Tu Pork Chops

Jing tu literally means "capital city." In China, that means Beijing, the home of this versatile pork chop dish — versatile because it's scrumptious served straight off the stove as well as at room temperature. If you can't find ¼-inch thick pork chops, buy thicker ones and pound them.

Preparation time: *15 minutes*

Cooking time: *10 minutes*

Yield: *4 to 6 servings*

2 tablespoons soy sauce

2 tablespoons wine

1½ tablespoons cornstarch

6 pork chops, about ¼ inch thick

¼ cup ketchup

¼ cup Sweet and Sour Sauce (see Chapter 7)

3 tablespoons Worcestershire sauce

1 tablespoon sugar

2 tablespoons cooking oil

1 To make the marinade, combine the soy sauce, wine, and cornstarch in a bowl. Add the pork chops and turn to coat. Let stand for 10 minutes.

2 To make the seasoning sauce, combine the ketchup, Sweet and Sour Sauce, Worcestershire sauce, and sugar in a small bowl.

3 Place a wide frying pan over high heat until hot. Add the oil, swirling to coat the sides. Add the pork chops and cook until golden brown, about 2-3 minutes per side. Reduce the heat to medium. Add the seasoning sauce; cook, stirring, until the sauce is reduced and thickens slightly, about 3 minutes.

Remember: Be sure to drain all the marinade from the pork chops before placing them in the pan. If you don't, the meat tends to "stew" in the lingering marinade juices, whereas its surface is actually supposed to sear from direct contact with the hot oil in the hot pan. If it doesn't sear, it doesn't caramelize. If it doesn't caramelize, it doesn't develop the same color or delicious flavor.

Sichuan Spareribs

Chinese-style spareribs, especially when they get a little Sichuan kick from chile garlic sauce and Sichuan peppercorn, can hold their own against Western-style barbecued baby back ribs any day. Give this recipe a try and taste for yourself.

To cut the marinating time and make it easier to work the flavor of that marinade (also known as Chinese barbecue sauce) into the ribs, combine the two in a tightly zippered bag and periodically give it a good shake as it marinates in the refrigerator.

Preparation time: *15 minutes*

Cooking time: *1 hour*

Yield: *4 servings*

2 pounds pork spareribs

2 tablespoons Chinese rice wine

2 tablespoons dark soy sauce

2 tablespoons hoisin sauce

1 tablespoon packed brown sugar

1 tablespoon minced garlic

2 teaspoons chile garlic sauce

½ teaspoon Chinese five-spice powder

2 tablespoons honey

1 teaspoon sesame oil

1 Cut the ribs between the bones to make individual pieces. Place them in a 3-quart pot and barely cover with water; bring to a boil. Reduce the heat, cover, and simmer until the ribs are tender, 45 to 50 minutes. Drain (reserve the liquid for other uses) and let cool.

2 Make the marinade by combining the rice wine, dark soy sauce, hoisin sauce, brown sugar, garlic, chile garlic sauce, and five-spice powder in a large bowl. Add the pork and stir to coat. Cover and refrigerate, turning occasionally, for 30 minutes or as long as overnight.

3 Lift the ribs from the marinade and place them on a rack in a foil-lined pan; reserve the marinade. To the reserved marinade, add the honey and sesame oil.

4 Broil the ribs until golden brown, 2 to 3 minutes per side, basting with the reserved marinade.

Martin Says: Whenever I simmer pork ribs, or anything else with flavor-packed bones, I save the stock that's left over. It gives a whole new dimension to soups that call for chicken broth. If I want only half of that new dimension, I combine the rib broth with chicken broth to make a half-pork/half-chicken broth mixture. Either way works.

Pork with Bean Threads

Chinese cooks have mastered the art of turning modest ground meat into very impressive meals, as this recipe for ground pork with bean threads proves. The mildly piquant sauce (piquant thanks to some chile garlic sauce) makes the dish a perfect candidate for a garnish of red jalapeño or Fresno chile, seeded, finely diced, and sprinkled on top.

By the way, "pork with bean threads" also goes by the name "ants climbing up a tree."

Preparation time: *10 to 15 minutes*

Cooking time: *10 minutes*

Yield: *4 servings*

4 ounces bean thread noodles	*2 teaspoons chile garlic sauce*
½ pound ground pork	*3 green onions, chopped*
2 tablespoons dark soy sauce	*2 teaspoons sesame oil*
1 cup chicken broth	*1 tablespoon cooking oil*
1 tablespoon rice vinegar	*1 tablespoon minced ginger*
1 tablespoon packed brown sugar	

1 Soak the bean thread noodles in warm water to cover until softened, about 5 minutes; drain. Cut the noodles in half and set aside.

2 Combine the pork with the dark soy sauce and mix well. Let stand for 10 minutes.

3 Make the sauce by combining the chicken broth, rice vinegar, brown sugar, chile garlic sauce, green onions, and sesame oil in a small bowl.

4 Place a wok over high heat until hot. Add the cooking oil, swirling to coat the sides. Add the ginger and cook, stirring until fragrant, about 10 seconds. Add the pork and stir-fry for 2 minutes.

5 Add the bean thread noodles and the sauce; stir for 30 seconds. Reduce the heat to low. Cover and cook until most of the sauce has been absorbed, 3 to 5 minutes. Serve immediately.

Martin Says: I'm always on the lookout for one-dish meals for those times when I'm in a hurry and really hungry. Pork with bean threads fits the bill in my book, combining lightly saucy ground meat with a starch in the form of the mung bean noodles. If you're hankering for some simple steamed white rice, the pork-and-sauce part of the recipe makes a great topping for that as well — just remember to change the dish's name from "ants climbing up a tree" to "ants skiing down a snowy hill."

Steamed Cabbage Rolls

Do you ever wonder why the cuisines of so many different cultures include at least some version of stuffed cabbage rolls? One bite of these tasty packets — plump with ground pork, shrimp, and crunchy water chestnuts and topped with a sauce made with the steaming juices — and you'll understand why they're such winners in China.

If you're a little rusty as to how to actually roll the cabbage rolls, the steps as illustrated in Figure 12-1 should help clear things up for you.

Preparation time: 1 hour

Cooking time: 15 minutes

Yield: 14 rolls

7 large cabbage leaves

½ pound ground pork

¼ pound medium raw shrimp, shelled, deveined, and coarsely chopped

½ cup minced water chestnuts

¼ cup minced green onions

2 tablespoons wine

2 tablespoons soy sauce

¼ teaspoon white pepper

1 teaspoon chile garlic sauce

¾ cup chicken broth

1 tablespoon oyster-flavored sauce

2 tablespoons cornstarch dissolved in 4 tablespoons water

1 Bring a pot of water to a boil; blanch the cabbage leaves just until slightly limp, 5 to 7 minutes. Drain, rinse with cold water, and drain again. Cut the leaves in half and discard the thick center rib.

2 Make the filling by combining the ground pork, shrimp, water chestnuts, green onions, wine, soy sauce, and white pepper in a bowl.

3 Make the sauce by combining the chile garlic sauce, chicken broth, and oyster-flavored sauce in a small saucepan.

4 To make each roll: Place a cabbage leaf on a clean, flat work surface with the stem end facing you. Spread about 1 tablespoon of the filling in a band near the bottom of the leaf. Roll the leaf tightly to enclose the filling. Arrange the rolls on a heatproof dish in a single layer.

5 Prepare a wok for steaming (see Chapter 5). Steam the rolls over high heat until the filling is no longer pink, 12 to 14 minutes. When the rolls are cooked, transfer them to a serving platter. Pour the steaming juices into the saucepan with the sauce. Bring to a boil. Add the cornstarch solution and cook, stirring, until the sauce boils and thickens.

6 To serve, pour the sauce over the rolls.

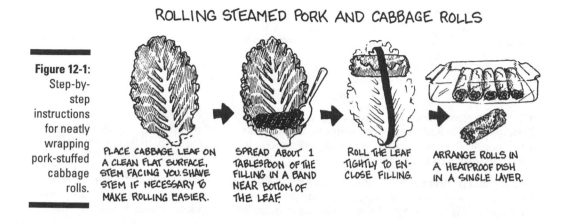

ROLLING STEAMED PORK AND CABBAGE ROLLS

Figure 12-1:
Step-by-step instructions for neatly wrapping pork-stuffed cabbage rolls.

PLACE CABBAGE LEAF ON A CLEAN FLAT SURFACE, STEM FACING YOU. SHAVE STEM IF NECESSARY TO MAKE ROLLING EASIER.

SPREAD ABOUT 1 TABLESPOON OF THE FILLING IN A BAND NEAR BOTTOM OF THE LEAF.

ROLL THE LEAF TIGHTLY TO ENCLOSE FILLING.

ARRANGE ROLLS IN A HEATPROOF DISH IN A SINGLE LAYER.

Tip: Regular head cabbage, which is the best choice for this recipe, is very dense and compact, and the leaves are sometimes hard to remove without tearing. Try this trick to keep your cabbage leaves in one piece: Core the cabbage with a paring knife. Meanwhile, heat a pot of water to boiling. Slide the whole head of cabbage into the water and blanch for 1 minute; remove from the pot. Now that the cabbage has softened from blanching, easily lift off as many large leaves as you need. Remove the heart of the remaining cabbage, rinse with cold water until it's cooled, and save it for another recipe.

Remember: The recipe recommends that you blanch the individual cabbage leaves for 1 to 2 minutes before rolling. If you decide instead to blanch the whole head of cabbage as outlined in the preceding tip, reduce the blanch time for the individual leaves to just 1 minute.

Char siu: Barbecued pork for all purposes

Just as Westerners can grab a hot dog at a food stand or deli, Chinese diners-on-the-run can pick up some *char siu*, Cantonese barbecued pork, from their favorite deli when they need a quick bite. And if I had to pick between a frank in a ketchupy bun and sweet savory chunks of heaven, well, you know where my loyalty lies.

Chefs roast these strips of pork — marinated in a glaze of soy and hoisin sauces, sugar syrup, and warm spices — over a pan of water so that dripping fat creates steam to moisten the meat during the roasting process. When it's done, chefs cut the brick red, glistening treats into chunks that shoppers purchase by the pound, by the kilos, or, in my case, by the truckload.

I always say the more you buy, the better. Consider char siu's versatility: You can serve it hot or cold, stir it into soups, toss it into stir-fries and fried rice dishes, or stuff it into pillowy Chinese buns. For me, char siu is also the perfect finger food. I just have to be careful not to bite off any fingers in my frenzy.

Shanghai Meatballs

In Shanghai, cooks prepare a classic dish of huge meatballs resting on a bed of napa cabbage. They call it "Lion's Head Meatballs" because the hefty meatballs are well on their way to being as big as — you guessed it — a lion's head.

It's just another example of the Chinese knack for giving foods catchy, figurative names. Perhaps such creativity stems from our ability to see food as something more artistic — more poetic — than a gathering of ingredients on a plate. Then again, these meatballs really do look like lions' heads.

I've shrunken those heads some for this recipe — they're now more in the range of kittens' heads — and have changed the name to preserve the true meaning of "Lion's Head Meatballs." And although the name is tame, the wildly delicious flavor is still the same.

Preparation time: *25 minutes*

Cooking time: *25 minutes*

Yield: *6 to 8 servings*

¼ pound regular-firm tofu, drained

1 pound ground pork

1 egg yolk, lightly beaten

2 tablespoons oyster-flavored sauce

2 teaspoons minced ginger

Cooking oil for deep-frying

8 ounces napa cabbage, cut into 3-inch lengths

6 fresh shiitake mushrooms, quartered

1 cup thinly sliced carrots

¾ cup chicken broth

2 tablespoons Chinese rice wine

1 tablespoon soy sauce

1 teaspoon sesame oil

2 green onions, cut into 1-inch lengths

2 teaspoons cornstarch dissolved in 1 tablespoon water

1 Prepare the meatballs: Mash the tofu in a bowl. Place the tofu in a clean towel and squeeze to remove the excess liquid. Return to the bowl and add the ground pork, egg yolk, oyster-flavored sauce, and ginger; mix well. Divide the mixture into 12 equal portions. Roll each portion into a ball.

2 In a wok, heat the cooking oil for deep-frying to 350°. Deep-fry the meatballs, 6 at a time, turning frequently, until browned on all sides, 3 to 4 minutes. Remove with a slotted spoon and drain on paper towels.

3 Heat a wok over high heat until hot. Add 1 tablespoon oil, swirling to coat the sides. Add the cabbage; toss until tender-crisp, about 2 minutes. Add the meatballs, mushrooms, carrots, chicken broth, rice wine, soy sauce, and sesame oil. Reduce the heat to medium; cover and braise for 15 minutes. Add the green onions and cornstarch solution; cook, stirring, until the sauce boils and thickens.

Chinese Pork Chops

Here's another Chinese twist on pork chops — a popular cut of meat in the West. The marinade has a nice balance of sweetness from the sugar, aromatic spice from the white pepper and Chinese five-spice powder, and nutty richness from the sesame oil.

Preparation time: 15 minutes

Cooking time: 10 minutes

Yield: 4 servings

2 tablespoons chicken broth

1 tablespoon soy sauce

2 teaspoons sugar

2 teaspoons sesame oil

¼ teaspoon white pepper

¼ teaspoon Chinese five-spice powder

4 pork chops, about ½ inch thick, pounded lightly

1½ tablespoons cooking oil

1 cup thinly sliced onion

3 green onions, sliced

1 Make the marinade by combining the chicken broth, soy sauce, sugar, 1 teaspoon of the sesame oil, white pepper, and five-spice powder in a bowl. Add the pork chops and turn to coat. Let stand for 10 minutes.

2 Place a wide frying pan over high heat until hot. Add the cooking oil, swirling to coat the sides. Remove the pork chops from the marinade and place in the pan. Cook, covered, until the meat is no longer pink, about 3 minutes per side. Remove and place on a serving platter.

3 Add the onion to the pan and cook, stirring until the onion is soft, about 3 minutes. Add the green onions and the remaining 1 teaspoon sesame oil. Serve onions over the pork chops.

What's Your Beef?

My theory is that American-Chinese restaurants are responsible for a widely held misconception about Chinese cuisine in North America. The popularity of dishes such as broccoli beef, beef and tomatoes, and tangerine peel beef — all wonderful recipes in their own right — may give the dining public the impression that the Chinese eat a lot of beef.

In fact, they don't. Beef's high cost and limited supply make it a luxurious dish for most Chinese diners. Furthermore, many don't care too much for beef's strong flavor and fibrous texture (as compared to pork's). Environmental and economic forces in China are not ideal for cattle roundups either. Most of China cannot dedicate precious land to grazing cattle when the same-sized plot can grow a larger crop of vegetables and grains. This fact may explain why beef appears more often in northern regions that are less populated and have grazing room to spare.

And though cows, oxen, and water buffalo have been a part of Chinese culture for centuries, they've traditionally earned their keep as beasts of burden rather than as dinners. Modern farm machinery is still out of reach for many small-scale rice farmers, so they can ill afford to turn their family plow — often, the family cow — into beef jerky.

Better Beef for a Chinese Meal

Given that they've had to work with tougher cuts of meat (often from retired water buffalo), Chinese chefs turned to clever cleaver techniques and quick cooking methods to make beef more palatable. Thinly slicing flank steak across the grain and marinating the strips in oyster-flavored sauce before stir-frying (the Cantonese way) help tenderize the stringy fibers. Deep-frying beef to a crispy-chewy finish also makes tougher parts easier to ingest. And, of course, mincing or grinding beef for potstickers and other dumplings completely sidesteps the poor-texture issue.

Although marinated and crosscut flank steak works well for stir-fry, I suggest more tender parts of the round and even the shoulder for other beef dishes. (Ask your supermarket's meat department manager to direct you to those more tender choices.) They contain plenty of collagen that, when braised or stewed for a long time, melts into the cooking liquid and sauce to give it a rich, mouth-pleasing, gelatinous texture that I absolutely adore. Even though the round may cost you a little more than some other cuts, the texture and flavor are more than worth the higher price.

Fortunately for you, America's beef industry provides high-quality, tender cuts of beef that don't require sneaky techniques to make up for shortcomings in flavor and texture. So you have no excuse not to beef up your Chinese menu.

Tomato Beef

Tomatoes aren't exactly native to China, but the country has fallen in love with them anyway. North Americans have also fallen in love with some of China's typical tomato-containing dishes, and tomato beef may be their favorite. Serve this stir-fry with some stir-fried noodles, and you have an easy tomato-beef chow mien.

Preparation time: *20 minutes*

Cooking time: *About 7 minutes*

Yield: *4 servings*

2 tablespoons oyster-flavored sauce

2 tablespoons Chinese rice wine

¾ pound beef (tri-tip or New York steak), cut into ½-inch cubes

⅓ cup chicken broth

3 tablespoons ketchup

1 tablespoon hoisin sauce

1 tablespoon packed brown sugar

1 teaspoon chile garlic sauce

1½ tablespoons cooking oil

1 cup diced green bell pepper (1-inch pieces)

1 medium tomato, cut into 8 wedges and then halved

1 To make the marinade, combine the oyster-flavored sauce and rice wine in a bowl. Add the beef and stir to coat. Let stand for 10 minutes.

2 To make the sauce, combine the chicken broth, ketchup, hoisin sauce, brown sugar, and chile garlic sauce in a bowl.

3 Place a wok over high heat until hot. Add the oil, swirling to coat the sides. Add the beef and stir-fry until no longer pink, about 1½ to 2 minutes. Add the bell pepper and tomato; stir-fry for 1 minute. Add the sauce and bring to a boil.

Remember: Obviously, sweet, ripe, bright red tomatoes are best for this dish. If the only ones you can find are anemic-looking at best, you may want to wait until the summer crop comes in before you make it. But if you absolutely need your tomato beef right now, you can get by with a firm, not-quite-so-sweet tomato because stir-frying softens it some and the mild tomatoey sweetness from the ketchup and sugar in the sauce makes up for what the tomato lacks.

Tangerine Beef

The wonderfully aromatic, lightly citrusy flavor in this stir-fry actually comes from an unattractive ingredient: dried tangerine peel. But who cares if dried tangerine peel is gnarled, brittle, and dusty-orange-colored — if it can make a dish taste this good, its flaws deserve to be forgiven! Just garnish the finished stir-fry with orange segments and sliced green onions rather than the dried peel itself.

By the way, if any pieces of peel have plenty of thick, white pith on their undersides, scrape it off with a knife after you soak the peels — that white pith can be pretty bitter.

Preparation time: *20 minutes*

Cooking time: *10 minutes*

Yield: *4 to 6 servings*

1 piece (about 2-inch square) dried tangerine peel (optional)

2 tablespoons dark soy sauce

1 teaspoon cornstarch

¾ pound beef tri-tip or flank steak, thinly sliced across the grain

¼ cup chicken broth

¼ cup orange juice

1 tablespoon soy sauce

2 tablespoons cooking oil

2 cloves garlic, sliced

1 tablespoon crystallized ginger, chopped

2 teaspoons cornstarch dissolved in 1 tablespoon water

1 can (11 ounces) mandarin oranges, drained

1 Soak the tangerine peel in warm water to cover until softened, about 20 minutes; drain. Thinly slice the peel.

2 Make the marinade by combining the dark soy sauce and cornstarch in a bowl. Add the beef and stir to coat. Let stand for 10 minutes.

3 Make the sauce by combining the chicken broth, orange juice, and soy sauce in a bowl.

4 Place a wok over high heat until hot. Add the oil, swirling to coat the sides. Add the garlic; cook, stirring, until fragrant, about 10 seconds. Add the beef and stir-fry until barely pink, about 1 minute. Add the tangerine peel; stir-fry for an additional 1 minute. Remove the beef from the wok.

5 Add the sauce to the wok; bring to a boil. Add the ginger and the cornstarch solution and cook, stirring, until the sauce boils and thickens. Return the beef to the wok; add the oranges and stir to coat well.

Tip: Dried tangerine peel is available in plastic packages in the Asian section of supermarkets. If you live near a store with a well-stocked bulk section, you might find some there, too. Dried orange peel makes a good substitute if you can't find tangerine. Soak dried tangerine peel before using and scrape away the bitter white pith on the peel's underside with a knife. Store the dried peels in a jar with a tightly fitting lid or in a zippered bag in a cool, dry place for up to several months.

Remember: This is one recipe in which fresh is not necessarily best: Definitely use canned mandarin orange segments here. Fresh ones contain active bromelin, an enzyme that breaks down the naturally occurring gelatin in beef and gives it an unappetizing, mushy texture. The heat of the canning process effectively deactivates the enzyme, making canned mandarin segments a safer bet for perfectly textured tangerine beef.

Making the grade: Meat grading and the Chinese cook

Meat goes through obligatory inspection by the U.S. Department of Agriculture (USDA) before it's sold to consumers. Most meat packers also submit their product to voluntary grading. USDA graders base quality designations on the animal's age, degree of muscle marbling, texture, color, and appearance. Grades of Prime, Choice, or Select (there are actually eight grades, but these are the most common) are the result. But what does each grade really tell you about the meat on your plate? Here's a basic description of each:

✔ Prime meat is generally considered top of the line and is actually hard to find in supermarkets because most of it goes directly to restaurants. The grade indicates that the meat has an optimum balance of fat and lean, as evidenced by its even marbling. The result: a juicier, more flavorful, and tender cut of meat.

✔ Choice meats are the most common kind at grocery stores. Although it has less fat than Prime meat, a Choice cut is still a good option for diners who like their meats juicy and flavorful.

✔ Select grading is the government's answer to consumers' search for leaner meat. These cuts have considerably less fat and marbling than Choice or Prime and are good bets if you're on a lowfat or low-cholesterol diet. Just bear in mind that Select meats won't be as tender, flavorful, or juicy as the other grades.

Broccoli Beef

Even the most committed "broccoliphobe" will have a hard time resisting this popular restaurant dish. And because it's so easy to prepare, it makes a great quick and nutritious lunch when served over plain steamed rice. Try it — it'll make your mother proud.

Your mother will also be pleased to know that you're eating broccoli, which is good for you. It has fiber, vitamin C, beta carotene, and plenty of other nutritious compounds. But you may not know that by combining the vitamin C in the broccoli with the iron in the beef, you make the dish even more nutritious. It turns out that iron and vitamin C work "synergistically" with one another in the body, each one making it easier for the body to absorb and use the other. It's a perfect example of culinary cooperation.

Preparation time: *15 minutes*

Cooking time: *6 minutes*

Yield: *4 servings*

1 tablespoon soy sauce

1 tablespoon Chinese rice wine

2 teaspoons cornstarch

¾ pound tri-tip or flank steak, thinly sliced across the grain

2 tablespoons oyster-flavored sauce

1 tablespoon dark soy sauce

1 teaspoon sesame oil

2 tablespoons cooking oil

2 cloves garlic, thinly sliced

8 ounces broccoli florets

¾ cup chicken broth

1 Make the marinade by combining the soy sauce, rice wine, and cornstarch in a bowl. Add the beef and stir to coat. Let stand for 10 minutes. Make the sauce by combining the oyster-flavored sauce, dark soy sauce, and sesame oil in a bowl.

2 Place a wok over high heat until hot. Add the cooking oil, swirling to coat the sides. Add the garlic and cook, stirring, until fragrant, about 10 seconds. Add the beef; stir-fry until barely pink, about 1 minute. Add the sauce and cook for 1 minute. Remove the beef and place in the center of a serving plate.

3 Add the broccoli and chicken broth to the wok. Cook until the broccoli is tender-crisp, about 3 minutes. Place around the beef and serve.

Beef Steak Over Glass Noodles

The herbs and ingredients common to Southeast Asian cuisines such as Vietnamese easily spread across the borders and into the kitchens of southern China. As a result, mint — a favorite in Vietnamese kitchens — finds its way into many of the area's dishes. I incorporate some of this zesty herb into a recipe that pairs flank steak with glass noodles — also known as cellophane or bean thread noodles.

No matter what you call them, these noodles add a pleasingly pliant, smooth texture to the dish, setting up a nice contrast with the crunchy nuts and bright flavor notes of the mint. Quickly simmering the glassy noodles with chicken broth and soy sauce infuses them with an extra facet of flavor as well.

Preparation time: *25 minutes*

Cooking time: *8 minutes*

Yield: *4 to 6 servings*

1 tablespoon Chinese rice wine	*4 ounces bean thread noodles*
2 teaspoons dark soy sauce	*1 cup chicken broth*
2 teaspoons soy sauce	*1 tablespoon soy sauce*
2 teaspoons cornstarch	*1½ tablespoons cooking oil*
1 teaspoon chopped mint leaves	*¼ cup chopped toasted nuts (peanuts or walnuts)*
¼ teaspoon ground black pepper	
¼ teaspoon sugar	*1 teaspoon chopped mint leaves*
¾ pound flank steak, sliced into 3-inch pieces, ¼ inch thick	

1 Make the marinade by combining the rice wine, dark soy sauce, 2 teaspoons soy sauce, cornstarch, mint leaves, pepper, and sugar in a bowl. Add the beef and stir to coat. Let stand for 10 minutes.

2 Soak the noodles in warm water to soften, about 5 minutes.

3 Place a wok over high heat until hot. Add the chicken broth, 1 tablespoon soy sauce, and noodles; cook until soft, about 3 minutes. Place the noodles on a serving platter.

4 Return the wok to high heat. Add the cooking oil, swirling to coat the sides. Add the beef and stir-fry until no longer pink, about 1 minute on each side.

5 To serve, place the beef on top of the noodles. Garnish with the toasted nuts and mint.

Spicy Beef with Leeks

By this point, you probably have the impression that any Chinese cook who loves beef had better learn to love flank steak. Fortunately, that's not tough (nor is flank steak). After all, flank steak really is the perfect cut of beef for stir-fries. Slicing it across the grain — in other words, slicing perpendicular to the direction that the meat's fibers run — creates strips that remain moist and tender through the high temperatures and short cooking times characteristic of stir-frying.

I also give you the option of using tri-tip, another handy cut of beef for stir-fries. For the story behind this native Californian cut, see the sidebar "Getting tipped off on tri-tip," later in the chapter.

Preparation time: *15 minutes*

Cooking time: *About 9 minutes*

Yield: *4 servings*

2 tablespoons soy sauce	*2 tablespoons hoisin sauce*
1 tablespoon Chinese rice wine	*2 teaspoons chile garlic sauce*
1 tablespoon cornstarch	*1 teaspoon sesame oil*
¾ pound flank steak or tri-tip beef, cut into ½-inch cubes	*2 leeks, white parts only*
	3 tablespoons cooking oil
2 tablespoons Chinese black vinegar or balsamic vinegar	*4 to 6 small dried red chiles, torn in half*

1 Make the marinade by combining the soy sauce, rice wine, and cornstarch in a bowl. Add the beef and stir to coat. Let stand for 10 minutes.

2 Make the sauce by combining the vinegar, hoisin sauce, chile garlic sauce, and sesame oil in a bowl.

3 Wash the leeks well. Cut them in half lengthwise and then into 1-inch pieces.

4 Place a wok over high heat until hot. Add 1½ tablespoons of the cooking oil, swirling to coat the sides. Add the chiles and stir-fry until fragrant, about 1 minute. Add the beef and stir-fry until no longer pink, 1 to 2 minutes. Remove the beef from the wok.

5 Return the wok to high heat until hot. Add the remaining 1½ tablespoons oil, swirling to coat the sides. Add the leeks and stir-fry until slightly softened, about 3 minutes. Add the sauce; bring it to a boil and cook until the sauce reduces slightly. Return the beef to the wok and mix well.

Variation: I add a spicy kick to this recipe with the inclusion of dried red chiles. But if you'd like a little less heat, reduce the amount according to your tongue's tolerance, or omit the chiles entirely.

Tip: When stir-frying the leeks, you may want to add a couple tablespoons of chicken broth to the wok. This extra bit of moisture lets the leeks steam a little, releasing their juices and cooking them down to a moist, tender texture. Another leek hint: Clean them thoroughly, rinsing between the leek's layers with plenty of running water. These vegetables are notorious for harboring sand and grit, and only by cleaning deeply within their "leaves" can you make sure that the sand ends up in the sink and not in the serving dish.

An appeal to the senses: Dried tangerine peel

Sichuan's spice box is packed with more than just chile peppers and Sichuan peppercorns. Plenty of warm — rather than hot — spices and seasonings round out the flavorful tapestry of the region's cuisine. One such milder Sichuan seasoning is dried tangerine peel.

It may not be too pretty to look at — it's a gnarled, brittle, rusty orange-colored peel. But when soaked, rid of its bitter white pith (see the tip with the Tangerine Beef recipe in this chapter), and added to braised dishes, stews, and sauces, it releases a warm, aromatic citrus fragrance that you may not be able to put your finger on. Believe me, that mysterious flavor is all in the peel.

Although dried orange peel makes a decent substitute for tangerine, if you can't find either, why not dry your own? Next time you eat a tangerine (or an orange), save the peel, cut it into smaller pieces, scrape away as much white underside as you can, and lay flat on a tray. Leave the tray out to sun- or air-dry for a few days or until the pieces have dried and toughened to a leathery texture. (Cover with a thin, breathable towel to keep bugs and dirt away, if you wish.) Then store the pieces in an airtight jar or zippered bag.

Beef Stew

Every culture has its cold-weather comfort foods, and on a winter day in China, a big, comforting bowl of Chinese beef stew like this can come to the rescue. Serve it over rice or, better yet, given its hearty leanings, over some filling noodles that beg to be slurped and twirled with the aromatic broth.

Don't let the long cooking time fool you. This is really an easy dish to make. There's very little prep work involved: some cutting of vegetables, crushing of ginger and garlic, and cubing of beef is about it. But you can even eliminate that last step by having the butcher cut cubes of stew beef for you. Because most of the approximately 1-hour-and-45-minute cooking time is hands-off, keep your hands off and relax as the stew's comforting fragrance and warmth fill your kitchen.

The long, slow cooking makes the beef falling-apart tender, and the addition of daikon, potatoes, and carrots adds a healthful burst of color. (To find out how to roll cut these vegetables, turn to Chapter 5.) It's like a heating blanket for your insides.

Preparation time: *18 minutes*

Cooking time: *1 hour and 45 minutes*

Yield: *4 servings*

1 pound boneless beef chuck, cut into 1-inch cubes

2½ cups chicken broth

3 tablespoons dark soy sauce

1 tablespoon sugar

1 piece dried tangerine peel (about 2-inch square)

1 whole star anise

8 thin slices ginger, lightly crushed

2 cloves garlic, lightly crushed

1½ cups roll-cut daikon

1 cup roll-cut russet potatoes

1 cup roll-cut carrots

1 tablespoon cornstarch dissolved in 2 tablespoons water

1 Place the beef in a 3-quart pan. Add the chicken broth and the dark soy sauce, sugar, tangerine peel, anise, ginger, and garlic; bring to a boil. Reduce the heat to low, cover, and simmer for 1 hour.

2 Add the daikon, potato, and carrots, stirring to coat the vegetables with the pan juices. Cover and simmer until the meat and vegetables are tender when pierced, 25 to 30 minutes. Add the cornstarch solution and cook until the sauce boils and thickens.

Tip: Normally, you'd want to soak the dried tangerine peel to soften it before adding it to a dish. But because the dried peel in this recipe softens and releases its fragrance and flavor as it simmers with the stew, you can skip the presoaking.

Tip: If the stew has too much liquid for your liking, even after it's simmered for the specified time, drain off enough to achieve the consistency you want and freeze that liquid for use in your next beef stew. As you're preparing Stew Number 2 (or Number 3, Number 4, and so on), defrost the liquid in the refrigerator, bring to a boil in a saucepan, and add a solution of equal parts cornstarch and water. Boil and stir until slightly thickened and then stir it into your newly developing stew.

Getting tipped off on tri-tip

If you have to consult a guide to meat butchery to figure out what a tri-tip is, you're probably not a Californian. Wildly popular in California's kitchens, restaurants, and backyard barbecues, tri-tip remains a relatively unheard-of cut of beef in some other North American locations. But after one bite of a moist, flavorful grilled or roasted tri-tip, you'll be convinced why its star is on the rise.

Tri-tip is actually a large, boneless, triangular hunk of meat trimmed from the tip of the bottom sirloin. For a long time, butchers considered it scrap and relegated it to either hamburger or stew-meat duty, or simply threw it away altogether.

But as the story goes, during the 1950s, a butcher in a town on California's central coast wound up with more tri-tip than he needed. Creative butcher that he was, he experimented with different seasoning and cooking combinations that he hoped would turn a cut with a shoe-leather reputation into something worth holding onto.

Surprisingly enough, a short stint on a rotisserie grill yielded a tri-tip that wasn't only flavorful but also was so moist and tender that you didn't have to chew it "till the cows came home." Many credit the thick layer of fat that lies along one side of the tri-tip for holding in the juices and keeping the meat well lubricated, so to speak.

After this discovery, the secret of tri-tip didn't even make it to other parts of California for a while. But now California's markets sell it proudly, and during barbecue season, grill aficionados practically make a run on the meat counters for it. Restaurants also enjoy serving it, particularly when they can feature it in two-fisted tri-tip sandwiches and in hearty Western roasts. It's a versatile, delicious meat, and if you're lucky, you'll soon find it in your supermarket's meat counter, too.

Uncle Philip's Beef Tri-Tip

My neighbor, Uncle Philip (whose wife, Auntie Jessica, created the chicken wing recipe in Chapter 8), gave me this fabulously easy dish that takes next to no time to put together. Serve it hot out of the broiler or stash it in the refrigerator overnight for great tri-tip sandwiches the following day. It's a real winner at parties, too — as Uncle Philip should know, because he sure has a lot of them. If the weather permits and you have access to a grill, cook the marinated tri-tip that way. It's the perfect addition to any backyard barbecue.

Preparation time: *25 minutes, plus up to 4 hours of marinating time*

Cooking time: *20 minutes*

Yield: *4 to 6 servings*

2 pounds beef tri-tip	*1 cup chopped cilantro*
1½ cups dry red wine	*¼ cup minced ginger*
¼ cup soy sauce	*3 tablespoons minced garlic*
2 tablespoons dark soy sauce	*½ head small iceberg lettuce, julienned*
2 tablespoons sugar	

1 Place the beef in a resealable plastic bag. Make the marinade by combining the wine, soy sauce, dark soy sauce, sugar, cilantro, ginger, and garlic in a bowl. Pour the marinade over the beef; seal the bag. Place in the refrigerator for 4 hours or overnight, turning the bag occasionally.

2 Lift the meat from the marinade and place it on a rack in a foil-lined pan about 6 inches away from the broiler. Broil the tri-tip for 8 to 10 minutes on each side. Remove from the oven and let the tri-tip rest for up to 20 minutes before carving.

3 Serve it over a bed of lettuce.

Tip: This marinade is so flavorful that it'd be a shame to toss it out after it's done its job on the tri-tip. To make a delicious au jus, simply pour the marinade into a saucepan and bring it to a boil. Simmer for about 5 minutes to develop the flavor's richness and to make the marinade safe to serve as a sauce, and it's ready.

On the Lamb

Lamb has many more fans in the West than in China, where diners deem its flavor too strong and its texture too fibrous for their sensitive palates. Many actually find lamb's gamey scent and toughness even more objectionable than beef's. Lamb was introduced into the Chinese diet via the Mongolian and Muslim connection from the North and West. Even today, the average Chinese in southern China isn't completely warmed up to it, and restaurants serve it only as something of a novelty, almost exclusively in the appropriately named Mongolian hotpot (see the recipe in this section).

Chinese cooks most often slice lamb thinly or braise it with flavorings strong enough to stand up to its aroma, helping make the meat more acceptable to Chinese tastes and more amenable to Chinese recipes. Pairing lamb with aromatic vegetables such as garlic and onions and seasonings including ginger and bean paste — ingredients common to northern and Beijing-style dishes — usually does the trick. Clever Chinese chefs also use wine and pungent Chinese five-spice powder (see Chapter 4) to disguise the strong aroma. When all else fails, you can always use the nose clamp!

I admit that I'm a latecomer to the fan club for lamb, but I've been making up for lost time ever since. I've developed recipes that showcase the tender and subtly flavored lamb available in the West. The leg and loin are great for cutting into chunks that you can braise or red-cook, as well as for slicing into thin strips ideal for Mongolian hotpot. Although the recipes here still capitalize on the advantages of coupling lamb with onions and other aromatic vegetables, the pairings serve less to cover up undesirable flavors than to enhance tasty ones.

Mongolian Lamb in Hotpot

What a great party dish this makes. Fondue parties may have had their heyday during the '70s, but if I had my way, a wave of Mongolian hotpot parties would sweep the nation right now.

The concept really is similar to fondue (or is fondue similar to Mongolian hotpot?): Just dip a variety of ingredients into boiling, flavored broth, let them cook for a few seconds, and then fish them out with a little basketlike strainer instead of those fondue forks that always seem to drop whatever you grab with them. (See the typical set-up for Mongolian hotpot in Figure 12-2.) Enjoy with a dipping sauce; the All-Purpose Dipping Sauce in Chapter 7 works well, and if you'd like something thicker, sesame seed paste is a traditional favorite.

Like stone soup, Mongolian hotpot gets better the more you add to it. Each ingredient lends its own distinct flavor to the broth, making it more complex as the meal goes on.

Preparation time: 45 minutes

Cooking time: Time you need to finish cooking and eating at the table at your leisure

Yield: 4 to 6 servings

8 cups chicken broth	¾ pound tender boneless lamb
2 slices ginger, lightly crushed	1 pound mixed leafy green vegetables, such as spinach and napa cabbage, cut into bite-size pieces
1 stalk green onion, cut into 1½-inch pieces	
4 ounces dried bean thread noodles	1 package (16 ounces) soft tofu, drained and cut into 1-inch cubes

1 Place the broth, ginger, and the green onions in a large pot; bring to a boil. Reduce the heat, cover, and simmer for 30 minutes. Discard the ginger.

2 Soak the noodles in warm water to cover until softened, about 5 minutes; drain. Cut the noodles into 4-inch lengths.

3 Cut the lamb into thin slices. Arrange the noodles, lamb, vegetables, and tofu attractively on a large platter. Cover and chill until ready to cook.

4 Reheat the broth to simmering. Set a Mongolian hotpot or an electric wok in the center of a table. Pour 6 cups of the broth into a hotpot and adjust the heat so that the broth simmers gently. Each diner cooks his or her choice of the ingredients in the broth and seasons it with a dipping sauce. Add more of the broth as you go along.

TRADITIONAL TABLE SETTING FOR MONGOLIAN HOTPOT

RAW EGGS

GREEN ONION

BEAN THREAD NOODLES

CILANTRO

SAUCE

LAMB

BEAN SPROUTS

TOFU PUFFS

Figure 12-2:
A traditional set-up for Mongolian hotpot.

SAUCE

GREENS

Tip: A successful Mongolian Lamb in Hotpot depends on having paper-thin slices of tender lamb that cook quickly and effortlessly in the simmering broth. Make those slices so thin that you can read this recipe right through by slightly freezing the lamb before you slice it. Pop the lamb into the freezer until it's firm but still yields to a knife. This solid texture makes obtaining precise, thin slices more manageable than it would be with warm meat, which is inevitably too soft and elastic.

Regional Note: This dish's northern origin makes lamb an obvious part of Mongolian hotpot meals. But the boiling broth does just as good a job of cooking thin slices of pork and beef, and even shellfish. In fact, as the dish traveled south and gained popularity in seafood-loving regions such as Guangzhou, it became more and more common to see shrimp in a Mongolian hotpot along with lamb and other regulars. If you have a soft spot for seafood — or pork or beef — include it in your own hotpot spread.

Tip: What can you do if you don't have a Mongolian hotpot, as show in Figure 12-2? Go ahead and make it all the same, but substitute an electric wok that you can use table-side, or even a portable gas stove on which you can place a large pot with low enough sides to allow diners easy access to its contents.

Lamb with Green Onions

This recipe pairs lamb with a flavorful marinade of rice wine and soy, as well as with pungent garlic and green onions — all of which show off the lamb's flavor to its best advantage. The smoky-sweet flavor of the hoisin sauce also helps make this dish a hit.

Preparation time: *15 minutes*

Cooking time: *15 minutes*

Yield: *4 servings*

1 tablespoon soy sauce	*2 tablespoons hoisin sauce*
1 tablespoon Chinese rice wine	*2 tablespoons cooking oil*
2 teaspoons cornstarch	*1 tablespoon minced garlic*
¾ pound boneless lamb (leg or loin), cut into thin slices across the grain	*¾ cup julienned red bell pepper*
	4 green onions, cut into 1½-inch pieces
2 tablespoons chicken broth	

1 Make the marinade by combining the soy sauce, rice wine, and cornstarch in a bowl. Add the meat to the marinade; stir to coat. Let stand for 10 minutes.

2 Make the sauce by combining the chicken broth and hoisin sauce in a small bowl.

3 Place a wok over high heat until hot. Add the oil, swirling to coat the sides. Add the garlic and cook, stirring, until fragrant, about 10 seconds. Add the lamb and stir-fry until barely pink, 2 to 3 minutes. Add the red pepper and cook for 1 minute.

4 Add the green onions; stir-fry for 1 minute. Add the sauce and bring to a boil; cook until the sauce reduces slightly.

Chapter 13

Healthy Tofu and Eggscellent Ideas

In This Chapter

▶ Working wonders with tofu

▶ Eating eggs at meals other than breakfast

Recipes in This Chapter

▶ Tofu with Spicy Tomato Sauce

▶ Tofu with Ham and Napa Cabbage

▶ Tofu with Shrimp

▶ Monk's Choice Tofu

▶ Ma Po Tofu

▶ Tofu and Spinach

▶ Tofu Puffs with Three-Color Vegetables

▶ Tofu with Mushrooms and Cashews

▶ Scrambled Eggs with Crabmeat

▶ Tomato Eggs

▶ Steamed Eggs

▶ Egg Fu Young

▶ Tea-Flavored Eggs

Chinese cooking at times makes strange bedfellows. Consider the frequent coupling in Chinese cuisine of eggs and tofu. Now what do eggs — poultry products — have to do with tofu, a soybean derivative? Aside from being potent sources of non-meat protein, both are true "culinary chameleons" in the Chinese kitchen. Tofu and eggs don't have assertive tastes or textures of their own, so both can assume the many different forms and flavors called for by different recipes. Such subtlety and variety are the strong suits of eggs and tofu. Because China hasn't always been a land of plenty, securing reliable and inexpensive protein sources, especially ones that can imitate the foods they're meant to replace, has been a lifesaver for millions.

In the case of tofu (also known as bean curd), this classic Asian ingredient has gained popularity the world over despite its arguably bland flavor, texture, and shape. After trying a few inventive dishes made with this multifaceted product, skeptical Westerners are quickly convinced that you can't judge this book by its nondescript cover. Tofu agrees with almost any cooking method: The Chinese steam it, chill it, braise it, stir-fry, and deep-fry it. They scoop out its center to make a pocket for a variety of savory fillings. I especially love tofu's uncanny ability to adopt the flavor of whatever sauce or ingredient it's served with. This makes tofu the perfect "cheat meat" and a favorite of many vegetarians and meat eaters (including yours truly) alike. But meat mimicry is only the tip of the iceberg when it comes to cooking tofu. As unassuming as it may seem, tofu is a true culinary powerhouse.

Eggs, like tofu, also make for easy shape shifting. In the West, we fry, scramble, hard-boil, poach, and bake them. Chinese chefs do all that and add a little steam power as well. They also whip them into rich sauces or stir them into soups to create gossamer egg threads. Really, what *can't* you do with eggs? The Chinese eat them throughout the whole day: as thin omelets sliced into stir-fries, as hearty egg pancakes topped with vegetables and sauce, mixed into noodle and wrapper doughs, and steeped whole in tea for a quick snack. Over the centuries, Chinese chefs have developed countless incredible uses for this egg-citing treat. No wonder all the hens in China looked so tired.

Taking a Look at Tofu

While tofu isn't exactly the cottage cheese curds Little Miss Muffet made famous, the two foods actually share some similarities, particularly in how they're made. Tofu making began as a cottage industry in China more than 2,000 years ago. Legend has it that someone "discovered" tofu when he or she (no one really knows) added a natural coagulant called *nigari* to flavor a batch of cooked soybean puree.

How tofu is made

Much of that "cottage" tradition has survived over the years. Today, towns big and small all over China all have their traditional tofu factories — usually just the part of the tofu maker's house where the trays, vats, and other tofu-making equipment are stored. Of course, you'll also find many modernized industrial manufacturing plants. After all, it takes a lot of soy to cater to China's market of a billion-plus tofu fanatics!

In truth, the entire tofu-making process is pretty simple — that is, if you have the right equipment and a steady supply of gypsum (a calcium-containing mineral and important tofu-making ingredient). But why sweat it when virtually every supermarket nowadays carries a fresh supply of tofu, nicely prepared and neatly packaged for your convenience? Now, for the true tofu adventurers — or those who happen to have some extra gypsum lying around — here's a tofu-production primer:

1. **The dried soybeans are soaked in water overnight and drained.**

2. **The beans are ground to a powder while a little boiling water is poured over them.**

   This process produces a mash with the texture of mashed potatoes.

3. **In order to denature a soybean enzyme that, in its native form, makes the soy protein indigestible, the soybean mash is simmered in water for about 10 minutes.**

4. **The slurry is filtered, separating its liquid "whey" — packaged and sold as soymilk — from the soy pulp solids, which themselves go into making soy flour, animal feed, and even fertilizer.**

5. **To coagulate the liquid soymilk, gypsum salt, a hydrated form of calcium sulfate mined for thousands of years in Chinese mountain quarries, is added.**

   This process creates curds that float to the liquid's surface, leaving the clear whey behind.

6. **The curds are harvested from the whey and placed in perforated molds lined with cheesecloth for further draining.**

7. **After the molds are covered and weighted, the curds rest for several hours or until enough whey has drained to leave a block with a dense, cheeselike texture whose firmness varies depending on how much whey has drained.**

8. **The manufacturers keep the blocks of tofu but pour the leftover whey into the pig trough or petunia bed.**

   Remember, nothing goes to waste.

These steps provide a nutshell description of how to make firmer varieties of tofu. Soft tofu is manufactured in an entirely different process. It isn't pressed during production, the liquid whey is mixed with coagulant, and the mixture is poured into tubs until set to a custardy and silky consistency.

Tofu texture variations

Tofu textures run the gamut from silken-soft and creamy to as solid as hard cheese. And although I give you a brief introduction to the different types in Chapter 4, I examine them in more depth here so you'll know when to use which. Check out the illustrations of the different types of tofu in Figure 13-1. Here's a list of the varieties of tofu:

Figure 13-1: Some examples of the different types of tofu, from regular tofu to pressed blocks and fried puffs.

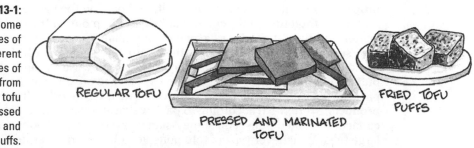

REGULAR TOFU

PRESSED AND MARINATED TOFU

FRIED TOFU PUFFS

- **Soft tofu**, also known as silken or silken-style tofu, has a smooth, delicate texture and works best in gently simmered soups and desserts, where it plays a role similar to that of custard. I even like to puree it into sauces and dressings to add body and texture. But because of its delicacy, it doesn't hold its shape in recipes that require a lot of stirring or high temperatures. In other words, it isn't amenable to stir-frying, long braising, or deep-frying. But if you need a tofu that adds puddinglike creaminess to a dish, soft tofu is your best choice.

- **Regular and firm tofu** both have dense structures and slightly spongy interiors. As the name implies, firm tofu is denser and more solid than regular. Beware, however, that the textural difference between the two types can be hazy. One brand's "regular" could be firmer than the next brand's "firm." (Try a few brands and settle on the one you like most.) Both regular and firm work well in high heat — stir-frying, braising, and deep-frying — so you can use them interchangeably. Should you need a firmer tofu than the one you've chosen, just drain it a little bit more in your own kitchen. Follow the directions in the sidebar "Down the drain: Draining tofu yourself" in this chapter.

- **Pressed tofu** is drained and pressed for a very long time to make it even firmer and drier than "firm." It's very different from the previously mentioned type of tofu. Whereas soft tofu is similar to custard, and firm and regular varieties resemble a firm cream cheese, pressed tofu has a texture most like an aged Swiss. The extensive loss of whey gives it a compact, flattened appearance. You can buy it in flat, square cakes or 1-inch-thick bricks. It has a very dense internal structure that some describe as chewy and meatlike. This texture makes pressed tofu a great ingredient in vegetarian dishes. Its firmness lets it stand up to just about any cooking method without losing its shape or texture. Try the types that are marinated with different seasonings such as soy sauce, Chinese five-spice powder, or sesame oil — you can distinguish these from plain ones by their darkly colored surfaces or, of course, by reading their labels. Try marinating some pressed tofu in your own favorite spice mixture for extra flavor. Just remember to place any unused portion of pressed tofu in a zippered plastic bag and refrigerate it for up to a week.

- **Fried tofu puffs** really illustrate this deceptively simple soy ingredient's versatility. Deep-frying makes the tofu cubes lightly crispy and golden brown on the outside, and spongy, soft, and pale on the inside. For a fun way to try fried tofu puffs, cut off one edge, scoop out a little of the center, and then stuff with a savory shrimp filling or some rice mixed with sesame seeds. Before sliding them into soups and noodle dishes or adding them whole to stews and claypots, you may want to blanch the puffs in boiling water to rid of any excess surface oil. You can find plastic packages of tofu puffs in refrigerator cases next to the other fresh tofu products; store them according to package directions. You can also find canned, seasoned puffs, and some Asian markets even sell loose puffs in large tubs. Whichever type of tofu puffs you choose, refrigerate them in tightly sealed containers for up to a week — if you don't eat them before then. They also freeze well for a few months.

Frozen and fermented tofu?

Considering that the entire tofu-making process is itself a form of preservation, isn't it kind of redundant to preserve the curds even more by freezing or fermenting them? Not at all. Freezing and fermenting fresh tofu actually add a whole new flavor and textural wrinkle to it, revealing yet another of its many "faces." Unlike cheesy-textured fresh tofu, frozen tofu is more rubbery, porous and similar in texture to ground beef, believe it or not. It also changes from a pearly white color to creamy beige. Most frozen tofus on the market in China have been frozen via industrial methods, but you can easily freeze your own tofu at home. Home freezing doesn't produce exactly the same results, but it's a great approximation. Just drain firm or regular tofu — both work best for freezing — according to the instructions found in the sidebar "Down the drain: Draining tofu yourself," and put it in the freezer until it's solid. Before you use the tofu, you'll have to thaw and rehydrate it, which you can do by dousing it with boiling water and letting it "steep" for 5 to 10 minutes until defrosted. Wring out the tofu as you would a sponge and proceed with your recipe.

As for fermented tofu, it comes in jars and has a soft, smooth, custardy texture and a mildly pungent, winey aroma. Generally, you'll find it in white and red varieties. The white kind gets its flavor from sesame oil, rice wine, and maybe a little chile. Red fermented tofu is flavored with rice wine, chile, red rice, and sometimes rose essence; its red color comes from oil infused with the brick-red seeds of the annatto tree. Because the white variety is a bit saltier, it boosts the flavor of leafy greens and works well as a side dish. The red variety works well in stews and claypot dishes, especially those with chicken, pork, or duck. Both kinds are pretty strongly flavored, so remember to use them sparingly. Although fermented tofu may not be too easy to find in your neighborhood supermarket, it's a common item on the shelves of a Chinese grocery store.

Tofu preparations

I love tofu because of its ease of preparation. In fact, you can eat it straight from the package. This feature opens tofu up to a wide worlds of salads, cold appetizers, and no-cook wonders. I love experiencing the textures of the different types of tofu, and I really appreciate its subtle flavor. Try munching on marinated pressed tofu as a healthy, protein-packed snack, and I bet you'll soon find it tough to get through a tofu recipe without sampling at least half of what's supposed to go into the dish.

As much as I like it cold, I am even more impressed by the complete metamorphosis tofu gets from a quick turn in a wok, or how slow simmering in broth can turn it into a totally different treat. I'm sure that the crispy, light-as-air feel of a fried tofu puff or the contrast between the slightly caramelized bottom and still-soft center of a stir-fried chunk will tempt you just as much as it does me. So give the following recipes a try, and in no time, you'll join ranks with me in the army of a billion-plus tofu fanatics.

Tofu with Spicy Tomato Sauce

With zucchini, tomatoes, and garlic, this recipe comes close to passing for an Italian one. But the tofu, oyster-flavored sauce, chile garlic sauce, and ginger bring it securely back within the ranks of Chinese cuisine. Personally, I think the combination of ingredients makes for a delicious blending of flavors.

Preparation time: 20 minutes

Cooking time: 6 minutes

Yield: 4 to 6 servings

⅓ cup chicken broth

¼ cup ketchup

1 tablespoon oyster-flavored sauce

1 teaspoon chile garlic sauce

1 tablespoon cooking oil

1 teaspoon minced garlic

1 teaspoon minced ginger

1 small zucchini, cut in half lengthwise and then roll cut

2 small tomatoes, cut into ¾-inch cubes

1 package (16 ounces) regular tofu, drained and cut into ½-inch cubes

1 Make the sauce by combining the chicken broth, ketchup, oyster-flavored sauce, and chile garlic sauce in a bowl.

2 Place a wok over high heat until hot. Add the oil, swirling to coat the sides. Add the garlic and ginger; cook, stirring, until fragrant, about 10 seconds. Add the zucchini and tomatoes; stir-fry until the zucchini is tender-crisp, about 1 minute.

3 Reduce the heat to medium. Add the tofu and sauce; cover and bring to a boil for 30 seconds. Uncover and continue to cook until the sauce reduces slightly.

Tip: Letting the tofu drain on paper towels before you add it to a recipe is always a good idea. No matter how well the manufacturer drained it, you almost always have whey left over that you don't want diluting your dish. In fact, letting it drain overnight on paper towels in the refrigerator gives you the best results. For more heavy-duty draining needs — for example, when the manufacturer's idea of "firm" is your idea of "soft" — follow the draining procedures in the sidebar "Down the drain: Draining tofu yourself."

Tip: Tofu cooking requires a delicate touch — stir too vigorously, and you'll wind up with a bunch of misshapen pieces rather than individual tofu cubes. To keep your tofu in good shape, remember one magic word: toss. Instead of stirring the tofu itself, shake and toss the wok or pan, tipping the tofu toward the opposite edge of the wok and then gently flipping the contents back toward yourself. Be careful not to flip them onto yourself or the stove. This is the same technique known to expert pancake flippers, so if you have that skill down, you should have no trouble stir-frying tofu to perfection. But if you're a little hesitant to flip your way to perfect tofu, stirring gently with a pair of chopsticks gets you there just the same, albeit via a different route.

Tofu with Ham and Napa Cabbage

Ham, dried shrimp, and tofu: These three excellent protein sources come together in this healthful dish. And in addition to being good for you, the ingredients pack plenty of savory flavor and balanced texture — from the chewy dried shrimp (see the sidebar "Little shrimp, big flavor," later in this chapter) to the slightly yielding tofu.

Preparation time: *30 minutes*

Cooking time: *8 minutes*

Yield: *4 servings*

1 tablespoon dried shrimp

1 tablespoon cooking oil

4 cloves garlic, lightly crushed

2 tablespoons julienned Virginia ham

1 pound napa cabbage, cut into bite-sized pieces

3 tablespoons chicken broth

⅛ teaspoon salt

⅛ teaspoon white pepper

1 package (16 ounces) firm tofu, drained and cut into ½-inch cubes

1 teaspoon cornstarch dissolved in 1 tablespoon water

1 Soak the dried shrimp in warm water until softened, about 15 minutes; drain and coarsely chop.

2 Place a wok over medium heat until hot. Add the oil, swirling to coat the sides. Add the garlic and cook, stirring, until fragrant, about 10 seconds.

3 Add the shrimp and cook for 1 minute. Add the ham and napa cabbage; stir-fry for 1 minute. Cover and cook for an additional 2 minutes.

4 Add the chicken broth, salt, and white pepper; bring to a boil. Add the tofu and cook for about 30 seconds. Add the cornstarch solution and cook, stirring, until the sauce boils and thickens.

Tofu with Shrimp

The color contrast of the pink shrimp and green peas makes this dish a feast for the eyes as well as for the taste buds. And the delicious combination of shrimp and tofu proves that tofu deserves a spot in meat eaters' kitchens, too. Hey, there's enough tofu out there for all of us to share!

Preparation time: *10 minutes*

Cooking time: *7 minutes*

Yield: *4 servings*

6 ounces medium raw shrimp, shelled and deveined

1 teaspoon cornstarch

⅓ cup chicken broth

1 tablespoon Chinese rice wine

2 teaspoons chile garlic sauce

1½ teaspoons hoisin sauce

1 teaspoon sesame oil

1 tablespoon cooking oil

4 pieces thinly sliced ginger

½ cup frozen peas, thawed

1 package (16 ounces) firm tofu, drained and cut into ½-inch cubes

1 teaspoon cornstarch dissolved in 2 teaspoons water

1 Combine the shrimp and cornstarch in a bowl; toss to coat. Let stand for 10 minutes.

2 Make the sauce by combining the chicken broth, rice wine, chile garlic sauce, hoisin sauce, and sesame oil in a bowl.

3 Place a wok over high heat until hot. Add the cooking oil, swirling to coat the sides. Add the ginger and cook, stirring, until fragrant, about 10 seconds. Add the shrimp and stir-fry until the shrimp turn slightly pink, about 30 seconds. Add the peas and stir-fry for an additional 1 minute.

4 Add the tofu and toss gently for 1 minute. Add the sauce; bring it to a boil. Add the cornstarch solution and cook, stirring, until the sauce boils and thickens.

Remember: When shopping for tofu — or any ingredient, for that matter — remember this important rule: It should look clean and smell fresh when you buy it. Although you can't smell tofu that's packaged in tightly sealed containers, you can at least give it a good look-see. Dirty gray or brown tofu is a no-no, unless of course, it's brown because it's marinated pressed tofu. If you buy bulk tofu from tubs of water, a sour smell coming from those tubs is a sure sign of contamination. Shop elsewhere. After you've refrigerated your tofu, remember to change the water in which you store it (see Chapter 4 for tofu storage recommendations). The fresher the water, the longer the tofu remains fresh itself.

Down the drain: Draining tofu yourself

Tofu manufacturers drain most of the whey from firm and regular tofu, but the degree of draining varies from brand to brand. Furthermore, the need for different degrees of draining varies with different tofu recipes. Now a quick take-home tofu lesson: You can drain it more at home if the cube that you've bought is too soft for its recipe. Tofu aficionados all have their own favorite draining methods, but here's my pick for the easiest way to do it:

1. Cut the block of tofu in half horizontally as you would a roll for a sandwich (a technique known as parallel cutting, which I describe in Chapter 5), making two slabs, each about 1 inch thick.

2. Wrap these pieces in paper towels or a lint-free kitchen towel, or you can even sandwich them between two double layers of coffee filters.

3. Weight the wrapped blocks with a flat object such as a coffee can, frying pan, or cutting board placed on top and let them sit for 30 minutes to a couple hours. The countertop is a fine spot for shorter draining times, but if you plan to keep your tofu under wraps for a while, put the weighted pieces in the refrigerator. Periodically check on the texture of tofu and, when it reaches the firmness you need, unwrap it and continue with the recipe.

Little shrimp, big flavor

What do you get when you preserve tiny shrimp in brine and then dry them until they become pungent and slightly chewy? Dried shrimp, that's what. You may have seen small plastic bags of these curled, slightly shriveled, and bright coral shrimp in the Asian or Latino section of your supermarket.

Chinese cooks love using dried shrimp because of the unique flavor — fresh shrimp simply can't compare — that they give to soups, dumplings, and rice dishes, among others. They're great choose-your-own ingredients for *any* fried rice creation.

Soak them until softened before adding to braised and stir-fried dishes. When used in soups, they need no presoaking. Their flavor may seem arresting at first, but you'll quickly develop a liking for that distinctive texture and sharp, salty taste — so much so that you may end up snacking on them as I do.

Choose packages with bright, uniformly sized, coral-colored shrimp. Avoid flaky, spotted, gray, or pale shrimp because those characteristics are signs of age and poor flavor. Once you open the package, store the remaining dried shrimp in a tightly sealed container in a cool, dry place for up to several months.

Monk's Choice Tofu

This recipe, which wins favor with Buddhist monks, features chewy bean thread noodles and dried mushrooms mingled with puffy fried tofu. The monks enjoy it so much not only because it's scrumptious but also because, as vegetarians, they rely on tofu as a source of protein.

Now, I've spent some time with monks during my travels in Asia, and I can tell you that "living like a monk" doesn't necessarily mean leading a spartan life of sacrifice — these monks often eat better than I do, with or without meat! I've gleaned some of my most valuable cooking lessons from the wisdom of Buddhist monks.

Preparation time: *30 minutes*

Cooking time: *About 18 minutes*

Yield: *4 servings*

1 ounce dried bean thread noodles	*Cooking oil for deep-frying*
6 dried black mushrooms	*1 package (16 ounces) firm tofu, drained, dried well, and cut into triangles*
4 dried cloud ears (see Chapter 4)	
¾ cup chicken broth	*2 teaspoons minced garlic*
2 tablespoons oyster-flavored sauce	*½ cup thinly sliced carrots*
1 tablespoon Chinese rice wine	*1 whole baby bok choy, quartered lengthwise*
1 teaspoon sesame oil	

1 In separate bowls, soak the noodles, mushrooms, and cloud ears in warm water to cover until softened, about 5 minutes for the noodles and 20 minutes for the mushrooms and cloud ears; drain. Leave the noodles long. Discard the mushroom stems and cut the caps in half. Cut the cloud ears into ½-inch pieces.

2 Make the sauce by combining the chicken broth, oyster-flavored sauce, rice wine, and sesame oil in a bowl.

3 In a wok, heat the oil for deep-frying to 360°. Deep-fry the tofu, a few pieces at a time, turning occasionally, until golden brown, about 2 minutes on each side. Remove with a slotted spoon; drain on paper towels.

4 Place a wok over high heat until hot. Add 1 tablespoon of the cooking oil, swirling to coat the sides. Add the garlic and cook, stirring, until fragrant, about 10 seconds. Add the mushrooms, cloud ears, and carrots; stir-fry for 1 minute. Add the sauce and bring it to a boil.

5 Return the tofu to the wok; add the baby bok choy and the noodles. Reduce the heat, and cook, stirring occasionally, until the baby bok choy is tender-crisp and the noodles absorb most of the liquid, about 3 minutes.

Tip: To cut the tofu into triangles, first cut the block into 12 equally sized pieces and then cut each piece diagonally into triangles.

Tip: If your market sells tofu in a tub of water, and you can't tell whether the tofu got firm or soft, go ahead and give the cubes a quick but gentle poke. A smooth surface and easily yielding response tell you that you're dealing with soft, whereas firm tofu provides your finger with some resistance. If you don't feel comfortable with the touch method — or if other shoppers are giving you questioning stares — just look closely at the surface of the cubes: Soft tofu looks very smooth and shiny, while regular and firm varieties have woven textures on their outer surfaces from the pressing cloths; regular and firm also look a little more grainy on their cut surfaces.

Tofu to your health

As much as we'd like one, there is simply no one perfect food. But the general health profile of the Chinese population hints that if there were such a thing, it just may be tofu. At times of famine and malnutrition in China, soy products, including tofu, came to the rescue. And it seems that each new scientific finding adds another gold star to tofu's impressive resume of health benefits.

Modern nutritional analysis shows that the high-quality vegetable protein in soy products such as tofu contains all the amino acids needed to make it a "complete" protein. Tofu is also relatively high in calcium, which has helped maintain strong bones in China, an especially important benefit because milk isn't a popular beverage among the Chinese. Tofu and soymilk are also fortifying foods for young, growing bodies. The easy digestibility of soymilk has made it popular with mothers in China and abroad — when you have an infant with a dairy allergy, having safe and nutritious soymilk as a dairy substitute can make the difference between an all-nighter by the crib and a good night's rest. And of course, tofu's low fat and sodium contents, not to mention its total lack of cholesterol, make it a favorite among those watching their weight as well as their hearts.

Beyond these well-established nutrition facts, researchers are beginning to discover plenty more good news about tofu and soy. Health professionals and scientists have long known that breast and prostate cancer rates are much lower in Asia than in the West. And although many factors may contribute to this phenomenon, a healthful vegetable-rich diet and a passion for soy products cannot be ignored. Medical investigators have found that some soy products contain estrogen-like compounds — *isoflavones* — which may possess cancer-fighting qualities. Research findings are so encouraging that doctors are looking into the compounds' possible benefits on lowering serum cholesterol levels and reducing heart disease and osteoporosis risk, too.

Researchers haven't yet fully figured out just what makes isoflavones so helpful in fighting disease, or how much soy that people need daily to enjoy the cancer-fighting benefits. But I wouldn't wait for a doctor's prescription before adding a healthy helping of soy to my diet, and neither should you.

Ma Po Tofu

It's story time! The name of this classic Sichuanese dish actually means "pockmarked grandmother's bean curd," which doesn't quite do its deliciously bold flavors justice. But according to legend, hundreds of years ago, a pockmarked grandmother in Sichuan was known for her generosity to travelers and townsfolk despite being very poor herself. She also ran a tofu stall where she served the only dish she could afford to make — a combination of tofu cakes, a little ground meat, and the local spices and seasonings.

Although her specialty had obviously humble origins, it was nothing to be ashamed of. Not only was her dish inexpensive and nutritious, but those who ate it thought it so unforgettable that Chinese cooks still make it centuries later, and it remains a regular item on Chinese restaurant menus today.

Preparation time: *15 minutes*

Cooking time: *5 minutes*

Yield: *4 servings*

6 ounces ground pork	*1 teaspoon sesame oil*
1 tablespoon oyster-flavored sauce	*2 tablespoons cooking oil*
½ cup chicken broth	*1 teaspoon minced garlic*
1 tablespoon soy sauce	*1 teaspoon minced ginger*
1 tablespoon white distilled vinegar	*1 package (16 ounces) soft tofu, drained and cut into ½-inch cubes*
2 teaspoons sugar	
1 teaspoon dried chile flakes	*1½ teaspoons cornstarch dissolved in 1 tablespoon water*

1 Combine the ground pork and oyster-flavored sauce in a bowl. Let stand 10 minutes.

2 Make the sauce by combining the chicken broth, soy sauce, vinegar, sugar, chile flakes, and sesame oil in a bowl.

3 Place a wok over high heat until hot. Add the cooking oil, swirling to coat the sides. Add the garlic and ginger; cook, stirring until fragrant, about 10 seconds. Add the pork and stir-fry until lightly browned and crumbly, about 2 minutes. Add the sauce and bring it to a boil. Reduce the heat to medium and cook for 2 minutes.

4 Add the tofu and bring to a boil. Cook for 1 minute. Add the cornstarch solution and cook, stirring, until the sauce boils and thickens.

Remember: Be gentle when draining soft tofu. You won't want to press it with a coffee can or cutting board as described in the draining instructions in the sidebar "Down the drain: Draining tofu yourself"; that much weight will completely smash the delicate, custardy curds.

Potstickers; Steamed Shrimp and Chive Dumplings (both from Chapter 8)

Egg Flower Soup (Chapter 9);
Fried Rice (Chapter 15)

Shrimp and Scallops with
Snow Peas (Chapter 10);
Steamed Rice (Chapter 15)

Steamed Whole Fish (Chapter 10)

Seafood Casserole (Chapter 10)

Spicy Salt Shrimp (Chapter 10);
Three Mushrooms (Chapter 14)

Steamed Cabbage Rolls (Chapter 8)

Chinese Roast
Chicken (Chapter 11)

Lemon Chicken (Chapter 11); Stir-Fried
Assorted Vegetables (Chapter 14)

Jing Tu Pork Chops (Chapter 12)

Tangerine Beef (Chapter 12)

Tomato Beef (Chapter 12); Tofu Puffs with Three-Color Vegetables (Chapter 13)

Mongolian Lamb in
Hotpot (Chapter 12)

Claypot Chicken and
Mushroom Rice (Chapter 11)

Ja Jiang Mein (Chapter 15)

Lychee Ice Cream; Caramelized Bananas (both from Chapter 16)

Tofu and Spinach

If you've never tried pressed tofu, this recipe, which pairs its firm texture with tender spinach, gives fabulous results.

Because some types of pressed tofu are flavored with marinades or spices, you may want to use that kind in this recipe. But remember that you have to adjust the seasonings in the sauce according to the pressed tofu's seasonings. What's the best way to do this? Taste some of the pressed tofu and judge from there how to alter the oyster-flavored sauce, sugar, or chicken broth to suit your tastes. It's all a matter of training the tongue!

Preparation time: *12 minutes*

Cooking time: *5 minutes*

Yield: *4 servings*

2 tablespoons black vinegar or balsamic vinegar

1 teaspoon sesame oil

½ teaspoon salt

¼ teaspoon pepper

1 tablespoon cooking oil

4 cloves garlic, sliced

1 pound spinach, washed and drained well

½ cup thinly sliced carrots

4 ounces pressed tofu, cut into ¼-x-1-x-½-inch pieces

⅓ cup chicken broth

¼ cup glazed walnuts

1 Make the sauce by combining the vinegar, sesame oil, salt, and pepper in a bowl.

2 Place a wok over medium-high heat until hot. Add the cooking oil, swirling to coat the sides. Add the garlic and cook, stirring, until fragrant, about 10 seconds. Add the spinach, carrots, and tofu; stir-fry for 1 minute. Add the chicken broth and stir to mix well. Add the sauce; cover and cook until the spinach is wilted, about 4 minutes. Discard the excess liquid and place on a serving platter. Garnish with the glazed walnuts.

Variation: Fresh, young pea shoots really work well in this dish, so if you can find some at a farmers market or Asian grocery store, give them a try. Also, to make it a meatier meal, add strips of ham with the vegetables and tofu.

Variation: Pressed tofu is such a delicious treat, as well as an important part of this recipe. But many Western supermarkets don't carry this distinctly Asian ingredient. If that's the case in your neighborhood, make your own pressed and marinated tofu by pressing half a block of fresh tofu as instructed in the sidebar "Down the drain: Draining tofu yourself," leaving it to drain overnight. Then marinate it in ½ cup of dark soy sauce for 2 to 3 hours. Using about 1 tablespoon cooking oil, pan-fry the tofu until golden brown and pleasingly caramelized on the outside.

Tofu Puffs with Three-Color Vegetables

Here's a chance for you to give light, spongy tofu puffs a try. In this case, I braise them with a flavorful sauce and vibrant vegetables. Just make sure to leave the puffs whole when you cook them; slicing causes them to absorb so much of the braising liquid that they become soggy.

Also, the quail eggs in this recipe may seem like an exotic surprise to you, but they're actually quite common in all sorts of Chinese dishes and in Chinese markets, along with plenty of other "exotic" eggs.

Preparation time: *10 minutes*

Cooking time: *20 minutes*

Yield: *4 to 6 servings*

½ cup All-Purpose Stir-Fry Sauce (see Chapter 7)

¼ cup water

1 tablespoon cooking oil

1 cup sugar snap peas, stem ends snapped off and fibrous strings removed

¾ cup thinly sliced carrots

½ cup water chestnuts

8 tofu puffs

½ cup shelled hardboiled quail eggs or canned quail eggs (optional)

1 To make the sauce, combine the All-Purpose Stir-Fry Sauce and water in a bowl.

2 Place a wok over high heat until hot. Add the oil, swirling to coat the sides. Add the sugar snap peas and carrots; stir-fry until the vegetables are tender-crisp, about 1 minute. Add the water chestnuts and tofu puffs; stir-fry for 1 minute.

3 Add the sauce and, if desired, the quail eggs. Reduce the heat to medium; cover and braise for 3 minutes.

Variation: Technically, the addition of quail eggs knocks this recipe off the list of vegetarian dishes. So if you're looking for a completely vegetarian dish, just leave the eggs out and use button mushrooms instead. They have a similar shape and texture but don't have any ties to the animal kingdom.

Tofu with Mushrooms and Cashews

The tantalizing textures in this dish run the gamut: It has light, airy pieces of fried tofu; chewy, tender button mushrooms; and crunchy roasted cashews. Combine all that with the bright green of the asparagus spears and the sweet-savory flavors of the stir-fry sauce, and you have a recipe that's a feast for all the senses.

Preparation time: 15 minutes

Cooking time: 12 minutes

Yield: 4 servings

½ cup chicken broth

1 tablespoon hoisin sauce

2 teaspoons soy sauce

1 teaspoon sesame oil

Cooking oil for deep-frying

1 package (16 ounces) regular tofu, drained, dried well, and cut into ½-inch cubes

1 teaspoon minced garlic

6 asparagus spears, cut at an angle into 1-inch pieces

6 medium white button mushrooms, quartered

½ cup roasted cashews

1 To make the sauce, combine the chicken broth, hoisin sauce, soy sauce, and sesame oil in a bowl.

2 In a wok, heat the oil for deep-frying to 360°. Deep-fry the tofu, a few pieces at a time, turning occasionally, until golden brown, about 2 minutes on each side. Remove with a slotted spoon; drain on paper towels.

3 Place a wok over high heat until hot. Add 1 tablespoon of the oil, swirling to coat the sides. Add the garlic and cook, stirring, until fragrant, about 10 seconds. Add the asparagus; toss for about 30 seconds. Add the mushrooms and cook for 1 minute.

4 Add the tofu and sauce. Bring to a boil; cook until the sauce reduces slightly. Add the cashews and stir to coat.

More Than It's Cracked Up to Be: The Egg in Chinese Cuisine

The egg: It's not just for breakfast anymore. In China, it never was *just* for breakfast in the first place. Chinese egg cookery doesn't stick to the Western "sunny-side up at sunrise" philosophy. Instead, Chinese cooks spread the wealth of eggs to all times of day and all sorts of dishes. And the love of eggs is not restricted to chicken eggs either. Duck, quail, and pigeon are all fair game in the Chinese kitchen.

Eggs are also valuable ingredients in marinades. I sometimes mix egg whites with cornstarch in my poultry and seafood marinades. This ingredient gives the finished dish a smooth, velvety texture. What's more, the egg coating that sticks to the meat after you drain it from the marinade acts as a sort of temperature "shield" for the underlying flesh, sealing in its natural juices and protecting it from oversearing.

A quick look at eggs' nutritional benefits gives even more reasons for their popularity. High in complete protein, minerals, and vitamins A, D, E, K, and the B-complex, and low in saturated fat, eggs have gotten the nod from Western nutritionists as a wise dietary choice. But for centuries, the Chinese have known how good for you eggs really are. Case in point: Pickled eggs are welcome gifts for new mothers who, according to tradition, must "restore" their bodies during a month of post-labor recuperation.

Of course, no discussion on the notable role of eggs in Chinese cuisine and culture is complete without mentioning the egg's symbolic importance. In addition to the obvious links to birth and life — red-dyed eggs celebrate a baby's first full month — the contrast of white and yolk symbolizes the principle of yin (the white) and yang (the yolk). Eggs also symbolize prosperity, and tea-soaked eggs "roll in" good luck during Chinese New Year. Whether they're lucky or not, I absolutely crave their smoky-tea flavor and gorgeous marbled appearance. In my kitchen, every day is Chinese New Year.

Walking on eggshells: Safety tips for dealing with eggs

Ironically, all the protein, vitamins, and minerals that make eggs so nutritious for humans also make them the perfect food for bacteria. *Salmonella* bacteria that set up shop in chickens' intestinal tracts can make their way onto eggshells and from there onto the egg itself when you crack the shell. Although egg packagers normally clean their eggs, some stubborn bacteria can cling to the shells. Don't gamble with your health. Pay close attention to health safety tips on selection and storage, and you'll enjoy a safe egg-eating experience.

Choosing the freshest eggs

A childhood of fresh-from-the-coop eggs has left me a little biased toward those homegrown beauties. And even though I no longer have a chicken coop in my backyard (the Jacuzzi got in the way), I still insist on using only the freshest eggs possible. An older egg doesn't taste as good, and both yolk and white flatten and thin with time. Then there are the concerns over safety. Here are some tips for buying high-quality, fresh, and *safe* eggs:

- ✔ **Take a look at the freshness dating on the egg's package.** This obvious sign of freshness tells you the date that the eggs were packaged. Make sure to use the eggs within 4 to 5 weeks of that date.

- ✔ **Dig to the back of the supermarket egg case.** The temperature is generally lower back there, and cold eggs are fresher, safer eggs. When you consider that most supermarket egg cases aren't as cold as they should be, the little extra effort this takes is worth it.

- ✔ **Check the eggs while they're in the carton to make sure that the shells are clean and uncracked.** Dirty, cracked shells not only indicate contamination but also are a waste of money.

- ✔ **Choose grade AA or A eggs.** Actually, these may be the only grades that your supermarket sells. The differences between the two grades are so slight — both have thick, clear whites and firm yolks — that either works well in any application.

- ✔ **If you do have access to farm-fresh eggs, congratulations, but make sure that the folks on the farm keep them cold and clean.** If they don't, you're better off buying from the supermarket.

What's one good thing about older eggs? When hard-boiled, their shells are actually easier to peel. So as long as you've followed the storage and safe-handling suggestions mentioned in this section, go ahead and hard-boil those older eggs.

Out, out, darned spot! Blood spots in eggs

Plenty of people get a little unsettled when they find a blood spot in an egg, but there's no cause for alarm. This doesn't mean that the egg was laid by a cursed hen, and it doesn't mean that the egg was fertilized either. Actually, it just means that a blood vessel burst on the yolk's surface — a normal occurrence that doesn't affect the safety or flavor of the egg. If you don't like looking at the spot, just scrape it off or scoop it out and continue with the recipe.

Safe handling for eggs, from storage through service

The clock on an egg's shelf life starts ticking long before you bring the eggs home from the store. Remember that nothing deteriorates the quality of fresh eggs quicker than careless storage and handling. Properly treated eggs keep for up to 4 to 5 weeks beyond their packaging date. Check out these tips to get the most mileage out of your next egg hunt.

✓ **Haste makes taste, and freshness, in eggs.** In other words, don't sign up for a city tour when you're heading home from the store with your eggs. Get home as quickly as you can — obeying the speed limit, of course — and put those eggs in the fridge.

✓ **Store eggs below 40° at a relative humidity between 70 percent and 80 percent.** Believe it or not, eggs age more quickly during just one day at room temperature than they do during an entire week refrigerated at 40°.

✓ **The best spot in the refrigerator for storing eggs is in their original carton.** Those cute little refrigerator egg pockets may be selling points at the appliance store, but you're better off using them to chill limes. The pressed paper-pulp and polystyrene cartons manufactured for eggs actually protect flavor and freshness much better.

✓ **Keep eggs away from other strongly flavored foods in the refrigerator.** Because they have porous shells, eggs can easily absorb any surrounding flavors — another reason why you should keep them in their original carton.

✓ **Stick to the 4- to- 5-week shelf life standard with fresh, refrigerated eggs.** I may sound redundant, but I want you to remember this point.

✓ **As always, thoroughly wash hands, kitchen tools, cutting surfaces, and equipment with hot, soapy water before and after working with eggs.**

✓ **Mind the temperature when cooking eggs.** By keeping a whole egg at 140° for 3.5 minutes, you've effectively pasteurized it, and that's the best way to kill bacteria. Also, store cooked egg dishes either below 40° or above 145° — never in between — and don't leave them at room temperature for longer than an hour.

✓ **Let the daredevils eat raw eggs.** Although plenty of people crack raw eggs into their Caesar salad dressings or protein shakes, they're taking chances with their health. The choice is ultimately up to you. But when cooking for the young, pregnant, elderly, or those with compromised immune systems, it's best to serve your eggs fully cooked.

Great egg preparations

Endless culinary possibilities and a great taste make this perfectly packaged food a favorite with Chinese diners.

Scrambled Eggs with Crabmeat

Breakfast, lunch, dinner, or even dessert, if you're so inclined — it's hard to think of a time when you *wouldn't* want to enjoy this light dish of eggs scrambled with tender crabmeat.

Of course, fresh crabmeat is best. But if it's not available, substitute shrimp, artificial crab, or any other seafood you like, and you'll still create a sensational scramble. It's especially tasty paired with a mimosa (equal parts champagne and orange juice) during Sunday brunch.

Preparation time: *10 minutes*

Cooking time: *5 minutes*

Yield: *4 servings*

6 large eggs, lightly beaten	*⅛ teaspoon salt*
6 ounces crabmeat	*⅛ teaspoon sugar*
1 tablespoon soy sauce	*¼ cup minced cilantro*
1 teaspoon sesame oil	*2 green onions, sliced at an angle*
¼ teaspoon white pepper	*2 tablespoons cooking oil*

1 Combine all the ingredients except the cooking oil in a bowl. Lightly beat to mix well.

2 Place a nonstick frying pan over medium-high heat until hot. Add the cooking oil, swirling to coat the sides. Pour the egg mixture into the pan and spread it over the bottom of the pan. When the eggs start to set, push the cooked egg to the side, letting the uncooked mixture run back to the heated surface of the pan. Continue to push back with the spatula until no more egg mixture runs out. Serve immediately.

Tomato Eggs

This is one of my all-time favorite quick dishes. It's easy to make in a hurry and calls for only a few basic ingredients that are probably already lurking around somewhere in the back of your refrigerator.

Preparation time: *20 minutes*

Cooking time: *6 minutes*

Yield: *4 servings*

¼ cup chicken broth	*2½ tablespoons cooking oil*
¼ cup ketchup	*5 eggs, lightly beaten*
2 tablespoons soy sauce	*1 green onion, thinly sliced*
2 teaspoons packed brown sugar	*2 medium tomatoes, peeled, seeded, and cut into 1-inch cubes*
2 teaspoons chile garlic sauce	

1 To make the sauce, combine the chicken broth, ketchup, soy sauce, brown sugar, and chile garlic sauce in a bowl.

2 Place a wok over high heat until hot. Add the oil, swirling to coat the sides. Add the eggs, green onion, and tomatoes; stir until the eggs are slightly set, about 1 minute.

3 Add the sauce; stir to combine for 1 minute.

Tip: I recommend that you seed the tomatoes for this recipe. Chinese cooks normally take this extra step, and I really think that the smoother texture it creates is worth the effort. Doing so also gets rid of excess tomato juice that can dilute the final dish. To seed a tomato, simply slice the tomato in half and scoop out the seeds and juices with a teaspoon or your fingers (the most effective tools in the kitchen). Or, if the tomato is on the ripe side, gently squeeze out the seeds and juices, being careful not to bruise the tomato itself.

Variation: What can you do with all those extra seeds and juices that you squeezed from the tomato? Add them to one of those blended veggie drinks that are so popular these days, or save them for the marinara sauce you'll make when you need a break from all this Chinese food. Me? I plant them. My tomato patch is a by-product of my smooth seedless tomato dishes.

Tip: Blanching makes all the difference in removing the peel from a tomato without turning the tomato to mush in the process. Bring a pot of water to a boil. Make an X on the bottom (non-stem end) of the tomatoes with a paring knife. Add the tomatoes to the boiling water for a few seconds. You'll see the skin start to peel off slightly on its own, beginning at that X spot. As soon as that happens, remove the tomatoes from the water and immediately plunge them into a bowl of ice water to stop the cooking. The skin should peel off easily at this point.

Steamed Eggs

This flanlike dish of steamed eggs is a smooth, custardy indulgence. If you'd like to add a little meaty substance to its silkiness, toss some small shrimp or shredded ham into the beaten eggs before steaming.

Preparation time: *15 minutes*

Cooking time: *15 minutes*

Yield: *4 servings*

4 large eggs, lightly beaten

1¾ cups water

2 tablespoons soy sauce

1 teaspoon cooking oil

1 tablespoon chopped green onion

1 In a heatproof glass pie dish, beat the eggs with the water until thoroughly mixed.

2 Make a seasoning mixture by combining the soy sauce, cooking oil, and green onion in a small microwave-safe bowl.

3 Prepare a wok for steaming (see Chapter 3). Place the pie dish in a wok, cover, and steam over high heat until the eggs are set, about 13 minutes.

4 Heat the seasoning mixture in the microwave for 15 seconds to warm it up; pour it over the "flan" and serve hot.

Tip: To ensure a smooth custard with no bubbles on top, lay two wooden chopsticks across opposite edges of the wok's rim and then carefully and securely rest the lid on them. Doing so creates a small air vent that allows excess steam to escape so it won't condense back onto the flan.

Remember: After about 8 minutes, check on how the flan is cooking by lightly touching the top with one of the chopsticks. It should feel stiff and resistant at the edges but still be a little soft and yielding at the surface's center. If this is the case, after about 5 more minutes, depending on the strength of your burner, the eggs should be ready.

Martin Says: How did I determine how much water to mix with the eggs for this flan? The way Mom taught me, that's how. She, and many other Chinese home cooks, use the eggshell method: Fill one half of a cracked eggshell with water three times for each egg, and you'll get the right amount for the whole dish. These days, what with measuring cups and all, I've figured that three half-shells of water per egg works out to at least 1¾ cups water for the 4 eggs in this recipe. Make sure you use enough, or the flan will turn out stiff.

Egg Fu Young

Egg fu young, basically a Chinese take on the omelet, now shows up on Chinese restaurant menus all over. And though it has become pretty Americanized over the years, the name *fu young*, which means "peony flower," still has special traditional meaning in China.

In fact, beautiful women in China were described as having the "face of a peony." But before you call anyone "*fu young* face," make sure they know that you mean it as a compliment.

Preparation time: *25 minutes*

Cooking time: *35 minutes*

Yield: *4 servings*

4 fresh white button mushrooms, cleaned and coarsely chopped

6 ounces small raw shrimp, shelled, deveined, and finely chopped

6 ounces bean sprouts

1 green onion, thinly sliced

1 teaspoon cornstarch

3 teaspoons sesame oil

⅛ teaspoon white pepper

4 large eggs, lightly beaten

1 cup chicken broth

1 tablespoon dark soy sauce

1 tablespoon soy sauce

½ teaspoon chile garlic sauce

4 tablespoons cooking oil

1 tablespoon cornstarch dissolved in 1½ tablespoons water

1 Combine the mushrooms, shrimp, bean sprouts, onion, cornstarch, 1 teaspoon of the sesame oil, and the white pepper in a large bowl. Stir in the eggs and mix well.

2 To make the sauce, combine the chicken broth, dark soy sauce, soy sauce, the remaining 2 teaspoons sesame oil, and the chile garlic sauce in a small pan. Set aside.

3 Place an 8-inch nonstick frying pan over medium heat until hot. Add 1 tablespoon of the cooking oil, swirling to coat the sides. Pour one-fourth of the egg mixture into the pan and cook. As the edges begin to set, lift with a spatula and shake or tilt the pan to let the eggs flow underneath, swirling the eggs to prevent sticking. When the eggs no longer flow freely, about 2 minutes, turn the omelet over and brown lightly on the other side, about 1 minute. Repeat with the remaining oil and egg mixture.

4 Bring the sauce to a boil over medium-high heat. Add the cornstarch solution and cook, stirring, until the sauce boils and thickens.

5 Slide the omelet onto a warm serving plate and pour the sauce over it.

Variation: You can substitute ½ cup diced cooked ham or ½ cup crabmeat for the shrimp, or you can omit it entirely and make a meat-free fu young.

CULTURAL TIDBIT

Freshness in the days before refrigeration: Chinese preserved eggs

Keeping eggs at a steady 40° without a refrigerator is a tricky job, yet the Chinese have eaten eggs for centuries, and there weren't a lot of refrigerators back in those days. So how did they manage not to get sick?

Simple preservation. The Chinese developed a handful of creative preservation techniques that can keep bacteria from over-running eggs. In the case of tea-simmered eggs, not only did simmering kill harmful bacteria and extend shelf life a few days, but simmering in tea added a smoky, aromatic flavor to the eggs that Chinese adore. A more unusual technique used to make sweet

and salty preserved duck eggs involves pickling them in a salty brine after first packing them in a preservative mixture of lime and ashes. Although the end result may not seem too appetizing to Western sensibilities, these eggs are true delicacies in China, and they can be kept at room temperature for a long time.

And, of course, I can't imagine a better-preserved egg than the "thousand-year-old" egg. Okay, maybe they're not *really* one thousand years old, but considering that you can still eat them a good four to five months after they're preserved, they deserve the exaggerated title.

An egg of a different color: Are brown eggs better than white?

In recent years, brown eggs have become increasingly popular in Western markets. They've actually been widely available in China for a long time, along with speckled eggs and other multicolored varieties. Are there any real differences among them other than appearance?

Yes. Brown eggs are laid by a different breed of hens. But as far as nutritional content, flavor, and quality, they are remarkably similar to white eggs. And once you've removed the egg from its shell, I bet that you can't tell one from the other.

Tea-Flavored Eggs

These stunning, marbleized eggs remind me of a Chinese version of Easter eggs. Actually, fans of Chinese opera like to eat them as snacks, purchased from street vendors, while they pass the time during intermission.

They're surprisingly easy to make, with an even more surprising tea flavor. Prepare them at least a day in advance to allow the tea's flavor enough time to permeate.

Preparation time: _20 minutes_

Cooking time: _50 minutes_

Yield: _4 to 6 servings_

8 eggs	_3 tablespoons black tea leaves_
¼ cup dark soy sauce	_3 tablespoons packed brown sugar_
3 tablespoons soy sauce	_1 teaspoon Chinese five-spice powder_
3 green onions, crushed	_2 whole star anise_
4 to 5 slices ginger, lightly crushed	

1 Place the eggs in a 2-quart pot and cover with cold water. Over medium-low heat, simmer the eggs for 10 minutes. Cool the eggs under cold running water. Gently tap each egg all over with a spoon until hairline cracks form over the entire shell. Do not remove the shells.

2 Return the eggs to the pot. Add the remaining ingredients and enough water to cover the eggs. Heat to simmering; cover and continue to simmer over low heat for 45 minutes. Let the eggs cool and then refrigerate the eggs in the seasoning liquid for at least 8 hours or overnight, or up to 2 days.

3 To serve, remove the eggs from the seasoning (discard the liquid) and shell the eggs; leave them whole or cut them into quarters.

Tip: Be gentle when tapping the eggshells. You want to create fine cracks that allow in just enough of the cooking liquid to flavor and marbleize the eggs. You don't want to peel them.

Remember: Tea leaves, like spices, lose their potency as they age. For that reason, use fresher tea leaves or tea bags in this recipe; they'll release more flavor and create more memorable marbled eggs.

Chapter 14

The Green Revolution: Cooking Vegetables the Chinese Way

In This Chapter

▶ Getting acquainted with Chinese vegetables
▶ Cooking vegetables the right way

Recipes in This Chapter

▶ Braised Bamboo Shoots with Bok Choy
▶ Stir-Fried Assorted Vegetables
▶ Asparagus with Baby Corn and Oyster-Flavored Sauce
▶ Ivory and Jade (Cauliflower and Broccoli with Creamy Egg White)
▶ Sautéed Green Beans
▶ Three Mushrooms
▶ Eggplants with Spicy Sauce
▶ Swiss Chard with Tender Pork Slices
▶ Chinatown Chop Suey

🍴 ◗ ◔ 🥢 🌿

*T*he Chinese have always been a step ahead of their time. Although Western nutritionists, doctors, and medical researchers now tell people to eat at least five servings of fruits and vegetables each day, the Chinese have been doing just that for thousands of years. And they never needed the coaxing of medical professionals to get them to do it either. Why? Because, when prepared the Chinese way — rapidly cooked and with an eye toward preserving their natural flavors — vegetables are just too delicious to resist. Whether stockpiling a winter's-worth of rugged, Tianjin cabbage or quickly stir-frying fresh, delicate pea shoots from a backyard garden in Guangzhou, the Chinese have a million reasons (and recipes) to eat their veggies. Their mothers see to it. Mine certainly did.

A typical restaurant in the West may serve its guests a big, thick steak with just a spoonful of mashed potatoes and maybe a skimpy stalk of broccoli on the side. But if that kind of meal were served to a typical Chinese diner, it would go right back to the kitchen. A typical Chinese meal stars a variety of crisp, fresh vegetables — brightly colored greens and peppers, slender Asian eggplants, and exotic mushrooms and fungi that may look strange but still taste truly heavenly. Meats, if included in the cast at all, play more of a supporting role in this culinary production. They're there to accompany the lead vegetables on a stage whose set decoration is nothing more than a subtly designed sauce.

You can trace this fond regard for vegetables back to China's Buddhist and Taoist roots. Although not all Chinese Buddhists follow strict tenets of vegetarianism at all times, they choose meatless meals for special festival dinners and as a form of bodily and spiritual cleansing. Similarly, Taoist thinking holds that meat's strong yin element throws diners' internal balance significantly off-kilter. To reinstall the yin-yang harmony (a topic that I discuss in more detail in Chapter 1), the philosophy recommends that you go on a meat-free diet from time to time. Since Taoist deities are supposedly all yang, heavy doses of yin from meaty meals will probably upset them. But there's no reason to offend the heavens with so many fruits and vegetables at the ready.

The economic factor also plays a role in China's emphasis on vegetables. China has never been the wealthiest of countries. And sometimes — whether because of disease, war, political upheaval, or famine — agriculture has provided the only means of feeding the country's masses. Why raise a few head of cattle or small herd of sheep on land that could support a much larger and more sustainable crop of grain or produce?

All these reasons have combined to make Chinese chefs the world's foremost experts at turning a few humble shoots and roots into scrumptious delicacies that leave even the most skeptical Western diners begging not for another slab of steak but for another plateful of greens. With some careful shopping, light seasoning, and simple cooking, you too can throw your own "Green Party"!

Who's Who in the World of Chinese Vegetables

A green revolution is going on in Western supermarkets. When you drop by the produce section of your local grocery, don't be surprised to find bean sprouts, napa cabbage, and even fresh gingerroot among the potatoes, apples, and corn on the cob. The steady growth of Asian-American communities across the country and the emphasis on healthy vegetable-based diets have resulted in a dramatic rise in consumer demands for characteristically Chinese vegetables previously undiscovered by North American shoppers.

To make yourself even more savvy as to how Chinese broccoli and Chinese eggplants differ from their Western cousins, consult the following primer and check out Figure 14-1, which gives you some visual clues about who's who. Both should help you better navigate the produce aisles of your local market as well as those at your Chinatown grocer's.

Figure 14-1:
Some of the items you'll find on your next trip to the produce section.

Bean sprouts (Ah cai; dou ya)

Although these silver-white stalks with their yellow heads and long tails aren't exactly exotic to most North American diners anymore, they're nevertheless classic ingredients in Chinese stir-fries, soups, and noodle dishes, and they deserve a closer look.

Most bean sprouts, if left to grow to maturity, would sprout into either soy or mung beans. The soy bean sprouts — the rarer of the two — have larger heads and are crunchier than the more-delicate mung bean sprouts. But regardless of parentage, bean sprouts are completely edible and surprisingly tasty.

When you buy them at the market, seek out dry, firm, and unbroken white bean sprouts. Rinse them with water to clean them and remove any unwanted woody green seed hulls before using. Although they're best consumed the day of purchase, you can refrigerate them for up to a couple days in a plastic bag with one end kept open for ventilation.

Bok choy (Bok choy; xiao bai cai)

With its crunchy, white, mildly tangy stalks and soft, peppery, green leaves, bok choy has really grown in popularity and availability in the West recently. Today, I'm hard-pressed to find a grocery store that doesn't carry at least one variety of this loose-leafed cabbage. Baby bok choy is a smaller and younger version of the full-grown bok choy, while the similarly petite Shanghai bok choy has lovely jade green, curved leaves and spoon-shaped stalks. Both of these smaller varieties are sweeter and less tough than regular bok choy.

For simplicity in nutrition and taste, you can't beat a plate of bright green, freshly steamed or stir-fried bok choy. Just season it lightly with a little garlic and soy sauce, and its naturally sweet flavor comes through beautifully. Trim the stems and diagonally slice the large stalks before cooking. Leave baby or Shanghai varieties whole or sliced in half lengthwise.

When buying bok choy, look for firm stalks and bright leaves that are free of blemishes. The baby and Shanghai varieties are often sold in small bundles of three or four each. Refrigerate all types for up to a week.

Chinese broccoli (Gai lan; jie lan)

You should have no trouble telling Chinese broccoli from Western broccoli because the two look nothing alike. Chinese broccoli, with its tiny white flowers and dusty green stems and leaves, resembles leafy vegetables such as mustard greens or kale. Light steaming or stir-frying brings out its slightly bitter-sweet taste. My favorite Chinese broccoli treatment is a plate of steamed stalks and leaves seasoned with a little oyster-flavored sauce — nothing's more Cantonese than that!

Don't worry about peeling the tender stems of Chinese broccoli unless they appear thicker and tougher than you'd like — the sure sign of an older bunch. Because the stems take a little longer to cook, start them first and add the delicate leaves toward the end. Whenever possible, pick young broccoli with slender stems and unblemished leaves. It can be refrigerated for up to a week.

Chinese chives (Gou choy; jiu lai)

Once you get past the differences between Chinese and Western chives — not too tough a task because they're very different in both appearance and flavor — you then get to choose among a number of varieties within the group of Chinese chives themselves. For one, you have the green chives, which resemble long (about 9 inches), wide blades of grass. Yellow chives are shorter and less fibrous, with a mild onion-garlic flavor and aroma. Finally, flowering chives, the longest of the group, averaging about a foot, have the firmest, crispest stalks and little edible flowering buds at the tips.

Cut the chives into 1-inch lengths and sprinkle them into any Chinese dish. Here are some of my tips for mixing and matching the chive to the recipe:

- ✔ Yellow chives complement noodle dishes well.
- ✔ Marinated beef stir-fries always improve with some of the flowering types of chives.
- ✔ A dim sum meal isn't complete without some steamed buns or dumplings filled with minced green chives and shrimp.

Just remember to keep the breath mints handy whenever you enjoy these pungent herbs — their memory definitely lingers on the palate for some time after you take your last swallow.

Look for Chinese chives in bunches during summer and spring. I've increasingly found them in Western supermarkets on occasion during their high season, so keep your fingers crossed that your local store carries them at those times as well. If not, farmers markets and Chinese markets are always good bets for scoring a supply. To store them, wrap the bundles in a damp paper towel and place in a plastic bag. Store the bag in the refrigerator, where the chives will keep for several days. Do keep in mind that their flavor actually strengthens with time, however.

Chinese eggplants (Aike gwa; qie zi)

Compared to their plump Italian cousins, Chinese eggplants, generally 3 to 9 inches long and white to lavender in color, look like they're on a diet. Actually, their tubular shape makes them ideal for roll cutting (a technique I describe in Chapter 5), and their slimmer size makes them a more convenient choice for single diners who are cooking for one.

Another distinction that sets Chinese eggplants apart from most of the larger Western kinds: Their relative sweetness and tender texture make peeling and salting to eliminate bitter juices unnecessary. Just roll cut, slice, or cube them for stir-fries or braised dishes, or cut them in half lengthwise or fan-cut them for grilling.

Choose Chinese eggplants that are smooth, firm, and unblemished. They're best used the day of purchase, but if loosely wrapped in plastic and refrigerated, they will last for up to several days.

Cilantro (Yim sike; yuan xi)

An herb by any other name . . . just may be cilantro! This herb goes by so many names — cilantro, Chinese parsley, and coriander, to list its most common aliases — that it's no wonder many people confuse it with other herbs in the produce section.

But whatever you do, don't confuse cilantro with Italian parsley. The former has wider, flatter leaves and a characteristic aroma that some say is reminiscent of salsa or even soap. In my opinion, the aroma is actually reminiscent of Chinese food, because versatile cilantro gives such a distinctive flavor to Chinese soups, salads, dim sum stuffings, and steamed fish. Try it in your next stir-fry or stir-fry sauce recipe.

Choose bright, perky bunches of cilantro with fresh, crisp leaves and stems. If you can find bunches with the roots left on, use them, too, to give a more concentrated flavor. To store cilantro, stand the bunch in a glass of water, loosely cover the tops with a plastic bag, and refrigerate for up to several days.

Daikon (Law bok; lou bu)

In the West, people normally think of turnips as being squatty, somewhat top-shaped vegetables with bushy green leaves and a rosy red blush. But in Asia, turnips look more like pale, bleached-out, oversized carrots (they run about 2 to 3 inches in diameter and can be over a foot long). Known as the daikon, or occasionally the giant white radish, they nonetheless have the same sweet, peppery flavor and refreshing crunch as their Western cousins. Shred daikon and toss it into salads and soups. A characteristically Chinese treatment involves cutting it into chunks and adding it to stews and claypot dishes. Peel its tough, bitter skin before cooking or eating raw.

When choosing a daikon, look for one on the short side with a firm, smooth surface. The larger they are, the more fibrous they tend to be. Wrap the daikon in plastic to prevent moisture loss, and refrigerate for up to a couple weeks.

Napa cabbage (Siu choy; da bai cai)

Chinese napa cabbage has a short, football-shaped body with sweet, creamy white stalks ending in lacy, ruffled, pale green leaves. It's interchangeable with heartier Western cabbage in most recipes, but its tender leaves warrant shorter cooking, and its delicacy makes it a much more appealing choice. Just cut the stalks and leaves into small pieces and stir-fry until slightly wilted and crisp-tender. Thinly sliced napa cabbage also makes a nice addition to soups and stews; just simmer until translucent and silky-textured.

Napa cabbage is a seasonal vegetable, but thanks to advances in agricultural science, it's now available in stores throughout the year. Look for cabbages with moist, pale green leaves that have no browning around the edges. If you see any black spots near the base of the stalks, don't worry about them — they're just the result of unpredictable and variable growing conditions. Being a cabbage, napa cabbage is naturally heartier than other vegetables and will keep in the refrigerator for a couple weeks.

Snow peas (Hor lan dou; xue dou)

Order a stir-fry or soup at a Chinese restaurant, and you'll likely be treated to the bright green color, sweet taste, and crisp-tender texture of snow peas. Because of their tenderness, you needn't bother shelling them before eating. Instead, just snap off the stem ends and remove the fibrous strings that run along the pods' sides. Boil, steam, or stir-fry them until crisp-tender and add them to any dish that could use some bright green color and springtime flavor.

Be sure to pick young snow peas carefully, choosing those that are bright green, flat, crisp, and blemish-free. Discard the ones that are wilted, thick-skinned, overly plump, or discolored. Those old-timers will be too tough and fibrous to enjoy. Snow peas will keep in your refrigerator for about a week.

Taro root (Woo tou; yu tou)

If you've ever had taro root — the brownish, hairy-looking, rough-skinned root that ranges in size from a golf ball to a melon — it was probably at a luau as the mashed Hawaiian dish poi. But Chinese cooks have uncovered plenty of other ways to showcase this starchy vegetable, with its sweet, nutty flavor and whitish gray to light purple flesh.

In addition to boiling and steaming taro to make a mash or puree, you can also blend it into stuffings, shred and deep-fry it, or cut it into chunks to simmer in a stew or braised dish. Basically, treat the taro as you would a potato, pairing it with rich seasonings and sauces to make a hearty meal. Just remember to peel taro root, and always cook it before serving — raw taro root is inedible. You may also want to wear rubber gloves when handling taro root because its juices are known to irritate some people's skin.

Look for firm taro roots that are free of dents, wrinkles, blemishes, and mold. Store taro roots in a cool, dry place. They'll keep for about a week.

Winter melon (Doan gwa; dong gua)

The first time that you spot a winter melon, you may think that it's a dusty green, overgrown pumpkin. But don't let the appearance, or the chalky white bloom that covers the melon skin, fool you — winter melons are better eaten than turned into jack-o-lanterns. Their inner flesh is pale green to milky white and has a faint, sweet-peppery taste. Just make sure that you remove the tangled web of seeds at the center of the melons before you cook them.

And you must cook winter melons; these gourds are never eaten raw. Remove the seeds and rind, thinly slice the flesh, and steam or simmer it in soups. Because it has a relatively bland flavor, you'll probably want to pair winter melon with more flavorful ingredients, such as dried black mushrooms or Chinese sausages, in soups and stir-fries.

Mature water melons can weigh from 8 to 10 pounds and measure from 12 to 15 inches long. Because of such proportions, produce managers at Asian markets often cut and individually wrap sections of winter melon for sale. For first-time users, these smaller "sample" sizes may be just the thing (although after one taste of a soothing winter melon soup, you'll probably be back in the store for the whole melon the next day). Store uncut winter melon in a cool, dry place for up to a month. Wrap cut melon in plastic wrap and refrigerate for up to several days.

Yard-long beans (Dou gog; dou jiao)

Okay, maybe these beans aren't all a full yard long. But at up to 18 inches, they're pretty long nonetheless. The pencil-thin beans range in color from pale to dark green and have a shiny but somewhat bumpy surface. Although firm and crunchy when young and fresh, they're still flexible and long enough for produce managers to tie into knots for presentation at the store. When blanched until softened, they become even more flexible. Try serving long bean knots as a side dish with roasted meats and poultry.

Cut the long beans into 1½-inch to 2-inch pieces and stir-fry. Their sweet flavor and dry, crunchy bite set them apart from other green beans, which tend toward the juicy and crisp. Just trim the stem ends before cooking. And guess what: There are no strings to remove! An ingredient with no strings attached — how about that?

You can probably find yard-long beans year-round, but they're at their peak during summer. Buy young beans with few blemishes and wrinkles. Avoid the older, longer beans because they're tougher and more fibrous. You can keep bundles of yard-long beans in your refrigerator for about a week.

How to Get the Most Out of Your Vegetables While Cooking Them the Least

Years of practice at cooking vegetables have taught Chinese cooks that a light touch with flavor and texture works best when you're preparing fresh vegetables. So if you grew up with overboiled mushy green beans or anemic-looking canned corn, take heart that Chinese vegetable cooks have a lesson to teach you that will direct your diet toward much greener pastures.

So what do you do if you find yourself the proud owner of a big bunch of spinach, bok choy, napa cabbage, or any other leafy, green vegetable? If it's fresh and bright green, you do as little with it as possible, just as the crack vegetable chefs in Guangzhou do. You don't even need a recipe. Just follow these suggestions:

1. **Give the leaves a good rinse in cool water and drain them thoroughly; a salad spinner helps with this step.**

2. **Chop the leaves into pieces a few inches long, making sure to keep the lengths fairly similar among all the pieces — doing so ensures even cooking.**

   If the stalks seem tender enough, go ahead and chop those, too, cutting the stalks at an angle to expose more surface area to heat during cooking.

3. **Prepare yourself for stir-frying, heating your wok beforehand and adding just enough oil to lightly coat the amount of greens you want to cook.**

   After the oil starts steaming a bit, gently tilt your wok to distribute it evenly across the surface. It doesn't hurt to drop in a clove of crushed garlic and a few slices of fresh ginger for flavor before adding the main ingredients.

   Keep in mind the three cardinal rules of stir-frying that I explain more fully in Chapter 5: Have all your ingredients prepared and organized beforehand, make sure that your wok is smoking hot when you add the food, and stir, stir, stir.

4. **Take the plunge: Add the vegetables to the ready-to-go wok and toss them immediately to fully coat with the oil.**

   Keep tossing and pay attention to how they begin softening and changing color — not *wilting*, but rather just gently *relaxing* — all the while releasing their own earthy aroma.

5. **Add your choice of seasoning: Pepper, salt, and sugar are foolproof options.**

   Then add a little bit of water or broth and put a lid on it — the wok, that is — to initiate the steaming that finishes the vegetable-cooking process.

6. **Within a couple minutes, lift that lid and feast your eyes on one of the simplest and most delightful culinary creations nature offers: fresh, green vegetables redolent with their own natural juices and aromas.**

   Taste and adjust the seasoning according to your liking, add a sauce during the final couple minutes if you wish, and get ready to eat!

Of course, other, more elaborate recipes are out there — and in this chapter — for you to try. But remember that the Chinese have cooked their greens for millennia by following these simple steps. If they could do it, so can you.

The healing garden: A long tradition of Chinese herbalism

The West is finally catching on to age-old Chinese medical practices that treat and, more importantly, prevent illness via a judicious use of vegetables, herbs, seeds, and roots. They have proven effective at staving off any number of minor and major maladies. Check the labels of your favorite sports drink or energy bar, and you may be surprised to find "mysterious" ingredients such as ginseng, gingko, and gotu kola. But long before you ever took your first bite of a Muscle Bar, Chinese herbalists employed these items in tonics and infusions to restore and maintain the good health of their patients. In fact, more than 2,000 years ago, the Chinese Imperial Court created the position of Official Food Doctor, proving that the first line of defense in the war against sickness was drawn in the country's kitchens.

In recent years, the Western medical establishment is beginning to view the Chinese way of "food as medicine" with less skepticism. For as much a mix of myth, mysticism and art as Chinese herbal medicine may seem, plenty of healthy Chinese rely on it to keep them that way. And recent clinical research into the chemical and physiological basis of Chinese herbalism's curative effects has surprised Western scientists, showing that much of Chinese medicine's potency has a solid scientific base that concurs with Western medical knowledge. Maybe that's why you may find it difficult to differentiate among the markets, pharmacies, and herbal shops in Chinatown — they're really not that different from each other after all.

A simple plate of greens, Chinese mushrooms, and natural herbs can cleanse your body, nourish your soul, _and_ provide a treat for your taste buds at the same time. Follow my suggestions in the following table for finding some of the healthiest and tastiest produce ingredients with which to stock your kitchen shelves and bathroom medicine cabinet.

Ingredient	Reported Health Effect
Bird's nest	Excellent for clearing troubled complexions; has youth-restoring value
Bitter almonds	Good for respiratory ailments including coughing and asthma
Bitter melon	Cooling yin food; cleanses blood
Black pepper	Eases intestinal and stomach pain; cures diarrhea
Carrots	Just as mother always told you, improve eyesight
Dried tangerine peel	Superb yin food; very cooling
Dried black mushrooms	Stimulate the immune system; promote circulation; help reduce cholesterol levels
Chinese spinach (_een choi_)	High in protein; removes excess moisture from body
Garlic	Eases digestion, regulates circulatory system
Ginger	Soothes common cold symptoms; eases stomach pain; warming yang food
Gingko biloba	Increases mental capacity; sharpens mental functioning
Ginseng	Powerhouse ingredient: promotes energy and sexual vitality; cleanses the blood and lymphatic fluid; aids general immune response
Lotus seeds	Supposedly bring good luck when eaten (not exactly a medical property, but it can't hurt)
Jujubes (red Chinese dates)	Soothe nerves; known as "food of harmony"
Rice wine	Eases symptoms of rheumatism, muscle aches, and chest discomfort
Snow fungus	Has complexion-clearing properties
Soybean and soy products	Very high in protein; may help prevent heart disease and certain forms of cancer
Star anise	Aids digestion; has warming yang energy; associated with long life
Walnuts and walnut oil	Supply vitamins and nutrients, including vitamin E; contain energizing fats
Winter melon	Cooling yin food; excellent for soothing overheated bodies during summer
Wolfberries	Have palliative effect on headaches; refresh and cleanse body's systems

Braised Bamboo Shoots with Bok Choy

Here's a simple stir-fry to start you off. The combination of classic Chinese vegetables creates a distinctive dish that sings with its ingredients' flavors.

Some types of bok choy are rather short; I recommend those shorter types for this dish. The shorter ones allow you to sidestep cutting the leaves and stalks into crosswise chunks. Just slice them lengthwise into longer pieces that each combine the different colors and textures of the stalks and leaves.

Preparation time: *25 minutes*

Cooking time: *20 minutes*

Yield: *4 servings*

½ cup chicken broth

¼ teaspoon sugar

3 tablespoons oyster-flavored sauce

1 tablespoon cooking oil

1 clove garlic, crushed

3 slices ginger, crushed

8 to 12 medium fresh shiitake mushrooms

2 whole bamboo shoots, cut into 8 pieces, lengthwise

3 baby bok choy, cut in half, lengthwise

1 teaspoon cornstarch dissolved in 2 teaspoons water

1 To make the sauce, combine the chicken broth, sugar, and oyster-flavored sauce in a bowl. Place a wok over high heat until hot. Add the oil, swirling to coat the sides. Add the garlic and ginger; cook, stirring until fragrant, about 10 seconds. Add the mushrooms and stir-fry for 1 minute. Add the bamboo shoots; stir-fry for an additional 1 minute. Add the sauce; stir to mix thoroughly.

2 Reduce the heat to medium; cover and braise for 6 minutes. Add the baby bok choy; cover and cook for 2 to 3 minutes. Add the cornstarch solution and cook, stirring until the sauce boils and thickens.

Tip: Although you're probably most familiar with canned sliced bamboo shoots, you can also find canned whole bamboo shoots or even fresh ones in tubs of water at Asian markets. The whole shoots are usually cone-shaped and about the size of an average palm. Try them in this recipe if you can find some. Just cut the shoots into quarters and then into eighths before adding them to the stir-fry.

Martin Says: Six minutes may seem like a long time to cook tender Chinese vegetables, but I like to let this dish braise in the sauce for a bit because it helps the flavors permeate the whole dish. And because you add the bok choy near the end of cooking, it doesn't lose its texture.

Stir-Fried Assorted Vegetables

Crisp and crunchy stir-fried vegetables are a delight to have at every dinner table. This recipe contains an assortment that you should find easily in any grocery store's produce department. I picked these particular ones not only for their great flavor (made even greater with a little All-Purpose Stir-Fry Sauce from Chapter 7) but also for their bright, rainbow colors.

Preparation time: *15 minutes*

Cooking time: *10 minutes*

Yield: *4 to 6 servings*

½ cup All-Purpose Stir-Fry Sauce

¼ cup chicken broth

2 tablespoons cooking oil

3 cloves garlic, lightly crushed

½ cup thinly sliced carrots

½ cup julienned red bell pepper

1 cup broccoli florets

1 large zucchini, roll cut

1 cup small white mushrooms, cleaned and halved

1 To make the sauce, combine the stir-fry sauce and the chicken broth in a bowl.

2 Place a wok over high heat until hot. Add the oil, swirling to coat the sides. Add the garlic and cook, stirring until fragrant, about 10 seconds. Add the carrots and red pepper; stir-fry for 2 minutes. Add the broccoli, zucchini, and white mushrooms; stir-fry for 2 minutes. Add the sauce and bring it to a boil, stirring until the vegetables are tender-crisp, about 3 minutes.

Variation: If you'd like, gently toss a few cubes of firm tofu with the vegetables in this dish. Tofu not only adds healthful protein but also gives the recipe a little more substance and bulk. And tofu's yielding texture provides the perfect counterpoint to the crunchy vegetables.

Asparagus with Baby Corn and Oyster-Flavored Sauce

I always look forward to experiencing the change of seasons with my taste buds. For example, the first stalks of tender green asparagus never fail to remind me that spring is in the air. When I can get my hands on some of the early crop, I give it this classic Cantonese treatment: a touch of garlic and ginger, oyster-flavored sauce, and a hint of sesame oil.

But if the asparagus isn't quite ready to come out of hiding yet, choose whatever greens are fresh and in season. Gai lan, bok choy, pea shoots, and even spinach make great matches with these simple seasonings.

Preparation time: *12 minutes*

Cooking time: *5 minutes*

Yield: *4 servings*

1¼ pounds asparagus spears	*2 tablespoons cooking oil*
3 tablespoons oyster-flavored sauce	*2 cloves garlic, crushed*
3 tablespoons chicken broth	*1 slice ginger (⅛-inch), crushed*
1 teaspoon sesame oil	*1 can (8 ounces) baby corn, drained*

1 Trim the asparagus and cut the spears at an angle into 1½-inch pieces.

2 To make the sauce, combine the oyster-flavored sauce, chicken broth, and sesame oil in a bowl.

3 Place a wok over high heat until hot. Add the cooking oil, swirling to coat the sides. Add the garlic and ginger; cook, stirring, until fragrant, about 10 seconds. Add the asparagus, corn, and sauce; cover and cook until asparagus is tender-crisp, about 2 minutes.

Remember: Be sure to cook the asparagus lightly to preserve its crunch. Nothing is more disappointing than witnessing crisp, fresh asparagus lose its textural gusto.

Ivory and Jade (Cauliflower and Broccoli with Creamy Egg White)

Feast your eyes upon this colorful combination of cauliflower, broccoli, and a creamy sauce, and you'll know why it has such a descriptive, metaphoric name.

The sauce, which includes a slurry of milk and cornstarch, now shows up in a number of Chinese dishes. However, given that the Chinese diet hasn't historically embraced dairy products, it isn't quite traditionally Chinese itself. Nevertheless, with the influx of all sorts of Western foods, from pizza and ice cream to macaroni and cheese, dairy foods are starting to make their way into Chinese dishes more often. If the results are always as tasty as in this dish, I say keep those Western influences coming.

Preparation time: *12 minutes*

Cooking time: *12 minutes*

Yield: *4 to 6 servings*

¾ teaspoon salt

½ teaspoon sugar

10 ounces cauliflower florets

8 ounces broccoli florets

1 cup chicken broth

⅛ teaspoon white pepper

1½ tablespoons cornstarch dissolved in ½ cup milk

1 teaspoon toasted black sesame seeds

1 teaspoon toasted white sesame seeds

1 Bring a pot of water to a boil; add ½ teaspoon of the salt and ¼ teaspoon of the sugar. Add the cauliflower and broccoli florets; blanch until tender-crisp, about 4 minutes. Drain and rinse in cold water; drain again.

2 To make the sauce, combine the chicken broth, the remaining ¼ teaspoon sugar, the remaining ¼ teaspoon salt, and the white pepper in a medium saucepan; bring to a boil. Add the cornstarch solution, cook, stirring, until the sauce boils and thickens. Return the vegetables to the sauce and heat through.

3 To serve, arrange the cauliflower on one side of the plate and the broccoli on the other side. Garnish the cauliflower with black sesame seeds and the broccoli with the white sesame seeds.

Variation: If you have difficulty digesting dairy products or simply choose not to consume dairy products at all, you can certainly substitute unflavored, unsweetened soymilk for the dairy milk in this recipe.

Sautéed Green Beans

In this dish, I tweak the traditional cooking method of "dry-frying," in which cooks first deep-fry vegetables and then stir-fry them to produce a chewy texture. My version cuts out the middle man, in a way, simply asking you to shallow-fry the green beans in a quantity of oil that's somewhere between that of deep-frying and stir-frying. It's easier, quicker, and cleaner and still gives the beans a unique chewy texture.

This dish hails from the Hunan region, near Sichuan, in western China. But luckily for you, it's now available in Chinese restaurants of every regional stripe.

Preparation time: 15 minutes

Cooking time: 15 minutes

Yield: 4 servings

1½ tablespoons soy sauce	¼ cup cooking oil for shallow-frying
⅛ teaspoon white pepper	6 cloves garlic, thinly sliced
6 ounces ground pork	2 tablespoons hoisin sauce
¼ cup shredded Sichuan preserved vegetables	1 tablespoon dark soy sauce
	1 teaspoon sesame oil
½ pound green beans, ends and strings removed	

1 To make the marinade, combine the soy sauce and white pepper in a bowl. Add the pork; stir to coat. Let stand for 10 minutes.

2 Rinse the Sichuan preserved vegetables; coarsely chop.

3 Rinse and drain the green beans; cut into 3-inch lengths.

4 Place a wok over high heat until hot. Add the cooking oil, swirling to coat the sides. When the oil is smoking, shallow-fry the green beans until slightly wrinkled, 5 to 6 minutes; remove and drain on paper towels.

5 Remove all but 1 tablespoon of the cooking oil. Add the garlic and cook, stirring until fragrant, about 10 seconds. Add the ground pork; stir-fry until the pork changes color, about 1 minute. Add the preserved vegetables and stir-fry for 30 seconds.

6 Return the green beans to the wok; add the hoisin sauce, dark soy sauce, and sesame oil. Stir to mix well.

Variation: If your grocery store's produce market carries them, or if you have access to a well-stocked farmers market, pick up some yard-long beans to use in this recipe. They have a taste and texture that's a bit different from regular green beans, and if you haven't experienced them before, this is a great dish in which to do so. And guess what: With Chinese yard-long beans, there are no strings attached — literally! These stringless beans make the chore of removing those fibrous strands a distant memory.

Variation: Traditionally, cooks include dried shrimp in this dish to give it a more robust flavor. (See the sidebar on dried shrimp in Chapter 13.) If you'd like to do the same, soak them first in warm water for about 15 minutes. Then drain and coarsely chop the shrimp, adding them to the wok after the ground pork has lost its pink color.

Three Mushrooms

Welcome to the wonderful world of mushrooms! This simple dish — the name says it all — introduces you to three different mushrooms, each with its own distinct texture and flavor. Really, it's all about those different textures and flavors that intermingle in your mouth when you combine mushrooms in this way.

You don't have to stop at just three, either. If you'd like, add some soaked and sliced dried black mushrooms to the stir-fry as well.

Preparation time: 12 minutes

Cooking time: 6 minutes

Yield: 4 servings

2 tablespoons cooking oil

8 basil leaves

8 to 10 fresh shiitake mushrooms, halved (quartered if large)

1 cup small button mushrooms

1 can (15 ounces) straw mushrooms, unpeeled and drained

⅓ cup chicken broth

1 tablespoon oyster-flavored sauce

1 tablespoon dark soy sauce

½ teaspoon cornstarch dissolved in 2 teaspoons water

1 Place a wok over high heat until hot. Add the oil, swirling to coat the sides. Add the basil leaves and cook, stirring until fragrant, about 10 seconds. Add the shiitake, button, and straw mushrooms and chicken broth; mix well. Cover and cook for about 2 minutes.

2 Add the oyster-flavored sauce and dark soy sauce; cook for 1 minute. Add the cornstarch solution and cook, stirring, until the sauce boils and thickens.

Eggplants with Spicy Sauce

The mild, neutral flavor of eggplant pairs well with a potent sauce. This one gets its spice from a generous dose of chile garlic sauce that's balanced with some dark soy sauce, sugar, and rice vinegar. The combination of flavors, colors (you can't beat that eggplant-purple), and textures really makes this Chinese vegetable creation stand out.

Preparation time: 20 minutes

Cooking time: 25 minutes

Yield: 4 servings

6 ounces ground pork

1 tablespoon soy sauce

⅔ cup chicken broth

3 tablespoons dark soy sauce

2 tablespoons black vinegar

1 tablespoon hoisin sauce

1 tablespoon chile garlic sauce

1 teaspoon sesame oil

3 tablespoons cooking oil

1 pound Asian eggplants, roll cut

6 cloves garlic, sliced

½ cup basil leaves

¾ teaspoon cornstarch dissolved in 1 teaspoon water

1 Combine the pork with the soy sauce in a bowl; let stand for 10 minutes.

2 To make the sauce, combine the chicken broth, dark soy sauce, vinegar, hoisin sauce, chile garlic sauce, and sesame oil in a bowl.

3 Place a wok over high heat until hot. Add 2 tablespoons of the cooking oil, swirling to coat the sides. Add the eggplants until lightly browned, about 4 to 5 minutes. Remove and set aside.

4 Return the wok to high heat until hot. Add the remaining 1 tablespoon cooking oil, swirling to coat the sides. Add the garlic and basil; cook, stirring, until fragrant, about 10 seconds. Add the pork and stir-fry for 2 minutes. Return the eggplants to the wok and add the sauce; stir to mix well. Reduce the heat to medium. Cover and simmer until the eggplants are tender, 10 to 12 minutes. Add the cornstarch solution and cook, stirring, until the sauce boils and thickens.

Variation: Thankfully, Asian eggplants are becoming more and more available in Western supermarkets; they're the perfect size for a light and simple dish for one. But if these slender purple jewels are still few and far between in your area, a larger Italian "globe" eggplant, cut into bite-size pieces, can take their place.

Tip: Because eggplants, as well as zucchini and mushrooms, have a tendency to absorb more oil during cooking than some less porous vegetables, you may find that you have to top off the oil in the wok as you're stir-frying these vegetables. If it's looking pretty dry in there, and the eggplant pieces are beginning to stick, add a little bit more oil. And use a light hand; more than a few drops will turn the eggplant greasy.

Better shredder: Another handy knife-handling technique

The Chinatown Chop Suey recipe in this chapter mentions using diced cabbage, but if you're looking for another way to prepare your cabbage for this and a whole host of other cabbage-containing dishes, try your hand at shredding. It's actually a pretty common knife technique in Chinese cuisine, and it's perfect for making thin, fairly uniform slivers out of an ingredient. Here's how to do it:

1. Begin as you would for matchstick or julienne cutting (see Chapter 5), by first slicing the ingredient into thin slices.

2. Stack the slices evenly.

3. Cut vertically through the stacked slices, creating thin shreds of the ingredient — thinner, even, than matchsticks.

Plenty of other ingredients take well to shredding, including carrots, zucchini, ginger, bamboo shoots, and cucumber. Just remember that when shredding several ingredients that are destined for the same dish, keep the shred size uniform to ensure that they all cook evenly.

Swiss Chard with Tender Pork Slices

Despite Swiss chard's European sounding name, it's actually a very popular green in China, where it's called *jui na choy*. Judging by this title, which roughly translates to "pig's food," you may think its popularity is highest in the pigpen. But make no mistake about it: Chinese humans — myself included — go hog-wild for Swiss chard. I once ate the stuff every day for four consecutive years!

Preparation time: *18 minutes*

Cooking time: *6 minutes*

Yield: *4 servings*

1 teaspoon soy sauce	*1 tablespoon Chinese rice wine*
1 teaspoon cornstarch	*1 teaspoon sesame oil*
⅛ teaspoon white pepper	*2 tablespoons cooking oil*
4 ounces thinly sliced pork	*2 teaspoons minced garlic*
3 tablespoons chicken broth	*8 ounces Swiss chard, cut into 2-inch lengths*
2 tablespoons oyster-flavored sauce	

1 To make the marinade, combine the soy sauce, cornstarch, and white pepper in a bowl. Add the pork and stir to coat. Let stand for 10 minutes.

2 To make the sauce, combine the chicken broth, oyster-flavored sauce, rice wine, and sesame oil in a bowl.

3 Place a wok over high heat until hot. Add 1 tablespoon of the cooking oil, swirling to coat the sides. Add the garlic and cook, stirring until fragrant, about 10 seconds. Add the Swiss chard and sauté until slightly soft, about 2 minutes. Remove and place on a serving plate.

4 Return the wok to high heat until hot. Add the remaining 1 tablespoon oil, swirling to coat the sides. Add the pork; stir-fry until lightly browned, about 2 minutes. Add the sauce and cook, stirring until it boils and reduces slightly. Pour over the Swiss chard and serve immediately.

Chinatown Chop Suey

"Miscellaneous odds and ends." That's the literal translation of the Cantonese words *chop suey,* and the combination of ingredients in this recipe for chop suey fits the bill perfectly. In fact, chop suey is a dish that really doesn't need a recipe at all. All you need is a refrigerator and pantry full of leftover vegetables, some seasonings and sauces, and even meat if you'd like, and you have the makings for your very own version of chop suey.

A typical survey of my kitchen would likely yield the ingredients in this recipe. If you see something there you don't have or don't like, substitute it with something you do have and do like. And if you want to make a full meal out of your chop suey, pair it with rice or noodles to get a simple, hearty dish that puts miscellaneous odds and ends in a whole new light.

Preparation time: *20 minutes*

Cooking time: *10 minutes*

Yield: *4 servings*

¾ cup chicken broth

2 tablespoons oyster-flavored sauce

1½ tablespoons Chinese rice wine

2 tablespoons cooking oil

1 tablespoon minced garlic

6 ounces boneless lean pork, thinly sliced

2 heaping cups diced green cabbage
(1-inch pieces)

½ cup sliced water chestnuts

⅔ cup thinly sliced carrots

1 cup bean sprouts

2 green onions, cut at an angle into 1-inch lengths

1 tablespoon cornstarch dissolved in 2 tablespoons water

1 To make the sauce, combine the chicken broth, oyster-flavored sauce, and rice wine in a bowl.

2 Place a wok over high heat until hot. Add the cooking oil, swirling to coat the sides. Add the garlic and cook, stirring, until fragrant, about 10 seconds. Add the pork and stir-fry until lightly browned, about 2 minutes.

3 Add the cabbage, water chestnuts, and carrots. Stir-fry until tender-crisp, about 2 minutes. Add the bean sprouts and stir to mix well. Add the sauce and bring it to a boil. Add the cornstarch solution and cook, stirring, until the sauce boils and thickens.

Chapter 15

Rice Bowls and Oodles of Noodles

· ·

In This Chapter

▶ Discovering varieties of rice

▶ Making the perfect rice recipe

▶ Noteworthy noodles

▶ Stirring up noodle dishes

· ·

Recipes in This Chapter

▶ Perfect Steamed Rice

▶ Perfect Steamed Glutinous Rice

▶ Fried Rice

▶ Sweet Precious Glutinous Rice

▶ Claypot Chicken and Mushroom Rice

▶ Easy-to-Make Chow Mein

▶ Hong Kong-Style Pan-Fried Noodles

▶ Chinese Chicken Noodle Soup

▶ Singapore Rice Noodles

▶ Beef Chow Fun

▶ Ja Jiang Mein

▶ Eight Treasures Noodle Soup

▶ Shanghai Fried Noodles

🦃 🝆 ⊘ 🝆 ⇗

*I*n China, rice reigns in the hot, humid paddies down south while amber waves of grain sway over the colder, drier plains up north. The same trend holds true when it comes to how the Chinese eats their main grains, rice and wheat. Old habits die hard even in this age of modern transportation and mass communication. Even at a time when traditional regional favorites are no longer restricted to their place of origin, inhabitants of southern China continue to pledge their allegiance to rice, while northerners don't let a day go by without enjoying some hearty noodles, dumplings, breads, or steamed buns made from wheat.

My recommendation to you: Take advantage of the wealth of both north and south. Rice and wheat (and rice and wheat products) make up the bulk of the Chinese diet, and all the creative rice and noodle dishes that showcase these humble starches make carbo-loading a delicious idea. But if steamed and fried is all you know of rice, or if your idea of a Chinese noodle is the one Confucius used to come up with all those great sayings, you have some pleasant surprises in store.

Rice to the Occasion

Chi le fan mei you? Have you eaten rice yet? The next time a Chinese friend asks you this, don't take it literally. The question is actually a common greeting — as well as proof of how intrinsically linked rice is with Chinese well-being, culture, and even language. In fact, the word for rice, *fan*, has come to mean "food" in conversational contexts. Rice, for many Chinese, is a way of life.

After all, when you've got billions of people to feed, rice makes an obvious staple. Why? Consider the following:

- ✔ Rice provides more calories per acre than any other crop except potatoes.
- ✔ Rice yields are typically high in the south's wet weather and often-flooded rice paddies.
- ✔ It's relatively inexpensive.
- ✔ As the recipes in this chapter prove, it's extremely versatile and can serve as the foundation for truly scrumptious meals.

In southern China, people eat rice with just about any meal, usually steaming or boiling it to a semidry and fluffy consistency — wet and gluey is not the way to serve rice in Guangzhou. *Unless*, that is, you're serving the thick, soupy rice porridge, called jook, that's as well loved and common on Cantonese breakfast tables as cereal is on North American ones. As for northern Chinese and Shanghainese, they exploit rice's ability to soak up and complement whatever they put atop it by serving plenty of sauces and other embellishments along with the grain.

In China, rice is such an important part of meals that any accompanying meat, fish, and vegetables dishes (what might be considered the main courses in the West) are really just icing on the cake — or better yet, icing on the rice. Rice creates a "cushion" that tones down the richness of heavier dishes, while its starchiness bulks up lighter ones. (See Chapter 17 for more on the role of rice in the Chinese family meal.) And though white rice is the most popular, the Chinese claim to grow and eat over 3,000 different rice varieties, including brown rice. That's probably an inflated number, but it is a testament to rice's role in the cuisine all the same. Some have said that rice is the foundation of all other tastes. This sounds about right to me.

Which Rice Will Suffice?

Although simple white rice seems about as basic as you can get, the wide variety of rice cultivated and consumed in China proves that there's a lot more to this humble grain than meets the eye. But before you panic and run out to buy dozens of rice bins for your kitchen, just remember that the most common types of rice fall within three fundamental categories:

Is "white" right when it comes to rice?

For China, white rice is the top choice. In fact, most of Asia prefers white rice over all other varieties, which range in color from pink and red to black. And as much as nutritionists may lament the age-old practice of "polishing" rice to a smooth, pearly whiteness, white rice isn't going away any time soon.

White rice actually begins its life brown. Remove the inedible outer hull, and you have the brown rice that nutritionists prefer. And why are they so enthusiastic about making polished rice a thing of the past? Because to turn brown rice white, processors must remove the bran and germ as well as the hull, which means removing the fiber, vitamin E, phosphorus, and B-complex vitamins

such as thiamin, niacin, and riboflavin that the bran and germ contain. And although most white rice in the United States is enriched with B vitamins and iron to make up for some of the nutritional losses, the rice eaten in China and other parts of Asia, for the most part, is not.

But it's not fair to blame white rice for any nutrient deficiencies China has suffered over the years. After all, a quick consideration of the rest of its diet — fresh produce, lean meats and seafood, and high-quality protein from vegetable sources such as soy — proves that where white rice falls short in the nutrition department, plenty of other dietary powerhouses can pick up the slack.

Long-grain rice (*Jim mike; chan mi*)

Most southern Chinese turn to long-grain rice for everyday — and every-meal — use. Of all the rice varieties, it is the least starchy, which means that it cooks up dry and fluffy, with grains that separate easily. This quality makes long-grain rice the top choice for classic fried rice.

In your local markets, you can find several varieties of long-grain rice, all of which work well in Chinese dishes. Here are the more aromatic kinds that you should try:

- ✔ **Basmati rice:** It has an unmistakable, nutty aroma that will turn your kitchen into an olfactory oasis whenever you cook it. Once the traditional rice of India and the Middle East, basmati now grows extensively on Texan farms.

- ✔ **Jasmine rice:** This is the most common import from Thailand, and its floral aroma lives up to its name. It's a perfect candidate for most Chinese long-grain rice dishes, too.

You're more likely to find jasmine and basmati rice in the Asian foods section of your grocery store rather than in the regular rice and beans aisle, although some supermarket shelf stockers are beginning to make the switch. After you open the bag or box, store uncooked rice in a tightly sealed container in a cool, dry place for up to several months. Place cooled, cooked rice in a container with a tight lid and store it in the refrigerator for up to several days. Just drizzle a little water into the container and reheat the rice in the microwave. Or, of course, use it in the fried rice recipes that appear later in the chapter.

Perfect Steamed Rice

Electric-rice-cooker-challenged, take heart! You too can make the fluffy, long-grain rice that you thought came only from Chinese restaurants — and you can make it the old-fashioned way. Just follow the stove-top instructions below. (They come straight from the best rice cook I know: Mom.)

Preparation time: 3 minutes

Cooking time: 16 minutes, plus 10 minutes for the rice to rest

Yield: 4 servings

2 cups long-grain rice   3 cups cold water

1 Rinse the rice; repeat 2 or 3 times until the water is clear; drain well.

2 Place the rice in a 3-quart saucepan with a tight-fitting lid; add the water. Bring to a boil, uncovered, and cook over high heat for 2 minutes. Reduce the heat to low; cover and simmer for 9 minutes. Remove from the heat and let it stand, covered, for 10 minutes. Remove the cover and fluff the rice with a fork.

Remember: Good rice comes to those who wait. Treasure those last 10 or so minutes of "sitting" time, as you let the cooked rice rest off the heat with the cover on. This technique leaves you with firm, fluffy rice; serve it too soon, and it will be soggy and overly starchy.

Martin Says: Chinese tradition says that adding salt to rice brings good luck and prosperity, and I see no reason why you shouldn't toss a pinch into the pot before bringing the water to a boil.

Medium-grain rice (Fong loi mike; fung lai mi)

Shorter than long-grain, medium-grain rice has fans in eastern China and Taiwan, as well as in Korea and Japan, where its higher starch content makes it sticky enough for sushi. When cooked (as you would long-grain rice, but with slightly less water), medium-grain rice is nuttier tasting and shinier than long-grain, as well as stickier and softer. To make it less sticky, use even less water in preparation.

Most supermarket rice and beans aisles carry medium-grain rice in various-sized plastic and paper bags, as well as in woven sacks with a variety of labels. Store raw medium-grain rice the same way you would long-grain: in a tightly sealed container in a cool, dry place. It will keep for months. Place cooled, cooked rice in a container with a tight lid and store in the refrigerator for up to several days. Reheat it as you would long-grain rice.

Glutinous rice (Nor mike; nuo mi)

A variety of short-grain rice, uncooked glutinous rice resembles tiny, opaque, oblong pearls. Follow the cooking instructions in the recipe for Perfect Steamed Glutinous Rice in this chapter, or just cook it according to package directions — chefs normally steam, rather than boil, glutinous rice. — Either way, it becomes soft, moist, translucent, sticky, and slightly sweet. No wonder it also goes by the names "sticky rice" and "sweet rice."

In Chinese cuisine, glutinous rice appears most often in dim sum and dessert items such as lotus wraps and rice puddings. It also makes an appearance in savory dishes such as salty *jungdz* — sticky rice wrapped in bamboo leaves and stuffed with salted duck eggs and roast pork. This is a popular treat during the Dragon Boat festival, although I like to eat it year-round. Glutinous rice's starchiness and natural tendency to stick together as a soft paste make it perfect for puddings and fillings. Before steaming or boiling glutinous rice, do as the pros do and plump the grains a bit by soaking them in water for several hours to overnight.

You can find glutinous rice in the rice and beans section and the Asian food aisle of your supermarket. Store any uncooked rice in a tightly sealed container in a cool, dry place, and it will keep for several months. Placed cooled cooked rice in a container with a tightly fitting lid and store in the refrigerator for up to several days, reheating it as you would long-grain and medium-grain rice.

If you bought the rice in a big bag imported from Asia, you may want to pick through the sack or bag first to weed out any rice hulls or pebbles that sneaked in from the paddy. Some less expensive types of rice also benefit from rinsing and draining several times before cooking. This is actually an old tradition in China, where the rhythmic motions of soaking the rice and rubbing the grains until the water runs clear is a calming, meditative process. However, because many rice producers in North America process the rice free of foreign materials and enrich it with water-soluble B vitamins, you may want to check the package directions and nutrition label before you rinse all that nutrition down the drain.

Perfect Steamed Glutinous Rice

Steaming glutinous rice to a perfectly moist and sticky finish can be a bit of a — ahem — sticky proposition, especially considering that many bags of imported glutinous rice either don't have cooking instructions or print the instructions in Chinese or Japanese.

But you don't need a crash course in Mandarin to make glutinous rice. Steaming glutinous rice is shockingly easy. Just follow these instructions, and you'll be a glutinous glutton in no time.

Preparation time: *Up to 8 hours or overnight for soaking the rice*

Cooking time: *25 minutes*

Yield: *4 servings*

1½ cups Chinese glutinous rice   *2 tablespoons water, for sprinkling*

1 Soak the glutinous rice for at least 8 hours or overnight; drain.

2 Prepare a wok for steaming (see Chapter 3).

3 Place the glutinous rice in a heatproof glass dish. Steam over high heat for 25 minutes. Sprinkle with some water at 10-minute intervals to retain the moisture.

Remember: Give the glutinous rice ample time to soak and absorb plenty of water — overnight is best. Doing so gives the plump little grains a chance to become even plumper, making the final dish moist and soft.

What to Make with Your Perfectly Cooked Rice

Master the technique for making perfectly cooked rice, with a little help from the recipes above, and you open up a treasure chest of rice dishes that's as deep as your imagination allows. With more than half the world's population eating rice at least once a day, cooks have obviously figured out some delicious ways of doing just that. Personally, I think these dishes are among the best.

Fried Rice

Leftovers get a makeover in this answer to the age-old question "What do I do with last night's rice?" Actually, the fluffy, slightly dry texture of fried rice practically depends on your using day-old — or at least not-straight-from-the-stove-or-steamer — rice. Freshly cooked rice still contains so much moisture that when you stir-fry it with all the other ingredients, you end up with a wet, clumpy dish.

Break up the clumps that form in the leftover rice by gently rubbing the grains between your fingers or breaking them apart with a wooden spoon or rubber scraper before stir-frying. Separate grains stir-fry more quickly and evenly than huge clumps.

Preparation time: *15 minutes*

Cooking time: *8 minutes*

Yield: *4 servings*

3 tablespoons cooking oil

2 eggs, lightly beaten

¼ teaspoon salt

⅛ teaspoon white pepper

3 cups cold, cooked long-grain rice, fluffed

¾ cup diced char siu (store-bought or made with recipe in Chapter 12)

¾ cup frozen peas and carrots, thawed

1½ tablespoons soy sauce

4 green onions, thinly sliced

1 Place a wok over high heat until hot. Add 2 tablespoons of the oil, swirling to coat the sides. Add the eggs, salt, and white pepper; cook until lightly scrambled. Use a spatula to move the eggs to the side. Add the remaining 1 tablespoon oil. Add the rice; stir for 2 minutes.

2 Add the char siu and peas and carrots; stir to mix well. Add the soy sauce and green onions; stir-fry for 1 minute.

Variation: After making fried rice for a while, you can cast recipes aside. Fried rice is really meant to be one of those do-it-yourself dishes, so whatever looks good in your pantry is a potential fried rice ingredient. I chose the particular ingredients for this dish with the goal in mind of creating a fried rice like those you get at Chinese restaurants. As you become more familiar with Chinese cuisine, take some chances and create your own fried rice dishes by using regional or seasonal ingredients. For instance, if you'd like fried rice with shrimp, it's a short order to fill: Before you add the eggs, quickly stir-fry some shrimp until they begin to curl and turn pink. Set them aside, proceed with the fried rice recipe, and return the shrimp to the wok for a quick heat-through before serving.

Sweet Precious Glutinous Rice

This dish makes a beautiful presentation when you invert it out of the bowl in which it steams — it looks almost like a pearly, jewel-studded pudding. Dim sum restaurants serve a variety of steamed rice dishes similar to this, all of which take advantage of the dense, soft, and slightly chewy texture of cooked glutinous rice.

Preparation time: *35 minutes*

Cooking time: *8 minutes*

Yield: *4 servings*

5 dried black mushrooms

1 tablespoon dried shrimp

1 tablespoon cooking oil

1 tablespoon minced garlic

1 Chinese sausage, coarsely diced

3 cups cooked Perfect Steamed Glutinous Rice (see recipe in this chapter)

1 tablespoon chopped cilantro

2 tablespoons soy sauce

1 teaspoon sesame oil

1 green onion, chopped (optional)

1 In separate bowls, soak the mushrooms and dried shrimp in warm water until softened, about 20 minutes; drain. Discard the mushroom stems and coarsely chop the caps. Coarsely chop the dried shrimp.

2 Place a wok over high heat until hot. Add the cooking oil, swirling to coat the sides. Add the garlic and cook, stirring, until fragrant, about 10 seconds. Add the sausage, mushrooms, and shrimp; stir-fry for about 2 minutes. Add the rice and cilantro; stir to mix well. Season with the soy sauce and sesame oil.

3 Prepare a wok for steaming (see Chapters 3 and 5). Place the rice mixture in a bowl (about 6 inches in diameter and 4 inches deep), and steam over high heat for about 10 minutes. Invert onto a serving plate. If desired, garnish with the green onion.

Tip: Here's the quickest way to dice Chinese sausage: Cut the links into ¼-inch slices and then coarsely chop. That's all there is to it.

Claypot Chicken and Mushroom Rice

Here's a chance to use the claypot introduced in Chapter 3. It's the perfect Chinese casserole dish, and this recipe makes the perfect Chinese casserole. Volunteer to make this flavorful one-pot meal the next time you're invited to a potluck.

Preparation time: 20 minutes

Cooking time: 40 minutes

Yield: 4 servings

6 dried black mushrooms

2 tablespoons oyster-flavored sauce

2 teaspoons Chinese rice wine

6 chicken drummettes

2 to 3 tablespoons soy sauce

1 teaspoon sesame oil

1 tablespoon cooking oil

3 pieces thinly sliced ginger, lightly crushed

2½ cups plus ¼ cup chicken broth

1½ cups long-grain rice

2 Chinese sausages, cut into thirds

1 Soak the mushrooms in warm water until softened, about 20 minutes; drain. Discard the stems and cut the caps in half.

2 Make a marinade by combining the oyster-flavored sauce and rice wine in a bowl; add the chicken and stir to coat. Let stand for 10 minutes.

3 Combine the soy sauce and sesame oil in a small dish; set aside.

4 Place a wok over high heat until hot. Add the cooking oil, swirling to coat the sides. Add the ginger and cook, stirring until fragrant, about 10 seconds. Add the chicken and stir-fry until lightly browned, about 3 minutes. Add the mushrooms and the ¼ cup of chicken broth; stir for 1 minute. Reduce the heat to low, cover, and simmer until the chicken is cooked, about 5 minutes. Set aside.

5 Place a claypot over low heat; gradually increase the heat to medium-high. Add the rice and the 2 ½ cups chicken broth; increase the heat to high and bring it to a boil. Reduce the heat to low; cover and cook until the water level is just below the top of the rice, about 15 minutes.

6 Place the chicken, mushrooms, and sausages over the top of the rice; cover and continue cooking for an additional 15 minutes. (Rice will be tender and flavors intermingled).

7 Drizzle the soy sauce mixture over the top.

Noodling Around

Rice may be nice, but in the north and west of China, noodles are nicer. In fact, in much of northern China, where it's too cold and dry to grow rice, noodles are so common that, to a southerner like myself, rice seems downright rare in comparison. (Not until the Mongol invasions and the introduction of northerners to the imperial court did southern Chinese gourmets stop dismissing noodles as peasant food and finally allow them at their rice-filled tables.)

Fortunately, noodles have swept across China just as easily as rice — converting taste buds along the way and leaving a legacy of hearty noodle soups as well as braised, fried, and tossed noodle dishes in all regions.

Traditionally thought of as snacks and small meals in the south, noodles still make classic lunchtime dishes in southern homes and restaurants. When I was a child, that was the only time of day that my mother would make noodles, no matter how much I begged. But in northern China, they're fair game any time of day. Here's a brief sampling of some of the different styles in which Chinese serve and eat noodles:

- ✔ Warmed in stews, soups, and casseroles
- ✔ Stir-fried with vegetables and meats
- ✔ Fried into a crispy pancake shape and topped with meat or vegetables and a sauce
- ✔ Simply boiled and tossed with a sauce and any other appealing ingredients
- ✔ Chilled with a light dressing as a cooling snack during hot weather

If these suggestions get your appetite going, the recipes that follow will do more of the same.

And though you may be most familiar with China's wheat-based noodles, southern Chinese use rice flour to make rice noodles. Even mung bean flour becomes the thin, glassy noodles known as cellophane noodles or bean threads. All these noodles come in different shapes and sizes. Whether flat, round, wide, or thin, or in sheets, ribbons, strings, or strands, Chinese noodles add oodles of variety to Chinese meals.

Choose a Noodle, Any Noodle

Whether the Italians invented noodles or Marco Polo just took them home to Venice from their rightful birthplace in China, there's no question that the Chinese love their noodles and have for centuries. The shapes of their noodles may not vary as much as do those of Italian pasta — you won't see pasta shaped like bow ties or wagon wheels in China, for example. However, the different ingredients used to make Chinese noodles do set one variety apart from the next. Here are some basic descriptions of what you'll find in Chinese markets and on Chinese restaurant menus. See Figure 15-1 for illustrations of these noodles.

Fresh egg noodles (Darn min; ji dan mein)

Of all the Chinese noodles, fresh egg noodles bear the strongest resemblance to Western pasta, although some striking differences still distinguish the two. For example, although Italian pasta is made from semolina flour and some-times eggs, Chinese noodle makers use regular wheat flour and, almost always, eggs. Wheat grows plentifully in China's north, much more so than rice, and these wheat-based noodles enjoy considerable popularity in their home turf and throughout China.

Like Italian pasta, Chinese egg noodles come in both fresh and dried forms and in a wide range of widths, lengths, and flavors. If you can find fresh Chinese egg noodles, more power to you. You only need to lightly blanch them before stir-frying with vegetables and chicken to make the classic *chow mein* – literally, "stir-fried noodles". (Boil the dried version fully to rehydrate them first) Toss cooked noodles with stir-fried meat and vegetables to create *lo mein*, or tossed noodle dishes. Pan-fry cooked egg noodles into a crispy, browned pancake shape, top them with meat or vegetables and a sauce, and bingo — you've created a classic noodle treat that's a favorite in Hong Kong. Of course, egg noodles make perfect accompaniments to savory braised meats with hearty northern Chinese sauces. And don't forget to add Chinese egg noodles to hot soups and cool, lightly dressed salads.

Many stores carry fresh and dried egg noodles in plastic packages and cello-phane-wrapped boxes. Store fresh noodles in the refrigerator for up to a week or freeze them for up to several months. Keep dried egg noodles in an unopened package or, after opening, in a tightly sealed container in a cool, dry place. They'll keep for several months.

Be picky when purchasing fresh Chinese egg noodles. Take a good look through the package and pass up those bundles that appear stuck together in gluey lumps. These noodles are probably too moist and may not separate fully when plunged into boiling water. Try to get as good an idea as you can of the noodles' texture through the package, as well, *gently* poking and squeez-ing the plastic-wrapped noodles. If they feel (and look) stiff and dry, they may crack into pieces when you cook them.

Long live the noodle!

What's the one dish that's a must at Chinese birthday, anniversary, New Year's, and wedding celebrations? No, it's not cake. It's noodles — long-life noodles, to be precise. In the rich world of Chinese food symbolism, noodles enjoy a very auspicious position, and for good reason: Chinese noodles are long (especially the hand-made *la mein*.) That length has grown to symbolize a long, unbroken life, whether the life belongs to a person, a career, a relationship, or even an imperial dynasty. What better way to celebrate a long life than with a big bowl of long-life noodles?

Chinese cooks take great care not to break or cut noodles when preparing them for a banquet or celebration. (Gently stirring and tossing them with chopsticks as they cook helps.) You should do the same once those noodles get to your table. Slurp them with care and try as hard as you can to safely suck each strand into your mouth in one piece. If you cut a noodle with your teeth, legend has it that you'll similarly shorten the life of whomever or whatever you're cele-brating. But according to my own legend, you'll just have an easier time eating the noodles.

Shanghai noodles are a thicker style of round noodle that, as their name sug-gests, originated in Shanghai. Because they're larger and more filling than the thinner types, they deserve a hearty, more richly flavored sauce, which is just the kind that Shanghai cooks are known for making. Boil Shanghai noo-dles until tender and serve with a rich sauce of your own choosing. Because they're normally available fresh, follow the shopping and storage instructions for fresh noodles mentioned earlier in this section.

Fresh rice noodles (Seen hor fun; xian he fen)

Although not quite as common in American-Chinese restaurants as chow mein, chow fun, or the stir-fried Chinese rice noodle dish that's an easy find in any Chinatown, makes a delicious, richly textured treat. When fresh, these characteristically southern Chinese noodles are soft and pliable and have a milky white color. They're made from long-grain rice flour and water and come in whole folded sheets that you cut to your desired thickness, or in ready-cut strips ranging in width from a couple inches to thin, linguine-like strands. Both types have a light coating of oil to keep the notoriously sticky noodles from sticking together. To remove this coating, you need only rinse them gently with hot water.

After rinsing, stir-fry the strips to create a crispy-edged, soft-centered, chewy treat that tastes and feels wonderfully rich to the palate. A Chinese restaurant favorite that's worth trying is beef chow fun — you can even try it in your own kitchen by using the recipe found later in this chapter. Experiment with your own flavor combinations. The mild taste of rice noodles goes well with just about anything.

Look for fresh rice noodles in plastic bags or plastic-wrapped foam trays in the refrigerated sections of Asian markets. Choose those that are soft and spongy to the touch, and try to use them the day of purchase, when they're softest and freshest. If doing so is not an option, store them in the refrigerator for up to several days. Refrigeration may stiffen them, so remember to soften them with hot water before cooking.

Dried rice noodles (Gon hor fun; gan he fen)

Not everyone is lucky enough to live near a Chinatown with fresh noodle shops, so fresh rice noodles may be something of a luxury or a purely restaurant-based treat for many. But if you're keen to make your own rice noodle dishes, you can find dried ones in an increasing number of supermarket Asian food sections. Made from the same rice flour as the fresh kind, these translucent, brittle sticks and ribbons are firmer than fresh, but are still excellent alternatives for those of us who just can't live without our rice noodles.

Before stir-frying them or using them in soups, soak dried rice noodles in warm water to soften — a half hour to an hour is all they need. Thinner varieties of dried rice noodles also deep-fry nicely; separate a bundle into small handfuls and deep-fry each one individually until it puffs and expands. Then use the crispy nets to garnish stir-fries and salads.

You'll find dried rice noodles in varying widths and lengths in plastic packages in Asian markets and the Asian food section of supermarkets. Store opened packages in tightly sealed containers in a cool, dry place. They'll keep for several months.

Cellophane or bean thread noodles (Fun xi; fen si)

These semi-transparent noodles made from mung bean flour look like coils of fishing line, but you wouldn't want to leave them in the tackle box. Their mild flavor and slightly elastic consistency perfectly complement soups and casseroles with thick sauces and rich seasonings that cling to the noodles' surfaces. Chinese grocery stores often carry different lengths and thicknesses of these noodles (also called Chinese vermicelli, or *fun xi*), so go ahead and have fun with your fun xi.

Before adding bean thread noodles to a dish, soak to soften them in plenty of warm water. If the dish itself has a lot of liquid and calls for long simmering, you can add the noodles while they're still a bit firm. But don't use dry noodles right out of the bag — they'll absorb so much liquid from whatever dish you're cooking that they'll leave it dry. You can also deep-fry dried cellophane noodles as you would dried rice noodles, separating a bundle and adding a handful at a time to hot oil. They also make great salad garnishes.

You can find bean thread noodles in plastic packages that often hold a number of individual noodle bundles. Store opened packages in a container with a tightly fitting lid in a cool, dry place for several months.

Figure 15-1:
Use your noodle, and this illustration, to guide you through the choices in Chinese noodles — from bean thread and egg to fresh and dried rice flour varieties.

FRESH

RICE NOODLES

DRIED

BEAN THREAD NOODLES   EGG NOODLES   RICE NOODLES

Noodle Recipes

The following recipes show you what to do with your noodles.

Easy-to-Make Chow Mein

Actually, the whole point of chow mein ("stir-fried noodles" in Cantonese) is that it should be easy to make — a quick stir and toss, and there you have it. Remember, once you get down the basics of stir frying, you're free to invent whatever chow mein creations strike your fancy. As with fried rice, what you put in this noodle dish is really up to you. Use this recipe to get your imagination (and your appetite) going.

Preparation time: *20 minutes*

Cooking time: *12 minutes*

Yield: *4 servings*

8 ounces fresh or dried Chinese egg noodles	*½ teaspoon sugar*
	3 tablespoons cooking oil
6 ounces lean pork, thinly sliced	*2 teaspoons minced garlic*
1 tablespoon oyster-flavored sauce	*3 bok choy (or any leafy Chinese greens), cut into 1½-inch pieces*
½ cup chicken broth	
2 tablespoons dark soy sauce	*1½ cups bean sprouts*
2 teaspoons sesame oil	*3 green onions, cut into 2-inch pieces*

1 In a large pot of boiling water, cook the noodles according to the package directions until barely tender to the bite; drain, rinse with cold water, and drain again.

2 Combine the pork and the oyster-flavored sauce in a bowl; stir to coat. Let stand for 10 minutes.

3 Make a sauce by combining the chicken broth, dark soy sauce, sesame oil, and sugar in a small bowl.

4 Place a wok over high heat until hot. Add the cooking oil, swirling to coat the sides. Add the garlic and cook, stirring, until fragrant, about 10 seconds. Add the pork and stir-fry for 2 minutes.

5 Add the noodles and sauce; gently toss until heated through. Add the bok choy, bean sprouts, and green onions; cook for 2 minutes, stirring to mix well.

Remember: Just as fried rice is great for using leftover rice, chow mein is a perfect opportunity for doing something with leftover noodles. However, unlike fried rice — which requires rice that's not brand-spanking new — chow mein comes out just as well with freshly cooked noodles.

Variation: To save time, keep plenty of All-Purpose Stir-Fry Sauce or Hot and Spicy Stir-Fry Sauce, both from Chapter 7, on hand. Instead of making the sauce in the recipe, just add ⅓ cup chicken broth to ½ cup of either sauce and toss it with the noodles.

Hong Kong-Style Pan-Fried Noodles

It's no wonder that this classic noodle creation from Hong Kong has almost as many fans in the West as it does in its rightful birthplace. The "pancake" of fried noodles topped with saucy meat and vegetables (or whatever else you like) has a smoky, caramelized flavor and a rich, crisply textured surface that no one can resist. Also, the pancake's combination of crispy outside and soft inside is the perfect embodiment of culinary balance of yin and yang.

Preparation time: *25 minutes*

Cooking time: *45 minutes*

Yield: *4 servings*

6 ounces medium raw shrimp, shelled and deveined

6 ounces sea scallops, halved horizontally

⅛ teaspoon white pepper

1¼ cups chicken broth

2 tablespoons oyster-flavored sauce

1 teaspoon sesame oil

¼ teaspoon sugar

1 tablespoon cornstarch

8 ounces fresh thin egg noodles

¼ cup cooking oil

1 tablespoon minced garlic

1 teaspoon minced ginger

4 fresh shiitake mushrooms, sliced

3 baby bok choy, quartered lengthwise

1 Combine the shrimp, scallops, and white pepper in a bowl.

2 Make a sauce by combining the chicken broth, oyster-flavored sauce, sesame oil, sugar, and cornstarch in a small bowl.

3 In a large pot of boiling water, cook the noodles according to the package instructions; drain, rinse with cold water, and drain again.

4 Place a 10- to 12-inch nonstick frying pan over medium-high heat until hot. Add 1 tablespoon of the cooking oil, swirling to coat the sides. Spread the noodles in the pan and press lightly to make a firm cake. Cook until the bottom is golden brown, about 5 minutes. Turn the pancake over, add 1 more tablespoon of the cooking oil around the edges of the pan, and cook until the other side is golden brown, 3 to 4 minutes. Remove to a serving plate and keep warm.

5 Place a wok over high heat until hot. Add 1 tablespoon of the cooking oil, swirling to coat the sides. Add the garlic and ginger; cook, stirring, until fragrant, about 10 seconds. Add the shrimp and scallops; stir-fry until the shrimp turn pink and the scallops are slightly firm, about 2 minutes. Remove and set aside.

6 Add the remaining 1 tablespoon cooking oil to the wok over high heat, swirling to coat the sides. Add the mushrooms; cook for 1 minute. Add the sauce and bring it to a boil. Add the baby bok choy; cover and cook for 1 minute. Return the seafood to the wok and stir to heat through. Pour on top of the noodle pancake and serve.

Chinese Chicken Noodle Soup

This is *not* your mom's chicken noodle soup, although it's just as good for the soul — and for the body — as any lovingly prepared, home-cooked chicken noodle soup ever could be. It's also a great place for you to put that Chinese chicken broth from Chapter 9 to use.

Preparation time: 18 minutes

Cooking time: 10 minutes

Yield: 4 servings

6 to 8 ounces boneless, skinless chicken, thinly sliced

1 tablespoon plus ½ teaspoon soy sauce

8 ounces thin fresh egg noodles

6 cups chicken broth

⅛ teaspoon white pepper

¼ cup thinly sliced carrots

2 cups spinach leaves

6 medium white mushrooms

2 teaspoons cornstarch dissolved in 1 tablespoon water

1 teaspoon sesame oil

1 Combine the chicken and ½ teaspoon soy sauce in a bowl; stir to coat. Let stand for 10 minutes.

2 In a large pot of boiling water, cook the noodles according to the package directions until tender to the bite; drain, rinse with cold water, and drain again. Divide equally among 4 individual bowls; set aside.

3 Bring the broth, 1 tablespoon soy sauce, and white pepper to a boil in a large pot. Reduce the heat to low. Add the chicken and simmer for 3 minutes. Add the carrots, spinach, and mushrooms; cook for a further 2 minutes. Add the cornstarch solution; cook, stirring until the soup thickens slightly. Stir in the sesame oil. Ladle the soup over the noodles.

Variation: If you'd like, use thin, dried rice noodles in this soup. Soak them first to soften and then boil to remove any powdery residue of rice flour. Add to the simmering soup. You can also put them in individual soup bowls and ladle the soup over the top.

Remember: A little garnish of green onion rounds can really add a shot of color, flavor, and aroma to this sublime soup.

Singapore Rice Noodles

How's this for a culinary journey? The curry flavors that characterize this noodle dish hail originally from India. From there, they traveled to Singapore, where they blended their own spicy signature with the Chinese dishes that Chinese immigrants brought to Singapore in the mid-1800s. Today, the curried rice-noodle dish has spread to Chinese restaurants around the world, where its name, Singapore rice noodles, still pays homage to its origin.

Preparation time: *25 minutes*

Cooking time: *14 minutes*

Yield: *4 servings*

8 ounces dried rice vermicelli	*2 teaspoons minced garlic*
2 tablespoons curry powder	*½ cup julienned onion*
1 teaspoon turmeric powder	*½ cup julienned carrots*
½ cup chicken broth	*1 cup bean sprouts*
2 tablespoons cooking oil	*3 ounces julienned char siu (store-bought or see Chapter 12)*
1 egg, lightly beaten	

1 Soak the rice vermicelli in warm water until softened, 6 to 8 minutes.

2 Make a curry mixture by combining the curry powder, turmeric powder, and chicken broth in a bowl.

3 Place a wok over high heat until hot. Add 2 teaspoons of the oil, swirling to coat the sides. Add the egg; cook to make an omelet that is slightly browned. Remove from the wok; cut into ¼-inch strips.

4 Return the wok to high heat until hot. Add the remaining oil, swirling to coat the sides. Add the garlic and cook, stirring until fragrant, about 10 seconds. Add the onion and carrots; stir-fry for 1 minute. Add the rice vermicelli and toss for 1 minute. Add the curry mixture and cook, tossing to coat thoroughly, until the vermicelli is slightly softened. Use chopsticks in one hand and a spatula in the other to lift the noodles up to combine them with the vegetables.

5 Add the bean sprouts and the char siu; stir for 2 minutes. Garnish with the omelet strips.

Beef Chow Fun

This one's a real restaurant favorite. The salty-sweet sauce provides the perfect foil for the chewy, richly textured rice noodles. To jump-start that sauce's flavor even more, stir a little crushed red pepper into the dish near the end of the cooking time.

Preparation time: *30 minutes*

Cooking time: *10 minutes*

Yield: *4 servings*

½ *pound dried wide rice noodles*

3 *tablespoons dark soy sauce*

1 *teaspoon Chinese rice wine*

1 *teaspoon cornstarch*

6 *ounces flank steak, thinly sliced across the grain*

½ *cup chicken broth*

3 *tablespoons cooking oil*

1½ *cups sliced onions*

3 *green onions, cut into 1-inch pieces*

1 Soak the noodles in warm water until softened, about 30 minutes; drain.

2 Make a marinade by combining 1 tablespoon of the dark soy sauce, the rice wine, and cornstarch in a small bowl; add the beef and stir to coat. Let stand for 10 minutes.

3 Make a sauce by combining the chicken broth and the remaining 2 tablespoons dark soy sauce in a bowl.

4 Place a wok over high heat until hot. Add 2 tablespoons of the oil, swirling to coat the sides. Add the noodles and stir for 1 minute. Add half the sauce and cook, stirring, until the noodles are evenly coated. Remove and set aside.

5 Place the wok over medium-high heat until hot. Add the remaining 1 tablespoon oil, swirling to coat the sides. Add the onions and stir-fry for 1 minute. Add the flank steak and the green onions; stir-fry until the beef is no longer pink, about 1 to 2 minutes. Return the noodles to the wok and toss gently. Add the remaining sauce to coat evenly and cook for about 2 minutes.

Variation: Great kudos to you if you can find fresh rice noodles for this dish instead of the usual dry variety. Remember that the fresh noodles don't need prior soaking to rehydrate them. A quick rinse with hot water separates them, removes their oily coating, and sufficiently softens them for cooking. Leave out that step, and you may end up with a big slab of mushy rice noodles.

Ja Jiang Mein

In northern China, people enjoy this flavorful noodle dish hot or at room temperature. Actually, because it's common practice for the noodles themselves to be cold, topping them with the warm meat and sauce sets up a pleasing temperature contrast. Enjoy this dish at whatever temperature you like for a quick breakfast, lunch, snack, or dinner. (Any time is noodle time in northern China.)

Chinese men like to cook this quick and easy dish when they invite dates over for a home-cooked meal. It's a Chinese version of *spaghetti bolognese* that they can always count on to impress a woman.

Preparation time: *40 minutes*

Cooking time: *8 minutes*

Yield: *4 to 6 servings*

½ cup chicken broth	*1 tablespoon cooking oil*
½ cup sweet bean paste	*1 tablespoon minced garlic*
1 tablespoon chile garlic sauce	*1 cup diced onion (½-inch)*
1 tablespoon soy sauce	*½ pound ground meat*
1 tablespoon plus 1 teaspoon sesame oil	*1 cup thinly julienned cucumber*
10 ounces dried wheat noodles or fresh egg noodles	*1 cup thinly julienned carrot*

1 Make a sauce by combining the chicken broth, sweet bean paste, garlic sauce, soy sauce, and the 1 teaspoon sesame oil in a small bowl.

2 In a large pot of boiling water, cook the noodles according to the package directions; drain, rinse with cold water, and drain again.

3 Place a wok over high heat until hot. Add the cooking oil, swirling to coat the sides. Add the garlic and cook, stirring, until fragrant, about 10 seconds. Add the onion and stir-fry until almost translucent, about 2 minutes. Add the meat and stir-fry until brown and crumbly, about 2 minutes. Add the sauce and cook until the sauce boils and thickens slightly, about 3 minutes.

4 Before serving, toss the noodles with the 1 tablespoon sesame oil to coat. Place on a serving plate and pour the sauce over the noodles; arrange the cucumber and carrot on the top.

Remember: Use an English or Japanese cucumber for a crispier, sweeter texture and taste. And when purchasing sweet bean paste — a salty-sweet paste made from fermented soybeans and sugar — don't confuse it with sweet bean sauce, which has a very different consistency. Pastes are thicker than sauces, and for this recipe, you want thick.

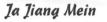

Eight Treasures Noodle Soup

Feel like having a delicious noodle soup? You won't want to miss this one. And the number eight is very special in Chinese culture, too: The Cantonese word for the number eight is *batt,* which sounds similar to the word *fatt,* which itself means "prosperity." Because symbolism is an inescapable part of Chinese cuisine and culture, you often find dishes that take advantage of eight's propitious link with prosperity by including eight tasty "treasures" in their recipe.

Preparation time: *30 minutes*

Cooking time: *15 minutes*

Yield: *4 servings*

6 pieces cloud ears	*½ teaspoon sugar*
1 pound fresh Chinese egg noodles	*1 cup thinly sliced carrots*
1 package julienned Sichuan preserved vegetables (about ¾ cup)	*¾ cup julienned red bell pepper*
8 ounces pressed tofu	*1 teaspoon cornstarch dissolved in 2 teaspoons water*
6 cups chicken broth	*2 cups julienned iceberg lettuce*
2 tablespoons oyster-flavored sauce	

1 Soak the cloud ears in warm water until softened, about 15 minutes; drain. Coarsely chop.

2 In a large pot of boiling water, cook the noodles according to the package directions. Drain, rinse with cold water, and drain again. Divide the noodles equally among 4 individual bowls; set aside.

3 Rinse the Sichuan preserved vegetables to get rid of the excess salt.

4 Cut the tofu into ½-x-1-x-¼-inch pieces.

5 Combine the cloud ears, chicken broth, oyster-flavored sauce, and sugar in a large pot; bring to a boil and cook for 3 minutes. Add the carrots, bell pepper, and Sichuan preserved vegetables; cook for 1 minute. Add the tofu and cornstarch solution; cook, stirring until the soup boils.

6 To serve, top the bowls of noodles with the lettuce. Ladle the soup over the noodles.

Variation: For those of you who enjoy a little meat or seafood with your noodle soup, just add strips or slices of your favorite protein to the pot when the broth comes to a boil. Continue cooking as the recipe directs.

Shanghai Fried Noodles

Although this recipe calls for 1 pound of thick, round Shanghai-style noodles, most packages are usually 3 to 4 ounces more or less than that. But because the 1-pound quantity in the recipe is only a guide, you can use the entire package if you want — or even half of it if you're not in a noodle mood. Just remember that if you use more noodles than the recipe calls for, the amount of meat, vegetables, and sauce specified will seem less generous. Vice versa, if you use a smaller amount of noodles.

Preparation time: 20 minutes

Cooking time: 8 minutes

Yield: 4 servings

1 pound fresh Shanghai noodles

1½ tablespoons Chinese rice wine

1½ teaspoons hoisin sauce

½ teaspoon cornstarch

6 ounces boneless, skinless chicken, julienned

3 tablespoons dark soy sauce

1 tablespoon soy sauce

½ teaspoon sugar

2 tablespoons cooking oil

½ teaspoon minced garlic

3 cups julienned napa cabbage

4 green onions, cut into 1-inch lengths

1 In a large pot of boiling water, cook the noodles according to the package directions until barely tender to the bite; drain, rinse with cold water, and drain again.

2 Make a marinade by combining the rice wine, hoisin sauce, and cornstarch in a bowl; add the chicken and stir to coat. Let stand for 10 minutes.

3 Make a sauce by combining the dark soy sauce, soy sauce, and sugar in a bowl.

4 Place a wok over high heat until hot. Add 1 tablespoon of the oil, swirling to coat the sides. Add the garlic and cook, stirring, until fragrant, about 10 seconds. Add the chicken; stir-fry for 3 minutes. Add the napa cabbage and stir-fry for a further 3 minutes. Remove to a plate.

5 Return the wok to high heat until hot. Add the remaining 1 tablespoon oil, swirling to coat the sides. Add the noodles and stir-fry for l minute. Add the green onions and sauce; stir for 1 minute. Return the chicken mixture to the wok and stir to heat through.

Variation: Because Shanghai noodles aren't easy to find in all markets, a good substitute, should you need one, is Japanese udon noodles.

Remember: Any noodles left in the package that you didn't cook? Save them for the next dish in a tightly zippered bag in the freezer.

Chapter 16

Sweet Sensations

In This Chapter

▶ Tasting traditional Eastern desserts

▶ Dishing up desserts with a Western influence

Recipes in This Chapter

▶ Almond Jelly with Fruit Cocktail

▶ Sweet Tapioca Pearls

▶ Steamed Sponge Cake

▶ Sweet Silken Tofu

▶ Almond Cookies

▶ Mango Pudding

▶ Caramelized Bananas

▶ Egg Custard Tarts

▶ Lychee Ice Cream

Chinese restaurant menus can run for pages, sometimes listing hundreds of dishes in all. Everything gets a fair shake — from soups and appetizers to meats and vegetables, from "sizzling platters" and claypot casseroles to countless interpretations on rice and noodles. But when it comes to desserts, you often find only the cursory plate of fortune cookies, maybe some caramelized bananas, or, as a sop to Westerners, ice cream.

Then again, after a deliciously satisfying Chinese meal, do you really need, or even want, a big slab of cheesecake? According to Chinese cuisine's balancing principles, an arsenal of light, mildly sweet, and usually fruit-based desserts is the more natural choice. Personally, I prefer to end a meal with a bowl of chilled fresh seasonal fruits, such as lychees and other tropical fruits. Dessert soups, served either chilled or warm, make refreshing finales, too; they often consist of tapioca pearls or sweetened nut pastes simmered in water, perhaps with a little coconut milk for flavor.

But just because you don't see as many desserts at a Chinese restaurant as you would at, say, a French one, don't assume that China doesn't have its own national sweet tooth. Visit any Chinatown bakery, and you'll find enough tarts, cakes, candies, pastries, and sweet paste-filled buns to put your dentist's six kids through college. The difference is that the Chinese prefer leaving the tour de force desserts to the specialists — and to those times when they're really hungry for them, which isn't normally after a full meal.

You can also experience the pleasures of selected Chinese sweets at dim sum teahouses. Many of those bakery-based specialties, as well as sweet rice puddings and jiggly almond, coconut, or fruit jellies, play supporting roles to a pot of hot jasmine tea.

The dessert recipes in this chapter contain a little bit of old and new and a little bit of East and West. By blending the best of China's lightly sweet philosophy with the richer Western dessert tradition, they do double duty as between-meal snacks and after-meal treats. Be sure to try your favorite Chinese restaurant standbys, but don't leave out the less familiar options — believe it or not, Sweet Silken Tofu makes a great dessert!

Eastern Traditions

If your idea of the ultimate treat is a gooey chocolate cake or a triple-decker sundae with the works, traditional Chinese desserts may seem a bit on the light side. But give them a chance, and you *will* become a Chinese sweetie in no time.

A clean, fresh sweetness comes naturally to China's many fruit-based desserts; you don't need a ton of sugar or cream to get those flavors. The smooth texture of the steamed and tofu-based desserts will awaken your palate to a different post-dining experience. Give them a try, and you may find that you don't miss the apple pie à la mode.

A fruitful endeavor

We Chinese were really on to something when we started serving simple chilled fruits for dessert. What could be easier than arranging ripe melon, orange, pineapple, and mango slices on a platter, and then sprinkling them with some juicy, seedless grapes (which have grown in China for centuries)?

Although many of China's favorite fruits also have legions of fans in the West, the following are a smattering of some that are popular in China but that you may not have thought to include in your last fruit salad:

✔ **Asian pears:** Combine the juiciness of a pear with an apple's crisp bite and you've got the popular Asian pear — appropriately called the apple pear. Although milder in flavor than either apples or pears, these squatty, round fruits with their dappled pale yellow skins are becoming very popular in the West.

✔ **Coconuts:** You may not think of them as fruits, but these versatile "nuts" definitely are. They're extremely popular in southern China and all over Southeast Asia, where cooks use the milk and rich cream from the fruit in curries, stews, and especially desserts. The liquid at the core of a fresh coconut, called the water, also makes a thirst-quenching drink. As for coconut flesh, you can dry, shred, flake, or sweeten it. But when I get my hands on a chunk of fresh, milky white coconut meat, there's nothing I'd rather do than eat it.

✔ **Kumquats:** If you've ever seen an oblong yellow-orange citrus fruit that looks like a doll-sized orange, you're in the company of the tart, refreshing kumquat. It's completely edible, so don't bother peeling it — hardly worth the effort, because that peel is actually tender and sweet itself. (Tender, sweet peel and tart flesh? Sounds like yin and yang to me.) Toss them with grapes and berries in a fruit salad, or slice them thinly as garnishes for salads and sweet or savory dishes. Take advantage of their symbolic associations, too: Being golden colored, they signify good fortune and joy and thus make classic New Year's treats.

✔ **Lychee:** Southern China should elect the lychee as its official King of Fruits. After all, the region already has a spring festival dedicated to these sweet fruits that are the size of large grapes. Fresh lychees have a lumpy, crimson red skin that, once removed, reveals a creamy white, juicy-crisp flesh underneath. If you can find fresh lychees (they're now grown in Florida, California, and Hawaii in addition to Thailand, Taiwan, and their native China), send me some because I can never get enough. The canned variety, though just not as good as fresh, is always available, peeled and pitted, in Asian sections of supermarkets.

✔ **Longan:** This "little brother of the lychee" has a sweet flavor and crisp, juicy texture similar to its sibling fruit's, although instead of a bumpy red peel, it's got a smooth brown shell. And like many little brothers, the longan is smaller than the lychee. Asian produce markets occasionally carry fresh longans in the summer, but Asian grocery stores stock the canned variety year-round.

✔ **Mandarin oranges:** With a name like mandarin oranges, these golden orange citrus fruits *must* be Chinese. Like tangerines, they've grown in China, particularly in the northwest, since ancient times. Their bright golden color — symbolic of wealth and prosperity — makes them popular gifts that friends offer to one another, while their mellowy sweet flavor makes them the perfect gifts for you to give yourself.

✔ **Persimmons:** Although their golden color symbolizes prosperity, smooth-skinned and creamy persimmons symbolize the start of autumn for me. Their flavor is almost a cross between plums and honey. Japanese varieties are squat and flat, while others are more acorn-shaped. You'll want to peel the latter before adding to a fruit salad or a fall fruit platter, while the flat kind are ready to eat as is. Although not a traditional Chinese treatment, a warm slice of persimmon quick bread is tough to beat, too. Remember that patience is a virtue with pointy-tipped persimmons — they're astringent, mealy, and practically inedible when unripe. For your next trip to paint the town red, you may also want to remember that Chinese legend says that persimmons cure drunkenness.

✔ **Pomelo:** These native Chinese citrus fruits look like overgrown yellow grapefruits. And like grapefruits, they have a thick skin with a bitter membrane. Unlike grapefruits, their flavor isn't as sour — it's more mildly sweet — and the flesh isn't as juicy either. You'll find them in store displays and on fruit platters served during Chinese New Year to take advantage of their symbolic links to good fortune in the coming year. Just peel and eat any time of year, and experience some of that good fortune and flavor yourself.

Almond Jelly with Fruit Cocktail

On a hot day in southern China, nothing cools me down better than a soothing bowl of almond-flavored jelly topped with fresh fruit and a light, simple syrup. I prefer using fresh tropical fruits from my childhood home — lychees, longan, and mango are a few of my favorites. For descriptions of these fruits, see the sidebar "A fruitful endeavor."

If you like, you can use canned fruit cocktail, an easy-to-find item that brings a little bit of the West to this Chinese treat. Then again, you can also use whatever fresh fruits are ripe for the choosing.

Preparation time: *5 minutes*

Cooking time: *10 minutes*

Yield: *4 to 6 servings*

3¼ cups plus ½ cup water	*4 envelopes unflavored gelatin*
1 cup milk	*½ cup plus 3 tablespoons sugar*
1 tablespoon almond extract	*1 can (15 ounces) fruit cocktail, drained*

1 To make the jelly: Bring the 3¼ cups water to a boil; add the milk and almond extract. Add the gelatin and the ½ cup sugar and stir until dissolved.

2 Pour the jelly mixture into a deep glass dish; chill in the refrigerator until it sets (about 2 hours).

3 To make the simple syrup: Bring the ½ cup water and the 3 tablespoons sugar to a boil to dissolve the sugar. Set aside to cool.

4 To serve: Cut the jelly into ½-inch cubes and place in a serving bowl. Spoon the fruit cocktail on top and pour the syrup over.

Sweet Tapioca Pearls

People usually have strong feelings about tapioca — and if you grew up on the gooey tapioca pudding cups served in school cafeterias, those feelings may be strongly negative. Get ready to redress your childhood tapioca issues with this delicious combination of starchy tapioca pearls and nutty-sweet taro root (yes, taro does make a great dessert; see Chapter 14 for a description of this versatile root). Serve it warm or chilled.

Don't succumb to the temptation of using quick-cooking tapioca in this recipe, because it simply won't give the same results as the pearls. Tapioca pearls are tapioca starch that has been processed into pellets ranging in size from about ⅛ to ¼ inch. They're essential to both the creamy, pearly texture of the dessert and to its lustrous name.

Preparation time: *25 minutes*

Cooking time: *30 minutes*

Yield: *4 to 6 servings*

6 cups water

2 cups (10 ounces) taro, cut into ¼-inch cubes

½ cup small tapioca pearls

1 cup sugar

1 cup coconut milk

⅛ teaspoon salt

1½ cups melon balls, about ¾ inch in diameter

1 In a large pot, bring 5 cups of the water to a boil. Add the taro and tapioca pearls; reduce the heat to medium. Cover and simmer for 25 minutes, adding additional water as needed.

2 When the tapioca pearls become translucent, add the sugar, coconut milk, and salt; cook for 3 minutes. Add the melon balls; cook to heat through, about 2 minutes.

Martin Says: With coconut milk, a full cup of sugar, and the starchy thickness of tapioca and taro, this dessert runs the risk of seeming pretty rich. But you'd be amazed what the little bit of salt I've added does to balance the sweetness. It gives the whole dish a more complex flavor.

Steamed Sponge Cake

Just as Chinese steamed buns raise a few Western eyebrows, steamed sponge cake may do the same. But this recipe for the Cantonese classic — straight from the kitchen of my good friend Trudy Cuan — makes a cake that's so light, fluffy, and pleasantly sweet that it'll have you raising your fork, instead of your eyebrows, for another bite.

Preparation time: 13 minutes

Cooking time: 20 minutes

Yield: One 9-inch round cake

4 large eggs	1 cup all-purpose flour
1 cup sugar	2 tablespoons cooking oil

1 Line the bottom of a 9-inch cake pan with plastic wrap and set aside.

2 Beat the eggs with an electric mixer until smooth, about 1 minute. Gradually add the sugar, beating well after each addition.

3 Slowly add ¼ cup flour at a time, mixing well after each addition. Continue to beat until fully incorporated. Add the cooking oil; beat to mix well.

4 Prepare a wok for steaming (see Chapters 3 and 5). Transfer the mixture into the cake pan. Set the pan into the wok; cover and steam for 20 minutes, or until a wooden pick inserted in the center comes out clean. Serve warm or cold.

Tip: Resist the temptation to lift the wok's lid and peek at your steaming cake. The condensation on the lid will drip onto the cake, making it soggy. To avoid having to lift the lid to add steaming water, use a little bit more than usual before you start and keep a pitcher of hot water handy in case you need it. Just carefully slide the lid to the side, leaving enough space for you to pour in the water. When the cake is done, quickly but gently lift and invert the lid to avoid splashing any condensation onto it.

Sweet Silken Tofu

You're at a dim sum restaurant, and a cart carrying a big wooden tub passes by. It stops at a neighboring table where a server scoops something soft and white out of the tub and into the diners' bowls, drizzling a light, clear syrup over the top. Wonder what they're getting? Better yet, want to make it at home?

That creamy concoction — somewhere in texture between a custard and a crème brûlée — is sweet silken tofu, one of my favorite simple desserts. In my version, I use brown sugar in the syrup, which gives the dish a slightly richer sweetness. The sprinkling of crushed peanuts accentuates that sweetness while providing a contrast to the velvety soft tofu.

Only silken or soft tofu, found in Asian grocery stores and the refrigerated cases of some supermarkets, will do in this recipe. Anything else is just too firm to create the creamy texture that makes this dessert such an indulgence.

Preparation time: *5 minutes*

Cooking time: *8 minutes*

Yield: *4 servings*

1 cup water	*1 package (16 ounces) silken tofu, drained*
½ cup packed brown sugar	*6 tablespoons crushed toasted peanuts*

1 Make a syrup by combining the water and brown sugar in a small saucepan; bring it to a boil. Reduce the heat to medium; simmer until slightly thickened, about 8 minutes.

2 To serve: Divide the tofu equally among 4 individual small bowls. Pour about 3 tablespoons syrup over each serving; sprinkle with 1½ tablespoons peanuts.

Western Influences

In the hotels and upscale restaurants of Hong Kong, Beijing, and China's metropolitan capitals, chefs from around the world bring their own influences to local traditional dishes and ingredients. Not surprisingly, the collaboration has produced innovative, mouthwatering desserts.

This culinary approach to "foreign affairs" spread from the big cities to local bakeries in smaller towns, in part because the results were so irresistible. From there, they returned to the Western world, where they satisfy sweet-toothed Western tastes quite handily. As I always say, there's no better way to achieve cultural diplomacy than through cuisine.

Almond Cookies

For some kids, the best part of a Chinese restaurant dinner comes when the server brings out a plate of flaky, crisp almond cookies. With this recipe, you can make them at home and give the little ones (the big ones, too!) a special treat in their lunch bags that they're sure to appreciate.

By using vegetable shortening instead of the lard that's often recommended in traditional Chinese versions, I make the cookies a little bit crispier — and a lot less cholesterol-packed. Let them cool on a rack on the kitchen counter to enhance that crispiness.

Preparation time: *20 minutes, plus 1 hour for the dough to rest*

Cooking time: *About 15 minutes per batch*

Yield: *About 32 cookies*

1¾ cups all-purpose flour	⅛ teaspoon salt
¾ teaspoon baking powder	1 egg, lightly beaten
½ teaspoon baking soda	2 teaspoons vanilla extract
1 cup solid vegetable shortening	1 teaspoon almond extract
½ cup granulated sugar	½ cup chopped blanched almonds
¼ cup packed brown sugar	32 almond halves

1 Sift the flour, baking powder, and baking soda into a bowl.

2 In a large bowl, beat the shortening, sugar, brown sugar, and salt with an electric mixer until fluffy. Add the egg and vanilla and almond extracts; beat until blended. Add the flour mixture; beat until fully incorporated. Add the chopped almonds and stir to mix well. Shape the dough into a ball, cover with plastic wrap, and refrigerate for at least 1 hour, or up to 2 days.

3 Preheat the oven to 350°. Roll about a tablespoon of the dough into a ball and place the balls 2 to 3 inches apart on a baking sheet. Press an almond half into the center of each ball.

4 Bake until golden brown, 14 to 16 minutes. Let cool on the baking sheet for 7 minutes and then transfer to a rack to cool completely.

Tip: Even desserts deserve garnishing. Sprinkle some toasted sesame seeds or even some finely chopped walnuts onto the cookies while they're still warm — they're the perfect accessory for these tempting treats.

Mango Pudding

The sweet perfume and smooth texture of mango turn a simple gelatin-based pudding into a sumptuous dessert. Served in individual ramekins, this pudding makes a particularly elegant presentation with an equally elegant flavor.

Preparation time: *12 minutes*

Cooking time: *3 minutes*

Yield: *4 servings*

2 mangoes, about 14 ounces each	*1 cup sugar*
1 cup water	*Lemon juice*
1 cup whole milk	*Lemon wedges (optional)*
1 package unflavored gelatin	

1 Peel the mangoes and cut the flesh from the pits. Cut enough flesh into ½-inch cubes to make 2 cups. Place the chopped fruit into the blender with the water and puree until smooth.

2 Combine the milk, gelatin, and sugar in a medium saucepan and bring to a simmer over medium-low heat. Stir well with a whisk to dissolve the gelatin, about 3 minutes. Remove from the heat. Pour the pureed mangoes into the pan and mix well. Pour the mixture into a 1-quart mold or divide among 4 individual 1-cup ramekins or custard cups. Cover and refrigerate until firm, 3 to 4 hours, or overnight.

3 Squeeze a few drops of lemon juice on the pudding before serving. Garnish with lemon wedges, if desired.

Tip: Use the ripest mangoes you can find to get maximum flavor.

Variation: If you're so inclined, make different flavors of fruit pudding with whatever sweet gems are ripe and ready. Just substitute a different fruit for the mango and proceed with the recipe.

Caramelized Bananas

This common Chinese restaurant dessert is just the kind of sticky situation that I crave, although "freezing" the fried bananas' syrupy coating with a dunk in ice water leaves you with less of a mess on your hands. What you *do* end up with is a crackly, cooled candy glaze surrounding soft, piping-hot bananas at the center — the best of both worlds.

Preparation time: *10 minutes*

Cooking time: *20 minutes*

Yield: *4 servings*

1 tablespoon sesame seeds	*Cooking oil for deep-frying*
¼ cup all-purpose flour	*7 tablespoons sugar*
1 egg, lightly beaten	*2½ tablespoons water*
4 firm bananas	*Ice cubes in cold water*

1 Place the sesame seeds in a small frying pan over medium heat, shaking the pan frequently, until lightly browned, about 3 minutes. Immediately remove from the pan to cool.

2 Place the flour and egg in separate dishes.

3 Peel and cut the bananas into thirds. Just before deep-frying, coat the bananas in the flour, then in the egg, and back to the flour, shaking off the excess.

4 In a wok, heat the oil for deep-frying to 360°. Using a pair of chopsticks or a slotted spoon, carefully lower the banana pieces into the hot oil. Deep-fry, a few pieces at a time, turning frequently, until golden brown, about 2 minutes. Remove with a slotted spoon and drain on paper towels.

5 To make the syrup, combine the sugar and water in a small saucepan. Cook over medium heat until the mixture caramelizes and turns to a pale straw color, about 8 minutes. (It is not necessary to stir, as the sugar should melt and incorporate into the water.) Immediately remove from the heat. (The syrup will continue to cook after you remove it from the heat, and the color will turn golden in a few seconds.)

6 Line a cookie sheet with wax paper or foil. Top with an oiled cooling rack. Lay the fried bananas on the rack, pour sugar syrup over bananas, and then sprinkle with the sesame seeds. Gently place the bananas on a lightly greased serving plate and serve immediately.

Tip: Even after you dunk the caramelized bananas into the ice water, they still may stick to the serving plate. Grease the dish with a little cooking oil or butter, and you won't leave any delicious bits stuck behind.

Regional Note: You may be more likely to find this dessert in northern-style Chinese restaurants, where the fruit of choice is actually sliced apples. I give it a southern, tropical spin with bananas, whose melting texture and buttery sweet flavor improve the dish, in my opinion. Create your own caramelized fruit dessert by using mangoes, pears, peaches, or whatever is ripe and fresh in your area. It's hard to find a fruit that won't benefit from this candied treatment.

Doing the mango tango

Mangoes may be delicious, but you sometimes have to work for that tasty reward. Peeling and deseeding a mango take a little practice, but with my tips, you'll never have to wait more than you can bear to savor this fruit's sweetness:

1. Stand the unpeeled mango on its pointy end with a narrow side facing you.

2. With a sharp knife placed slightly off the mango's center, steering clear of the large seed, slice vertically from top to bottom. Turn the mango around and make the same slice on the other side. Now you should have two cut slices of roughly equal size.

3. Lay the 2 slices cut side up on the counter and, using the tip of your knife, make diagonal cuts about ½ inch apart in a crosshatch pattern on the mango slices. Take care not to cut through the peel.

4. Hold the mango slices so that your thumbs rest on the skin, and press the slices with your thumbs to invert the mango. Doing so creates a mango "flower" as the cross-hatched sections separate from one another.

5. Trim away the peel, and the flesh will fall away into perfectly formed chunks. Repeat these steps with the other slice.

Egg Custard Tarts

The British have their afternoon tea and crumpets; the Cantonese have their midmorning tea and dim sum. Bring the two cultures and cuisines together on the island of Hong Kong, and you wind up with a scrumptious, one-of-a-kind collection of tea-time treats. These egg custard tarts, favorites among Hong Kong kids of all ages, are a perfect blend of the English expertise with pastry and a light Chinese hand with sweetness.

You can find the tarts in any dim sum restaurant or Chinatown bakery in North America. Once you get the hang of this recipe, you'll even be able to find them in your own kitchen — before everyone gobbles them up, at least.

Preparation time: *45 minutes, plus 2 hours for the dough to rest*

Cooking time: *35 minutes*

Yield: *14 tarts*

Pastry Dough	**Filling**
1¾ cups all-purpose flour	⅔ cup whole milk
½ cup vegetable shortening, chilled	⅓ cup heavy cream
¼ cup butter, chilled	⅔ cup sugar
1 egg	4 eggs
2 tablespoons ice water	1 teaspoon vanilla extract

1 Prepare the dough by placing the flour in a food processor. Cut the shortening and butter into ½-inch chunks and distribute over the flour. Process with on-off bursts until the fat particles are the size of peas.

2 Add the 1 egg and ice water. Process until the mixture just begins to form a ball. (Do not process completely to the ball stage, and don't worry if the dough has shortening streaks in it.) Remove the dough, shape into a patty 1 inch thick, and cover with plastic wrap. Chill for at least 1 hour, or up to 2 days.

3 To prepare the filling: Combine the milk, cream, and sugar in a small saucepan; place over medium-low heat until the sugar dissolves. Let cool in an ice bath. In a bowl, beat the 4 eggs slightly. Whisk in the milk mixture and vanilla extract, blending until smooth.

4 Preheat the oven to 300°. On a lightly floured board, roll out the pastry to about ¼ inch thick. Cut into fourteen 4-inch circles (reroll scraps and cut again if necessary). Fit the circles into 2½-inch tart molds. Lightly press the dough into the bottoms and sides of the molds and trim the edges.

5 Pour the filling into the pastry-lined molds to within ¼ inch of the top. Place the filled molds on a baking sheet; bake until a knife inserted in the center comes out clean, about 35 minutes. Place the molds on a rack and allow them to cool for 3 minutes. Remove the tarts from the molds. Serve warm or at room temperature.

Remember: When the butter in a pastry dough warms up, it softens and results in a tough pastry crust. So keep things as cold as possible while working with pastry dough. That means using ice water, working on a cold surface (marble pastry stones are ideal), making sure that your hands don't warm the dough too much, and keeping the dough in the refrigerator if you need to take a break. Just chill out, okay!

Cultural Note: Chinese call egg custard tarts *dan tat, dan* meaning "egg" and *tat* being the phonetic spelling of the way most Chinese pronounce "tart." Because tarts are Western imports to China, the language has no word of its own for the concept. The Chinese adoption of the English term is just another fine example of cultural and linguistic give-and-take.

Lychee Ice Cream

Yes, we all scream for ice cream, even in China. Although ice cream isn't a traditional dessert, the Chinese can't resist a cool, soothing bowl of ice cream any more than the rest of the world can. In China, we like to give it a Southeast Asian appeal with the addition of tropical fruits, like the lychee used in this recipe. Give it a try — it'll have you screaming for more, too.

I've tried this recipe with whole milk as well as 1 percent. You can use either kind and still come up with the same smooth and creamy frozen dessert.

Preparation time: *10 minutes*

Cooking time: *8 minutes*

Yield: *4 servings*

2 cups heavy cream

1 cup milk

¾ cup sugar

2 egg yolks, beaten

1½ cups seedless canned lychee, drained and diced

¼ cup fresh lemon juice

1 Combine the cream, milk, and sugar in a saucepan or double boiler; heat until warm and the sugar is completely dissolved. Add 1 cup of the cream mixture to the yolks while whisking lightly. Pour the egg mixture back into the cream mixture while continuing to whisk lightly.

2 Cook over medium heat, stirring constantly, until the back of your spoon is thinly coated, about 8 minutes. Do not allow it to boil, or the custard will curdle.

3 Add the lychee and lemon juice and let it cool in the refrigerator (overnight is fine).

4 Freeze in an electric or manual ice cream maker according to the manufacturer's instructions.

Tip: You can still prepare this ice cream even if you don't have an ice cream maker. It comes out just as well if you pour the ice cream custard into a cake pan or bowl and pop it in the freezer until frozen. Believe it or not, all the cream and milk in the recipe prevent the formation of too many ice crystals and result in a frozen concoction the consistency of a rich gelato.

Martin Says: In Step 1, I advise you to add a little bit of the warm cream to the egg yolks (a process that we call "tempering" in chef-speak) rather than dump the yolks into the simmering cream all at once. Do the latter, and you'll wind up with scrambled-egg-and-lychee ice cream, because the shock of the hot cream curdles the yolks just the same as a hot frying pan does. Gently introducing a portion of the cream into the eggs while stirring mixes the two ingredients to a silky-smooth consistency — and it keeps your temper at bay.

Chapter 17

Bringing It All Together: Full-Fledged Chinese Meals

In This Chapter

▶ Defining the Chinese family meal
▶ Planning menus for family meals of all sizes

Gathering the clan for a simple sit-down dinner isn't an easy task nowadays. The contemporary family is constantly on the go, trying to coordinate all those conflicting schedules. And let's face it, how many of us really have the time and energy to hover over a hot stove after a long day at work?

My solution is not to invest in a bigger microwave oven. No, tempt your family instead with a Chinese home-cooked meal that's as delicious as it is easy to whip up. The menus I've chosen will help you make colorful, quick, and delicious Chinese dishes that can hold their own with those from any Chinese restaurant. Whether you're making dinner for two or hosting a banquet for a dozen, dining Chinese-style is just the ticket. No doubt about it, Chinese food brings people together — my dining table is jam-packed every meal, and I honestly don't know half the people there.

The Chinese Family Meal

Chinese meals fall into two basic categories: the home-style meal and the formal banquet. Each has its own pattern of service, number and complexity of dishes, and appropriate occasions for serving it. Needless to say, home cooking is most familiar to all of us (I, for one, don't get invited to more than one banquet a week, if that), but even the most common and down-to-earth Chinese meal packs plenty of charm and grace. Here are some of the characteristics that define a classic Chinese home-style meal:

✔ **Chinese family meals are served family style.** Surprise. That means it's a communal affair where all the dishes appear on the table simultaneously for everyone to share, and all the diners help themselves to the goodies. No wonder so many Chinese households and restaurants have round tables: They're the fairest, easiest way for everyone to access the food.

✔ **All the dishes revolve around a grain as focus.** Rice plays this role most of the time, but in some regions (northern China, in particular), other starches such as noodles, millet, and steamed breads take on that role, too. The "main" dishes, delicious as they may be, are essentially there to flavor and complement the grain.

✔ **The meal usually includes four or five of these auxiliary dishes, composed of a combination of meat, fish, poultry, seasonal vegetables, tofu, or eggs.** This may seem like a lot of food, but spreading the dishes among everyone at the table prevents any one diner from overindulging. And because home-style dishes are simple and easy to make, a few auxiliary dishes don't take up a whole day of preparation.

✔ **Just because traditional Chinese family meals usually include four or five dishes, your own meal doesn't necessarily have to; serve as much or as little as is appropriate.** Depending on how many people you're feeding, the recipes can either be part of a multi-dish meal or can serve as main dishes for smaller groups. Use your own best judgment when planning how many dishes to make.

✔ **Soups cleanse the palate between dishes and aid digestion.** Therefore, they're not served *only* before the meal, as they often are in the West, but rather throughout and sometimes even after it. The clear soups can also do double duty as mealtime beverages.

✔ **As for desserts, most family dinners end with some fresh fruit and tea instead of a decadent cheesecake or pecan pie.** One of my favorite ways to cap off a meal: peeled and chilled lychees — translucent, juicy-fleshed fruits found in cans in the Asian food aisles of most supermarkets — served in a bowl on ice. Deeeelicious!! But, of course, at times something sweeter is called for; for those occasions, check out the recipes in Chapter 16.

Eating a Chinese meal

The Chinese have the most effective way to *consume* home-style meals. By contrasting and complementing tastes, textures, and ingredients, the Chinese chefs get the most bang out of each bite. Just grab your bowl of rice (the Chinese prefer to eat rice from bowls and not as a side dish on a dinner plate), take a bite, and then chase it with some meat, seafood, and vegetables, along with some of the sauce. Bring the bowl close to your mouth, and "shovel" the delectable combination in with your chopsticks. Follow that with a slurp of soup and then start again with a different mixture of rice and entrée.

By the way, slurping, sucking, and shoveling food won't get you sent to bed without dessert in China the way they can in the West. In fact, these perfectly permissible, even polite, practices are almost necessary when using chopsticks if you want to get all that rice and sauce into your mouth without spilling. And the Chinese penchant for steaming-hot soup makes slurping — and the slight cooling it gives the soup's surface — a must unless you have an asbestos tongue.

Communal, family-style dining, as practiced in China, isn't just a matter of convenience that lets all the diners get their share of the food before someone else does. It's actually very fundamental to the whole spirit of family togetherness that has helped hold Chinese culture together for thousands of years. The family that eats together stays together.

Making a marvelous menu: Planning a balanced Chinese meal

Now that you know the basics of a Chinese home-style dishes, shift your focus to orchestrating them into a simple, enjoyable dinner that everybody will love. This means getting to the heart of *how to plan a menu*. And whether you're making a small, romantic repast for two or feeding a crew of famished rugby players, the heart of putting together a home-cooked Chinese meal goes right back to our old friends: yin and yang.

Contrast, complement, balance: Whatever you call it, a good Chinese menu encompasses this dynamic duo of yin and yang. Keep that in mind, and you'll instinctively design meals that won't bore your guests or overwhelm the chef in the kitchen. These tips help you pick winners every time:

✔ **Use different ingredients to create contrast and complement.** Variety is the spice of life, after all. Think of the foods you have at your ready, and then mix them up. If you have an all-meat dish, make sure that an all-vegetable dish appears on the table, too. By tapping into a variety of ingredients, you inevitably work plenty of balance into the menu.

When it comes to vegetables, stick with the stuff that's fresh, seasonal, and local. You can't go wrong that way. Sure, you may want to contrast tender, delicate spring pea shoots in one dish with braised cold-weather cabbage in another, but you probably won't find both at their peaks at the same time. Plenty of other ingredients can create culinary balance, so choose the ones you know are fresh and at their prime, and look forward to enjoying the rest when their seasons roll around.

✔ **Contrast and complement flavor within and among dishes.** Sweet and sour, ginger and onion, and rice wine and soy are all classic pairings that allow one element's flavor to play off the other's. Serving too many subtle dishes will have your guests snoozing, while a 100-percent Sichuan, three-alarm chile feast is an obvious bad idea, too. So avoid extremes, and everybody will have an enjoyable dining experience.

If it works with the menu, serve the milder dishes at the beginning of the meal. Doing so keeps delicate flavors from getting lost among the saltier, tangier, spicier, and generally bolder dishes that come later.

✔ **Looks count, so choose dishes that balance colors, shapes, and sizes.** Who wants to eat a totally brown meal: braised pork in soy sauce, stir-fried mushrooms, and crispy-skinned roast duck, for example? Or a dish with nothing but finely shredded ingredients? These may taste great, but they won't satisfy visual appetites. By the same token, mix up the color scheme *on the dishes themselves* — in other words, don't serve pale steamed buns on a white plate.

✔ **Serve dishes that vary in texture.** Imagine these pairings: crackling roast duck skin and sumptuous, chewy rice noodles; crunchy stir-fried vegetables with smooth and silky tofu soup; crispy-fried salt and pepper prawns next to meltingly tender red-cooked pork. Are you drooling yet? Contrasting textures obviously keep the mouth awake, and contented.

✔ **Use a range of cooking methods.** Not only will a combination of stir-frying, steaming, braising, and deep-frying vary the flavors, textures, and colors, but it'll make the cooking go more smoothly, too. While a slow-simmering stew or roast is cooking, you can turn your attention to the hands-on dishes, such as the stir-fries.

The key to harmonizing the dishes in your Chinese home-style meal is to complement and contrast — not to clash. It's a subtle distinction, but one that you'll soon recognize as your skills and tastes develop. (The menus in this chapter help you, too.)

Sample Menus for Two, Four, and More

To give you a little jump start, I include a number of sample menus that are based on recipes in this book. Some of these menus are perfect for an intimate party of two, while others make enough for a houseful of hungry teenagers. All of them pay their respects to yin-yang balance as well as to good taste, so take your pick, pick up your chopsticks, and enjoy!

Rice and noodles are so integral to Chinese meals that I didn't explicitly list them in all the menus. Although a few of the menus contain suggestions for specific rice or noodle dishes, it's practically a given that a proper Chinese table will include enough steamed rice or boiled noodles to keep everyone's bowls full. Without brick-and-mortar ingredients such as these, you just can't build a solid Chinese meal.

Two's company

Chinese food is best when shared. But after a long day at work and a long commute home, the only thing you probably want to share are firm instructions for everyone to leave you alone. On nights like these, just mustering the energy to prepare a dinner for two can send even the most eager cooks running for the take-out menu.

The next time you and your partner retreat from the day's cares in the comfy cocoon of your home, don't immediately dial 1-800-TAKE-OUT. Tossing together a respectable Chinese meal for two is as easy as it is satisfying. You don't need to make multiple courses or dishes from every recipe category — poultry, seafood, meat, vegetables, and so on. The following menus for two prove that good meals come in small packages. They aren't the makings of an all-you-can-eat buffet, but they're balanced, packed with tasty dishes, and — a crucial point — hassle-free.

Table for two, please

All you need are three simple courses to get a fair sampling of an authentic Chinese meal — and these three restaurant classics give your dinner table a distinctly Chinese-restaurant feel. If three courses seem a little excessive for a quick dinner for two (okay, four courses if you count rice or noodles, but they're so easy to make that I'm tempted not to count them), you'll breathe a sigh of relief when you find out how embarrassingly simple each is. Prepare the soup and stir-fried chicken — both take only minutes — while peeling and slicing the oranges for dessert. I bet you'll be done before your favorite show's second commercial break.

- Egg Flower Soup (Chapter 9)
- Kung Pao Chicken (Chapter 11)
- Fresh, peeled orange wedges

The romantic dinner

Chinese food, especially home-cooked Chinese food, never fails to wow a first date. (The way to any romantic conquest's heart is through the aisles of a Chinese market, I always say.)

Jewel-colored ingredients, aromatic sauces, and a mixed bag of tempting textures will fool your crush into believing that you spent a lot more time and effort preparing the meal than you actually did. Although I recommend honesty in a relationship, especially at its outset, keeping your sweetheart in the dark about this little matter is forgivable in this case. Just don't tell my wife I said so.

- Shrimp Toast (Chapter 8)
- Oysters in Black Bean Sauce (Chapter 10)
- Chinatown Chop Suey (Chapter 14)
- Sweet Tapioca Pearls (Chapter 16)

The Chinese table

If you really want to go local when you make your Chinese home-style meal, don't stop with just the food. You must have the table covered as well — literally. The typical table setting for a Chinese family meal differs significantly from most Western settings, and for good reason: The differences in food and service require different accoutrements. Here's how to make your table look, and function, more like a Chinese one:

- Get a round table. This shape facilitates the communal style of dining and makes it easier to fit in those drop-in guests. It's a pretty egalitarian set-up, too: No one person can lay claim to being head of the table. If it's good enough for King Arthur and his court, it's good enough for the Chinese. (If a round table isn't a possibility, *lazy susans* — those round, spinning platters found in the center of many Chinese restaurant tables — are a good substitute.)

- Place the dishes of food in the table's center to give everyone easy access. If you use higher-edged bowls and tureens, place them in the center of the table. Surround them with the flatter platters. The reason: All the better to reach you with, my dear!

- Each dish gets its own serving dish and a pair of communal chopsticks or serving spoon with which to serve it. In the absence of communal servingware, just turn your own pair of chopsticks around and use the clean, thicker ends to grab food from the serving dish.

- Serve soups and rice from large communal serving bowls with large, communal serving spoons.

- For individual place settings, having an individual rice bowl and trusty pair of chopsticks for each is a must.

- Diners also get individual soup bowls and small, bowl-shaped soup spoons.

- The Chinese make no bones about scraping every last scrap of tasty meat off a pork or chicken bone — or out of a shrimp or clam shell, for that matter. For that reason, each guest also gets a saucer-sized side plate to hold those bones or shells, as well as to hold the soup spoon when it's not in use.

- And although the teapot may not make it to the table until the meal's over, you usually find small, handle-less teacups — or, more accurately, tea bowls — set out for everyone.

Just study the accompanying illustration of the Chinese table, take note of the tips in this sidebar, and you're set to set!

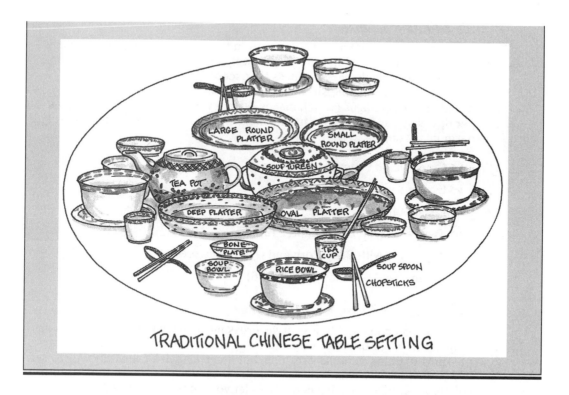

TRADITIONAL CHINESE TABLE SETTING

A feast for four

The combination family-style dinners at Chinese restaurants — you know, the ones with the set menus composed of a balance of different dishes — usually allow you to add extra choices based upon the number of people in your party. (For more on dining in Chinese restaurants, head to Chapter 18.) You can do the same when putting together Chinese menus in your own home, and the following suggestions give you ideas on how to do just that.

As your party grows from two to four, count on preparing a couple extra dishes to keep everyone's plate full. A more substantial menu makes sure that everyone is well-fed and also presents a wider mix of China's culinary gifts. The more people to feed, the more dishes everyone gets to sample, and the merrier everyone is in the end.

Just remember to keep the selection balanced; keeping it simple is only natural with the combinations I provide. Your kitchen will be earning repeat business in no time.

It's all in the balance

You can discover a lot about balance from this menu. The golden pancakes add a lively crispiness that plays against the moist, tender pork. That same pork has a pleasingly fiery richness that keeps the tangy-sweet lemon chicken from stealing the show. Round it out with a supper-time omelet, bright green asparagus (which makes getting your five servings of veggies per day easy), and candylike fried bananas. You have the makings of a truly harmonious meal.

- ✔ Green Onion Pancakes (Chapter 8)
- ✔ Egg Fu Young (Chapter 13)
- ✔ Lemon Chicken (Chapter 11)
- ✔ Twice-Cooked Pork (Chapter 12)
- ✔ Asparagus with Baby Corn and Oyster-Flavored Sauce (Chapter 14)
- ✔ Caramelized Bananas (Chapter 16)

All aboard a culinary journey for four

When you get cooking Chinese-style, crossing culinary borders becomes as easy as strolling from the refrigerator to the stove. This menu reads like a passport to China's culinary regions, but it certainly isn't the only way to satisfy your stomach's wanderlust. Consider these recipes inspiration for future culinary journeys. It's a big country — let your appetite explore!

- ✔ Cantonese Pickled Vegetables (Chapter 8)
- ✔ Hot and Sour Soup (Chapter 9)
- ✔ Broccoli Beef (Chapter 12)
- ✔ Hong Kong-Style Pan-Fried Noodles (Chapter 15)
- ✔ Almond Jelly with Fruit Cocktail (Chapter 16)

A table for six

A novice Chinese cook may find preparing a Chinese family-style meal for six a little overwhelming. I understand the concern: Bringing together such a combination of colors, textures, and flavors can seem deceptively complicated and time-consuming.

But don't be deceived. When the individual elements of a large meal are simple, putting them together is a snap as well. Wrapped dishes such as potstickers and wontons are easy to make ahead of time; sauces prepared in bulk and stored in the refrigerator shave minutes off a meal's preparation time; and the cooking techniques common to most Chinese dishes are inherently speedy. Try some of the menus in the following section, and you'll discover that, when preparing a spread for six, there's nothing to fear except washing the dishes when you're done.

Satisfaction for six

This menu has a little something for everyone: plump potstickers for dumpling fans; a healthful soup packed with fresh fish, tofu, and tender greens; steamed chicken and stir-fried lamb and beef for the meat eaters, and colorful vegetables and spicy tofu to satisfy those who eat a little closer to the earth. And for folks with room in their stomachs to spare, a sweet, creamy mango pudding finishes everything with a fitting flourish.

- Potstickers (Chapter 8)
- Fish Soup with Spinach and Tofu (Chapter 9)
- Gingered Chicken (Chapter 11)
- Lamb with Green Onions (Chapter 12)
- Beef Steak Over Glass Noodles (Chapter 12)
- Ma Po Tofu (Chapter 13)
- Stir-Fried Assorted Vegetables (Chapter 14)
- Fried Rice (Chapter 15)
- Mango Pudding (Chapter 16)

Textural tapestry

When preparing a menu to serve six, working the whole spectrum of textures into the package is easy, as this selection proves. By incorporating deep-fried, braised, stir-fried, and steamed dishes, you naturally create a contrast of mouthfeels that give the meal more palate appeal.

- Crispy Wontons (Chapter 8)
- Braised Fish Hunan Style (Chapter 10)
- Honey Garlic Chicken (Chapter 11)
- Steamed Cabbage Rolls (Chapter 12)
- Tofu and Spinach (Chapter 13)
- Fried Rice (Chapter 15)
- Lychee Ice Cream (Chapter 16)

Part IV
The Part of Tens

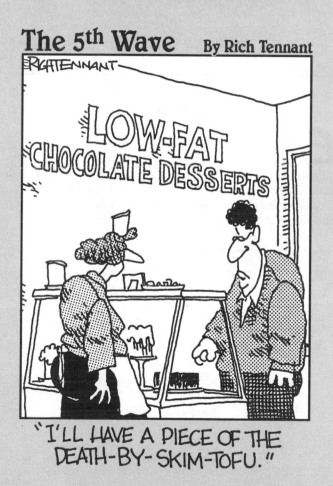

The 5th Wave   By Rich Tennant

"I'LL HAVE A PIECE OF THE DEATH-BY-SKIM-TOFU."

In this part . . .

Every *For Dummies* book ends with top-ten lists. It's a way to give you a little extra information in an easily digestable format. I offer you the commonsense scoop on successful Chinese cooking, some beverage tips for Chinese meals, additional resources for more information, and much more.

Chapter 18

Almost Ten Tips for Enjoying the Chinese Restaurant Experience

In This Chapter

▶ Understanding regional Chinese cooking styles

▶ Making sense of restaurant menus

▶ Eating dim sum

▶ Trying out some suggested menus

▶ Using chopsticks

A s delicious as their home-cooked meals may be, Chinese cooks take equal pleasure in dining out. With so many on-the-go food lovers, it's no wonder that Chinese communities the world over have all embraced a booming restaurant culture. The Chinese rendezvous at restaurants, use them for parties and banquets, and simply enjoy their quality times with their friends and family there. Thankfully, Chinese immigrants to the West have brought this philosophy, along with their sharp cooking skills, with them. Most Westerners had their first bite of Asian food in an American-Chinese restaurant. And while these restaurants may not always be the best representations of authentic Chinese cuisine, they're still the key ambassadors of Chinese food for most Westerners.

Making Sense of Regional Chinese Restaurants

In most of the West, you'll probably find the range of Chinese regional restaurants whittled down to three general options: Cantonese, Mandarin (also known as Northern or Peking), and Sichuan-Hunan restaurants. As for Shanghai-style establishments, they're rarer than the others, but if you're lucky, your neighborhood has one of its own. If it doesn't, don't be surprised if a local Shanghai restaurant pops up soon. And what about dim sum teahouses? They're essentially subsets of Cantonese restaurants specializing in dim sum, but serving a wider range of Cantonese dishes, too.

Cantonese (Southern-style)

Because most early Chinese-Americans hailed from southern China, most American-Chinese restaurants today have a distinct Cantonese flavor. Wherever the Cantonese have settled, they've given the gift of their recipes and culinary skill to their new neighbors, most often in the form of restaurants.

When dining at an American-Cantonese restaurant, sample specialties such as char siu (Cantonese roast pork), a perfectly prepared wonton soup, or Cantonese roast duck. Make a point of ordering a whole steamed fish accented with a little green onion and fragrant ginger slices, something Cantonese chefs prepare with aplomb. (Keep in mind that Cantonese chefs have peerless seafood-cooking skills, and when you see a big tank full of live, swimming fish upon entering a restaurant, you know you've found a little piece of Cantonese fish-dining heaven.) And remember to eat your vegetables, because nothing beats a plate of lightly stir-fried Chinese broccoli kissed with a hint of garlic and rice wine or oyster sauce.

Mandarin (Northern- or Beijing-style)

Whereas American-Cantonese restaurants epitomize relaxed, neighborhood dining, typical Mandarin-style restaurants characterize what many Westerners think of as the classic "imperial" Chinese restaurant, with hanging red lanterns, gilt columns, and sumptuously upholstered chairs. Granted, not all American-Mandarin restaurants are this elaborate, but they did arise out of a northern tradition of lavish culinary refinement and a catering to the Mandarins, or high-ranking public officials, who frequented the capital's grand restaurants.

And what should you include on that banquet menu? For starters, watching a waiter crack into the clay crust surrounding traditional beggar's chicken is always a show-stopper. Pair that with some silver thread buns and handmade noodles, and you've got the makings of a feast. Speaking of feasts, the culinary phenomenon of Peking duck has made Mandarin restaurants famous worldwide. And Mongolian hotpot, popular with those living near the China-Mongolia border, has wound up in northern-style restaurants almost by default. How's that for a happy accident? (Find a helpful description and illustration of this northern treat in Chapter 12.) Of course, don't forget to try the Beijing dumplings and potstickers.

Sichuan-Hunan

Chefs from Sichuan and nearby Hunan province, both landlocked in the heart of China, have brought a fondness for spicy foods to the wider world by way of their restaurants. Because large parts of these provinces are relatively remote from China's seaside ports, preservation by pickling and liberal use of chiles helps rations last longer. The pickling and the chiles also give their cuisine the spiciness that sets Sichuan-Hunan restaurants apart from the rest of the Chinese restaurants in North America today.

If you're a fan of fiery foods, tell the chef to go full-speed ahead, and Sichuan-Hunan restaurants will become nirvana for you. Among the menu items, you'll find plenty with flavors of garlic, onions, ginger, and the region's namesake Sichuan peppercorn. Try the smoked duck (Sichuan and Hunan chefs are masters at the art of smoking foods) if you're in for something not-too-spicy. For the adventuresome, or at least those with a higher heat threshold, try the spicy tofu dishes such as ma po tofu that have made a name for Sichuan-Hunan food. And even though all Chinese restaurants serve kung pao dishes (favorites with Western diners), none make them quite as well as do Sichuan-Hunan restaurants.

Shanghai

The cuisine of Shanghai, such an international city, has few representative restaurants in the West. Because the West hasn't seen as big an influx of immigration from Shanghai as it has from Guangzhou or northern China, the number of Shanghainese restaurants has come up short. But that's changing as Western communities of expatriate Shanghainese grow, and as more people discover their unavoidable culinary charms.

You've already discovered some of those charms if you've ever had a "drunken" dish such as drunken crab or the Drunken Chicken recipe in Chapter 11. (Shanghai's closeness to Shao Hsing, home of fabled rice wines, makes these wine-marinated dishes common.) Also, are you a fan of that classic restaurant-style fried rice with barbecue pork or Chinese sausage, shrimp, green peas, carrots, and scrambled egg slivers among other treats? It hails from Yangzhou, a city that's put its two cents into the blend of local regional specialties that make up Shanghainese cuisine. Some other Shanghai surprises to look for: lots of seafood specialties thanks to the region's relationship with its rivers; rich braised and red-cooked dishes full of rice wine and dark soy sauce (these make great family-style choices), and a healthy selection of scrumptious vegetable dishes.

Eating Your Heart Out: Dim Sum

No discussion of Chinese restaurants would be complete without a thorough treatment of dim sum, the endless collection of appetizer-sized, sweet and savory tea snacks popular throughout China, but originating in Guangzhou. Luckily for you, dim sum and the restaurants that specialize in it are becoming more popular to Westerners. Those outside China are starting to realize how irresistible dim sum — the words literally mean "touches the heart" — really is, as both a way of eating and of learning about the food, culture, and lifestyle of the Chinese.

If you find your way to a more traditional dim sum house, don't expect a server to take your order and then bring your dishes to the table. Instead, a stream of carts emerges from the kitchen, each piled with small bamboo or aluminum steamer baskets or little white plates containing all sorts of fresh dim sum, hot from the steamer or wok. Servers stroll past tables, stopping to entice diners with what's on their carts, and diners literally pick the items they want simply by pointing their fingers or nodding their heads.

So if a cart has those fluffy pork buns you've heard about, go ahead and let the server know you want them; you don't need to be fluent in Cantonese, because the "smile, point, and nod" technique gets the sentiment across clearly. If, on the other hand, nothing on this particular cart catches your eye, politely shake your head no and wait for the next ship to come in. And if you spy that special dish you crave on a cart across the room, don't be shy about flagging the server over to your table either.

To navigate your way through the wonderfully confusing world of dim sum, familiarize yourself with the dishes in the following dim sum primer (Table 18-1) and their illustrations in Figure 18-1. After all, if you don't see the dumpling or bun that touched your heart on your last trip to the restaurant, you should know how to ask for it by name.

Table 18-1	A Crash Course in Dim Sum		
Chinese Name	*American Name*	*Preparation Method*	*Description*
Char siu bao	Barbecued pork bun	Steamed	Fluffy steamed bread stuffed with slightly sweet barbecued pork
Gouk char siu bao	Barbecued pork bun	Baked	Slightly sweet barbecued pork stuffed into a golden brown, tender, baked bun

Chinese Name	American Name	Preparation Method	Description
Chun guen	Spring roll	Deep-fried	Thin, wheat-flour skins wrapped cigar-style around various fillings and fried to a golden crisp
Har dor see	Shrimp toast	Deep-fried	Small pieces of Western-style bread topped with minced shrimp and deep-fried
Har gau	Shrimp dumpling	Steamed	Tender shrimp and vegetables encased in a translucent wrapper
Siu mai	Pork dumpling	Steamed	Sack-shaped dumpling of minced pork and vegetables in a wheat-flour wrapper
Wor tip	Potstickers	Pan-fried	Various meats and vegetables encased in a wheat-flour dough that gets crispy on the bottom during pan-frying

Figure 18-1:
All this can be yours on the next trip to a dim sum restaurant!

A Not-So-Sticky Situation: Using Chopsticks

Before requesting a fork in your favorite Chinese restaurant, practice your chopstick drill at home. In no time flat, you, too, can be a chopstick expert, picking up slippery cashew nuts or thin, julienned pepper. All it takes is a little patience and lots and lots of practice. Chopstick wielding can become as natural to you as eating itself. You may also find that using chopsticks makes eating Chinese food more fun! Just follow these steps, shown in Figure 18-2.

USING CHOPSTICKS

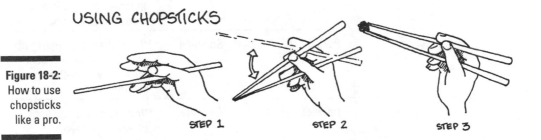

STEP 1   STEP 2   STEP 3

Figure 18-2:
How to use
chopsticks
like a pro.

1. **Place one chopstick through the crook formed by your thumb and index finger, letting it rest and remain stationary against the tip of your ring finger.**

2. **Hold the second stick, in the same hand as the first, as if you were holding a pencil, letting it pass under your index finger and holding it in place with your thumb.**

3. **Move the second chopstick up and down in a pivoting motion, bringing its tip into contact with that of the stationary stick; use this motion to grasp anything on your plate — even a teeny-tiny grain of rice.**

Chapter 19

Ten Commandments: Secrets to Your Success

In This Chapter

▶ Cooking with flexibility and creativity

▶ Using seasonal ingredients

▶ Relying on your senses (and your common sense)

▶ Having fun

*R*evealing these ten secrets to my culinary success was an easy decision for me, not because I'm so generous, but because these secrets aren't very secret at all. Come to think of it, they're not too commanding either.

Why not? For one thing, successful Chinese cooking is really an endeavor of the heart, the soul, and the senses. In other words, once you get in touch with those elements, you only need to know some basics about the cuisine's techniques, its flavors, and its philosophies to really start thinking like a Chinese cook. And guess what? You've already made a big dent in gaining that background if you've read the other chapters in this book. The rest is really pretty easy. So no more secrets and no more commandments — it's time to let common sense take over. Consider the following as reminders, should you need any.

Flexibility and Adaptation Are Key

Be flexible. Be spontaneous. Go with the flow. I've said this before, and I'll say it again, but that's only because it's one hallmark of real Chinese cooking. Some cooks follow recipes for a reason — they guide us toward tried-and-tested results and dishes we may never have attempted without a recipe in the first place. But no one should let a recipe become the one and only way of preparing a dish.

If the recipe calls for a pound of bok choy and you have just shy of three-quarters, or if neither you nor your grocery store has any bok choy at all on that particular day, don't throw in the towel. The dish won't be ruined if there isn't exactly a full pound of bok choy (you'll end up trimming away some of that weight anyway). And neither will it suffer if you were to substitute the bok choy with some spinach or mustard greens. In fact, you may even make it better. So switch the ingredients, make your own Chinese recipe, and you're one step closer to becoming a true Chinese cook. Already you're giving me a run for my money!

Let Your Creative Instincts Loose

Here's another justification for leaving recipes behind now and then: There are now so many exciting Chinese ingredients available in grocery stores, that letting yourself get lost among the selection is actually your ticket to an eye-opening culinary adventure. Meander the aisles and pick whatever Chinese vegetables, sauces, seasonings, seafood, meat, or poultry items strike your fancy. Then draw from the principles of yin-yang balance when combining the ingredients and try your hand at one or two of the cooking techniques I cover in this book. Before you know it, you're creating yet another authentically Chinese recipe. Half the fun is just deciding what to make.

And don't worry if what you've come up with isn't the most delicious stir-fry or claypot dish ever prepared. Believe me, if I'd let that hold me back when I was starting out, I wouldn't have made it past the appetizers. Cooking the Chinese way — which means planting your creative instincts securely in the captain's seat — is a matter of trial and error. Remember to keep your patience as close as you keep your trusty Chinese chef's knife.

Cook with the Seasons

The first time I had fresh strawberries in the middle of winter was a shocking experience for me. How did these ruby-colored summer gems make their way to a January table? I wondered. For starters, we now have hothouses; farms in South America, Australia, and Africa; agricultural advances; and worldwide shipping networks. The globalization of the dinner table means that we're eating foods from not only more global cuisines but also from more global gardens!

But not too long ago, you simply couldn't get spring greens in winter or winter root vegetables in spring, and in the more remote parts of China, things are still that way. But that doesn't mean that kitchens shut down for a good chunk of the year. As unbearable as it may seem to wait through winter for the delicacy of freshly stir-fried asparagus shoots, there's actually a good reason for bearing this culinary burden, even if you *can* find — and can afford — hothouse versions: Produce simply tastes better and is of higher quality when grown and harvested during its natural growing season. Those winter strawberries may have been a novelty for me, but they couldn't compare to the summer ones. And when produce has to travel long distances to get to market, it tends to arrive a little "road weary" anyway.

So as the nights become longer and the days shorter, shift your cooking mind-set away from bright bell peppers and summer squashes to all the hearty cabbages and winter squashes that can take summer produce's place. There's a time for everything — especially produce.

Let Your Senses Be Your Guide

As you increasingly base your shopping lists on the calendar, you'll notice that the in-season items make obviously better choices than hothouse versions of out-of-season produce. After all, the former are in their prime. Hydroponic tomatoes may be a nice convenience when winter's chill makes the backyard variety hard to come by, but they'll probably be paler in color and flavor and a little drier and mealier as well. On the other hand, notice how dense and hearty that winter cabbage looks with its crisp, clean leaves. Now, you tell me which one's the better choice. Sure, you may really want to make tomato beef, but is sacrificing the quality and flavor of the dish with second-rate ingredients really worth it? Considering how nice the cabbage looks in comparison, wouldn't pairing it with some tender, red-cooked chunks of pork make the better meal?

That's the whole idea behind buying with your senses. Again, it requires flexibility on your part to substitute fresh, tender green beans for asparagus when the latter is getting limp and slimy at the tips. Or give a cod steak a try if your fishmonger's sea bass selection doesn't quite pass muster. You get the picture. You won't end up with exactly the same dish, but I promise that it'll be better than if you'd settled for second best.

Taste as You Cook

If you really want cooking to become second nature to you, you have to use your senses in the kitchen, too. That may sound obvious, but it's surprising how many people prepare meals without really knowing what they're cooking. The best way to do that: Taste each dish repeatedly as you cook it. Now, you're not tasting for any particular "correct" flavors here, but rather just for the flavors that you like in your own food; you're going to be the one eating it, after all. You may feel that you're flying (or tasting) blind initially, especially because you may still be familiarizing yourself with the distinctive flavors of Chinese cuisine. But just as novice art fans learn to identify quality work, or at least work that appeals to them, through repeated exposure to art, your palate will instinctively recognize dishes that need more cilantro or could've used less soy sauce the more you taste them.

There are no rules here *except* for the ones that your own tongue makes — and that approach fits perfectly with the whole philosophy of Chinese cooking. After all, with an educated palate that knows which tastes work and which don't, adapting recipes to fit available ingredients, variable equipment, and changing numbers of servings becomes refreshingly easy and fun. In fact, one of the best ways to liberate yourself from a dependence on recipes is to give your palate some practice. If you can learn how to taste, learning how to cook can't be too far behind. Besides, getting to taste the fruits — and vegetables, seafood, meat, and poultry — of your labor is a fitting and filling reward.

Portions Aren't Set in Stone

This book gives you plenty of advice on serving sizes, from planning how many dishes to order or serve, to determining how many people you can feed with a particular recipe. Remember that these are all just suggestions. One family of four may devour twice as much as another family of six. And as Chapter 17 explains, Chinese-style dining follows different patterns and involves a different way of serving food than does Western dining anyway.

Suppose that you're preparing a Chinese family-style meal — making a number of dishes that each provide a counterpoint to rice. You'll eke out more servings from those dishes than if the meal were Western-style, with one central, often meat-based, item taking up most of the plate while the side dishes get what space is left. In general, figure that a Chinese dish served Western-style yields about two-thirds the number of servings it would as part of a Chinese meal. So, in the former case, increase recipe sizes accordingly unless you want to face a table full of hungry family or guests.

If you're looking for another way of serving Chinese dishes to suit your own eating style, consider turning your Chinese culinary creations into one-dish meals. Rice and noodles are perfect one-dish candidates. For example, a chow mein packed with mixed-and-matched meat and veggies, and a classic fried rice studded with peas, carrots, barbecued pork, and egg need little time and equipment to prepare and are about as flexible as you can get, in terms of ingredients and serving sizes. Depending on how hungry you are, you may be able to eat the whole thing yourself. And don't forget that topping some plain steamed rice with a simple stir-fry such as spicy beef and eggplant is also a great way to make a satisfying meal out of just a few simple ingredients.

Respect the Leftover

Those little take-out boxes (the perfect souvenirs from an evening at a Chinese restaurant), as well as the chow mein and fried rice mentioned in the section "Portions Aren't Set in Stone," prove that leftovers, at least in Chinese cuisine, are nothing to snub. Wise Chinese cooks are loathe to throw good food away, and we would all do well to follow their example. "Recycling" this food not only saves money but also provides creative cooks with a whole host of ingredients to turn into completely different dishes than what they were the night before. With leftovers, what's old really is new again.

That's because the Chinese style of serving leftovers isn't necessarily a matter of popping last night's meal into the microwave and then experiencing dinner deja vu. Instead, make the most of your leftovers by combining a bit of this and that with rice or noodles, a quick sauce, and even some fresh ingredients, and you've created a completely new dish. Anything goes.

In fact, fried rice got its start in Chinese kitchens as a new take on leftover food. Last night's rice, barbecued pork from the deli, fresh peas from the garden, and some stir-fried egg that didn't get eaten at breakfast all came together in a hot wok with some seasoning and became a famous dish with literally endless interpretations. That's a pretty impressive result for the humble leftover.

Know Thy Stovetop

All the recipes in this book list specific cooking and preparation times, and after preparing them many times myself, I can vouch that those times are accurate. But burner temperatures *do* vary. For example, gas burners characteristically heat to higher temperatures and allow for more precise heat control than do electric ones. So if you have an electric burner, keep in mind that a dish requiring medium-high heat may actually need high heat on your own stovetop.

Thicknesses of fish fillets, heat conductivities of different woks, temperatures in individual kitchens, and a number of other factors can throw off specific cooking times, too. But you don't need any conversion factors or new sets of cooking instructions to work with these variables. Just experiment a little. If your chunks of pork are larger than the recipe specifies, they'll take a little bit longer to cook than the recipe specifies as well. How much longer? Follow the recipe's recommendations and then check them for doneness. If they're still a little pink, give them a few more minutes in the wok. The same advice applies when you're cooking with different equipment or in different environments. The more you cook, the more you'll be able to gauge the extra — or reduced, depending on the situation — time requirements.

In the interest of health, err on the side of fully cooking meat, seafood, and poultry products if you have any question as to how much longer they should stay on the stove. I'm not advocating *over*cooking anything — tough, dry, and chewy meats are disagreeable to Chinese tastes — but rather just making sure that no trace of pink remains. It's a fine line, but one that you won't cross if you keep your eye on the stir-fry or, to be extra sure, on an instant-read thermometer. (As for overcooking vegetables, that's a serious violation on all counts. Don't even approach the line in that instance.)

Mind the Details

You're not going to want to garnish every dish you make. You don't need to either. And nothing is wrong with occasionally tossing looks aside and making a meal that, although delicious, may be better off eaten with eyes closed.

But that said, do remember that little things count, and garnishes and other eye-pleasers fall into this category. Maybe you're cooking only for yourself, and your mission is to make a tasty meal with a minimum of effort. Even then, you'd be surprised how a little attention to a dish's looks can not only perk you up but increase your overall enjoyment of the meal. All you need to do is choose an attractive plate, sprinkle some sesame seeds, or place a sprig of cilantro at the edge of a dish.

Of course, garnishes, attractive plate settings, and conscientious service all make a big impact when entertaining with food. Sure, the dishes will taste just as good without the special effects, and I doubt that anyone will notice whether there's a splash of sauce on the serving platter's rim. But when flavor, texture, and appearance meld with an evening of friendly togetherness, you'll realize that facing the devil that's in the details is worth it.

Share the Food; Share the Fun!

Chinese tables are round for a reason: so each person can share in the conversation, companionship, and culinary creations just as easily as the next. As this books shows, food is intrinsically linked with togetherness, celebration, and the Chinese way of life itself. And we all know that life needs a healthy dose of fun, right?

Chapter 20

Ten Martin-Tested Resources for Chinese Cuisine and Culture

· ·

In This Chapter

▶ Finding great Web sites

▶ Browsing at a market

▶ Identifying other sources for Chinese cooking supplies

· ·

Sure, this book is a comprehensive guide to Chinese cuisine. But there are still more recipes, ingredients, stories, and surprises about this fascinating cuisine and culture that I haven't covered. Get answers to all your questions and satisfy your curiosity at the same time with the resources in this chapter. They include brick-and-mortar companies, virtual communities, magazines, and everything in between. I've had positive experiences with all of them, so I'm eager to let you know about them as well. Whether you're strolling the supermarket aisles or surfing the Web in search of more juicy details about Chinese food and culture, this list is your ticket to enlightenment.

AsianConnections.com

For everything you've always wanted to know about Asia, head to www.asianconnections.com. Once you make your way through the interviews with Asian celebrities, Asian business news, community and cultural updates, travel information, and even the singles section, you may still have time to hop over to the food page for recipes (many courtesy of yours truly) and restaurant reviews aplenty.

Flavor & Fortune Magazine

In a world full of food-related newsletters, magazines, and webzines, you may wonder which ones to keep and which subscriptions to let slide. *Flavor & Fortune* magazine (one of the old-fashioned kinds; it comes by snail mail) definitely falls into the former category. This graceful quarterly is the first devoted entirely to Chinese cuisine and to "everything that advances the science and art of a cuisine consumed by more people worldwide than any other," as it says. I look forward to each issue's recipes, restaurant and cookbook reviews, trend reports, and articles on equipment, ingredients, health, and nutrition — all relating to the food of my home. It's put out by the Institute for the Advancement of the Science and Art of Chinese Cuisine, a group that's at the top of its game in reporting accurate and informative information. Pick up a subscription for yourself. Check *Flavor & Fortune*'s Web site, `www.flavorandfortune.com`, or contact the subscription department at *Flavor & Fortune*, Subscription Division, P.O. Box 91, Kings Park, NY, 11754. You can also fax inquires to 631-265-9126 or e-mail them to `flavorandfortune@hotmail.com`.

JFC International Inc.

I couldn't possibly give a full accounting of JFC International's Asian food products, because JFC has more than 8,500! Although I pity whoever has to keep track of all that inventory, I'm sure glad it's as extensive as it is. In addition to all the Japanese products it markets under the JFC, Hapi, and Hime names (you could open your own hibachi restaurant and sushi bar with what it offers), its Wel-Pac brand chow mein is excellent. Its Dynasty brand encompasses everything from oils, sauces, and canned goods to teas, dumpling wrappers, seasoning mixes, and even cookbooks. Headquartered in San Francisco, California, it really does earn its international name — you can find JFC products literally all over the world. Even that classic *Californian* creation, the fortune cookie, has made it back to China, thanks to JFC. Find out more at `www.jfc.com`.

Kikkoman, Inc.

When you've been making soy sauce for more than 300 years, you get pretty good at it. That's the case with Kikkoman, possibly the world's most popular soy sauce, and for good reason. Personally, I can always count on Kikkoman for high-quality soy sauce, brewed using natural, time-honored fermentation techniques. I won't settle for anything less in my recipes or on my table, where a bottle of the stuff is more common than salt and pepper. And although its name is synonymous with soy sauce, it also makes a variety of Japanese seasonings, including teriyaki sauce (soy sauce flavored with wine, sugar, and spices), mirin (sweetened Japanese rice wine for cooking), and ponzu (a Japanese-style salad dressing made from lemon juice, vinegar, and soy sauce). Its Web site (`www.kikkoman.co.jp/world/home/index.htm`) lists these and other products, recipes, soy sauce facts, and the company's history. There's even an "Edutainment Park" with activities for kids. Who knew soy sauce could be so exciting!

Lee Kum Kee

In 1888, Mr. Lee Kum Sheung started making oyster-flavored sauce on the southern coast of China. Over 100 years later, Lee Kum Kee, the company he founded, still produces a premium oyster-flavored sauce that's a permanent fixture in my kitchen. And that's not all the company does. It makes excellent standard cooking and dipping sauces — soy, hoisin, chile garlic, and black bean garlic, for starters — and sells convenient minced fresh ginger and garlic, a fine selection of oils, a brand-new line of one-step recipe sauce packets, and even canned abalone. Be sure to check out XO sauce, a gourmet condiment made from dried scallops and shrimp, ham, red chili pepper, and spices that's known as the "Caviar of the Orient." This spicy luxury is better than caviar, *and* less expensive. But don't take my word for it. Take theirs: Lee Kum Kee's Web site (www.lkk.com) gives a full listing of the company's product range. And because Mr. Lee Kum Sheung's family business now distributes to more than 60 countries on 6 continents, you can find his legendary oyster sauce in your own supermarket.

Melissa's

No matter where I am, I know that fresh, quality produce is only a click or a call away, thanks to Melissa's/World Variety Produce. Whether you're looking for winter melon or water chestnuts, these folks can give it to you. Not only do they lead the pack when it comes to Asian vegetables, but they're a top-rate source for fresh, exotic, and organic fruits and vegetables, as well as for specialty foods and authentic ingredients from around the world. Melissa's even has a tasty selection of Asian seasonings and sauces. You've probably sampled some of Melissa's products yourself — you can easily find them at supermarkets and specialty stores throughout the United States. You can find out more at www.melissas.com or by calling 800-588-0151.

99 Ranch Markets

When is a grocery store not just a grocery store? When it's a 99 Ranch Market. These independently operated Asian groceries sprinkled throughout California, Washington, Arizona, Nevada, Georgia, and Hawaii put the *super* in *supermarket.* (You can also find these stores in Indonesia, in case you need to run to the market on your next trip to Jakarta.) They carry everything you'd find in a normal grocery, from toothpaste to toilet paper, but they also have one of the widest selections of Asian sauces, snack foods, noodles, grains, teas, wines, breakfast cereals, housewares . . . I could go on. Their fresh meat and seafood counters always give my imagination plenty of dinner ideas to play with, and the produce section is the next best thing to an open-air Chinese market. Some of the stores even have full-service bakeries, Chinese delis, and take-out counters that give the genre a much-needed boost. Find out whether there's a 99 Ranch near you at www.99ranch.com.

Oriental Pantry

Oriental Pantry (www.orientalpantry.com) has an extensive online catalog of products ranging from housewares and groceries to books and gifts. Its selection of teas, fresh and dried seasonings, sauces, and even a variety of preserved meat and seafood products, such as Chinese sausage, dried shrimp, and and fish flakes, would make even a well-stocked Chinatown grocery blush. And I've only scratched the surface of what you can find on this easily navigable site. When it's time to stock your kitchen with more Chinese cooking equipment, Oriental Pantry provides a one-stop spot for finding it. Once you've gathered your ingredients and cooking equipment, check out the site's recipes for ways to use your new purchases. If you're so inclined, you can contact them via phone at 978-264-4576; it's located in Acton, Massachusetts, so call between 10 a.m. and 5 p.m. Eastern time, Monday through Saturday.

Roxy Trading Inc.

Whenever I get a craving for uniquely Chinese treats such as the ginger candy, sesame brittle, or preserved mango jellies that I enjoyed when I was young, Roxy Trading Inc. pulls through. But beyond these decadent little snacks that always make me wax nostalgiac for my days in Hong Kong, Roxy supplies a fine assortment of Asian sauces and seasonings, beverages and beverage mixes, and all the canned goods you could want. Straw mushroomes, lychees, an assortment of bamboo shoots, and plenty more only begin the list of products available. For more information, contact Roxy at 909-622-6888 or roxytrading@earthlink.net.

YanCanCook.com

Okay, I know this may seem like a shameless plug, but I have to point you toward www.yancancook.com. It's my first venture onto the World Wide Wok! I've loaded the site with Chinese recipes, as well as delicious dishes from other Asian outposts. You can find my favorite holiday meals there, too. I update everything regularly, so you'll never run out of items to make. The site also lets you follow my travels at the "travelogue" page, where you'll find stories and pictures from my latest journeys. And if you have questions about *anything* to do with Chinese food, cooking, holiday feasts, or anything else that's on your mind, use the "Wok Talk" feature as a posting board for inquiries. It's a great forum for your comments, suggestions, and your own personal cooking secrets as well. That's what makes this site so great for me: It allows me to interact with you in ways that a television screen or book simply doesn't. So come on over, and let's get interactive!

Chapter 21

Drink Up: Ten Tips for Drinking Tea and Wine with Chinese Food

In This Chapter

▶ Sorting out the teas

▶ Uncorking some wine tips

A Chinese cookbook wouldn't be complete without a nod to that most noble, most Chinese of beverages: tea. The French have their wines, the Italians their espresso, the Germans their beers, and the Americans their soft drinks, but thanks to China, we all have tea.

But many of us also like to drink wine with our meals, and the area of matching wines with Chinese food, in particular, is ripe for discovery because, historically, most people haven't given much thought to pairing Western, grape-based wines with Chinese foods. They've missed out! The sometimes spicy, sometimes savory, and always flavorful foods of the Chinese kitchen are just begging for that stellar wine match.

Four Bits of Info for the Tea Drinker

With 200-plus varieties of tea grown in China alone, you have to look elsewhere for a comprehensive guide to tea in its entirety. And as if all the varieties weren't enough, the many factors influencing the finished brew's quality, from water and soil types to altitude and climate, only complicate matters more. (By the way, mild, humid, and mountainous growing conditions yield the best leaves.)

However, distinctions among the way that tea leaves are treated after picking allow us to break down the basic types of Chinese teas into categories. The following list should help make sense of things:

✓ **Green, unfermented tea** comes from tea leaves that are sun-dried and roasted immediately after picking. They produce a pale-colored drink with clean, delicate flavors and aromas. Some examples include Dragon Well tea (prized for its soothing qualities), Gunpowder, and Lu An.

✓ **Semi-fermented tea**, also known as oolong tea, is a little fuller in body, color, and flavor than green tea, but it still retains some of the latter's delicate fragrance. As a result, this tea is a happy medium for those who find fermented teas too strong. No wonder it's probably the most commonly served tea in Chinese restaurants in the West.

✓ **Fermented, black teas** resemble the English breakfast teas familiar to so many North Americans and Europeans: They're darker, more full-bodied, and definitely more flavorful and aromatic. Long fermentation in humid air before roasting is the reason. Examples include Keemun and Yunnan teas and the famous Iron Goddess of Mercy from Fukien province.

✓ **Scented teas** are green and black varieties that are "perfumed" by blending them with fragrant flowers such as chrysanthemum, jasmine, and others. The curing methods used to make scented teas also affect their finished character; for example, curing with smoldering logs gives Lapsang Souchong tea a mild smokiness.

Six Wine-Related Tips

Wine and food buffs have learned to predict how certain wines behave with certain foods. They've turned these predictions into matching principles that can improve anyone's wining and dining success rate. Here's a rundown of the most important:

✓ **Focus on the similar and contrasting flavors.** This principle is the yin and yang of wine matching. Familiarize yourself with the flavor combination in a dish or focus on a particularly dominant flavor in, say, a sauce. You can then choose a wine with a similar flavor to mirror that in the dish and add depth to it. Then again, when you choose a wine with flavors very different from those in a dish, you bring in a whole new sensory element that changes your perception of the dish.

✓ **Pay attention to flavor intensities.** Whether you go with a similar or opposite flavor, remember that a light, delicate dish such as steamed whole white fish with ginger and green onion gets lost when paired with a bold and heavy red such as Cabernet Sauvignon or a similarly strong white such as some Chardonnays. And vice versa: A delicate, light, red Gamay wine or white Chenin Blanc gets lost in the midst of a hearty claypot beef stew; you may end up tasting all stew and no wine.

✔ **Foods have texture, and so do wines; make sure they match.** We often refer to this texture as "body," "mouthfeel," or "power." Think about body in terms of milk. Reds such as Pinot Noir and whites including Chenin Blanc are on the "skim" end of the body scale. More powerful wines with heavier "whole milk" textures, including some Chardonnays and reds such as Syrah, overpower lighter dishes like Cantonese pickled vegetables, Chinese chicken salad, and delicately steamed seafood treats. However, these powerful wines are great with chunky casseroles and complex claypot dishes when a delicate textured white wine just can't compete.

✔ **The cooking method helps make the match.** Just as with flavors and textures, cooking methods run from minimal and delicate (think of steamed chicken) to powerful and intense, as with Peking roast duck, barbecued pork ribs, and even Mongolian barbecue. The preparation of a dish changes its texture and flavor, so choose a wine with an intensity that takes those changes into account. For example, pair that steamed chicken with a delicate Chenin Blanc, and the caramelized, smoky roast duck with a bolder Syrah.

✔ **Make clever use of acidity, sweetness, and bubbles.** The refreshing tartness of white wines like Sauvignon Blancs and dry (as opposed to sweet) Rieslings contrasts with greasiness in deep-fried foods such as wontons or spring rolls, cleansing that greasiness from the palate; bubbles in sparkling wines perform the same feat. And when it comes to taming spiciness, the honeyed flavors of sweet wines and a sparkling wine's sparkles do a number on heat by creating a cooling contrast and acting as a heat buffer on your tongue.

✔ **Tame the tannins, the bitter astringent compounds in red wine.** To mellow their bitterness, offset their drying effects, and add complexity to the wine-and-food combination, drink tannic wines with protein-rich foods such as meats. The proteins combine with the tannins, taking the latter "out of service" on your palate. (Another way to tame the tannins: Set up a textural contrast by combining smooth, rich foods with tannic wines.)

Index

• Numbers •

99 Ranch Markets, 313

• A •

adaptation, 305–306
All-Purpose Black Bean Sauce, 90
All-Purpose Dipping Sauce, 92
All-Purpose Stir-Fry Sauce, 86
Almond Cookies, 280–281
Almond Jelly with Fruit Cocktail, 276
aluminum steamer, 30
American-Cantonese restaurants, 300
appetizers, 95–101
  Auntie Jessica's Party Chicken Wings,
    97
  Baked Pork Buns, 100
  Cantonese Pickled Vegetables, 98
  Chinese Chicken Salad, 99
  Sichuan Bang Bang Chicken, 156
Apple Wings, 77–78
AsianConnections.com Web site, 311
Asian pears, 274
Asparagus with Baby corn and Oyster-
    Flavored Sauce, 242
Auntie Jessica's Party Chicken Wings, 97

• B •

baby bok choy, 232
baby corn (Siu gum soeun; xiao jin sun),
    48–49
Baked Pork Buns, 100–101
baking sheets, 2
balance, 11

bamboo shoots (Tzook soeun; zhu
    sun), 49
bamboo steamer, 30
barbecued pork, 187
barbecued pork bun, 302
barbecuing, 69
basmati rice, 253
bean curd, 47. *See also* tofu
bean sprouts (Ah cai; dou ya), 231
beef, 190
  Beef Steak Over Glass Noodles, 195
  Beef Stew, 198–199
  Broccoli Beef, 194
  flank steak, 196
  Spicy Beef with Leeks, 196–197
  Tangerine Beef, 192
  tender cuts, 190
  Tomato Beef, 191
  tri-tip, 199
  Uncle Philip's Beef Tri-Tip, 200
Beef Chow Fun, 269
Beef Steak Over Glass Noodles, 195
Beef Stew, 198–199
beggar's chicken, 300
Beijing, 14–15
Bianyifang Restaurant, 15
black bean garlic, 313
black bean sauce (See shi zi jiang; tzup
    jeng), 38, 145
black pepper, 90
black vinegar (Hok tzo; hei cu), 44
blanching, 66–67
blue-black chickens, 169
bok choy (Bok choy; xiao bai chai), 232
boning chicken legs, 153–154

Braised Bamboo Shoots with Bok
    Choy, 240
Braised Fish Hunan Style, 130
braising, 67
Broccoli Beef, 194
brown rice, 253
buying ingredients
  locally, 11–12
  with your senses, 307

● *C* ●

Cabernet Sauvignon, 316
cake pan, 2
calcium sulfate, 207
Cantonese cooking, 17
Cantonese Pickled Vegetables, 98
Cantonese restaurants, 300
Caramelized Bananas, 282–283
caring for wok, 26
carved vegetable garnishes, 73
carving poultry, 163–164
cellophane or bean thread noodles (Fun
    xi; fen si), 263–264
Chardonnay wine, 316–317
Char Siu sauce (Tza siu jeng; cha shao
    jiang), 38, 181, 187
chef's knife, 2, 26–28
Chenin Blanc wine, 316–317
chicken, 147–148. *See also* poultry
  blue-black, 169
  boning legs, 153–154
  broth, 116
  carving, 163–164
  Chicken Curry, Cantonese Style, 162
  Chinese Roast Chicken, 168
  Claypot Chicken and Mushroom
      Rice, 259
  cutting up, 151–152
  Drunken Chicken, 157
  feet, 163
  Gingered Chicken, 167
  handling, 149–150

Honey Garlic Chicken, 159
  Kung Pao Chicken, 158–159
  Lemon Chicken, 160
  Moo Goo Gai Pan, 161
  oyster, 163
  parts not normally used, 163
  selecting, 148
  Sichuan Bang Bang Chicken, 156
  Soy Sauce Chicken, 166
  wings, 163
Chicken Curry, Cantonese Style, 162
Chicken Drummettes, 154–155
chile oil (Laut you; la you), 39, 92–93
chile pastes and sauces (Laut tziu jeng;
    la jiao jiang), 38–39
chile sauce, 313
Chili Pepper Flowers, 81–82
China
  Beijing, 14–15
  Guangzhou, 17–18
  Hangzhou, 16–17
  Jiangsu province, 16
  regional differences, 13
  Shanghai, 16–17
  Sichuan, 18–19
  Suzhou, 16, 17
  Yangcheng Lake, 16
  Yangtze Delta areas, 16
  Yangzhou, 16
  Zhejiang province, 16
Chinatown Chop Suey, 249
Chinatown markets, 36–37
Chinese
  cuisine and culture resources, 311–314
  finding ingredients, 36–37
  imperial cuisine, 78
  kitchens, 23
  medical practices, 238–239
Chinese broccoli (Gai lan; jie lan), 232
Chinese chefs, 9
Chinese chef's knife, 55
  grips, 56
  guide hand, 57

safety, 27–28
sharpening, 28
slicing, 57–58
Chinese Chicken Broth, 117
Chinese Chicken Noodle Soup, 267
Chinese Chicken Salad, 99
Chinese chives (Gou choy; jiu lai), 232–233
Chinese claypot, 31
Chinese cooking
  adaptation, 305–306
  balance, 11
  buying locally, 11–12
  buying with your senses, 307
  cooking times, 309–310
  creativity, 10, 306
  flexibility, 9, 305–306
  fresh ingredients, 12
  garnishes, 310
  geographic regions, 13–19
  growing vegetables, 12
  hard work, 10
  history of, 10
  improvising, 12
  leftovers, 309
  one-dish meals, 308
  portions, 308
  seasonal cooking, 11–12, 306–307
  sharing, 310
  tasting while cooking, 307–308
Chinese egg noodles, 261–262
Chinese eggplants (Aike gwa; qie zi), 233
Chinese five-spice powder (Ng heung fun; wu xiang fen), 45
Chinese hot mustard (Gai mut; jie mo), 45
Chinese meals
  home-style meal, 287–290
  sample menus, 290–295
Chinese Mustard Dip, 93
Chinese pantry
  basic ingredients, 53
  condiments and sauces, 37–44

finding essential ingredients, 36–37
herbs and spices, 44–47
long-lasting Chinese ingredients, 47–52
Chinese parsley, 234
Chinese Pork Chops, 189
Chinese preserved eggs, 227
Chinese red vinegar, 44
Chinese restaurants
  Dim Sum, 302–303
  regional, 299–301
Chinese Roast Chicken, 168
Chinese sausage (Larp tzoen; la chang), 48
Chinese vermicelli, 264
Chinkiang vinegar, 44
choice meat, 193
chopsticks, 32–33, 304
chow mien, 261
cilantro (Yim sike; yuan xi), 234
claypot, 2
claypot casserole, 31
Claypot Chicken and Mushroom Rice, 259
cleaning
  chopsticks, 33
  cutting board, 29
cloud ear fungus, 52
coconuts, 274
coffee grinders, 32
colander, 2
condiments, 37–44
  black vinegar (Hok tzo; hei cu), 44
  chile oil (Laut you; la you), 39
  dark soy sauce (Lo ceo; lao chou), 43
  hoisin sauce (Hoi seen jeng; hai xian jiang), 39
  rice vinegar (Bok tzo; mi cu), 43–44
  rice wine (Mike tziu; mi jiu), 40–41
  sesame oil (Ma you), 41
  sesame paste (Tzee ma jeng; zhi ma jiang), 42
  soy sauce (Jeng yeo; jiang you), 42

cooking
  barbecuing, 69
  blanching, 66–67
  braising, 67
  chopsticks, 33
  deep-frying, 67–68
  equipment, 2
  preparation for, 63–64
  red-cooking, 68
  roasting, 68
  seasonally, 11–12
  simmering, 67
  smoking, 69
  steaming, 66
  stir-frying, 64–65
  vegetables, 237–238
cooking techniques
  Chinese chef's knife, 55–57
  crushing, 61
  cubing/dicing/mincing, 59
  ingredient preparation, 55
  matchstick/julienne cutting, 57–58
  non-knife wielding techniques, 62–63
  roll cutting, 60
  scoring, 61–62
  slicing, 57–58
  soaking, 62
  tenderizing, 62
  toasting, 62–63
  velveting, 62
coriander, 234
cornstarch, 4
covered casserole, 2
Crispy Wontons, 106–107
crushing, 61
Cuan, Trudy, 278
cubing/dicing/mincing, 59
Cucumber Fan, 79
cutting boards, 27, 29

• D •

dark soy sauce (Lo ceo; lao chou), 43
deep-frying, 67–68
desserts, 273
  Almond Cookies, 280–281
  Almond Jelly with Fruit Cocktail, 276
  Caramelized Bananas, 282–283
  Eastern traditions, 274–279
  Egg Custard Tarts, 284–285
  family-style meal, 288
  Lychee Ice Cream, 286
  Mango Pudding, 281
  soups, 273
  Steamed Sponge Cake, 278
  Sweet Silken Tofu, 279
  Sweet Tapioca Pearls, 277
  Western influences, 279–286
deveining shrimp, 140
diakon (Law bok; lou bu), 234
diamonds, 172
dim sum, 95–96, 255, 302–303
  barbecued pork bun, 302
  Crispy Wontons, 106–107
  egg roll wrappers, 102
  Green Onion Pancakes, 112
  pork dumpling, 303
  Potstickers, 108–109, 303
  shrimp dumpling, 303
  Shrimp Toast, 113, 303
  Spring Rolls, 104–105, 303
  spring roll wrappers, 102–103
  Steamed Shrimp and Chive Dumplings,
     110–111
  wonton and potsticker wrappers, 103
  wrappers, 101–103
dips, 85, 91
  All-Purpose Dipping Sauce, 92
  Chile Oil, 92–93
  Chinese Mustard Dip, 93
  Sichuan Spicy Salt, 94
dough for baked pork buns, 101

dragon and phoenix garnishes, 80
Dragon Well tea, 16
draining tofu, 213
dried black fungus (Hok mook yee; gan mu er), 52
dried black mushrooms (Gon doan gu; gan dong gu), 51
dried rice noodles (Gon hor fun; gan he fen), 263
dried shrimp, 213
dried tangerine peel, 192–193, 197
Drunken Chicken, 157, 301
drunken crab, 301
duck, 169. *See also* poultry
  Peking roast duck, 170
  Pineapple Duck Stir-Fry, 171–172

• *E* •

E. coli, 62
Easy-to-Make Chow Mein, 264–265
Egg Custard Tarts, 284–285
Egg Flower Soup, 118
Egg Fu Young, 226–227
egg rolls, 102
egg roll wrappers, 102
Eggplants with Spicy Sauce, 246–247
eggs, 205–206, 220
  blood spots, 221
  brown versus white, 227
  Chinese preserved, 227
  choosing freshest, 221
  Egg Fu Young, 226–227
  marinades, 220
  nutritional benefits, 220
  older, 221
  safe handling, 222
  safety tips, 220–221
  Scrambled Eggs with Crabmeat, 223
  Steamed Eggs, 225
  symbolic importance, 220
  Tea-Flavored Eggs, 228
  Tomato Eggs, 224
Eight Treasures Noodle Soup, 271
elaborate garnishes, 72–73
electric rice cooker, 31–32
electric spice grinder, 32
electric wok, 25
English breakfast tea, 316

• *F* •

family-style meals
  auxiliary dishes, 288
  color schemes, 290
  contrast and complement, 289
  contrast and complement flavor, 290
  desserts, 288
  eating, 288–289
  grain as focus, 288
  planning, 289–290
  range of cooking methods, 290
  soups, 288
  varying texture, 290
fan (rice), 252
farmers market, 11
fermented, black tea, 316
fermenting tofu, 209
fillets, 133
finding Chinese ingredients, 36–37
firm tofu, 208
fish, 126. *See also* seafood and shellfish
  marinating, 4
fish markets, 126–127
Fish Soup with Spinach and Tofu, 119
Fish Steaks in Fragrant Sauce, 131
fish-farming industry, 126
fishing, 125
flank steak, 196
flat-bottom wok and lid, 2
Flavor & Fortune magazine, 311–312
Flavor & Fortune's Web site, 312

flexibility, 305–306
flowering chives, 233
folding
  potstickers, 109
  wontons, 107
food
  marinating, 4
  as medicine, 238–239
Forbidden City, 15
free-range poultry, 148
freezing tofu, 209
fresh egg noodles (Darn min; ji dan
    mien), 261–262
fresh ingredients, 12
fresh rice noodles (Seen hor fun; xian he
    fen), 262–263
freshly butchered poultry, 148
Fried Rice, 257
fried tofu puffs, 208
frozen
  poultry, 148
  seafood, 128
fruits, 229
  Asian pears, 274
  coconuts, 274
  kumquats, 274–275
  longan, 275
  lychee, 275
  Mandarin oranges, 275
  persimmons, 275
  pomelo, 275
fun xi, 264

• G •

Gamay wine, 316
garlic, 4, 313
  peeling, 61
garnishes, 71, 310
  Apple Wings, 77–78
  basic principles, 74–75
  Chili Pepper Flowers, 81–82

Chinese imperial cuisine, 78
Cucumber Fan, 79
diamonds, 172
dragon and phoenix, 80
elaborate, 72–73
Green Onion Brushes, 80
importance of, 78
selecting items for, 76
simple, 72
Tomato Rose, 76–77
tools for making, 75–76
gelation temperature, 91
giant white radish, 234
ginger (Geung; jiang), 45–46
  peeling, 61
Gingered Chicken, 167
glutinous rice (Nor mike; nuo mi),
    255–256
Great Hall of the People, 15
green, unfermented tea, 316
green chives, 232–233
Green Onion Brushes, 80
Green Onion Pancakes, 112
grinding spices and herbs, 32
growing vegetables, 12
Guangzhou, 17–18, 125
Gunpowder tea, 316
gypsum, 206
gypsum salt, 207

• H •

Hangzhou, 16–17
heavy Dutch oven, 2
herbal medicine, 238–239
herbs and spices, 44
  Chinese five-spice powder (Ng heung
      fun: wu xiang fen), 45
  Chinese hot mustard (Gai mut; jie
      mo), 45
  ginger (Geung; jiang), 45–46

Sichuan peppercorns (Fa tziu; hua jiao), 46
star anise (Bark gog; ba jiao), 46–47
hoisin sauce (Hoi seen jeng; hai xian jiang), 39, 85, 313
home-style meals, 287–290
  setting table for, 292
Honey Garlic Chicken, 159
Hong Kong-Style Pan-Fried Noodles, 266–267
Hot and Sour, 120
Hot and Spicy Stir-Fry Sauce, 87
Hundred-year-old eggs, 16

• I •

imperial chefs, 15
Imperial Palace, 15
improvising, 12
Iron Goddess of Mercy tea, 316
isoflavones, 215
Italian parsley, 234
Ivory and Jade (Cauliflower and Broccoli with Creamy Egg White), 243

• J •

Ja Jiang Mien, 270
jasmine rice, 253
JFC International, Inc., 312
Jiangsu province, 16
Jing Tu Pork Chops, 183
jook, 252
Julienned ingredients, 4
jungdz, 255

• K •

Keemun tea, 316
Kikkoman, Inc., 312
knives, sharpening, 28, 75
kosher poultry, 148

kumquats, 274–275
Kung Pao Chicken, 158–159

• L •

ladle, 29
lamb, 201
  Lamb with Green Onions, 204
  Mongolian Lamb in Hotpot, 202–203
Lamb with Green Onions, 204
Lapsang Souchong tea, 316
large, covered pot, 2
lazy susans, 292
Lee Kum Kee, 313
Lemon Chicken, 17, 160
Lion's Head meatballs, 16
liquid measuring cups, 2
local farmers market, 11
lo mien, 261
longan, 275
long-grain rice (Jim mike; chan mi), 253–254
long-lasting Chinese ingredients
  baby corn (Siu gum soeun; xiao jin sun), 48–49
  bamboo shoots (Tzook soeun; zhu sun), 49
  Chinese sausage (Larp tzoen; la chang), 48
  dried black fungus (Hok mook yee; gan mu er), 52
  dried black mushrooms (Gon doan gu; gan dong gu), 51
  straw mushrooms (Tzo gu; cao gu), 50
  Tofu (Dou fu; do fu), 47–48
  water chestnuts (Ma tike; ma ti), 49–50
long-life noodles, 262
lotus wraps, 255
Lu An tea, 316
lychee, 275
Lychee Ice Cream, 286

• M •

Mandarin oranges, 275
mangoes, 283
Mango Pudding, 281
Ma Po Tofu, 216, 301
mariculture, 126
marinades and eggs, 220
marinating food, 4
Master Sauce/Red-Cooking Sauce, 89
matchstick-cut ingredients, 4
matchstick/julienne cutting, 57–58
meals. *See* Chinese meals
meat
  color and general appearance, 174–175
  complementing and enhancing, 173
  cutting, 4
  cutting across grain, 174
  grading, 193
  marbling, 175
  marinating, 4
  mincing, 59
  parallel cutting, 60–61
  safe handling, 175–176
  sell-by or packed-on date, 175
  shopping for, 174–175
  types eaten in ancient China, 174
medium-grain rice (Fong loi mike; fung lai mi), 254–255
Melissa's/World Variety Produce, 313
metal spatula, 29
mincing meat, 59
mini food processor, 32
mirin, 312
mixing bowls, 2
mixing spoons, 2
Mongolian barbecue, 69
Mongolian Hotpot, 202–203
Mongolian Lamb in Hotpot, 202–203
Monk's Choice Tofu, 214–215
Moo Goo Gai Pan, 17, 161
muffin tin, 2
mung bean sprouts, 231
Mu Shu Pork, 180

• N •

napa cabbage (Siu Choy; da bai cai), 234–235
natural food stores and co-ops, 36
nigari, 206
noodles, 260, 290–291
  Beef Chow Fun, 269
  cellophane or bean thread noodles (Fun xi; fen si), 263–264
  Chinese Chicken Noodle Soup, 267
  dried rice noodles (Gon hor fun; gan he fen), 263
  Easy-to-Make Chow Mein, 264–265
  Eight Treasures Noodle Soup, 271
  fresh egg noodles (Darn min; ji dan mien), 261–262
  fresh rice noodles (Seen hor fun; xian he fen), 262–263
  Hong Kong-Style Pan-Fried Noodles, 266–267
  Ja Jiang Mein, 270
  long-life, 262
  Shanghai, 262
  Shanghai Fried Noodles, 272
  Singapore Rice Noodles, 268
  symbolism of, 262
  types, 260–264
nori, 119
Northern Chinese chefs, 15

• O •

oil blanching, 66–67
one-dish meals, 308
oolong tea, 316
organic poultry, 148
Oriental Pantry, 314
oyster-flavored sauce (Hou yeo; hao you), 40
Oysters in Black Bean Sauce, 145

• P •

Pan-Grilled Salmon Fillet with Black Bean Sauce, 134
parallel cutting, 60–61, 213
pastries, 5
peeling garlic, 61
peeling ginger, 61
Peking duck, 15, 170, 300
pepper, white *versus* black, 90
Perfect Steamed Glutinous Rice, 256
Perfect Steamed Rice, 254
persimmons, 275
pie dish, 2
Pineapple Duck Stir-Fry, 171–172
Pinot Noir wine, 317
planning family-style meal, 289–290
plum sauce (Suin mui jeng; suan mei chiang), 40
pomelo, 275
ponzu, 312
pork, 177
  Char Siu, 181, 187
  Chinese Pork Chops, 189
  Jing Tu Pork Chops, 183
  Mu Shu Pork, 180
  pork butt, 178
  Pork with Bean Threads, 185
  purchasing, 178
  Shanghai Meatballs, 188
  Sichuan Spareribs, 184
  Steamed Cabbage Rolls, 186–187
  Sweet and Sour Pork, 179
  Twice-Cooked Pork, 182–183
pork butt, 178
pork dumpling, 303
Pork with Bean Threads, 185
portions, 308
Potstickers, 105, 108–109, 303
poultry. *See also* chicken and duck
  carving, 163–164
  classification, 149
  cooking temperatures, 150
  free-range, 148
  freshly butchered, 148
  frozen, 148
  handling, 149–150
  kosher, 148
  marinating, 4
  organic, 148
  salmonella contamination, 149
  selecting, 148
  sell-by dates, 148
  skin color, 148
  storing, 149–150
  USDA stamps, 149
  whole *versus* precut, 148
pressed tofu, 217
prime meat, 193

• Q •

Qing dynasty, 15

• R •

red-cooked pork, 16
red-cooking, 68
reduced-sodium soy sauce, 43
regional Chinese restaurants
  Cantonese (Southern-style), 300
  Mandarin (Northern- or Beijing-style), 300
  Shanghai, 301
  Sichuan-Hunan, 301
regular tofu, 208
retrogradation, 91
rice, 251, 290–291
  basmati, 253
  brown, 253
  Claypot Chicken and Mushroom Rice, 259
  Fried Rice, 257

rice *(continued)*
  glutinous rice (Nor mike; nuo mi),
      255–256
  importance of, 252
  jasmine, 253
  long-grain rice (Jim mike; chan mi),
      253–254
  medium-grain rice (Fong loi mike; fung
      lai mi), 254–255
  Perfect Steamed Glutinous Rice, 256
  Perfect Steamed Rice, 254
  Sweet Precious Glutinous Rice, 258
  types, 252–256
  as way of life, 251–252
  white, 253
rice cookers, 31–32
rice porridge, 252
rice puddings, 255
rice vinegar (Bok tzo; mi cu), 43–44
rice wine (Mike tziu; mi jiu), 5, 40–41
Rieslings, 317
roasting, 68
roasting pan, 2
roll cutting, 60
rolling steamed pork and cabbage
      rolls, 187
romantic dinner, 291–292
round table, 292
round-bottom wok, 2
Roxy Trading Inc., 314

• S •

salads, Sichuan Bang Bang Chicken, 156
Salmonella, 62, 149, 220
salted fish, 16
sample menus
  balance, 294
  for four, 293–294
  romantic dinner, 291–292
  for six, 294–295
  for two, 291–292

saucepans, 2
sauces, 5, 85
  All-Purpose Black Bean Sauce, 90
  All-Purpose Stir-Fry Sauce, 86
  black bean sauce (See shi zhi jiang;
      tzup jeng), 38
  char Siu sauce (Tza Siu jeng; cha shao
      jiang), 38
  chile pastes and sauces (Laut tziu jeng;
      la jiao jiang), 38–39
  Chinese pantry, 37–44
  hoisin sauce (Hoi seen jeng; hai xian
      jiang), 39, 85
  Hot and Spicy Stir-Fry Sauce, 87
  Master Sauce/Red-Cooking Sauce, 89
  oyster-flavored sauce (Hou yeo; hao
      you), 40
  plum sauce (Suin mui jeng; suan mei
      chiang), 40
  slurries, 91
  starch-thickened, 91
  Sweet and Sour Sauce, 88
  thick and thin, 91
Sauteed Green Beans, 244–245
scented tea, 316
scoring, 61–62
  fish fillets, 136
Scrambled Eggs with Crabmeat, 223
seafood, 125–126. *See also* shellfish and
      fish
  black bean sauce, 145
  Braised Fish Hunan Style, 130
  choosing, 127–128
  cooking, 129
  deep-frying, 129
  fillets, 133
  Fish Steaks in Fragrant Sauce, 131
  freshness, 126
  frozen, 128
  handling, 128
  Pan-Grilled Salmon Fillet with Black
      Bean Sauce, 134

refrigeration, 128
scoring fish fillets, 136
seasoning, 129
shelling shrimp, 141
skin, 133
Smoke-Broiled Fish, 132
steaks, 133
Steamed Trout in Black Beans and
    Garlic, 136
Steamed Whole Fish, 135
types, 126
varieties, 129
seasonal cooking, 306–307
seasoning wok, 25
seaweed, 119
select meat, 193
semi-fermented tea, 316
sesame oil (Ma you), 41
sesame paste (Tzee ma jeng; zhi ma
    jiang), 42
Shanghai, 16–17
Shanghai bok choy, 232
Shanghai Fried Noodles, 272
Shanghai hairy crab, 16
Shanghai Meatballs, 188
Shanghai noodles, 262
Shanghainese restaurants, 301
Shao Hsing rice wine, 16, 301
sharing Chinese cooking, 310
sharpening Chinese chef's knife, 28
sharp knives, 75
shellfish, 137. *See also* seafood and fish
  deveining shrimp, 140
  marinating, 4
  Oysters in Black Bean Sauce, 145
  Seafood Casserole, 144
  shopping for, 137–138
  Shrimp and Scallops with Snow
      Peas, 143
  Spicy Salt Shrimp, 142
  storing, 138
  Sweet and Sour Shrimp, 139
shelling shrimp, 141

Sheung, Lee Kum, 313
shiitake mushrooms, 51
shopping language gap, 37
shredding, 247
shrimp, dried, 213
Shrimp and Scallops with Snow Peas, 143
shrimp dumpling, 303
Shrimp Toast, 113, 303
Sichuan, 18–19
Sichuan Bang Bang Chicken, 156
Sichuan peppercorns (Fa tziu; hua
    jiao), 46
Sichuan Spareribs, 184
Sichuan Spicy Salt, 94
Sichuan-Hunan restaurants, 301
silken-style tofu, 208
simmering, 67
simple garnishes, 72
Singapore Rice Noodles, 268
sizzling spareribs, 16
skimmer, 29–30
slicing, 57–58
slurries, 91
Smoke-Broiled Fish, 132
smoked duck, 301
smoking, 69
snow peas (Hor lan dou; xue dou), 235
soaking, 62
soft tofu, 208
soups, 115
  chicken broth, 116
  Chinese Chicken Broth, 117
  dessert, 273
  Egg Flower Soup, 118
  family-style meal, 288
  Fish Soup with Spinach and Tofu, 119
  Hot and Sour Soup, 120
  ingredients add to, 115–116
  leftovers, 116
  Sweet Corn and Crabmeat Soup, 121
  winter melon, 123
  Winter Melon Soup, 122
  Wonton Soup, 123

soy bean sprouts, 231
soy sauce (Jeng yeo; jiang you), 4, 42,
    312–313
Soy Sauce Chicken, 166
soymilk, 207, 215
spatula, 2, 29
spice grinders, 32
spices. *See* herbs and spices
Spicy Beef with Leeks, 196–197
Spicy Salt Shrimp, 142
Spring Rolls, 102, 104–105, 303
spring roll wrappers, 102–103
stainless steel steamers, 30
star anise (Bark gog; ba jiao), 46–47
starches, 91
steaks, 133
Steamed Cabbage Rolls, 186–187
Steamed Eggs, 225
Steamed Shrimp and Chive Dumplings,
    110–111
Steamed Sponge Cake, 278
Steamed Trout in Black Beans and
    Garlic, 136
Steamed Whole Fish, 135
steamers, 30, 66
steaming, 66
Stir-Fried Assorted Vegetables, 241
stir-frying, 64–65
    pork with marbling, 178
    small ingredients, 153
strainer, 29–30
straw mushrooms (Tzo gu; cao gu), 50
supermarkets, 36
sushi, 119
Suzhou, 16, 17
Swan Palace, 15
Sweet and Sour Pork, 179
Sweet and Sour Sauce, 88
Sweet and Sour Shrimp, 139
Sweet Corn and Crabmeat Soup, 121
Sweet Precious Glutinous Rice, 258
Sweet Silken Tofu, 279

Sweet Tapioca Pearls, 277
sweet vinegars, 16
Swiss Chard with Tender Pork Slices, 248
Syrah wine, 317

• T •

Tangerine Beef, 192
tannins, 317
Taoist, 230
taro root (Woo tou; yu tou), 235
tart molds, 2
tasting while cooking, 307–308
tea, 315
    English breakfast, 316
    fermented, black, 316
    green, unfermented, 316
    Gunpowder, 316
    Iron Goddess of Mercy, 316
    Keemun, 316
    Lapsang Souchong, 316
    Lu An, 316
    oolong, 316
    scented, 316
    semi-fermented, 316
    Yunnan, 316
Tea-Flavored Eggs, 228
tenderizer hammer, 62
tenderizing, 62
teriyaki sauce, 312
thick and thin sauces, 91
Three Mushrooms, 245
Tin Li Restaurant, 15
toasting, 62–63
tofu (Dou fu; do fu), 47–48, 205–206
    draining, 213
    fermenting, 209
    freezing, 209
    fried puffs, 208
    health benefits, 215
    making, 206–207
    Ma Po Tofu, 216
    Monk's Choice Tofu, 214–215

parallel cutting, 60–61
preparations, 209–210
pressed, 208, 217
regular and firm, 208
soft, 208
testing, 215
texture variations, 207–208
Tofu and Spinach, 217
Tofu Puffs with Three-Color
    Vegetables, 218
Tofu with Ham and Napa Cabbage, 211
Tofu with Mushrooms and Cashews, 219
Tofu with Shrimp, 212
Tofu with Spicy Tomato Sauce, 210–211
Tomato Beef, 191
Tomato Eggs, 224
Tomato Rose, 76–77
tools
    Chinese chef's knife, 26–28
    chopsticks, 32–33
    claypot casserole, 31
    cutting boards, 27, 29
    electric rice cooker, 31–32
    ladle, 29
    skimmer, 29–30
    spatula, 29
    spice grinders, 32
    steamer, 30
    strainer, 29–30
    wok, 23–26
tree ear fungus, 52
tri-tip, 199
turnips, 234
Twice-Cooked Pork, 182–183
typical Chinese kitchen, 23

• U •

Uncle Philip's Beef Tri-Tip, 200
USDA (United States Department of
    Agriculture), 149, 193

• V •

vegetables, 229, 289
    Asparagus with Baby corn and Oyster-
        Flavored Sauce, 242
    bean sprouts (Ah cai j dou ya), 231
    bok choy (Bok choy; xiao bai chai), 232
    Braised Bamboo Shoots with Bok
        Coy, 240
    Buddhists, 230
    Chinatown Chop Suey, 249
    Chinese broccoli (Gai Lan;jie lan), 232
    Chinese chives (Gou choy; jiu lai),
        232–233
    Chinese eggplants (Aike gwa; qie zi), 233
    cilantro (Yim sike; yuan xi), 234
    cooking, 237–238
    diakon (Law bok; lou bu), 234
    economics, 230
    Eggplants with Spicy Sauce, 246–247
    Ivory and Jade (Cauliflower and
        Broccoli with Creamy Egg White), 243
    napa cabbage (Siu Choy; da bai cai),
        234–235
    Sauteed Green Beans, 244–245
    shredding, 247
    snow peas (Hor lan dou; xue dou), 235
    Stir-Fried Assorted Vegetables, 241
    Swiss Chard with Tender Pork Slices, 248
    Taoist, 230
    taro root (Woo tou; yu tou), 235
    Three Mushrooms, 245
    winter melon (Doan gwa; dong gua), 236
    year-long beans (Dou gog; dou jiao), 236
velveting, 62

• W •

water chestnuts (Ma tike; ma ti), 49–50
Western influences, 279–286
Westlake fish, 16
wheat, 251

white pepper, 90
white rice, 253
wine
  acidity, sweetness, and bubbles, 317
  Cabernet Sauvignon, 316
  Chardonnays, 316–317
  Chenin Blanc, 316–317
  cooking method and, 317
  flavor intensities, 316
  Gamay, 316
  Pinot Noir, 317
  Rieslings, 317
  similar and contrasting flavors, 316
  Syrah, 317
  tannins, 317
  textures, 317
winter melon (Doan gwa; dong gua), 236
Winter Melon Soup, 122–123
wire racks, 2
wire strainer, 29–30
wire whisk, 2
wok, 23–26
  caring for, 26
  electric, 25
  lid, 24
  seasoning, 25
  selecting, 24–25
  shape, 24
  sizes, 24
  types, 24
  wok stand, 24
wonton and potsticker wrappers, 103
Wonton Soup, 123
wood ear fungus, 52
wrappers, 101–103

• X •

XO sauce, 313

• Y •

YanCanCook.com, 314
Yang, 11, 230
Yangcheng Lake, 16
Yangchow fried rice, 16
Yangtze River, 16, 19
Yangzhou, 16
year-long beans (Dou gog; dou jiao), 236
yellow chives, 233
Yellow River, 14
Yin, 11, 230
Yuan dynasty, 15
Yunnan tea, 316

• Z •

zest, 171–172
Zhejiang province, 16

Notes

Notes

IDG BOOKS WORLDWIDE BOOK REGISTRATION

Register This Book and Win!

We want to hear from you!

Visit **http://my2cents.dummies.com** to register this book and tell us how you liked it!

- ✔ Get entered in our monthly prize giveaway.

- ✔ Give us feedback about this book — tell us what you like best, what you like least, or maybe what you'd like to ask the author and us to change!

- ✔ Let us know any other *For Dummies*® topics that interest you.

Your feedback helps us determine what books to publish, tells us what coverage to add as we revise our books, and lets us know whether we're meeting your needs as a *For Dummies* reader. You're our most valuable resource, and what you have to say is important to us!

Not on the Web yet? It's easy to get started with *Dummies 101*®: *The Internet For Windows*® *98* or *The Internet For Dummies*® at local retailers everywhere.

Or let us know what you think by sending us a letter at the following address:

For Dummies Book Registration
Dummies Press
10475 Crosspoint Blvd.
Indianapolis, IN 46256

FOR DUMMIES™

BESTSELLING
BOOK SERIES